INTO THE MOUTHS OF BABES

D0168941

INTO THE MOUTHS OF BABES

AN ANTHOLOGY OF CHILDREN'S ABOLITIONIST LITERATURE

Deborah C. De Rosa

PRAEGER

Westport, Connecticut
London

Library of Congress Cataloging-in-Publication Data

Into the mouths of babes : an anthology of children's abolitionist literature / Deborah C. De Rosa.

    p. cm.

Includes bibliographical references and index.

ISBN 0–275–97951–2 (alk. paper)

1. Slavery—Literary collections. 2. Antislavery movements—Literary collections. 3. American literature—Women authors. 4. American literature—19th century. 5. Children's literature, American. 6. Didactic literature, American. I. De Rosa, Deborah C.

PS509.S436I58 2005
810.8'03552—dc22   2004022570

British Library Cataloguing in Publication Data is available.

Library of Congress Catalog Card Number: 2004022570
ISBN: 0–275–97951–2

First published in 2005

Praeger Publishers, 88 Post Road West, Westport, CT 06881
An imprint of Greenwood Publishing Group, Inc.
www.praeger.com

Printed in the United States of America

In memory of Rosa De Rosa
November 18, 1928–December 15, 2004.
Mom, you can never imagine how much we love you.

In joyful anticipation of Isabella Grace De Rosa.
Isabella Grace, I loved you yesterday, I love you today, I will love
you tomorrow.

CONTENTS

ILLUSTRATIONS

ACKNOWLEDGMENTS

LITTLE OF THE RECOVERY WORK of abolitionist juvenile literature would have been possible without the financial assistance of the Elizabeth Cady Stanton Foundation, the W. Bruce Lea Family, the University of North Carolina at Chapel Hill Off-Campus Graduate Research Grant, the Cairns Friends of Library at Madison Wisconsin Fellowship, the Barnard Alumnae Graduate Fellowship, the Senior Fellowship at the University of North Carolina, and the Graduate Council Research and Artistry Grant for the Summer 2001 from Northern Illinois University. These works were located in the archives at the Schomburg Collection, the Widener and Houghton Libraries at Harvard University, the Boston Athenaeum, the American Antiquarian Society, the Library Company of Philadelphia, and the Cairns Women's Collection at the University of Madison, Wisconsin.

I would like to acknowledge James Peltz (editor in chief) and Jennie R. Doling (rights and permissions editor) at SUNY Press for allowing me to exercise the fair use policy regarding the materials I discussed in *Domestic Abolitionism and Juvenile Literature, 1830–1860* (2003). Thanks must also go to the Dean of Liberal Arts and Science and the English Department at Northern Illinois University for providing the funding needed to obtain permissions and to reproduce the images included in this volume.

My sincere gratitude goes to Suzanne Staszak-Silva (and her new bundle of joy) at Greenwood Press, whose faith in this project brought it to completion. Karyn Slutsky's amazing attention to detail has resulted in a more accurate and complete volume.

This anthology also grew out of great patience from friends and colleagues who helped me to complete the challenging work of comparing original texts to the transcribed and then copyedited pages. My thanks go to Kai Zhang (my research assistant), Aaron Butler, Renee Blanchard-Culbertson, Eva and Maeve Thurman-Keup, James Hardgrove, Michael Ryder, Lise Schlosser, Sabina Sorgum, and Ibis Gomes-Vega (*ay Caramba*, are you devoted!). Thanks must also go to Aaron Butler, Kelli Lyon Johnson, Michael Ryder, and Lise Schlosser for reading, critiquing, and editing the introductory materials.

INTRODUCTION

THE RECOVERED ARCHIVAL JUVENILE ANTEBELLUM literature (alphabet books, poetry, short fiction, and "conversations") that constitutes this anthology reveals that nineteenth-century women who opposed slavery created a literary space and public forum for their views through the seemingly nonthreatening genre of children's literature. Historians and literary critics of children's literature, women's biography, literary and political history, the history of the book, as well as African American history and literature have overlooked these texts where women claimed a political voice during a conflicted cultural moment (De Rosa 1–5). This anthology restores that voice to domestic abolitionists like Elizabeth Margaret Chandler, Eliza Lee Cabot Follen, Ann Preston [Cousin Ann], Hannah and Mary Townsend, Jane Elizabeth (Hitchcock) Jones, and others who supplement and complicate the history of women's literary production.

Nineteenth-century American women lacked safe public platforms from which to voice their abolitionist views. Whenever they spoke publicly or published their concerns about slavery, they risked or received criticism for transgressing their gender roles. Lydia Maria Child experienced financial ruin and social ostracization when she published *An Appeal in Favor of That Class of American Called Africans* (Roberts 354; see also Bardes and Gossett *Declarations*, 41). Sarah Jane Clarke Lippincott lost her position as *Godey's Lady's Book* editorial associate when she wrote antislavery articles for *The National Era* (Gray 364; Born 305). Jane Grey Swisshelm "was attacked . . . because she dared to comment directly on politics, a topic perceived to be the domain of men only" (Okker 16). The Grimké sisters and Jane Elizabeth (Hitchcock) Jones encountered critical public receptions and mob violence when they spoke publicly against slavery. Visible, assertive, and vocal women like Child, Lippincott, Swisshelm, Jones, and the Grimkés violated the unwritten gender codes of female passivity, submissiveness, and piety. Yet, women like them wanted to participate in the public abolitionist debate. Given an obstacle, women found a way to bypass it. The recovered juvenile texts reveal that domestic abolitionists adopted all the genres acceptable for women authors (i.e., histories, sentimental fiction, domestic novels, and children's literature) and created juvenile abolitionist texts from their "domestic" perspective. This became a "safe" genre in which to cloak their political views in a nonthreatening discourse; after all, the texts were grounded in a domestic space: the nursery. This became their strategy for walking the tightrope of female propriety so that they could publish their anxieties about the peculiar institutions' (i.e., slavery) destruction of childhood innocence, family bonds, and democratic ideals.

Domestic abolitionists wrote for the nursery, but through publication, their sentiments reached a large and widespread public arena. They published their works with the American Sunday School Union, the American Anti-Slavery Society, the American Reform Tract and Book Society, as well as with various commercial publishers like Carter and Hendee, James Loring, James McKim, John P. Jewett, Lee and Shepard, Philip Cozans, and Vincent Dill, among others, from Boston, to New York, to Pennsylvania, and to midwestern cities like Cincinnati, Ohio (De Rosa 15–37). With the support of these publishers, domestic abolitionists forged a safe literary space within an often-hostile public arena.

In *Domestic Abolitionism and Juvenile Literature, 1830–1865*, I argue that these women authors employed three overarching images: the victimized slave child, the abolitionist mother-historian, and the young (white) abolitionist. First, several domestic abolitionists included in this anthology adopted the rhetoric popular in slave narratives, sentimental novels, and children's literature to create a pseudo-juvenile slave narrative (see Chapter 2 in *Domestic Abolitionism* for a complete treatment of this genre). By blending these genres, domestic abolitionists sought to arouse empathy in their young readers as they worked to express their anxiety about lost innocence through the voice of a previously marginalized character, the black slave child, as well as heroic slave mothers who revolt against the institution that threatens their child's innocence. From either the first or third person, these fictional slave children relate their experiences to inspire private tears in their readers. In some texts, the child's plight inspires fictional white and black mothers to rebel against slavery to protect the slave child's best interests. Thus, rather than offering readers a theoretical "male" view of abolitionist politics, women like Eliza Lee Cabot Follen, Ann Preston, Kate Barclay, Grandmother, and others created sentimental, domestic, and political narratives designed to inspire tears. However, these tears did not result in inactivity; instead they advanced activism: prayers, promises, or literal acts of intervention.

Second, some domestic abolitionists challenged slavery through the figure of the abolitionist mother-historian, who overtly critiques religious and political corruption, renounces the transmission of hypocritical patriotism, and corrects distorted representations of American history (see Chapter 3 in *Domestic Abolitionism* for a complete treatment of this character). The abolitionist mother-historian gives voice to the truth about slavery, thereby "writing" revisionist histories. Through the image of the mother as educator, domestic abolitionists could navigate the tightrope of abolitionist rhetoric by situating women in the roles of children's educators. This built on the eighteenth-century tradition of Republican motherhood, which argued that a mother's influence would shape patriotic citizens and develop America's moral character. But these mother-historians spoke *against* American politics and politicians. They sought to instill a reformist consciousness in the child, whom they hoped would carry these beliefs into adulthood and thereby rescue American democratic ideals. These women did not silence themselves; rather, they told their children listeners nontraditional history lessons to document slavery's brutalities and violations. They also critiqued the hypocrisy of July Fourth celebrations; the passage of the Fugitive Slave Law in 1850; Northerners who directly or indirectly supported slavery; Southern women who violated female proprieties as they engaged in acts of violence against slaves; those who did not speak out against slavery; and all violent (physical and psychological) treatment of slaves. Appearing to maintain the role of mother-educator, these politicized mother-historians overstepped women's designated private sphere as they voice quasi-seditious critiques of America's corrupt religious, political, and economic principles. Knowledge, nonconformity, and activism motivate the conversations in texts by Kate Barclay, Harriet Butts, Elizabeth Margaret Chandler, Eliza Follen, Jane Elizabeth (Hitchcock) Jones, S.C.C., and Matilda Thompson.

The third image that domestic abolitionists created is that of young abolitionists who ask and answer the question, "What can I do to end slavery?" (see Chapter 4 in *Domestic Abolitionism* for a complete treatment of this character). These stories shift attention away from the victimized slave child and the abolitionist mother-historian to images of white children who engage in behaviors to initiate, foster, or enact change, i.e., freedom for slaves. These images reflect the creation of real juvenile anti-slavery societies established in eastern and midwestern states (De Rosa 108–114). Similar to activities undertaken by adults in antislavery societies, children from these societies participated in petition campaigns, boycotted slave-made goods, and engaged in political discussions. Eliza Follen, Jane Elizabeth (Hitchcock) Jones, Harriet Beecher Stowe, Anna Richardson, and others adapted these real-life experiences to their fiction by fashioning images of children effecting change through activities ranging from familial and/or private reflection, to liberal, public activism. Most interesting is that prior to Harriet Beecher Stowe's creation of Little Eva in *Uncle Tom's Cabin* (1852), most of the images of young abolitionists were of boys. However, with Little Eva as a model, domestic abolitionists adopted and adapted her into the image of a young abolitionist girl with a strong voice and conscience geared to effect change.

This anthology functions as a form of resuscitation for antebellum women's politically motivated abolitionist fiction for children. The volume revives works by twenty American women and two British women ("bookends" of sorts since Opie wrote in the 1820s and Richardson in the late 1850s). Lois Brown has also recently edited *Memoir of James Jackson, the Attentive and Dutiful Scholar, Who Died in Boston, October 31, 1833, Aged Six Years and Eleven Months* (1835), by Susan Paul, an African American. Yet, more work must be done. The works of Eliza Weaver Bradburn, *Pity Poor Africa: A Dialogue for Children in Three Parts*; M.A.F., *Gertrude Lee; or, The Northern Cousin*; Maria Goodell Frost, *Gospel Fruits; or, Bible Christianity Illustrated; A Premium Essay* represent three novel-length juvenile abolitionist texts carefully preserved in rare book archives that await revival. William Lloyd Garrison compiled *Juvenile Poems, for the Use of Free American Children of Every Complexion*, which includes over thirty poems and stories by unidentified authors who submitted works to *The Liberator's* juvenile department, yet his volume has reached neither a general nor a scholarly modern audience. This anthology and the above-cited texts do not account for those other women (Northern, Southern, and African American) whose voices still remain silenced in children and women's collections held at rare book libraries. The lack of ready access and the long process of transcribing such works further hamper the important project of recovering literary works that offer important insights about forgotten women authors, their participation in their historical-political moment, and their literary production in nineteenth-century America. The recovered documents in this anthology give voice to these women and their writing, extend the boundaries of historical and literary criticism, and most importantly, raise questions about the existence of other notable and still silenced literature by women.

STATEMENT OF EDITORIAL PRACTICE

This anthology strives to reprint the individual texts as accurate repro-ductions of the originals. The editor has not changed the spelling, capi-talization, or punctuation to conform to modern standards. As a result, forms of address, such as *Mother* and *Father*, may appear in lower case in some texts and upper case in others. The same is true for terms like *Bible*, *He* (with reference to God), *North*, *South*, and several others. The editor has made silent corrections to obvious inconsistencies within individual texts—those perhaps due to original printers' errors—and she has noted egregious spelling errors with "[*sic*]."

AMELIA ALDERSON OPIE

(NOVEMBER 12, 1769–DECEMBER 2, 1853)

Daughter of Doctor James Alderson and Amelia Briggs from Norwich, England, Amelia Alderson Opie authored thirty-three volumes of fiction (moral "tales," short stories, drama, and so on) and four collections of poetry during the early nineteenth century, or Romantic period. Her husband, John Opie (the Cornish painter and member of the Royal Academy), encouraged her to write, especially when his art could not sustain them (Balfour 84; Simmons 265; Reiman vi). Furthermore, while she lived in London, she joined progressive literary salons known to William Godwin, John Aiken, Harriet Martineau, Mary Wollstonecraft, and Elizabeth Inchbold (Buck 879; Simmons 262; Reiman v). When her husband died suddenly in 1807, Opie returned to care for her father in Norwich, where she met William Wordsworth, Walter Scott, and Sarah Siddons (Simmons 265). Each of these relationships with contemporary literati impacted her work. Early in her career she wrote primarily domestic, sometimes sentimental, novels with female protagonists. Later, her affiliations with the Quaker Society of Friends resulted in increasingly didactic and moral tales. Because she was so prolific (and well connected), her works eventually reached American markets. Opie's abolitionist literature for children may have inspired American women authors to use children's literature as a means to express their antislavery views when doing so in the public arena would have been deemed inappropriate.

Scholars of nineteenth-century British literature consider Opie a foremother of the domestic novel and compare her to Maria Edgeworth, Fanny Burney, and Jane Austen (Kelly 198). Her best-known works, *The Father and Daughter, a Tale in Prose* (1801) and *Adeline Mowbray; or, The Mother and Daughter, a Tale* (1804), epitomize the sentimental, morally didactic, and realistic qualities of her fiction. Susan Staves suggests that *The Father and Daughter* exemplifies "the seduced maiden novel," a popular eighteenth-century form that depicts "a modest girl who strenuously resists invitations to illicit intercourse, yielding only after a protracted siege" (110, 115). Gary Kelly argues that many of Opie's young heroines hold a financial, social, or moral debt that causes much suffering; however, reconciliation often repays the "breach of duty" and indebtedness (199, 200). Opie's works fell in popularity as they became increasingly didactic, especially once she joined the Religious Society of Friends (Quakers) in 1824, after which time she "curtailed her active social and literary life" (Kelly 198; see also S. Howard 231; Simmons 264).

In addition to her sentimental, moral, and didactic rhetoric, Opie interweaves abolitionist opinions into several of her tales. Opie's mother[1] shared her abolitionist views with her daughter (Simmons 268) and thereby planted the seeds for Opie's support of antislavery ideas. *Valentine Eve* (1816) and "A Wife's Duty" (1820) make passing references to ex-slaves. *Adeline Mowbray* briefly address issues of race and power through the black fugitive slave, Savanna, who becomes the protagonist's servant after Adeline saves Savanna's husband from debtor's prison.[2] Roxanne Eberle argues that Opie diminishes the defiant black female because of the poorly replicated Caribbean dialect and "romantic racism" (141); however, she argues that Savanna "can serve as an empowering model for the psychologically shackled white British woman. Just when Adeline abandons her quest for self-ownership, Savanna enters the novel as an individual who has literally reclaimed herself from an economic and legal system which has considered her 'chattel'" (142). Unsurprisingly, when Opie deals with abolitionism more extensively, she receives more criticism than praise. In a discussion of the merits and failures of her poems, a contemporary reviewer criticizes *The Negro Boy's Tale*, stating:

> [M]uch more ought to have been made. His argument on the natural equality of the Negro, and his sarcasms against those who practice not what they preach, are more in the character of the poet, than of the supposed speaker. Even had they been natural, as addressed by any other person, they certainly are not, as addressed to her who had always been his friend. ("Review" 120)

Donald Reiman supports the 1802 reviewer's critique and goes so far as to dismiss Opie's abolitionist fiction:

> Her anti-slavery poems—though probably based on strong personal convictions—suffer from her obvious lack of firsthand knowledge of the

blacks for whom she has such intellectual sympathy. Her children's book on slavery, *The Black Man's Lament* [1826], may have brought some of the evils of West Indian slavery to the attention of school children, but—as its subtitle indicates—it could also serve as a training manual on how to operate a sugar plantation and refinery. And one of her most ridiculous poems to modern readers is "The Negro Boy's Lament," with its attempt to represent the speech of a slave. (viii)

Unfortunately, the 1802 reviewer and Reiman condemn Opie's abolitionist efforts rather than recognize her subversiveness.

In *The Negro Boy's Tale* (1824; the text reproduced here is the American printing), Opie offers children a narrative about West Indian slavery designed to instill an abhorrence of slavery and a desire to abolish it. Opie prefaces the poem with a brief history of the triangular trade, the slave's brutal middle passage experience, and the French, Spanish, and Portuguese participation in perpetuating slavery in the colonies despite the British Parliament's abolition of slavery in 1806. Opie facilitates her young readers' ability to respond compassionately to Zambo's story by giving them a white child, Anna, with whom to identify. Anna sympathetically listens as Zambo tells about his subjugation and desire to leave Jamaica, where he has been enslaved, his desire to return to England, where he would be free, and then sail for his homeland, where he can join his family (lines 2–4; 17–32). Through Zambo's first-person narrative, Opie critiques the brutally ruptured family bonds and the religious hypocrisy necessary to sustain slavery. She also acknowledges the purity of the slave's heart. Furthermore, Opie emboldens a young, white female to effect change. Although Anna recognizes her powerlessness (lines 109–112), she begs her father, Trevannion, to take Zambo with them to England or at least to make his plight as a slave less treacherous (lines 113–120). Trevannion refuses and instead forcefully takes Anna to the ship that will sail for England. When Zambo sees this, he swims to the ship but drowns in the process. Opie's voice surfaces in the final four stanzas emphasizing sorrow for the slaves and a call for abolitionism, thereby reinforcing the moral values and politically responsible behavior she hopes her readers will adopt.

The Negro Boy's Tale serves as an important precursor to other works in this anthology. Opie's attempt to document the slave trade, to critique its negative impact on the African's mental state and family unit, and to call white individuals to action sets the stage for American white women to express their abolitionist sentiments via children's literature.

THE NEGRO BOY'S TALE (1825?)

INTRODUCTION[3]

ADDRESS TO CHILDREN

My Dear Young Friends,

Dr. Watts, who wrote so many pretty hymns for your use, says, that "the children of the present age are the hope of the age to come"—meaning, that if your parents and preceptors instruct you in your duties, teaching you what to do, and what to avoid doing, you will be such wise and virtuous men and women, that you will make the world what we of the present generation wish it to be, but are not able to make it ourselves.

Therefore, as it is one of your Christian duties to abhor the cruelties practiced on poor Negro Slaves in the West India Islands, and to try, by every means possible, to put a stop to them when you grow up, I wish to make you acquainted with some important facts before you read my "Negro Boy's Tale"; which I republish by desire of the mother of sixteen children, who, finding that it interested them in the cause of the oppressed Africans, thought it might have the same effect on the children of others. I fear that she overrates its power: but, it is worth the trial; as I should be happy to assist, in any degree, the labours of such men as Clarkson, Wilberforce, William Smith, Fowell Buxton, and other philanthropists, who have served, and are still serving, our injured black brethren through good and evil report.[4]

When I first published my *Negro Boy's Tale*, the British Slave Trade was going on in all its horrors; that is, English, as well as other captains of trading vessels, went to the coasts of Africa, tempted the native inhabitants to kidnap and tear their fellow-countrymen from their families, that they might purchase them—then carry them away to their ships, and stow them like bales of goods, with scarcely room enough to breathe or move in. Many of these poor creatures died on the passage from harsh and ill treatment; some found an opportunity to jump overboard, happy to avoid such suffering by death; while those who lived to reach the colonies were put under task-masters, who scourged and tortured them till they did a certain quantity of work under a burning sun!

And this tyranny was exercised on those who were born as free as we are!—But, supposing that these slaves had been carried to a land better than their own, and "flowing with milk and honey," still no one had a right, even for their own good, to force them from their parents, their wives, their husbands, and their children. In the land of their fathers alone could they find happiness; and to tear them thence was contrary to the first principles of liberty, of justice, of the rights of man, and of CHRISTIANITY. But, in 1806, owing to the constant labours of the friends of the Abolition out of Parliament, and their eloquence in it, the detestable SLAVE TRADE was abolished by an act of our legislature. Still SLAVERY has continued in our colonies; and the friends of humanity have therefore been obliged to come forward again, with petition on petition, praying, that Slavery may be gradually, but effectually abolished, and the poor Negroes treated as we ever ought to treat our fellow-men and fellow-subjects.[5]

The cause of injured Africa had now gained a new champion in Thomas Fowell Buxton; and, on the 15th of May, 1823, he delivered a powerful speech in the House of Commons; the consequence of which was, that George Canning, one of the ministers of the crown, proposed and carried a resolution for a gradual amelioration of the condition of our slaves in the colonies.

But, in the meanwhile, the slave trade itself, though abolished by us, is still carried on by French, Spanish, and Portuguese traders, and dreadful cruelties are practiced by them on the slaves.[6]

Therefore, the rising generation must never lose sight of the wrongs of the Negroes, till they are completely redressed and ended; for the West Indian Slave is a *mere chattel*,—he is reduced to the condition of a beast of burden. He may be bought; divorced from his wife; separated from his children; worked hard, flogged, tortured, branded with a red-hot iron; and, under peculiar circumstances, even *murdered*, according to the arbitrary determination of his fellow-man.[7]

Therefore, dear Children, as Negroes can still be thus cruelly treated, you will allow that much remains to be done, and will eagerly, I trust, look forward to that time when you shall be old enough to endeavour to remove all the sufferings of your black fellow-creatures, as well as of sufferers over the whole world.

And "I implore you all, (to borrow the conclusion of the speech quoted above,) whatsoever situation you may occupy, never to relax your efforts in this holy cause, until that happy day shall arrive when every individual within the whole circuit of the British dominions shall be able to lift up his head with thankfulness and joy, and, say, Behold, I am free!"

Amelia Opie

"THE NEGRO BOY'S TALE"

'Haste! hoist the sails! fair blows the wind:
Jamaica, sultry land, adieu!
Away! and loitering Anna find!
I long dear England's shores to view.'

The sailors gladly haste on board;
Soon is Trevannion's voice obeyed,
And instant, at her father's word,
His menials seek the absent maid.

But where was 'loitering Anna' found? . . . .
Mute, listening to a Negro's prayer,
Who knew that sorrow's plaintive sound
Could always gain her ready ear; . . . .

Who knew, to soothe the slave's distress
Was gentle Anna's dearest joy;
And thence, an earnest suit to press,
To Anna flew the Negro boy.

'Missa,' poor Zambo cried, 'sweet land
Dey tell me dat you go to see,
Vere, soon as on de shore he stand,
De helpless Negro slave be free.

'Ah! dearest missa, you so kind!
Do take me to dat blessed shore,
Dat I mine own dear land may find,
And dose who love me see once more.

'Oh! ven no slave, a boat I buy,
For me a letel boat vould do,
And over wave again I fly
Mine own loved Negro-land to view.

'Oh! I should know it quick like tink, ...
No land so fine as dat I see,
And den perhaps upon de brink
My moder might be look for me! . . . .

'It is long time since lass ve meet,
Ven I vas take by bad Vite man,
And moder cry, and kiss his feet,
And shrieking after Zambo ran.

'O missa! long, how long, me feel
Upon mine arms her lass embrace!
Vile in de dark, dark ship, I dwell,
Long burn her tear upon my face.

'How glad me vas she did not see
De heavy chain my body bear;
Nor close, how close, ve crowded be;
Nor feel how bad, how sick, de air!

'Poor slaves! . . . . but I had best forget.
Dey say (but teaze me is deir joy)
Me grown so big dat ven ve meet
My moder vould not know her boy.

'Ah! sure 'tis false! But yet if no,
Ven I again my moder see,
Such joy I at her sight vould show
Dat she vould tink it must be me.

'Den, kindest missa, be my friend; . . . .
Yet dat indeed you long become;
But now one greatest favour lend, ...
O find me chance to see my home!

'And ven I'm in my moder's arms,
And tell de vonders I have know,
I'll say, most best of all de charms
Vas she who feel for Negro's woe.

'And she shall learn for you dat prayer
Dey teach to me to make me good;
Though men who sons from moders tear,
She'll tink, teach goodness never could.

'Dey say me should to oders do
Vat I vould have dem do to me; . . . .
But, if dey preach and practise too,
A Negro slave me should not be.

'Missa, dey say dat our black skin
Be ugly, ugly, to de sight;
But surely if dey look vidin,
Missa, de Negro's heart be vite.

'Yon cocoa-nut no smooth as silk,
But rough and ugly is de rind;

Ope it, sweet meat and sweeter milk
Vidin dat ugly coat ve find.

'Ah missa! smiling in your tear,
I see you know what I'd impart;
De cocoa husk de skin I vear,
De milk vidin be Zambo's heart.

'Dat heart love you, and dat good land
Vere every Negro slave be free, ...
Oh! if dat England understand
De Negro wrongs, how wrath she be!

'No doubt dat ship she never send
Poor harmless Negro slave to buy;
Nor vould she e'er de wretch befriend
Dat dare such cruel bargain try.

'O missa's God! dat country bless!'
(Here Anna's colour went and came;
But saints might share the pure distress,
For Anna blushed at others' shame.)

'But missa, say; shall I vid you
To dat sweet England now depart,
Once more mine own good country view,
And press my moder on my heart?'

Then on his knees poor Zambo fell,
While Anna tried to speak in vain:
Th' expecting boy she could not tell
He'd ne'er his mother see again.

But, while she stood in mournful thought,
Nearer and nearer voices came;
The servants 'loitering Anna' sought,
The echoes rang with Anna's name.

Ah! then, o'ercome with boding fear,
Poor Zambo seized her trembling hand,
'Mine only friend,' he cried, 'me fear,
You go, and me not see my land'.

Anna returned the artless grasp:
'I cannot grant thy suit', she cries;
'But I my father's knees will clasp,
Nor will I, till he hears me, rise.

'For, should thine anxious wish prove vain,
And thou no more thy country see,
Still, pity's hand might break thy chain,
And lighter bid thy labours be.

'Here wanton stripes, alas! are thine,
And tasks, far, far beyond thy powers;
But I'll my father's heart incline
To bear thee to more friendly shores.

'Come! to the beach! for me they wait!'
Then, grasping Zambo's sable hand,
Swift as the wind, with hope elate,
The lovely suppliant reached the sand.

But woe betides an ill-timed suit:
His temper soured by her delay,
Trevannion bade his child be mute,
Nor dare such fruitless hopes betray.

'I know', she cried, 'I cannot free
The numerous slaves that round me pine;
But one poor Negro's friend to be
Might (blessed thought!) might now be mine.'

But vainly Anna wept and prayed,
And Zambo knelt upon the shore;
Without reply, the pitying maid
Trevannion to the vessel bore.

Mean while, poor Zambo's cries to still,
And his indignant grief to tame,
Eager to act his brutal will,
The Negro's scourge-armed ruler came.

The whip is raised . . . . the lash descends . . . .
And Anna hears the sufferer's groan;
But while the air with shrieks she rends,
The signal's given . . . . the ship sails on.

That instant, by despair made bold,
Zambo one last great effort tried;
He burst from his tormentor's hold, ...
He plunged within the foaming tide.

The desperate deed Trevannion views,
And all his weak resentment flies;

'See, see! the vessel he pursues!
Help him, for mercy's sake!' he cries:

'Out with the boat! quick! throw a rope!
Wretches, how tardy is your aid!'
While, pale with dread, or flush'd with hope.
Anna the awful scene surveyed.

The boat is out, ... the rope is cast, ...
And Zambo struggles with the waves; ....
'Ha! he the boat approaches fast!
O father, we his life shall save!'

'But low, my child, and lower yet
His head appears; .... but sure he sees
The succour given .... and seems to meet
Th' opposing waves with greater ease: ....

'See, see! the boat, the rope, he nears;
I see him now his arm extend! ....
My Anna, dry those precious tears;
My child shall be *one Negro's friend!*'

Ah! Death was near, that hope to foil: ....
To reach the rope poor Zambo tries; ....
But, ere he grasps it, faint with toil,
The struggling victim sinks, and dies.

Anna, I mourn thy virtuous woe;
I mourn thy father's keen remorse;
But from my eyes no tears would flow
At sight of Zambo's silent corse: ....

The orphan from his mother torn,
And pining for his native shore, ...
Poor tortured slave ... poor wretch forlorn! ....
Can I his early death deplore? ....

I pity those who live and groan:
Columbia countless Zambos sees; ....
For swelled with many a wretch's moan
Is Western India's sultry breeze.

Come, Justice, come! in glory drest,
O come! the woe-worn Negro's friend, ...
The fiend-delighting trade arrest,
The Negro's chains asunder rend!

NOTES

1. Opie's mother died when Opie was fifteen years old.

2. See Eberle's discussion of the critical debate surrounding *Adeline Mowbray*, which she argues paints a portrait of a woman's sexual and intellectual transgressions. See also Carol Howard, "'The Story of the Pineapple': Sentimental Abolitionism and Moral Motherhood in Amelia Opie's *Adeline Mowbray*."

3. Opie's text also appears in *The Liberator* and Garrison's *Juvenile Poems, for the Use of Free American Children of Every Complexion*; however, that version does not include the "Address to Children."

4. Opie's note in the original text states: I believe that the late Granville Sharp, and some members of the Society of Friends, were the first to make exertions in behalf of the poor Negroes, and to oppose Slavery in all its branches; but the almost incredible labours of Thomas Clarkson have been the principal means of accomplishing what has hitherto been done to save and serve them. This benevolent man gave up his home and his comforts, and visited hundreds and hundreds of Slave Ships, in order to detect the barbarities which their peculiar construction was intended to effect, and he sailed and travelled thousands and thousands of miles to find out all the cruelties practiced on the passage and in the Islands, the blessing and protection of the Almighty attending him whithersoever he went.

5. Opie's note in the original text states: Thomas Cooper said in his examination before the Committee of the House of Commons, that he never saw a Negro uncovered who did not exhibit traces of the whip on his body. Others have said the same.

6. Opie's note in the original text states: In the Appendix to the Sixteenth Report of the Directors of the African Institution are the following facts.

> The *Rodeur* sailed from Havre on the 24th of January, 1819, for the Coast of Africa, to purchase slaves; when under the Line, it was perceived that the Negroes, who were heaped together in the hold, and between decks, had contracted a considerable inflammation in the eyes. They were successively brought on deck in order that they might breathe a purer air; but it was necessary to discontinue this practice, because they threw themselves into the sea locked in each other's arms.* On the arrival of the ship at Guadaloupe, the crew were in a most deplorable condition, for all except one sailor were deprived of sight. Of the Negroes, thirty-nine *had become blind*, and were *thrown overboard*, as being not fit to sell; twelve had lost one eye, and fourteen were more or less afflicted with spots on the cornea, or horny part of the eye.
>
> The traffic is still carried on with impunity, and conducted with more cruelty than ever; because the Slave Captains, to avoid detection, have recourse to the most atrocious expedients for getting rid of their captives. By the official reports relative to the *La Jeune Estelle*, (a slave ship) fourteen Negroes were on board. The vessel was stopped and examined, but no Negro could be found: a search was instituted, but in vain; at last a groan was heard issuing from a

cask. It was opened, and two young girls from ten to fourteen years of age were found nearly suffocated within it. *Several casks of the same form and size had been previously thrown overboard!*

*Being seized with *nostalgia,* or the *desire* (poor things!) of returning to their native country.

7. Opie's note in the original text states: Vide the speech of Joseph John Gurney, on British Colonial Slavery, delivered in January 1824, at a public meeting in Norwich.

SARAH JOSEPHA BUELL HALE

(OCTOBER 24, 1788–APRIL 30, 1879)

Poet, novelist, editor, and author of children's literature, Sarah Josepha Buell Hale represents one of the earliest recovered American women to reference slavery in children's literature. In sharp contrast to domestic abolitionists who subsequently created images of victimized slave children, abolitionist mother-historians, or abolitionist children, Hale expressed an indecisive position about slavery in her children's fiction. She embodies the Republican mother who encouraged children toward patriotism, not abolitionism.

Hale was born in Newport, New Hampshire, to Gordon Buell (a captain during the Revolutionary War) and Martha Whittlesey Buell. M. Sarah Smedman states that "[s]ubsequently studying Latin, philosophy, English, and classical literature with her brother Horatio, then a student at Dartmouth . . . , Hale acquired the equivalent of a college degree, a rare possession for a woman of her day. She put her talents to use [teaching] in a Newport private school" (209). In 1813, at the age of twenty-five, she married David Hale, a lawyer and Freemason, with whom she had five children. He encouraged Hale's writing and self-education. After his death in 1822, the Freemasons opened a millinery business to help Hale support herself; however, she left the business because she could earn an income from writing.

Hale's prolific literary production stemmed from her intent to use literature "to teach truth and to build character while imparting pleasure through story and verse" (Smedman 209). She published her first book of poems, *The Genius of Oblivion, and Other Original Poems* in 1823; however, her first novel, *Northwood: A Tale of New England* (1827), "the first American novel by a woman" (Smedman 209), secured her career as an author. Hale also served as editor for the *Ladies' Magazine and Literary*

Gazette, later renamed the *American Literary Magazine* (Boston, MA), from 1827 to 1836 and for *Godey's Lady's Book* (Philadelphia, PA) from 1837 to 1877. As *Godey's* editor for forty years, Hale played a major role in selecting original, contemporary American literary voices and in using the magazine to advance women's position in society through education. Always intent on blending character-building with pleasure, Hale edited numerous children's literature collections and published titles for children including "Mary Had a Little Lamb," *Poems for Our Children: Designed for Families, Sabbath Schools, and Infant Schools: Written to Inculcate Moral Truths and Various Sentiments* (1830), and *The School Song Book* (1834).

Following in her father's footsteps, Sarah was an ardent patriot but not an ardent abolitionist. She organized women to raise thirty-thousand dollars to complete the Bunker Hill Monument in Boston and campaigned for twenty-three years to institute Thanksgiving as a national holiday, a proclamation that Abraham Lincoln passed on October 3, 1863 (Schilpp and Murphy 34–48; Smedman 210; Okker 70–71, 84–109). Yet, when slavery divided the nation, Hale responded with reserved enthusiasm. Patricia Okker states, "Hale's own position [on slavery] reveals her division: although she opposed slavery, she rejected the abolition movement as too partisan. Yet in keeping with her association of women with morality, Hale did not remain silent on the subject" (80).[1] As editor of *Godey's Lady's Book*, she safeguarded its policy that "politics and economics [were] subjects inappropriate for women, [so the magazine] did not enter into the controversy between the states" (Smedman 210; see also Boyer 112; Okker 76; Finley 176). Outside of *Godey's* realm, however, Hale published two adult novels about slavery's immorality (Okker 81), *Northwood, A Tale of New England* (1827; revised, with a slightly different title, in 1852, to counter Stowe's *Uncle Tom's Cabin*) and *Liberia; or, Mr. Peyton's Experiments* (1853), in which she supported colonization rather than immediate emancipation.

Unlike the domestic abolitionists included in this anthology, Hale essentially excluded discussions about slavery from her prolific children's publications. The prefatory remark in *Poems for Our Children . . . Written to Inculcate Moral Truths and Virtuous Sentiments* reveals Hale as "an ardent patriot" (Schilpp and Murphy 38) and a teacher of familial, religious, and civic ideals. As evident in "My Country" and "Independence,"[2] Hale advocated patriotism in children because she downplayed the more problematic American past. For example, "My Country" champions patriotic idealism and relegates the violation of democratic liberties to an asterisk (after line 8) that states "All but two millions." Similarly, the ambiguity in "Independence," epitomizes the clash between presenting an idyllic versus a historically accurate record of American democracy. The first stanza celebrates men like Hale's father who fought for American independence during the Revolutionary War. She suggest that God will intercede to end oppression. But does that include the oppression African Americans endure under slavery? Hale's "ambiguity and inability to redefine patriotism in terms of historical accuracy perpetuates an inaccurate understanding of American freedom and accentuates the sadness that the narrator asks the celebrants to deny" (De Rosa 89). This stance contrasts to subsequent domestic abolitionists whose revisionist American histories for children expose the hypocrisy of American freedom in light of enslaving so many for racist and economic reasons.

FROM *POEMS FOR OUR CHILDREN: DESIGNED FOR FAMILIES, SABBATH SCHOOLS, AND INFANT SCHOOLS: WRITTEN TO INCULCATE MORAL TRUTHS AND VIRTUOUS SENTIMENTS* (1830)

"To all Good Children in the United States"

I wrote this book for you—to please and instruct you. . . . I intended, when I began to write this book, to furnish you with a few pretty songs and poems which would teach you truths, and, I hope, induce you to love truth and goodness. Children who love their parents and their home, can soon teach their hearts to love their God and their country.

"BIRDS"

If ever I see,
    On bush or tree,
Young birds in a pretty nest,
    I must not, in my play,
    Steal the birds away,
To grieve their mother's breast.

My mother I know,
    Would sorrow so,
Should I be stolen away—
    So I'll speak to the birds,
    In my softest words,
Nor hurt them in my play.

"MY COUNTRY"

America! my own dear land,—
O, 'tis a lovely land to me;
I thank my God that I was born
    Where man is *free!*

Our land—it is a glorious land—
And wide it spreads from sea to sea—
And sister States in Union join
    And all are *free.*[3]

And equal laws we all obey,—
To kings we never bend the knee—
We may not own no Lord but God
    Where all are *free.*

We've lofty hills and sunny vales
And streams that roll to either sea—[4]
And through this large and varied land
        Alike we're *free*.

You hear the sounds of healthful toil,
And youth's gay shout and childhood's glee,
And everyone in safety dwells
        And all are *free*.

We're brothers all from South to North,
One bond will draw us to agree—
We love this country of our birth—
        We love the *free*.

We love the name of Washington,
I lisped it on my father's knee—
And we shall ne'er forget the *name*
        While we are *free*.

My land, my own dear native Land,
Thou art a lovely land to me;
I bless my God that I was born
        Where man is *free*!

"INDEPENDENCE"

We come with hearts of gladness,
    To breathe our songs of praise,—
Let not a note of sadness
    Be blended in the lays;
For 'tis a hallowed story,
    The theme of Freedom's birth
Our *father's* deeds of glory
    Are echoed round the earth.

The sound is waxing stronger,
    And thrones and nations hear;
"Man may not triumph longer,
    For God, the Lord is near—"
And He will crush oppression,
    And raise the humble mind,
And give the earth's possession
    Among the good and kind.

And then shall sink the mountains,
   Where pride and power were crowned;
And peace, like gentle fountains,
   Shall shed its pureness round—
And then the world will hear us,
   And join our glorious la,
And songs of millions cheer us,
   On this our Nation's Day.

Soon Freedom's loud hosannas,
   Shall burst from every voice,
Till mountains and Savannas
   Rock back and sound—"Rejoice!"
To God, the king of heaven,
   Then consecrate the strain;—
Earth's fetters will be driven;
   And God the Lord will reign.

NOTES

1. For an informative, complex, and very insightful discussion of Hale's career and influence on America's literary scene, see Patricia Okker, *Our Sister Editors: Sarah J. Hale and the Tradition of Nineteenth-Century American Women Editors* (1995).

2. For a complete discussion of these poems, see De Rosa 87–89.

3. Hale's footnote in original text: All but two millions.

4. Hale's footnote in original text: Atlantic and Pacific Oceans.

FLORENCE

(BIOGRAPHY AND DATES UNAVAILABLE)

"THE INFANT ABOLITIONIST" (1834)

How often by a sinless child
May we of error be beguiled;
How oft a single, simple word
The scaled springs of thought have stirr'd
And waken'd feelings deep, to be
A lesson for futurity!

The gayest, most aerial thing,
That moves on earth without a wing,
Today such lesson taught to me.
How sweetly, yet unconscuiously,
The infant maiden, artless, mild,
Reproved her elder playmate's pride!
And yet the babe has only smiled
Three years by her fond mother's side.

They stood before a picture—one
Where dark 'neath Afric's burning sun,
A wild and lonely native lay:
The child's companion turn'd to say,
"There's an *old nigger*, Anne, see!,"
And pointed to the African;
The little one said quietly,
"I see he is a *colored man*."

Ah, well may sages bow to thee,
Loving and guileness infancy!
And sigh, amid their learned lore,

For one untaught delight of thine—
And feel they'd give their wisdom's store
To know again thy truth divine!

The boasted power of eloquence
Can sway the soul with magic art—
But simple words from innocence
May sink more deeply in the heart.

ELIZABETH MARGARET CHANDLER

(PSEUDONYMS: AGNES, MARGARET, EMILY, GERTRUDE, AND E.M.C.,
DECEMBER 24, 1807–NOVEMBER 2, 1834)

Elizabeth Margaret Chandler is perhaps one of the earliest American women to publish critiques of slavery's inhumanity and to support its immediate abolition; however, she did so by relying on pseudonyms such as Agnes, Margaret, Emily, Gertrude, and E.M.C. because of her "fear of publicity" (Bowerman 613). Chandler's modesty suited her to writing abolitionist texts for children because this genre permitted her to voice her political views without giving speeches at antislavery conventions or similar open forums.

Born to Margaret Evans (who died when Elizabeth was an infant) and Thomas Chandler (a farmer and doctor who died when Elizabeth was nine), Elizabeth and her two older brothers came from a highly respected family in Center, Delaware. After their mother's death, the family moved to Philadelphia. Elizabeth attended the Friends' School, where she later made acquaintances with leading abolitionists. Although she stopped attending school when she turned thirteen, she pursued her interests in reading and writing (Bowerman 613). From childhood, Chandler expressed a facility for writing poetry, which her friends and relatives started publishing when she was twelve. By age sixteen, Chandler's writings had already appeared in various newspapers (613) and they continued to do so for an additional eleven years as she advocated abolitionist ideas, especially to women and children from the Midwest to the northeast.

Chandler's upbringing in the Philadelphia Quaker community may have sparked her humanitarian and abolitionist interests. She joined Philadelphia's Female Anti-Slavery Society, but "did not, in consequence of her retired habits, take a very active part in its public proceedings" (Lundy 39). This female community and Chandler's love of writing fueled her abolitionist poetry, editorials, and essays. Her first antislavery

poem, "The Slave Ship" (1825) led to her affiliation with leading abolitionists. In a letter to Hannah Townsend, Chandler describes how, on
winning third prize in the *Casket*, the poem was reprinted in the *Genius
of Universal Emancipation* (Baltimore, MD), which led to her association
with its chief editor and publisher, Benjamin Lundy. After three years of
submissions to the *Genius*, Chandler worked as editor of the "Ladies
Repository" from 1829 to 1834 (Lundy 11–12). During this tenure, she
met William Lloyd Garrison, who coedited Lundy's *Genius*. To her advantage, Garrison subsequently published her poems in *The Liberator*
(Boston), which he founded in reaction against Lundy's support for colonization instead of immediate emancipation. Interestingly, even though
Chandler nurtured her affiliations with Garrison and Lundy, who published her works almost concurrently, she remained within more traditional female realms: the Ladies' Repository of Lundy's *Genius* and the
"Juvenile Department" of Garrison's *The Liberator*.[1]

Sarah Bowerman, Merton Dillon, Blanche Hersh, and Alma Lutz,
among others, have discussed Chandler's contributions to female abolitionist discourse; however, they have overlooked how her poems for children empower women and children abolitionists. Chandler's poems
depict mothers educating children about slavery as well as children en-
gaging in private or public antislavery protest. Chandler's poems, "What
Is a Slave, Mother?" (1831) and "Looking at the Soldiers" (1832), depict
children being (re)educated about slavery's inhumanity with the guidance of a mother who acts as both educator and revolutionary. For example, the image of the abolitionist mother-historian appears in "Looking
at the Soldiers," in which a child's fascination with a parade of marching soldiers sparks a mother-child dialogue that critiques American politics. The child's comments about the parade reveal his uncomplicated
American patriotism. However, his abolitionist mother-historian challenges his views by telling him that Americans celebrate their independence but enslave millions. By (re)educating the child, this mother
rewrites a chapter of American history. Furthermore, she asks her son to
reject the scene that masks America's hypocrisy, just as she turns her back
to it. This private but seditious abolitionist act fosters a new civic virtue
and an altered perception of American history (De Rosa 97). From the
safety of their homes and nurseries, Chandler's mother-figures unapolo-
getically endorse women and children's activism and civil disobedience.

Chandler also authored several poems in which children engage in private and public abolitionism without adult involvement. Chandler de-
velops a nonthreatening image of the child activist in "The Child's

Evening Hymn" (1831), one of the earliest poems to cast a fictional white child pleading for white masters to reject slavery. The child expresses gratitude for his family, but he also engages in a moment of private activism when he prays that God convert the slave owners and help the slaves. In contrast to images of abolitionist prayer, Chandler's "The Sugar-Plums" (1832), "Oh Press Me Not to Taste Again" (1832) and "Christmas" (1834) depict children who actively challenge slavery, much like children who joined juvenile antislavery societies (De Rosa 108–114). Just as Chandler encouraged members of the Ladies Free Produce Society to boycott slave-made goods (M. P. Jones, 6; Dillon, *Notable* 319), she depicts girls following this society's example. In each poem, a child deliberately deprives herself of sweets rather than support an economic system that violates religious principles and inflicts physical, familial, and emotional violence on African Americans. "Through her outspoken, young protagonists, Chandler gives young readers images of how even a child's private act can have public ramifications" (De Rosa 116).

One of the first American women to write abolitionist children's literature, Chandler establishes the tropes that appear repeatedly in subsequent works: the victimized slave child, the abolitionist mother-historian, and the abolitionist child.

"A LESSON FROM THE FLOWERS"² (1831)

Little maiden, little maiden!
With the spring's first blossoms laden,
Pause and list thee, while I tell
Words that thou should'st ponder well.
When thou pluck'd those glowing buds,
Saw'st thou none whom drenching floods,
Chilling winds, or blighting frost,
Rudely to the earth had tost—
Or which some rough foot had trod,
Crush'd and broken, to the sod,—
Till their leaves, all soil'd and stain'd,
Not a brilliant trace retain'd?
Yet had those been kindly rear'd,
They had bright as these appear'd.

Thou art in life's joyous spring,
Fair hopes round thee blossoming!
And the glad thoughts of thy breast
Sweet as perfume o'er thee rest:
Yet not all as young as thou,
Bright one! wear so free a brow.
There are some whose early years
Are all stain'd with hopeless tears,—
Some whose joys and griefs are slighted,
Some whose hearts are crush'd and blighted,
Till each sunny tint is lost
'Neath contempt's unkindly frost.

Little maiden, little maiden!
When thou seest one so laden
With the stains that wrong and wo
O'er the spirit's light will throw,
Past thou not with scornful eye
And unpausing footstep by;
For within thy shelter'd bower,
That had bloom'd as bright a flower.
Rather do thou lift its head
Gently from its rain-drench'd bed,
And with watchful care restore
All the brilliant hues it wore,
Till its grateful perfume be
Rich and sweet reward to thee.

"THE CHILD'S EVENING HYMN" (1831)

Father! while the daylight dies,
Hear our grateful voices rise:
For the blessings that we share,
For thy kindness and thy care,
For the joy that fills our breast;
For the love that makes us blest,
    We thank thee, Father.

For an earthly father's arm,
Shielding us from wrong and harm;
For a mother's watchful cares,
Mingled with her many prayers;
For the happy kindred band,
'Midst whose peaceful links we stand,
    We bless thee, Father.

Yet, while 'neath the evening skies,
Thus we bid our thanks arise,
Father! still we think of those,
Who are bow'd with many woes,
Whom no earthly parent's arm
Can protect from wrong and harm;
    The poor slaves, Father.

Ah! while we are richly blest,
They are wretched and distrest [sic]!
Outcasts in their native land,
Crush'd beneath oppression's hand,
Scarcely knowing even thee,
Mighty Lord of earth and sea!
    Oh save them, Father!

Touch the flinty hearts, that long
Have, remorseless, done them wrong;
Ope the eyes that long have been
Blind to every guilty scene;
That the slave—a slave no more—
Grateful thanks to thee may pour,
    And bless thee, Father.

"WHAT IS A SLAVE, MOTHER?" (1831)

What is a slave, mother? I heard you say
That word with a sorrowful voice one day;
And it came again to my thoughts last night
As I laid awake in the broad moon-light;
Methinks I have heard a story told
Of some poor men who are bought and sold,
And driven abroad with stripes to toil
The live-long day on a stranger's soil:
    Is this true, mother?

May children as young as I be sold,
And torn away from their mother's hold—
From home—from all they have loved and known,
To dwell in the great wild world alone,
Far, far away in some distant place,
Where they may never see their parent's face?
Ah? how I should weep to be torn from you!
Tell me, dear mother, can this be true?
    Alas, yes, my child.

Does the master love the slave child well,
That he takes away in his house to dwell?
Does he teach him all that he ought to know,
And wipe his tears when they sometimes flow—
And watch beside him in sickness and pain,
Till health comes back to his cheek again—
And kneel each night by his side to pray,
That God will keep him through life's rough way?
    Alas, no, my child.

Ah, then must the tales I have heard be true,
Of the cruel things that the masters do;
That the poor slaves often most creep to bed,
On their scatter'd straw, but scantily fed;
Be sometimes loaded with heavy chains;
And flogged till their blood the keen lash stains;
While none will care for their bitter cry,
Or soothe their hearts when their grief is high!
    It is so, my child.

And is it not, mother, a sinful thing,
The bosoms of others with pain to wring—
To bid them go labor and delve the soil,

And seize the reward of their weary toil?
For men to tear men from their homes away,
And sell them for gold like a lawful prey?
Oh, surely the land where such deeds are done,
Must be a most savage and wicked one!
    It is this, my child.

"THE SUGAR-PLUMS" (1832)

No, no, pretty sugar-plums! stay where you are!
Though my grandmother sent you to me from so far;
You look very nice, you would taste very sweet,
And I love you right well, yet not one will I eat.

For the poor slaves have labour'd far down in the south,
To make you so sweet and so nice for my mouth;
But I want no slaves toiling for me in the sun,
Driven on with the whip, till the long day is done.

Perhaps some poor slave child, that hoed up the ground,
Round the cane in whose rich juice your sweetness was found,
Was flogg'd, till his mother cried sadly to see,
And I'm sure I want nobody beaten for me.

So grandma, I thank you for being so kind,
But your present, to-day, is not much to my mind;
Though I love you so dearly, I choose not to eat
Even what you have sent me by slavery made sweet.

Thus said little Fanny, and skipp'd off to play,
Leaving all her nice sugar-plums just where they lay,
As merry as if they had gone in her mouth,
And she had not cared for the slaves of the south.

"OH PRESS ME NOT TO TASTE AGAIN" (1832)

Oh press me not to taste again
    Of those luxurious banquet sweets!
Or hide from view the dark red stain,
    That still my shuddering vision meets.

Away! 'tis loathsome! bear me hence!
    I cannot feed on human sighs,
Or feast with sweets my palate's sense,
    While blood is 'neath the fair disguise.

No, never let me taste again
  Of aught beside the coarsest fare,
Far rather, than my conscience stain,
  With the polluted luxuries there.

"LOOKING AT THE SOLDIERS" (1832)

"Mother, the trumpets are sounding to-day,
And the soldiers go by in their gallant array!
Their horses prance gaily, their banners float free,
Come, come to the window, dear mother, with me!

"Do you see how their bayonets gleam in the sun,
And their soldier-plumes nod, as they slowly march on?
And look to the regular tread of their feet!
Keeping time to the sound of the kettle-drum's beat.

"This, mother, you know, is a glorious day,
And Americans all should be joyous and gay;
For the Fourth of July saw our country set free;
But you look not delighted, dear mother, like me!"

"No, love; for that shining and brilliant display,
To me only tells of war's fearful array;
And I know that those bayonets, flashing so bright,
Were made in man's blood to be spoil'd of their light.

"And the music that swells up so sweet to the ear,
In a long gush of melody, joyous and clear,
Just as freely would pour out its wild thrilling flood,
To stir up men's hearts to the shedding of blood!

"Our country, my boy, as you tell me, is free,
But even that thought brings a sadness to me;
For less guilt would be hers, were her own fetter'd hand
Unable to loosen her slaves from their band.

"We joy that our country's light bonds have been broke,
But her sons wear, by thousands, a life-crushing yoke;
And yon bayonets, dear, would be sheathed in their breast,
Should they fling off the shackles that round them are prest.

"Even 'midst these triumphant rejoicings, to-day,
The slave-mother weeps for her babes, torn away,
'Midst the echoing burst of these shouts, to be sold,
Human forms as they are, for a pittance of gold!

"Can you wonder then, love, that your mother is sad,
Though yon show is so gay, and the crowd is so glad?
Or will not my boy turn with me from the sight,
To think of those slaves sunk in sorrow and night?"

"CHRISTMAS" (1834)

Mother, when Christmas comes once more,
   I do not wish that you
Should buy sweet things for me again,
   As you were used to do:

The taste of cakes and sugar-plums
   Is pleasant to me yet,
And temptingly the gay shops look,
   With their fresh stores outset.

But I have learn'd, dear mother,
   That the poor and wretched slave
Must toil to win their sweetness,
   From the cradle to the grave.

And when he faints with weariness
   Beneath the torrid sun,
The keen lash urges on his toil,
   Until the day is done.

But when the holy angels' hymn,
   On Judea's plains afar,
Peal'd sweetly on the shepherds' ear,
   'Neath Bethlehem's wondrous star,

They sung of glory to our God,—
   "Peace and good will to men,"—
For Christ, the Saviour of the world,
   Was born amidst them then.

And is it for His glory, men
   Are made to toil,
With weary limbs and breaking hearts,
   Upon another's soil?

That they are taught not of his law,
   To know his holy will,
And that He hates the deed of sin,
   And loves the righteous still?

And is it peace and love to men,
  To bind them with the chain,
And sell them like the beasts that feed
  Upon the grassy plain?

To tear their flesh with scourgings rude,
  And from the aching heart,
The ties to which it fondliest clings,
  For evermore to part?

And 'tis because of all this sin, my mother,
  That I shun
To taste the tempting sweets for which
  Such wickedness is done.

If men to men will be unjust, if slavery must be,
Mother, the chain must not be worn; the scourge
  Be plied for me.

"LITTLE SADO'S STORY" (1836)

Robert Sutcliff, in his book of travels in America, relates the incident which has suggested the following lines. Little Sado was an African boy, who was rescued from a slave-ship by a United States' frigate, and provided by the Pennsylvania Abolition Society with a home, in a respectable family, near Philadelphia.

"Although tended with the greatest tenderness," says Sutcliff, "yet he was often seen weeping at the recollection of his near connexions [sic]. He said that himself and sister were on a visit, at a relation's, and that after the family had retired to rest, they were suddenly alarmed at the dead of night, by a company of man-stealers breaking into their habitation. They were all carried off towards the sea, where they arrived at the end of three days, and were confined until the vessel sailed.

"Not long after this negro boy had been brought into S. P.'s family, he was taken ill of a bad fever; and for a time there appeared but little hopes [sic] of his recovery, although the best medical help was obtained, and every kindness and attention shown him.

"There being now scarcely any prospect of his recovery, his mistress was desirous of administering some religious consolation, and observed to him, as he had always been a very good boy, she had no doubt that if he died at this time, his spirit would be admitted into a state of eternal rest and peace. On hearing this he quickly replied, 'I know that if I die,

I shall be happy; for as soon as my body is dead, my spirit shall fly away
to my father and mother and sisters and brothers in Africa.' The boy recovered. His good conduct had gained the favour and respect of the
whole family, and I have no doubt that the care bestowed upon his education, will in due time afford him a brighter prospect of a future state
than that of returning to Africa."

"Why weep'st thou, gentle boy? Is not thy lot
Amidst a home of tenderness and friends
Who have been ever kind to thee? Thy heart
Should be too young for the world's bitterness,
And the deep grief, that even amidst thy smiles,
Seems scarce to be forgotten. Thou art good,
A very innocent and gentle boy,
And I would have thee happy. Is there aught
Thou lackest with us, Sado? Did I not,
In thy sore sickness, with a mother's care,
Watch by thy couch and nurse thee? Day by day
Have I not taught thee patiently? and more
Than earthly learning, show'd thee of the way
To win eternal happiness. A better hope
Than that which only look'd to Afric's shore,
To find thy future Heaven!"—

    "Yes, thou hast done all this,
And much more, lady! Thou hast been to me
A true and tireless friend, and may there be
    Laid up for thee a full reward of bliss,
In that bright Heaven of which I've heard thee tell,
Where God and all his holy angels dwell.

    "Yet how can I but weep
Whene'er I think upon the mother's eye,
That smiled to meet my glance in days gone by,
    And watch'd in tenderness above my sleep,
Now grown all dim with hopeless grief for me,
Who never more may home or parent see.

    " 'Twas on a bright sunny morn,
When with glad heart I sprang across the hills,
With my young sister, and beside the rills,
    Whose shining waves and clustering flowers were borne,
While at the cabin door my mother stood,
And watch'd our footsteps to the distant wood.

"She never saw us more—
For in the dead of night, while deep we slept
Within our uncle's home, the man-thieves crept
    With stealthy pace, like tigers, to our door.
And, bursting in, they dragg'd us far away,
A helpless, frighten'd, unresisting prey.

"Ah, lady, now thine eyes
Are wet with tears:—then wonder not I weep,
Within whose waking thoughts, or dreams of sleep,
    The memories of such scenes as this arise,
And worse than these, the constant thought of pain,
That I shall never see my home again.

"Three days they drove us on,
A weary, wretched, and despairing band,
Until with swollen limbs we reach'd the strand,
    Where 'neath the setting sun the sea-waves shone;
Then gasping in the slave-ship's hold we lay,
And wish'd each groan might bear our lives away.

"Ah, thou canst never know
Of all our sufferings in that loathsome den,
And from the cruel and hard-hearted men,
    Who mock'd at all our anguish and our woe;
Until at length thy country's ship came by,
And saved us from our depth of misery.

"Yet still, though not a slave,
I am a stranger in a stranger's land,
Far sever'd from my own dear kindred band,
    By many a wide-stretch'd plain and rolling wave;
And, although even with thee my lot is cast,
I cannot lose the memory of the past.

"Then wonder not I weep;
For never can my lost home be forgot;
Nor all the loved ones who have made that spot
    The heaven to which e'en yet, amid my sleep,
My hopes are sometimes turn'd—though thou hast taught
My waking hours a holier, better thought."

NOTES

1. Chandler also published her works in *The Liberty Minstrel*, *The Pearl*, the *Atlantic Souvenir*, and various gift books.

2. Reprinted in *The Liberator*'s Juvenile Department on May 14, 1831.

ELIZA LEE CABOT FOLLEN

(August 15, 1787–January 26, 1860)

Eliza Lee Cabot Follen, a prominent Bostonian,[1] abolitionist, editor, biographer, novelist, poet, playwright, and children's author, made significant contributions to abolitionist juvenile literature. Now remembered for "The Three Little Kittens" (in *Little Songs* 1833), Follen's catalog of children's literature includes *The Well-Spent Hour* (1827), *Sequel to "The Well-Spent Hour", or, The Birthday* (1832), *Hymns, Songs, and Fables, for Children* (1846), *Little Songs, for Little Boys and Girls* (1833), *The Liberty Cap* (1846), *Nursery Songs* (1839), *True Stories About Dogs and Cats* (1856), *May Morning and New Year's Eve* (1857), *Twilight Stories* (1858), a twelve-volume collection, and numerous other titles. She also edited *The Child's Friend* from 1843 to 1850. Phyllis Moe states, "Although her children's poetry is now almost forgotten, F[ollen] was a pioneer who turned from the harsh, morbid verse characteristic of early 19th-c. American children's poetry to rhymes frankly meant to give more pleasure than instruction" (59). Amidst Follen's pleasurable children's stories and poems, one finds abolitionist juvenile fiction that contains critical statements about slavery using recurrent tropes of domestic abolitionist juvenile fiction, namely, the victimized slave child, the heroic slave mother, the abolitionist mother-historian, and the abolitionist child.

Eliza Follen participated in various abolitionist efforts despite the denunciation from opponents who called her a radical. As "an active member of abolitionist society both in Boston and Cambridge, she lectured . . . and helped to organize antislavery bazaars to raise funds for the cause" (Schlesinger 166). In addition, Follen wrote prolifically about slavery. She authored "To Mothers in the Free States" (1855); edited the abolitionist annual, *The Liberty Bell*; and contributed several hymns and songs to the Anti-Slavery Tract collection.[2] Although literary critics and historians have recognized such titles, they have neglected to note that despite Follen's status as "a radical outcast" (MacCann 142), she included her abolitionist ideals throughout her literature for children. Perhaps, because she scattered her attacks on slavery within a gender-appropriate space of juvenile fiction, several Boston publishers continued to print her works and Americans continued to purchase them from 1830 until after Follen's death in 1860 (De Rosa 25–27).

In *Hymns, Songs, and Fables, for Young People* (1846; reprint here comes from the 1848 edition), Follen heightens consciousness about the slave child's plight by interspersing poems about slave children, namely, "Children in Slavery" and "The Little Slave's Wish,"[3] amidst those about white children's innocence. In "Children in Slavery,"[4] Follen contrasts a middle-class, white child's experience of happiness and uninhibited play with a slave child's lost innocence and mental distress. She establishes her abolitionist voice by asserting that the slave child's seemingly insignificant sadness will have negative national and global implications. Similarly, in "The Little Slave's Wish" (1846),[5] Follen creates a sentimental juvenile pseudo slave-narrative in which a slave-child's voice critiques slavery for rupturing the nineteenth-century notions of childhood innocence and American declarations of each individual's *right* to happiness. Having recognized his status as a slave, the child's questions reveal a budding preoccupation that he caused or that God ordained his suffering. The child's death wish suggests that he must alleviate his own emotional pain because he has no one to intercede on his behalf. Included amidst more traditional works in this collection, these two sentimental poems employ the slave child's voice to arouse sympathy intended to spur young white readers to abolitionist agendas.

In addition to images of violated childhood innocence, Follen's "Conscience—The Runaway Negro" (in *Sequel to "The Well-Spent Hour", or, The Birthday* [1832]) in part includes a sentimental juvenile pseudo slave-narrative that casts a fugitive slave mother as a heroic intercessor.[6] During Catherine Nelson's birthday celebration, her parents tell stories to Catherine and her siblings to awaken the children's moral and political consciousness. Mrs. Nelson tells the story of a cobbler who, after twenty years, confesses that he kept five dollars that he was overpaid for repairing a man's shoes. His dishonesty, however, stemmed from a desire to intercede for his poverty-stricken family. Mrs. Nelson's narrative parallels the story that Mr. Nelson tells about a slave mother who intercedes to preserve the family bonds. Trying to evade slave catchers, the slave mother and her sons live as fugitives for seven years as they wait for the

father's escape. Mr. Nelson describes the physical and mental strain that
this clandestine existence produces. When the father does not appear,
the mother surrenders. Ironically, on hearing her story, her former master's son, "in consideration of her sufferings, and from his grateful recollection of her kindness to him when a child, gave her and her boys their
freedom" (see 34). The juxtaposition of Mrs. Nelson and Mr. Nelson's
stories reveals how white families remain united despite economic crises
whereas slave families must contest the slavocracy to sustain their families. If a child reader does not sympathize with the slave's plight or recognize the slave's heroic nature, then Follen implicates him/her in the
institution that undermines America's cultural ideals.

In addition to creating images of rebellious slave mothers, Follen advocates that white mothers adopt an abolitionist mind-set. In "To Mothers in the Free States" (1855),[7] she modifies the eighteenth-century
ideology of "Republican motherhood" to the nineteenth-century principle of abolitionist motherhood. She calls mothers to "come to the rescue of this land" (4) by documenting its history of slavery. She states:

> When [the children] are of an age to understand and hear the sad story,
> she [the mother] will tell them of the wrongs done by the white man
> to the poor slave. She has kindled in the hearts of her children a love
> of justice, a hatred of tyranny, a passionate desire to take the part of
> the oppressed, which shall enlist them for life as the champions of their
> sorely injured, down trodden, colored brethren. Such a mother is an
> abiding inspiration to her children. Her son will not vote for the Fugi-
> tive Slave Law or the Nebraska Bill, nor become a kidnapping United
> States Commissioner! (3)

Follen's rhetoric reinforces the acceptability of the abolitionist mother-
historian because she acts not from political self-interest but from a desire to shape a generation that would rescue America's endangered
democratic principles.

Eliza Follen's collection *The Liberty Cap* (1837, 1840, and 1846) includes "Dialogue"[8] a story with an increasingly vocal and subversive abolitionist mother who gives her child accurate historical and political
information about slavery. When Robert informs his mother of stories he
has heard about Russians oppressing the Polish, she challenges his story
of distant, past oppression with a lesson in American current events. Although she admittedly attempts to arouse sympathy for the victims and
withholds information about some atrocities to protect Robert, the
mother condemns the inaccuracies and silences concerning America's

history of slavery. Follen's mother figure exposes the silenced history and simultaneously condemns the government that allows slavery and violence against Northern abolitionists. She tells Robert about slave children being separated from their parents, the intentional withholding of intellectual and religious education, as well as the violence inflicted on slave girls and fugitives. Her confidence and adamancy lead Robert and readers not only to revise their notions of cruel Russians, kind Americans, and benevolent fathers, but also to situate him/herself as a citizen of an oppressive community.

In "How Shall Children Do Good?" (1844), Eliza Follen specifically addresses what children can do about slavery. She claims that children can "study the perfect law of love and liberty" and learn that "these unhappy beings [slaves], are all the children of God" (see 45). She delays abolitionist activism until the child is older because "when his reason is strong, and his highest faculties are matured, he shall be prepared to live a life of self-denial and self-devotion, and to consecrate himself to the cause of humanity, to the service of his suffering brethren" (see 45). She stresses that arousing sympathy and empathy would shift children's perceptions away from viewing the slave as "other," the first step toward abolishing slavery. According to Follen, this mind-set would prepare children for the activism necessary to "ultimately restore domestic principles and American ideals" (De Rosa 77).

Contradicting her stance in "How Shall Children Do Good?" Follen's juvenile abolitionist literature celebrates young abolitionists. Follen's epistolary short story, "Picnic at Dedham" depicts the protagonist, Hal, differentiating himself from his parents' political views. After attending the August 1 celebration of slavery's abolition in the West Indies and hearing antislavery speeches, Hal writes to his parents, saying, "I never heard you or father speak of the 1st of August" (see 54). He also questions their antiabolitionist sentiments, saying, "When you and father speak of the fanaticism of the abolitionist, you can't mean this, I'm sure" (see 55). Challenging his parent's views, Hal adopts a newfound, abolitionist stance. His dramatic awakening is clear in that initially he hopes "that the time might come when we might be thanking God that our slaves were all free" (see 55–56). But, he ultimately desires to participate in the abolitionist process: "I think that if the men don't all do something about slavery soon, we boys had better see what we can do, for it is too wicked" (see 56). Thus, like the children who joined juvenile abolitionist societies, Hal affirms children's abolitionist activism.

Follen's "Soliloquy of Ellen's Squirrel and His Liberty;—Overheard by a Lover of Nature and a Friend of Ellen" (1846) and "Billy Rabbit to Mary" (1846) praise liberators and condemn oppressors, respectively. Follen's "Soliloquy"[9] praises children who liberate the oppressed. In "Soliloquy," an ex-slave squirrel can "taste of the joys that still are dear" (verse 1, line 4) and "make [a] winter's nest again" (verse 1, line 8) because Ellen has liberated it. Having gained what was previously denied to him but allowed to her, the squirrel teaches Ellen to appreciate her own freedom and celebrates her decision to restore its God-given freedom and American inalienable rights. In contrast, "Billy Rabbit to Mary"[10] represents Follen's critique of children who oppress others. Billy Rabbit critiques his former young mistress's proslavery behavior. As trickster-rhetorician, Billy justifies his escape, claiming it as normal to engage in unhindered childlike capers and to desire a family and a community. Follen suggests that the jubilant atmosphere that comes with liberation does not overshadow the ex-slave's resentment of his former owner. Although he begins the letter with "my dear Mary" (see 50) and signs the letter "your devoted, affectionate BILLY" (see 50), this fugitive ex-slave "sealed [the letter] with a thorn" (headnote), rather than a kiss. In this less-than-flattering portrait of Mary, Follen condemns those who perpetuate slavery and undermine the fallacy of benevolent masters and contented slaves.

Eliza Follen's abolitionist juvenile literature carefully imbeds abolitionist rhetoric in seemingly nonthreatening children's fiction. In so doing, she walked a tightrope to evade the criticism she received for otherwise voicing her abolitionist views.

FROM *SEQUEL TO "THE WELL-SPENT HOUR"*, OR, *THE BIRTHDAY* (1832)

CHAPTER VII
"CONSCIENCE—THE RUNAWAY NEGRO"

Mr. Nelson was the first to break the silence; "Come, my children," said he, "now for the stories. As you, Lucy, proposed the entertainment, as the youngest judge speaks first, suppose you begin."

"Oh no," said Lucy, "my story is not ready yet; let James begin."

"Nor mine either," said James; "I had rather not begin."

"I am in a still worse predicament," said Mr. Nelson; "I have not even thought of a story, and it would not be fair to call upon Catherine first."

"It seems to be left to me to begin," said Mrs. Nelson; "and rather than Lucy should not have her stories, I will try to remember an occurrence I witnessed, that I shall pass off for my story, and thus give you all time to prepare yourselves for something better deserving the name."

"There is the beautiful moon," said Lucy, "shining clear across the room through both the front windows; I can see every body's face; now is the time to begin, mother."

"My anecdote," said Mrs. Nelson, "has no interest, except what it derives from its truth, and from the moral it teaches; and may be told in a few words.

"Some years since, when I was passing the day at a friend's house in Boston, there was a ringing at the door, and a very poor but very respectable-looking man entered. I was struck with the serious, almost devotional expression of his face as soon as I saw him.

" 'I have come here,' said he to the gentleman of the house, 'to ask you where I may find your sister,—Jane, I think, was her Christian name. Have you such a sister, and where does she live?'

" 'She lives,' answered Mr. B. 'out of town, about four miles from Boston.'

" 'Then I can walk,' said the man, 'and return in the course of the evening.'

" 'Hardly,' Mr. B. replied; 'the roads are almost impassable. You had better take the stage if you must see her yourself; but I shall go there to-morrow; cannot I do your errand?'

" 'I would rather see her myself,' answered the man; 'I shall not be satisfied if I do not see her myself, and tonight; I should sleep better I think. I am too poor to ride, so I must walk.'

"'It seems strange,' said Mr. B., 'that you can have any thing to say to my sister that you cannot say to me; I will promise faithfully to deliver your message.'

"'I think,' said the man, after a long pause, 'I had better walk out; will you direct me, sir, to the house?'

"'It is now seven o'clock,' said Mr. B.; 'it is raining, and the snow and ice are ancle [sic] deep; and you look like a sick man.'

"'My home,' answered the stranger, 'is fifty miles from Boston; I must leave here tomorrow at day-light, and I cannot return till I have performed this duty. A friend brought me, and has promised to carry me home; but he goes tomorrow morning early. I wish I could see the lady; but, as I cannot, I must tell my errand to you. I must be willing,' said he, in a broken voice, 'to take all my punishment.' He looked pale as ashes as he went on. 'Twenty years ago, sir, I made some shoes for your father's family, and called at his house for my pay. He was sick, and sent his daughter to the door with the money. In paying me, she accidentally gave me two five-dollar bills instead of one. I saw it; I was the father of a young family; I was very poor; I was tempted; and I received the money, knowing and feeling that it was dishonest. I could not forget my sin, till at last I determined I would return the money as soon as I had the means. Then I fell sick, and I have never since had five dollars that I could call my own. Every thing has gone wrong with me; and the thought of my dishonesty still follows me wherever I go. I have not now five dollars in the world. I am sick and I am poor; but I thought if I could see the lady I took the money from, and confess my sin to her, and she would forgive, that then I should feel more certain that God would forgive me, and my mind would be easier. My character, with my town's people, stands fair. It is hard to confess this my sin before so many; but I must take my shame as a just punishment. If ever I have the means, I will restore the money; but I still hope for her forgiveness, though I cannot make restitution.'

"The gentleman assured him that he knew that his sister would freely and gladly forgive him, and would not desire him to restore the money. He would assure him, in her and in his deceased father's name, of their forgiveness, and that he could not but honor him for the proof he had given of the sincerity of his repentance.

"The poor man looked weak and exhausted, but much happier; and, thanking the gentleman for his kindness, left the house.

"There were three or four of Mr. B.'s children present, and their mother, and myself, to witness this poor man's confession of his offence; and I think I may say that we all felt nothing but respect for him, and thus learned the great lesson, that it is not money, or success, or importance in the world, or even a perfect freedom from sin, that is necessary to insure respect; but that it is a simple and earnest desire after perfection, a free confession and a true and hearty repentance of sin, that constitutes the true dignity of such weak and tempted beings as we all are."

"How much better he must have felt when he went away," said Lucy.

"And how glad Mr. B. must have been," said Catherine, "to be able to comfort him."

"But I hope," said James, "I shall never have to make such a confession."

"Though you may not have exactly such a confession to make, James," said his mother, "you remember that you may still have to confess faults, that, in you, are perhaps as great offences as what this poor man had committed, when you consider what his, and what your temptations are; and you ought only to desire to be able to imitate him in his truly manly as well as Christian conduct."

"I think, children," said Mr. Nelson, after a short pause, "that I must try to imitate your mother's magnanimity, and relate, without much preparation, a story that has just come to my mind, which interested me very deeply at the time, and which I heard told by the person who is the subject of it.

"Some years ago I was on a journey, and was passing a few days at Newbern in North Carolina. A gentleman one morning came into the inn where I had taken lodgings, and said that a negro woman and two boys had just been brought into town and carried to the public house opposite, and that they were the strangest looking objects he had ever seen. He asked two or three gentlemen, and amongst them myself, to go with him and see them. I followed him, and we found a young woman with her two children, miserably clothed and sadly emaciated. The mother had an expression of deep sorrow in her face, and the children started and looked up as we entered, as if they were upon the point of running away. When we spoke to them they made no answer, and when their mother repeated our questions to them, which she did in a low tone, they answered her in a whisper. They neither of them stood up, but squatted down close by their mother.

"After the mother and children had taken food, for they were hungry, the poor woman was induced by our entreaties to relate her story, which was this.

"Her owner (for she was a slave), about seven years before that time, had removed to the Western country and carried with him all his slaves except her, who, rather than be separated from her husband who was owned by another person, ran away with her two children, one a nursing infant, and completely escaped the vigilance of her pursuers.

"This part of the state abounds in marshes and fens, overgrown with weeds, and interspersed in some places with stumps of pine trees. In one of these dreary retreats she found means to conceal herself, and to obtain subsistence for herself and children, partly by her own exertions, and partly by the assistance of her husband, who occasionally made her a visit and brought them food.

"The manner in which this poor woman concealed herself and her children from discovery, was very curious. By the strictest care and discipline she prevented them from ever crying aloud. She never allowed a sound above a whisper. This may appear strange and difficult to believe, but it is certainly true; and as a proof that there was no deception in her account, I afterwards satisfactorily ascertained, that when they had been in town for more than a month in the company of noisy children, they were not known in a single instance to raise their voices higher than a soft whisper. Another proof of the truth of her account, was the appearance of the children. It was with great difficulty they could stand or walk erect, as their mother had always kept them in the posture in which they then were by her side, squatting down and taking up as little space as possible. When they did attempt to walk, it was with a low stoop, the bust inclining forward, and with a hasty step like that of a partridge. But their favorite position was that in which we first saw them. In this posture they could remain for hours without any apparent weariness, and, at a given signal, would move, one after the other, with great facility, and, at the same time, with so much caution that not the least noise could be heard from their footsteps.

"The account she gave us of their means of subsistence was very extraordinary. Sometimes, she said, her husband would fail to bring them supplies; and whether the fear of detection, or conscientious motives, prevented her from intruding on the rights of others, I could not ascertain; but, in this dreadful exigence, she would, for the support of herself and children, have recourse to expedients which nothing but the most pressing necessity could have suggested.

"Frogs and terrapins were considered as rare dainties, and even snakes were gladly taken to satisfy the calls of hunger. It was the custom, said this poor negro woman, in their little family, when they made up a fire in the night, which was only in the coldest nights of winter, for one to sit up while the others slept. As soon as the youngest was old enough, he took his turn. The one who watched had a double duty to perform, not only to stand sentinel and give the alarm in case of danger, but to watch for mice and catch them for food; which was effected in the following manner. The young watchman spread a few grains of corn, or peas, or crumbs of bread, on the ground; over these he placed an old handkerchief, and then kept perfectly still. A mouse would soon creep out from his hole in search of a repast; but as soon as the little fellow saw him fairly under the cloth, he would very dexterously clap down his hands upon the thief, and secure him for their breakfast the next morning. He often succeeded in catching a number.

"They not only eagerly devoured all the mice they could catch in this way, but they made use of the skins; they carefully preserved them, picked off the hair or fur, and mixed it with locks of wool or cotton that they picked up in the bushes, where it had been blown by accident, and made themselves stockings and mittens of it. These little boys, taught by their mother, managed to spin it into yarn by means of a stick about six or eight inches long. This they held in the left hand, while, in the right, they kept the materials to be spun. They gave us a specimen of their adroitness in this art; and the youngest of them could manage his stick with surprising dexterity. Several pairs of stockings and mittens were shown us, which the mother of these little negroes had knit of the yarn they had made during their sad, though voluntary, exile from the rest of the world.

"How much longer this poor mother with her children would have remained in the comfortless savannas of North Carolina, I know not, had she not been deserted by her husband. His visits ceased, she knew not why. Deprived of the only solace she had in the world, and of the scanty subsistence she received from his hands, her situation became too miserable to be endured. For seven years she had patiently borne cold, and hunger, and perpetual anxiety, for she had her husband to comfort her; but now she lost all hope, she lost her courage, she lost her fear of slavery for herself and her boys. Emaciated by hunger, she crept with them to the public road, and gave up herself and her two little boys, her only treasures, to the first person she saw, who happened to be a man with his cart going into town.

"My feelings," said Mr. Nelson, "were divided between my compassion for this poor woman and her suffering children, and my admiration of the noble fortitude they had displayed during this long period of privation and misery, of their ingenuity, their self-denial, their self-control; but more than all I honored, and admired the tender and faithful affection that had enabled a weak woman to endure with patience and constancy such evils from simple devoted love for her husband. The thought that she was deprived of this blessing, which had taken the place to her of all others, was more affecting to me than any part of her story.

"Numbers visited her and her children. I could not but hope that every one who saw her and heard her story, and who had ever failed to do honor to the immortal nature of the negro, or had been unfaithful in his own affections, might come away instructed and rebuked by the example of this humble, living martyr to affection.

"A purse was immediately made up to provide for the present comfort of her and her boys. I learned afterwards that a gentleman who heard her tell her story, and who happened to know that her master was dead, wrote an account of her to his son, who, in consideration of her sufferings, and from his grateful recollection of her kindness to him when a child, gave her and her boys their freedom."

HOW SHALL CHILDREN DO GOOD? (1844)

Children often say, "How can we do any good? We should like to do some good to the poor, but how can we? We do not possess any thing of our own. We go to our father and mother, and they give us something to give to the poor; but it is not our gift, and if they tell us what to do for them, it is not our thought, it was all their plan; it cannot be called our charity." The children are right; they cannot give, they cannot form intelligent and practical plans for the relief of the sufferers in this world. I knew a little girl who felt so much pain because she had nothing to give, that she was in the habit every day, of asking her mother to give her what she thought right for her to eat, and then she set apart a certain portion of it, to give to the poor, who came to the house to ask alms, and she felt, and she had a right to feel, that she gave something that was her own; and she had earned this pleasure by self-sacrifice, and though it may seem a small thing, it was in fact a great principle that she illustrated.

But it is certainly true, that giving, in the common acceptation of the term, is not in the power of children; they have not the means, and if they had, they have not the discretion and wisdom that is required to bestow favors. What they have, either of money or of wisdom, they receive from those on whom they depend.

But have children then nothing to give? Can they do no good in the world? Do they receive all, and bestow nothing? Are they quite cut off from the enjoyment of that purest of all pleasures, the feeling that one heavy heart is the lighter for their love and kindness? May they not cherish the divine ambition to bless others less happy than themselves? May they not be allowed to bring their little urns also, and pour them into the stream of human joy? Oh yes! children may do much: Life, true life, happiness, like Joseph's coat, is of many colors. They can always give that, which every human heart craves and welcomes, and which every happy child possesses in its own right, and can bestow upon another. Love flows from the heart of a little child as purely, and as freely, as from the heart of the profoundest philosopher, and it is like the dew of heaven upon the parched ground, it can revive the failing heart and wake up the flowers of life in the most barren places; it can lighten the heaviest load; it seems like the voice of God to his suffering children, bidding them not to despair.

Suppose yourself a sufferer from extreme poverty, and that some one who considered it a duty to help you, gives you such aid as you need, but coldly, and unkindly, with no word of sympathy or pity for you, and another, perhaps a poor little child, breaks its small crust of bread, and gives you half of it with words of love, and tears of sorrow that he has no more to give;—who would you feel was your true benefactor?

What is the worst and bitterest feeling in the heart of the sufferer? It is often the idea that he is an outcast, that no one cares for him, that the feast of life is spread out for all but him. All the happy turn away from him. Give him food, and give him clothes, and if you do not give him kindness and sympathy, he regards them not. Make him feel that you recognize him as your brother, and the meanest flower that you may chance to drop at his feet would be precious to him. But you will say, "How can I feel towards all the poor sufferers in the world?" I reply, "How did Jesus learn to feel for all mankind?" He doubtless during his childhood and early youth studied the great law of the brotherhood of man, till that divine love grew in his heart, which prepared him for his heavenly ministry, and then he poured it forth in all its fullness upon the sufferers around him. "Tell John," he said to the messengers who would know if he was the Christ, "that the blind see, the lame walk, the lepers are cleansed, the deaf hear, the dead are raised, to the poor the gospel is preached." This he considered the proof that God sent him. There are so many cruel distinctions among men, that it requires an effort to see, and believe, and remember, that we are all equally the children of God. Even in this, our country, where there is enough for all, children are daily born in damp, dark cellars to an inheritance of miserable poverty and pain: and worse still, hundreds are daily born to slavery, doomed to have all their rights trampled upon, to be bought and sold like four-footed animals: is it not work enough for a child, to learn that these unhappy beings, are all the children of God; that they have a claim upon him as their brothers and sisters, and they are calling for help from every Christian heart? Is it not work enough for the child, in his early days, so to study the perfect law of love and liberty, that when his reason is strong, and his highest faculties are matured, he shall be prepared to live a life of self-denial and self-devotion, and to consecrate himself to the cause of humanity, to the service of his suffering brethren?

We hear nothing of the *works* of Jesus when he was a child, we only hear of him as a learner in the temple, hearing and asking questions. A friend of children has said, "To learn to listen to the voice of instruction, and to render it more instructive still by asking questions, this is the beginning of true wisdom. To hear and to ask, is the special duty and chief occupation of childhood and youth. To children therefore, to the young, the example of Jesus, sitting in the temple among the wisest of his nation is peculiarly interesting and useful. In the course of education which divine Providence has laid out for the successive generations of man, it is the calling of the young, not only to overtake those who have set out before them in the way of perfection, but to outrun them in the course." If this should be the work, and is the duty of children, what is the duty of the parents? Are they faithful in this part of the education of children of which we have been speaking? They would have them enter college with honor, and they provide them with competent teachers; they would have them dance well, and they take pains to secure the most accomplished teacher for this purpose. So in religion, as far as it relates to the creed, none but the right faith is allowed; but how many parents are there, who think they are bound to teach to their children the divine science of philanthropy, the true love of man, telling them day by day the simple story of human brotherhood as taught by Jesus, and the duties that grow out of it, and so prepare them for those duties? Do they teach them this law of universal love repeating line upon line, precept upon precept? and thus kindle in their young hearts a flame that shall never be extinguished till they shall

"Labor with a glorious great intent,
And never rest, until they forth have brought
The eternal brood of glory excellent."

To perform deeds that shall bless others, must be held up to children as their great reward, when they by faithful study of truth and duty, and the surer enlightenment of a life of purity and love, shall become wise enough, perhaps, to know how to do good to their suffering brethren; and good enough, to deserve the joy.

In the mean time, the love that is growing in their hearts will, like an inward sun, illumine their whole being, and unconsciously they will bless all around them.

Therefore, to a child who came to ask me how he should do any good, I would say, "Seek daily and hourly to *be* good. When you are called upon to make any little sacrifice for the good of another, make it cheerfully, freely. Do what you can; and complain not if it is but little. But remember that in all things, life is at present only your school time. Cherish the desire to bless others, and the holy work shall ere long be given you to do. Learn to look upon every human being as equally with yourself the child of God, however degraded he may be, however the world may cast him off. So that when the ministry of your life here begins, (for everyone is a minister of either good or evil) you may be ready to stretch forth the arms of your love towards all your fellow men, and say in the words of your Divine Teacher: "Behold my mother, and my brethren."

F.L.F.

FROM *HYMNS, SONGS, AND FABLES, FOR YOUNG PEOPLE* (1846)

"REMEMBER THE SLAVE"

Mother! whene'er around your child
   You clasp your arms in love,
And when, with grateful joy, you raise
   Your eyes to God above,

Think of the negro mother, when
   Her child is torn away,
Sold for a little slave,—O, then
   For that poor mother pray!

Father! whene'er your happy boys
   You look upon with pride,
And pray to see them when you're old,
   All blooming by your side,

Think of that father's withered heart,
   The father of a slave,
Who asks a pitying God to give
   His little son a grave.

Brothers and sisters! who with joy
   Meet round the social hearth,
And talk of home and happy days,
   And laugh in careless mirth,

Remember, too, the poor young slave,
   Who never felt your joy,
Who, early old, has never known
   The bliss to be a boy.

Ye Christians! ministers of Him
   Who came to make men free,
When, at the Almighty Maker's throne,
   You bend the suppliant knee,

From the deep fountains of your soul
   Then let your prayers ascend
For the poor slave, who hardly knows
   That God is still his friend.

Let all who know that God is just,
   That Jesus came to save,

Unite in the most holy cause
  Of the forsaken slave.

"CHILDREN IN SLAVERY"

When children play the livelong day,
  Like birds and butterflies,
As free and gay sport life away,
  And know not care nor sighs;

Then earth and air seem fresh and fair,
  All peace below, above;
Life's flowers are there, and everywhere
  Is innocence and love.

When children pray with fear all day,
  A blight must be at hand;
Then joys decay, and birds of prey
  Are hovering o'er the land.

When young hearts weep as they go to sleep,
  Then all the world seems sad;
The flesh must creep, and woes are deep,
  When children are not glad.

"THE LITTLE SLAVE'S WISH"

I wish I was that little bird
  Up in the bright blue sky,
That sings and flies just where he will,
  And no one asks him why.

I wish I was that little brook
  That runs so swift along,
Through pretty flowers, and shining stones,
  Singing a merry song.

I wish I was a butterfly,
  Without a fear or care,
Spreading my many-colored wings,
  Like a flower in the air.

I wish I was that wild, wild deer,
  That I saw the other day,
Who through the dark green forest flew,
  Like an arrow far away.

I wish I was that little cloud
  By the gentle south-wind driven,
Floating along so calm and bright
  Up to the gates of heaven.

I'd rather be a savage beast,
  And dwell in a gloomy cave,
And shake the forest when I roared,
  Than what I am,—a slave.

My mother calls me her good boy,
  My father calls me brave;
What wicked action have I done
  That I should be a slave?

They tell me God is very good,
  That his right arm can save;
O, is it, can it, be his will
  That I should be a slave?

O, how much better 't is to die,
  And lie down in the grave,
Than 't is to be what I am now,—
  A little negro slave!

"SOLILOQUY OF ELLEN'S SQUIRREL, ON RECEIVING HIS LIBERTY;—OVERHEARD BY A LOVER OF NATURE AND A FRIEND OF ELLEN"

Was that the music of the wind,
  That whispered in my trembling ear?
And can I, free and unconfined
  Taste of the joys that still are dear?

And can I skip from tree to tree,
  And fly along the flowery plain,
Light as the wind, as fleet, as free,
  And make my winter's nest again?

O, yes! my joyful, trembling heart,
  The song you heard from yonder tree,
Which made awakening memory start,
  Was the sweet sound of Liberty!

Dear Ellen, many thanks I owe
  For tenderest care bestowed on me;
But most my gratitude will flow
  For your best gift—sweet Liberty!

Oft in your gayest, happiest hour,
  When all your youthful heart beats high,
And, hastening on from flower to flower,
  You taste the sweets of Liberty,

The thought that you have set me free,
  That I can skip and dance like you,
To your kind, tender heart shall be
  As pure a joy as e'er you knew.

Scarce can my wakening sense believe
  The sounds I hear, the sights I see;
Dear Ellen, once again receive
  Your Squirrel's thanks for Liberty.

"BILLY RABBIT TO MARY"

Billy Rabbit was a little rabbit which a boy caught in the woods, and gave to a little girl of the name of Mary. She was very attentive to the little prisoner, gave him an abundance of good things to eat, and tried her best to make him happy; but all in vain. After many attempts, he at last succeeded in making his escape, and instantly disappeared in the woods. In the course of the day, the following letter, sealed with a sharp thorn, was received by his friend Mary.

Artichoke Woods

  You thought, my dear Mary, you had Billy fast,
But I tried very hard, and escaped you at last;
The chance was so tempting, I thought I would *nab* it,—
It was not very naughty, I'm sure, in a rabbit.
O, let not your kind heart be angry with me;
But think what a joy it is to be free,
To see the green woods, to feel the fresh air,
To skip, and to play, and to run everywhere.
The food that you gave me was pleasant and sweet,
But I'd rather be free, though with nothing to eat.

  O, how glad they all were to see me come back,
And every one wanted to give me a smack.

Dick knocked over Brownie, and jumped over Bun,
And the neighbors came in to witness the fun.
My father said something, but could not be heard;
My mother looked at me, but spoke not a word;
And while she was looking, her eyes became pink,
And she shed a few tears, I verily think.

   To him, who a hole, or a palace inhabits,
To all sorts of beings, to men, and to rabbits,
Ah! dear to us all is sweet Liberty,
Especially, Mary, to you and to me.
So I hope you'll forgive me for sending this letter,
To tell you I'm safe, and feel so much better,
Cut all sorts of capers, and act very silly,
And am your devoted, affectionate

                                                 BILLY

THE LIBERTY CAP (1846)

"THE LIBERTY CAP"

It was a custom of the Romans when a slave was made free to take him to the temple of the goddess Feronia, and there to place upon his head a cap in sign of his liberation, and ever after the goddess, in whose temple the ceremony was performed was supposed to be his guardian and protector.

The Romans lived before the time of the great teacher of our religion, and with but little of the light of the pure and perfect truth he taught. They were men of war and blood, who believed that the strong should use the weak for their own selfish purposes, and who really knew no better: and so they *believed* that slavery was right, though they did not believe, as some who *call themselves* Christians say they do, that their Gods had marked one race of men with a black skin to point them out as slaves. Their slaves were the captives they took in war and their descendants, without distinction of color.

We *pretend* to be a Christian nation, to believe the religion of him who told us to do *as we would be done by*, who said that the substance of religion was to love God with all our heart and *our neighbor as ourselves*, and that our neighbor was the poor and the suffering and the oppressed, who told us that God was our *Father* and that we were *all* brethren, who told us to love one another even as God loved us. I say we pretend to believe this: every week we hear it preached; we call ourselves Christians, and pity the Bey of Tunis, though he has freed all the slaves in his dominions, because he is a heathen. And yet in our country are three millions of our brethren, groaning under a slavery far worse than that of the heathen and bloody Romans. We hold them in bondage—we ourselves—for their pretended masters could not keep them if it were not for our help. Yes, we even go to war and fight bloody battles to defend and perpetuate this infamous wickedness.

Shall we do it any longer? Shall there not be in all this Christian land, one temple where the bondman can find freedom? Here where we profess to love our brethren, shall there be no guardian spirit, to go forth with its holy influence, for the protection of the suffering and oppressed? Yes. Let that temple be our hearts. Let that spirit be our words and deeds, mighty with all the power of truth and right. Let us not cease from laboring till the Cap of Liberty shall be placed upon the head of every slave, and their guardian shall be a better than the heathen goddess, even the spirit of him who preached perfect peace and perfect love.

W.P.A.

West Roxbury, May 9, 1846.

"AM I NOT A MAN AND A BROTHER?"

My country that nobly could dare
    The hand of oppression to brave,
Oh how the foul stain canst thou bear
    Of being the land of the slave?

His groans, and the clank of his chains
    Shall rise with the shout of the free,
And turn into discord the strains
    They raise, God of mercy, to Thee.

The proud knee at His altar they bend,
    On God as their Father they call;
They call Him their Father and Friend,
    And forget He's the Father of all.

His children He does not forget,
    His mercy, His power can save;
And sure as God liveth, he yet
    Will liberty give to the slave.

Oh talk not of freedom and peace
    With the blood of the slave on your sod;
Till the groans of the negro shall cease
    Hope not for a blessing from God.

He asks, Am not I man?
    He pleads, Am not I a brother?
Then dare not, and hope not you can
    The cry of humanity smother.

'T will be heard from the south to the north,
    In our halls and in poverty's shed;
'Twill go like a hurricane forth
    And wake up the living and dead.

The dead whom the white man has slain,
    They cry from the ground and the waves;
They once cried for mercy in vain,
    They plead for their brothers the slaves.

Oh let them, my country, be heard,
  Be the land of the free and the brave,
And send forth the glorious word,
  This is not the land of the slave.

"PICNIC AT DEDHAM"

—, August 3, 1843.

Dear Mother,

  You asked me when I left you, to write to you; I well remember what a choaky feeling I had in my throat, when I was standing in our porch, and I felt your arm round my neck, as you said, "You will write often to me, Hal," and yet I have written only once. Well! I mean to make up now, and write you a real long letter; and one reason is, I have got something to write about. Uncle told us the day before yesterday that he was going to take us the next day, to the pic-nic at Dedham, for they were going to celebrate the first of August, and he must be there. I did not think much what it was all for, but I knew it was a holiday, and that was enough for me.

  You may be sure I was up betimes: we started soon after seven; uncle let me drive; George you know is a little chap, and he sat on the back seat with aunt. We got to Dedham a little after nine, and went directly to the Town Hall; there we found a great many people round the door, and a long stream of folks just arrived from Boston in the cars, and there was Dr. Bowditch and a number of other gentlemen with stars on their coats, arranging them so as to form a procession. They had ever so many beautiful banners. Uncle joined them, and left me in the wagon with aunt. After the procession was formed, they turned and passed directly by us, so that I saw every thing; and what was the best of the whole, the band of music was formed entirely of boys, and they played first rate. They walked so slowly that I could see what was on their banners, and read the inscriptions; I cannot remember all, but I do some of them.

  One had on it a fine figure of a black man, with his arms thrown up, exultingly, and his broken chains falling to the ground, and his foot upon a whip; the words over him were, "This is the Lord's doing," and underneath, "Slavery abolished in the West Indies, August 1st, 1834, Laus Deo." The figure was finely done, and the poor negro's face was full of joy; I thought it almost handsome, and mother I do wonder that I never heard you or father speak of the 1st of August. The next one I remember was a banner borne by a boy about my age; on it were these words,

"Shall a republic which could not bear the bondage of a King, cradle a bondage which a King has abolished?" Aunt told me that the boy who bore this banner, was the son of the man who wrote the words, and that his father had gone to that land where there was no slavery, and I felt, mother, that if I had been so unhappy as to lose my father, I should love to carry a banner with his words on it, for I should feel as if I was doing something to carry on his work.

Another banner had a liberty cap on it, with these words, "God never made a tyrant or a slave." Another, "Our fanaticism"; "All men are created free and equal." "Thou shalt love thy neighbor as thyself." When you and father speak of the fanaticism of the abolitionists, you can't mean this, I'm sure. Another banner had these words on it, "The Almighty has no attribute that can take sides with the slaveholder," and Thomas Jefferson's name under them: and yet Jefferson held slaves, and so did Washington, but Washington freed his in his last will.

One more I particularly noticed, for our friend Dr. Channing's name was on it. These were the words, "The Union: we will yield every thing to it but truth, honor, and liberty: These we will never yield." I forgot to mention that one banner had on it the initials of [William Lloyd] Garrison's name surrounded with an oaken wreath; and underneath it this inscription, "I am in earnest! I will not equivocate! I will not excuse! I will not retreat a single inch, and I will be heard!" Uncle helped me remember this. Well! The whole procession, men, women, and children, all marched to the boys' music, which was real good, to a fine large pine grove about half a mile off. We went round by another road so as to get there first and see them enter: they passed under a beautiful arch of oak leaves and evergreens, and slowly ascended the side of a hill covered with seats, under the tall pines which made a fine amphitheater; at the foot was a raised platform for the speakers, round which they placed the banners, and pictures, which I forgot to tell you about. After all had taken their places, Dr. Bowditch called for three cheers for the glorious occasion that had called them together, and oh! mother, they made the old grove ring well with their hurras [sic], and how the hats and handkerchiefs did fly round! My great straw hat did good service, and you know I can make a pretty good noise when I try for it. Then they sang a beautiful hymn written by Mr. Pierpont, and then Mr. Allen prayed, he did not, as you say, make a prayer, he prayed: it was heart work, his prayer, I'm sure. While he was praying I looked far, far up into the clear blue sky through the openings in the trees, and I never felt so much as if God heard our prayers; and oh, how I did wish that the time might come when we might be thanking God that our slaves were all free. Then some appropriate passages from the Bible were read. After this they sang another hymn written by Mr. James Lowell, and mother it was very beautiful, I have got it for you, and you must read it. After this Mr. Pierpont spoke, he was very entertaining, he put it to vote which was most likely to make men work, cash or lash—cash had the vote: he told us that freedom was working as well for the masters as for the slaves. Mr. Sietson spoke beautifully, but mother, some how or other he always makes me laugh. I can't tell you much about the speeches, at last the same boy that carried the banner recited a poem called "The Christian Slave." Mr. Pierpont told the audience that when they put up a slave on the auction table, the auctioneer would sometimes mention that she or he was a Christian, in order to get a higher price, and this was the subject of the poem—it made my blood run cold to think of selling Christians. The boy spoke well enough, and I think that if the men don't all do something about slavery soon, we boys had better see what we can do, for it is too wicked.

After this came the collation, we had to walk in a procession and place ourselves four or five deep at the table, and then get what we could; I hoped to get some of aunt's cake that we carried with us, but I did not, though I got enough of somebody's else; for they put the children forward, and I remembered, mother, to help my neighbors, arn't [sic] you glad of that?

After dinner there was a great deal more speaking and some real good singing; but what pleased me most was an address from a man who had been a slave. He was as white as I am, and a fine looking fellow: he spoke very well: he said that they had all come together to rejoice that eight hundred thousand human beings who had been slaves were made freemen, but if they knew what he knew, and had felt as he had what slavery was, they would gladly all meet to rejoice that one single man was free; then he spoke of what slavery was, and oh, dear mother, I never felt so about slavery before; every boy ought to know what American slavery is. When the whole was over, and it was time to go, they all joined together before they parted, in singing "Old Hundred." Now dear mother just imagine a grand large grove of tall pine trees, with their branches crossing each other, so as to look like the arches of a grand cathedral, with the blue sky for a ceiling, and at least fifteen hundred people joining most of them with their voices, and all looking as if they did with their hearts in singing "From all who dwell below the sky," and to that glorious old tune: it seemed to me as if the spirit of old Martin Luther was there. I never had such a feeling of awe in my life. I wanted you and father to be there; I never felt so religious; England may be forgiven a thousand sins for this one act. Why do not all Christians rejoice on this day?

When we were all seated in the wagon again, and on our way home, I told uncle that I had had a beautiful time. He said that "it was the most glorious day in the year to him:" "greater," I said, "than the fourth of July." "Yes," he said, "because it celebrated a bloodless victory, it was won by persevering love and justice, against selfishness and tyranny. It is such a victory as this Hal, that we abolitionists strive for, pray for, and are willing to suffer for." Then uncle told aunt an anecdote he had just heard, that I think mother, you will like to hear. He said that "five years ago on this same day, the 1st of August, a blind old man, a minister of religion, wished very much that there should be some public celebration of the event that was then taking place in the West Indies, that we republicans should join these eight hundred thousand souls in thanks to God, that they were free, that they were acknowledged to be men. The good man could not inspire those around him with his feelings about it; but all the more did he keep the hour holy in his own heart, so he and his daughter sat up that night till the clock struck twelve, and then he asked her to play a solemn tune on the piano, and the blind old man and his child sang by themselves at midnight a song of thankfulness and praise to God, that at that moment the chains of slavery were unloosed from eight hundred thousand of their fellow beings, and that they were restored to the rights and dignity of men. "Surely," said uncle, "those two weak voices in the stillness of that solemn night, were heard with more favor by the Almighty, than the roaring of our cannons, and the peals of our bells on the fourth of July"—and mother, I could not help thinking so too. Is not this a good long letter? I hope you will not think it is too long, but I could not help telling you all about the first of August.

I shall never forget it. Give my love to father.

Your affectionate son,
HAL.

"LINES ON HEARING OF THE TERROR OF THE CHILDREN OF THE SLAVES AT THE THOUGHT OF BEING SOLD"

When children play the livelong day
  Like birds and butterflies,
As free and gay sport life away,
  And know not care or sighs,

Then all the air seems fresh and fair,
  Around, below, above,
Life's flowers are there, and everywhere
  Is innocence and love.

When children pray with fear all day
  A blight must be at hand;
Then joys decay, and birds of prey
  Are hovering o'er the land.
When young hearts weep as they go to sleep,
  Then all the world is sad,
The flesh must creep and woes are deep,
  When children are not glad.

"DIALOGUE"

"I have been to aunt Elizabeth's this afternoon," said a warm hearted boy to his mother, "and have heard a Polish gentleman tell her of the cruelties inflicted upon his countrymen by the Russian emperor. Why, mother, they are too horrible to believe; and because they have made an effort lately to recover their freedom, the emperor has offered a large reward for the head of every Polish nobleman, and a great many hundred heads have been carried to him. The poor Poles have no liberty, they are banished to Siberia for the least offence, and they make the Polish girls marry Russians whether they like them or not."

"I do pity the poor Poles, and I do hate the Russians."

"And so do I pity the Poles," said the mother; "but, Robert, there is a nation as wicked and cruel as the Russians that you perhaps have not read any complete history of, and which you ought to know something about, and in many respects I think them worse than the emperor of Russia. No correct history has yet been written of this people, for their historians are afraid to tell the truth of them because they fear the people would be angry and not read their books. Shame on them for their mean cowardice and want of principle! A few of their poor exiles, like this Polish gentleman, tell of their wicked deeds, and now and then a traveller goes there, and brings back information about them, but if he is not very cautious while there, his life would be in danger. They are a very extraordinary people, and the Christian world is but just getting acquainted with their true character and history. Shall I tell you about them, Robert, and then you shall judge whether the Russians are any worse than they?"

"Do, mother," said the boy.

"These wicked people, Robert, have agreed among themselves to take a certain number of their infants as soon as they are born, when they cannot help themselves, and condemn them to the most wretched life that a human being can endure. They say to each one of these poor innocents, 'Although the good God has sent you into his beautiful world that you may be happy and enjoy existence, and learn to know and love him, and by your obedience to his laws here, make yourself fit for a higher state of existence, yet we will as far as we are able, deprive you of all these blessings. The mother that bore you and has suffered so much pain for you, on whose bosom you are now lying, to whose eyes you are looking up with such trusting love, shall have no right over you, we will take you from her when we please for our own purposes. If you are a boy, when you grow strong and your father feels proud of his boy, then we will tear you from his arms and send you for our advantage among strangers, who may be cruel to you if they will. If you are a girl your fate shall be yet worse, and your mother who now presses you to her heart shall pray for your death. If your father or mother should dare to defend you, death shall be their reward. You shall never learn to read: all that good and wise men have uttered, all their inspiring and inspired words embalmed in books, you shall know nothing of; you shall wear the meanest clothing; you shall be fed as the horses and pigs are fed; there shall be no true love for you; you shall marry and unmarry at our bidding, for your husband, or your wife shall not belong to you, but to us; the light of your intellect shall be darkened, the fire of your soul shall be quenched, your spirit shall be broken. We will shut out from you the knowledge of the Universal Parent; you shall know God only as a tyrant, not as your Father in Heaven. Life shall be hateful to you if you have a soul.'"

"Horrible, mother, horrible! Can this be true of any people?"

"Yes, my son, and this is not all. When in spite of all their efforts commencing at the cradle to extinguish the souls of these poor, helpless beings, some of them when they are grown up come to a sense of their own rights and try to escape from these savages, they hunt them with dogs and shoot them down like wild beasts. And if their victims do escape, they do as the emperor of Russia does, they offer a reward to whoever will bring them back, not, to be sure for their heads, because their heads would not be of any service to them, but alive that they may have possession of them, and use them for their own purposes, and then they often punish them for having run away, so severely that death would be preferable."

"Mother," said Robert, "this is too horrible; what people can be so wicked? Where is this country?"

"You are living in it, my son; you are one of its citizens; your father pays taxes to support the government which sanctions and defends these crimes against innocent beings. This country is now at war, as you know, with Mexico who has abolished slavery, for the purpose of making this infamous system more secure and extending it farther."

"Mother," said Robert, "I knew we had slaves, and I always thought slavery was wicked, but I never knew it was so bad. I never thought of their treating children so; I supposed they were kind to children."

"They are, I suppose, as kind to them as they are to little pigs, but they are defrauded of all the rights of intellectual and immortal beings. I have not told you half of its horrors. I would not harrow up your young heart by a relation of all the slaves have to endure, of all their bodily sufferings, of horrors too bad to think of. But all I have told you is strictly true."

"Whom, mother, do you mean by the exiles who relate these things?"

"Whoever, Robert, dares to tell the whole truth about slavery, and says he will have nothing more to do with it in any way, is an exile from that part of our country where these wicked things are done. A Polish nobleman would be as safe with the emperor of Russia as an abolitionist in our Southern States. Georgia has offered a reward of five thousand dollars for the head of William Lloyd Garrison. And even here in the free States, abolitionists are spoken ill of and the world hates them, and the friends of the Southern slaveholders say all sorts of evil things against them."

"Are our men here willing to bear these things, mother?"

"All but the abolitionists submit quietly to them, and some even vindicate Southern slavery."

"What do the abolitionists do, mother, what can they do against slavery?"

"I will tell you, Robert, what they do, and what they have done, and what they wish to do; but I must defer this to another time, and then I will tell you all about the abolitionists and their purposes."

"AGRIPPA"

In the village of Stockbridge lives a black man by the name of Agrippa Hull, who served in the Revolutionary War. At the close of it he was honorably discharged; in testimony of which he shows a certificate signed by General Washington. He was for some years the servant of General

Kosciusko, of whose generous and humane character he speaks with grateful love and admiration.

Agrippa has an uncommonly fine head, and is remarkable for his excellent understanding and good character. By his industry he has become possessed of a valuable farm, which he now, at the age of seventy-six, cultivates himself. He is eminent for his piety, and those who have heard him speak at conference meetings which he is in the habit of attending with his white neighbors, say that in prayer he is distinguished for fervor and eloquence, and for the peculiar originality and richness of his language.

The acuteness and wisdom of his views upon most subjects, and the wit and force of his illustrations, make his conversation so impressive that you remember what he has said, long after you have parted from him. During an interview of perhaps half an hour with him, I was so struck with his remarks that as soon as he left me, I wrote down his very words, as I here transcribe them, without any alteration or embellishment.

When I expressed to Agrippa my opinion upon the subject of prejudice against color, he said,

"When there is a flock of sheep, and some black ones among them, I always think that, if they behave well, they have as good a right to be fed as the white ones. God will not ask what is our color, but what has been our conduct. The Almighty made all colors. If we find fault with the work, we find fault with the workman. His works are all good. A black, ugly bottle may have just as good spirits in it as the cut glass decanter. Not the cover of the book, but what the book contains is the question. Many a good book has dark covers. Which is the worst, the white black man, or the black white man? When a white man says any hard thing to me about my color, I tell him I pity him, but I ask him which is the worst, to be black outside, or in? When a black man is treated ill on account of his color by a white man, and he bears it patiently and only pities him, I think that he has a chance to take a very high place over the white man."

"Once," said Agrippa, "when I was a servant to a gentleman who was very overbearing and haughty, we both went to the same church. One Sunday, a mulatto gentleman, by the name of Haynes, preached. When we came out of meeting, my master said to me, 'Well Agrippa, how do you like nigger preaching?' 'Sir,' I answered, 'he was half black and half white; I liked my half; how did you like yours?'"

Upon the assertion that the slaveholders cannot abolish slavery, Agrippa said, "No one is obliged to do wrong. When the drunkard says he cannot live without spirit, I tell him to take temperate things for a time, and see if he is not better. It is his will that is in fault. There is no necessity to do wrong. God never makes us do wrong."

He put his hand on a little boy's head, and said, "I love children; I love to see them well brought up. It is a good thing to feed the minds of children."

When speaking of the abolitionists, he said, "It will be a great while before the abolitionists can succeed in their purpose; but they will do great good to the black men by inducing them to keep down their bad feelings, because they know that they will have help at last."

"The abolitionists have the great happiness of working for a cause in which they know that they will have God on their side."

In a cause the merit of which depends upon the question whether the black man is a man, no further testimony is needed than the remarks of Agrippa; and what greater encouragement can the abolitionists desire than that contained in his words, "God is on their side"?

From *May Morning and New Year's Eve*
(ca. 1857)

"MAY MORNING"

It is the evening before the first of May, and the boys are looking forward to a May-day festival with the children in the neighborhood.

Mrs. Chilton read aloud these beautiful lines of Milton:—

Now the bright morning star, Day's harbinger,
Comes dancing from the east, and leads with her
The flowery May, who from her green lap throws
The yellow cowslip, and the pale primrose.
Hail beauteous May that dost inspire
Mirth, and youth, and warm desire;
Woods and groves are of thy dressing,
Hill and dale doth boast thy blessing.
Thus we salute thee with our early song,
And welcome thee, and wish thee long.[11]

"How beautiful!" said Frank and Harry.

"Suppose, Mother," said Harry, "it should rain, and hail, and snow to-morrow, for it looks like it now, and then you know we cannot go into the woods and gather flowers; and all our plans will be spoiled."

"Why, then, my dear, we must enjoy May morning as the great poet did, after he lost his sight, with our mind's eye; and you must bear your disappointment patiently."

"Easier said than done, Mother," said Harry. "Why, only think of all our preparations, and the beautiful wreath you made for Lizzy Evans, who is to be queen of the May, and how pretty she would look in it, and then think of the dinner in the woods, we all sitting round in a circle, and she and the king of the May in the midst of us, and Ned Brown playing on his flageolet; and then you know we are all to walk home in procession, and have a dance at his mother's after tea."

"You will not lose your dance, Harry," said his mother, "if it should hail, and rain, and snow; but, on the contrary, enjoy it all the more, for then you will not be fatigued by a long walk; and Lizzy can wear the wreath at any rate."

"I don't care for the fatigue, Mother; I want to be in the woods and gather the flowers with my own hands and smell them as I gather them in the fresh air, and hear the birds sing; and to scream as loud as I please, and kick up my heels, and not hear anyone say, 'Don't make such a noise, Harry.' I guess Milton did not take as much pleasure in writing poetry about the spring after he became blind. But please read his May Song again, Mother." She read it again.

"I think he must have felt as glad when he wrote it," said Harry, "as I hope to feel tomorrow.—'Comes dancing from the east'—how beautiful it is! What a pity he ever lost his sight!"

"Milton," said the mother, "made such a good use of his eyes while he could see, that he laid up stores of beautiful images, which he remembered when he could no longer use his bodily eyes. The poetry he wrote when he was blind shows the most accurate observation of the outward appearances of things, of shades of color, and of all those beauties which only sight could have taught him. It is worth while, boys, for you to imitate him in this, while you admire his poetry."

May morning came. It did not hail, or rain, or snow. The sun shone brightly. The birds seemed to know as well as the children that it was the first of May. The country village in which Mrs. Chilton lived was as noisy as a martin box, at break of day, when doubtless, though we poor wingless bipeds don't understand what the birds are chattering about, they are planning their work and their amusements for the day—and why not?

Soon after sunrise, all the children from far and near, dressed in their holiday clothes, with little baskets of provisions, all assembled on a little green before Mrs. Grey's house, and were ready to set out for the woods, about two miles distant. Ned Brown had his flageolet, and another boy had a drum. Lizzy Evans received the wreath, which made her queen of the May, and Frank, being the tallest boy, was chosen king. And now off they all set, in high glee, happy as only children can be.

Mrs. Chilton, and the teacher of the village school had promised the children to join them at the dinner hour, which was twelve. Just about eleven, the clouds began to gather. Nevertheless, the ladies kept their promise, and set out for the wood. The threatened shower came up, and they took refuge in an old empty barn, where they had not been many minutes before all the children, one after the other, came dripping in, some laughing, some small ones crying. Soon, however, the laughers prevailed; and, after showing their flowers, of which they had collected many, they set themselves to work to spread out the dinner, in the most attractive way possible, and make what amends they could for the unlucky chance of the rain. An old milk stool was appropriated to the queen. It had not even the accustomed number of three legs to support it, so that the poor queen had to endure the anxiety of a tottering throne, and learned experimentally some of the pains of royalty. The king took possession of an old barrel that had lost both ends, and sitting astride upon it, Bacchus fashion he took his place by the side of the poor queen on her two-legged stool, upon which she was exercising all the art of balancing that she had acquired in one quarter at dancing school, hoping against hope that she might keep her dignity from rolling on the barn floor. Just as his Maymajesty was fairly seated on the barrel, it, all at once, fell in, smash, and he was half covered with old hoops and staves. Whereupon the queen laughed so immoderately as to lose her balance, and thus both rolled in the dust. In the mean time, the other children, who had no dignity to support, had spread their little repast on an old sledge. Mrs. Chilton, who had brought a table-cloth, assisted them. Dinner was now announced. The queen declared she could support her throne no longer, and she and the king, both forgetting their royalty, sat down with the others on the hay-strewn floor and discussed apples, cake, &c., &c.

Unfortunately the rain lasted longer than the dinner; every scrap that was eatable of their provisions was consumed; and now the children all looked around with that peculiar, beseeching, half-discontented look, which is their wont to have on such occasions, as much as to say, "What shall we do next?" Grown people who have been much with children, know full well that there is no peace when such symptoms appear, under such circumstances, unless, before the king of misrule begins his reign, something is proposed of a composing tendency for turbulent spirits. Accordingly, Mrs. Chilton asked the children if they had ever heard of the Mayday ball which is given every year to the children in Washington. "No," was the answer. She said she had been at one, and she would tell all about it.

"It is held in a large public hall, decorated for the purpose. All the children in Washington and Georgetown are invited to attend; all have an equal right to go, ignorant and educated, poor and rich; no matter how poor, if the girls can get a neat white frock, and the boys a decent dress, they are all admitted; everyone wears a wreath of flowers, or has a bouquet in his hand or bosom. The children assemble very early, and dance as much as they please, to the music of a fine band, and all partake of some simple refreshment, provided for them, before they return home. They number often over a thousand, and as they are all moving together to the music, they look like a dancing flower garden. I said all the children, rich and poor, in Washington. I wish it were so; but there are many poor children who are never invited to this festival. No one dresses one of them in a nice white frock on May morning, and puts a wreath of flowers on her head, and a nosegay in her hands, and says to her, 'Go, dance, sing, and rejoice with the other children in God's beautiful world.'"

"Why not?" asked the listening children.

"They are slaves—they are negroes!" replied Mrs. Chilton.

"It is a shame; it is wicked," cried Frank and Harry, and all the rest.

"When you are men and women," said Mrs. Chilton, "you may do much for the poor slaves. Remember them then, and do not forget them now. All can do something for them, even little children.

"Now I will tell you a story that was related to me by a gentleman who knew it to be true. I knew, he said, a little boy, who was one of the best little fellows that ever lived. He was gentle and kind to his companions, obedient to his parents, good to all. His home was in a small country village, but he was very fond of wandering into the neighboring fields, when his tasks were all over. There, if he saw a young bird that had fallen to the ground before it could fly, he would pick it up gently, and put it back in its nest. I have often seen him step aside, lest he should tread on an ant-hill, and thus destroy the industrious little creatures' habitation. If a child smaller than he was carrying a heavy bundle or basket, Harry would always offer to help him. Was anyone hurt, or unhappy, Harry was quick to give aid and sympathy; ever ready to defend the weak, feared not the strong. For every harsh word, Harry gave a kind one in return. I have known him to carry more than half his breakfast to a little lame boy whose mother was very poor. Harry was brave and true; he would confess his own faults, he would hide those of others. He had a thirst for knowledge. He got all his lessons well at school, and he stood high in his class. But what he was particularly remarkable for, was his love of all beautiful things, and most especially of wild flowers. He would make wreaths of them and give them to his mother, and he was very fond of putting one on my study table, when he could contrive to place it there without my seeing him. Harry knew all the green nooks where the houstonia was to be found in the early spring, and it was he that ever brought me the beautiful gentian that opens its fringed petals in the middle of the chilly October day. On Sunday, and on all holidays, Harry always had a flower or a bit of green in the button-hole of his jacket. Every sunny window in his mother's house had an old teapot or broken pitcher in it, containing one of Harry's plants whose bright blossoms hid defects and infirmities. He also loved music passionately; he whistled so sweetly that it was a delight to hear him. Yet there was something in his notes that always went to your heart and made you sad, they were so mournful.

"Often in the summer time, he would go, towards evening, into the fields and lie down in the long grass; and there he would look straight up into the clear deep blue sky, and whistle such plaintive tunes, that, beautiful as they were, it made your heart ache to hear them. You could not see him, and it seemed as if you were listening to the song of a spirit.

"Alas! Harry was not happy; God's glorious world was all around him; his soul was tuned to the harmony of heaven, and yet his young heart ached; and tears—bitter, scalding tears—often ran down his smooth, round cheek, and then he would run and hide his head in his mother's lap, that blessed home for a troubled spirit.

"One day, I discovered the cause of Harry's melancholy. I was returning from a walk, and saw him at a little brook that ran behind my house, washing his face and hands vehemently, and rubbing them very hard. I then remembered that I had often seen him there doing the same thing."

"It seems to me, Harry," I said, "that your face and hands are clean now; why do you rub your face so violently?"

"I am trying," he said, "to wash away this color. I can never be happy till I get rid of this color. If I wash me a great deal, will it not come off at last? The boys will not play with me; they do not love me because I am of this color; they are all white. Why, if God is good, did he not make me white?" And he wept bitterly.

"Poor dear little boy!" I said, and took him in my arms and pressed him to my heart! "God is good; it is man that is cruel." The little fellow was soothed and strengthened by my sympathy, and the counsel I gave him.

Not long after this, it was May-day, and all the children of the village went out into the fields to gather flowers, to dress themselves for a little dance they were to have in the evening. Every boy and girl in the village, except Harry, was of the party. They set off early in the morning, and they ran gayly over hills and meadows, and hunted busily for flowers; but the spring had been cold, and they could not find many. They were returning home, wearied, and rather chilled and disheartened, when they saw Harry coming out of the woods with a large bunch of flowers in his hand. One of the boys called out to him, "Well, nigger, where did you get all your flowers?" Harry went on and made no answer. "Come, stop, darky," said the hard-hearted boy, "stop, and let's have your flowers; here's three cents for them."

"I don't wish to sell them," said Harry; "they are all for my mother."

"A nigger carry flowers to his mother! that's a good one! Come, boys, let's take them from him; they are as much our flowers as his; he has gathered more than his share;" and he approached Harry to seize his flowers.

"For shame, Tom, for shame!" cried out many of the children, and one of the larger boys came forward and stood by Harry. "Touch him if you dare, Tom. You have got to knock me down first." The cruel boy, who was, of course, a coward, fell back, and some of the little children gathered around Harry to look at the flowers.

"Don't mind that naughty boy, Harry," said one little girl, and slid her little hand into his. Harry's anger was always conquered by one word of kindness. "Where did you get all your flowers?" asked the children.

"I will show you," replied Harry, "if you will follow me."

They all shouted, "Let's go, let's go; show us the way, Harry;" and off they set.

Harry ran like a quail through bush and brier, and over rocks and stone walls, till he came to a hill covered with a wood. "On the other side of this hill," said he, "we shall find them." In a very few minutes the children were all there. There they saw a warm, sunny hollow; through it ran a little brook, and all around were massive rocks and pretty nooks; and there were the birds singing loudly, and there were cowslips, and anemones, and houstonias, and violets, and all in great profusion. The boy who had insulted Harry hung back ashamed. Harry quietly said to him, "Here, under this little tree, is a beautiful bed of violets, and there are anemones." Harry tasted of the pleasure of doing good for evil. The boy who had defended him walked by him, and talked kindly to him.

"How good it was in you to show us the flowers!" said the little girl who had taken Harry's hand, and whose apron he had filled with flowers. How happy now was poor Harry!

All the children gathered that morning as many flowers as they desired. Some carried home only perishable earthly flowers in their hands; others, immortal flowers in their hearts. The village children went to their dance, and were very happy. Harry spent the rest of the day and the evening in his mother's cottage, alone with her, and amused himself with making wreaths of his flowers. But he said he had never passed so happy a May-day. A loving heart, like Una's beauty, 'can make a sunshine in a shady place.'"

The clouds had now passed away. One of the boys proposed to pass a vote of thanks to the old barn, for the hospitable shelter it had afforded during the shower. This was received and passed with acclamations. Frank and Lizzy, or rather the king and queen of the May, declared that they had no thanks to offer to the old barrel or the milk stool. It was too wet to go into the woods again; so they formed a procession, and with their flowers in their hands, and such music as they had, returned gayly home.

The children all enjoyed the dance in the evening; but there were some hearts there, young and merry as they were, that made a solemn vow never to forget those of whom they had heard that day,—"them that are in bonds."

NOTES

1. Although her merchant father, Samuel Cabot, sometimes had difficulty supporting his thirteen children, Follen still received considerable intellectual stimulation through the family's ties to many prominent Bostonians (Schlesinger 157), especially Harriet Martineau, William Ellery Channing, and Catharine Sedgwick. In Sedgwick's home, Eliza met the German refugee and her future husband, Charles Follen, whom she married in 1828 (Schlesinger 157, 158). They remained in Boston's intellectual circles because Charles Follen taught German and gymnastics at Harvard.

2. Her submission to the Anti-Slavery Tracts collection includes: "Remember the Slave," "Where Is Thy Brother," "And the Days of Thy Mourning Shall Be Ended," "Lord Deliver," "The Land of the Free and the Home of the Brave" and "Auld Lang Syne."

3. For a complete analysis of these poems, see De Rosa 46–48.

4. "Children in Slavery" appeared as "Lines on Hearing of the Terror of the Children of the Slaves at the Thought of Being Sold" in *The Liberty Cap* (1846) and as "On Hearing of the Sadness of the Slave-Children from the Fear of Being Sold" for the American Anti-Slavery Society's Tracts collection.

5. "The Little Slave's Wish" (1846) appeared thirteen years later as "The Slave Boy's Wish" in Julia Coleman's "Little Lewis: The Story of a Slave Boy" (1859), which identifies Follen by name.

6. For a complete analysis of this text, see De Rosa 62–64.

7. For a complete analysis of this text, see De Rosa 84.

8. For a complete analysis of this text, see De Rosa 98–99.

9. For a complete analysis of this poem, see De Rosa 119–120.

10. For a complete analysis of this poem, see De Rosa 118–119.

11. From "Song on May Morning," by John Milton.

HANNAH AND MARY TOWNSEND

(DEFINITIVE DATES UNAVAILABLE)

In *Domestic Abolitionism and Juvenile Literature, 1830–1865*, I attributed *The Anti-Slavery Alphabet*[1] (1847), a unique text for educating children and encouraging them to become abolitionists, to Hannah Townsend Longstreth (1801–1865), the daughter of Joseph Townsend and Elizabeth Clark, and the wife of Daniel Longstreth. Hannah Townsend (Longstreth) helped Benjamin Lundy edit Elizabeth Margaret Chandler's collection, *The Poetical Works of Elizabeth Margaret Chandler*. However, recently recovered materials suggest that she did not author the alphabet book. Rather, according to Doris O'Keefe (senior cataloger for Rare Books at the American Antiquarian Society), the January 29, 1847, issue of William Lloyd Garrison's *The Liberator* attributes *The Anti-Slavery Alphabet* to Hannah and Mary Townsend, Quakers of Philadelphia. Hannah (born on July 17, 1812) and Mary (born on May 14, 1814) were the daughters of Charles Townsend and Priscilla Kirk (O'Keefe; Stone 617). Since Charles was Joseph's brother, Hannah and Mary were cousins to Hannah Townsend (Longstreth). The Townsends had a long and complex family history, which began with Bartholomew Longstreth, a Quaker who left England and settled in Pennsylvania in 1699 (Jordan 1532). The complex, weblike Townsend and Longstreth family tree is best left to genealogists like John Jordan.

Hannah and Mary Townsend's *The Anti-Slavery Alphabet*[2] represents a unique example of the materials that domestic abolitionists published. Parents who purchased this alphabet book at both the 1846 and 1847 Philadelphia Anti-Slavery Fairs were perhaps not surprised by this atypical approach that indoctrinates children into activism. Hannah and Mary Townsend's opening poetic plea, "To Our Little Readers," suggests that children have the power to fight slavery by speaking to their friends, by boycotting slave-made goods, and by pleading to slave-owners to end the purchase and sale of slaves. The alphabet book then presents the vocabulary necessary to engage in such activities. Rather than learn that "A" is for "Adam" (as the *New England Primer* teaches), or that "A" is for "Apple" (the most common designation for even modern alphabet books), children learn that "A" stands for "Abolitionist," which the quatrain defines. Each subsequent letter describes specific features related to the peculiar institution: from slave "D"rivers, to fierce "H"ounds, to the "V"essels used to transport slaves to America. The Townsend sisters also offer images of slavery's victims, speaking of them as "B"rothers, "I"nfants, and "P"arents, whose bonds the slave auction ruptures. Thus, their alphabet book arouses consciousness about the political, economic, religious, and familial crises that slavery spawns and spurs young children to effect its abolition.

THE ANTI-SLAVERY ALPHABET (1847)[3]

"TO OUR LITTLE READERS"

Listen, little children, all,
Listen to our earnest call:
You are very young, 'tis true,
But there's much that you can do.
Even you can plead with men
That they buy not slaves again,
And that those they have may be
Quickly set at liberty.
They may hearken what *you* say,
Though from *us* they turn away.
Sometimes, when from school you walk,
You can with your playmates talk,
Tell them of the slave child's fate,
Motherless and desolate.
And you can refuse to take
Candy, sweetmeat, pie or cake,
Saying "no"—unless 'tis free—
"The slave shall not work for me."
Thus, dear little children, each
May some useful lesson teach;
Thus each one may help to free
This fair land from slavery.

A is an Abolitionist—
    A man who wants to free
The wretched slave   and give to all
    An equal liberty.

B is a Brother with a skin
    Of somewhat darker hue,
But in our Heavenly Father's sight,
    He is as dear as you.

C is the Cotton-field, to which
    This injured brother's driven,
When, as the white man's *slave*, he toils
    From early morn till even.

D is the Driver, cold and stern,
    Who follows, whip in hand,

To punish those who dare to rest,
　　Or disobey command.

E is the Eagle, soaring high;
　　An emblem of the free;
But, while we chain our brother man,
　　Our type he cannot be.

F is the heart-sick Fugitive,
　　The slave who runs away,
And travels through the dreary night,
　　But hides himself by day.

G is the Gong, whose rolling sound,
　　Before the morning light,
Calls up the little sleeping slave,
　　To labor until night.

H is the Hound his master trained,
　　And called to scent the track
Of the unhappy fugitive,
　　And bring him trembling back.

I is the Infant, from the arms
　　Of its fond mother torn,
And, at a public auction, sold
　　With horses, cows, and corn.

J is the Jail, upon whose floor
　　That wretched mother lay,
Until her cruel master came,
　　And carried her away.

K is the Kidnapper, who stole
　　That little child and mother—
Shrieking, it clung around her, but
　　He tore them from each other.

L is the Lash, that brutally
　　He swung around its head,
Threatening that "if it cried again,
　　He'd whip it till 'twas dead."

M is the Merchant of the north,
　　Who buys what slaves produce—
So they are stolen, whipped and worked,
　　For his, and for our use.

N is the Negro, rambling free
    In his far distant home,
Delighting 'neath the palm trees' shade
    And cocoa-nut to roam.

O is the Orange tree, that bloomed
    Beside his cabin door,
When white men stole him from his home
    To see it never more.

P is the Parent, sorrowing,
    And weeping all alone—
The child he loved to lean upon,
    His only son, is gone!

Q is the Quarter, where the slave
    On coarsest food is fed,
And where, with toil and sorrow worn,
    He seeks his wretched bed.

R is the "Rice-swamp, dank and lone,"
    Where, weary, day by day,
He labors till the fever wastes
    His strength and life away.

S is the Sugar, that the slave
    Is toiling hard to make,
To put into your pie and tea,
    Your candy, and your cake.

T is the rank Tobacco plant,
    Raised by slave labor too:
A poisonous and nasty thing,
    For gentlemen to chew.

U is for Upper Canada,
    Where the poor slave has found
Rest after all his wanderings,
    For it is British ground!

V is the Vessel, in whose dark,
    Noisome, and stifling hold,
Hundreds of Africans are packed,
    Brought o'er the seas, and sold.

W is the Whipping post,
    To which the slave is bound,

While on his naked back, the lash
   Makes many a bleeding wound.

X is for Xerxes,[4] famed of yore;
   A warrior stern was he.
He fought with swords; let truth and love
   Our only weapons be.

Y is for Youth—the time for all
   Bravely to war with sin;
And think not it can ever be
   Too early to begin.

Z is a Zealous man, sincere,
   Faithful, and just, and true;
An earnest pleader for the slave—
   Will you not be so too?

NOTES

1. For an analysis of the historical context and textual analysis of this text, see De Rosa 22–23, and 117.

2. This text starkly contrasts with Abel C. Thomas (Iron Gray), *The Gospel of Slavery: Primer of Freedom* (1864). Thomas employs more sophisticated and critical poetic language and imagery in his alphabet book, perhaps designed for an older audience. Each of Thomas's entries includes a printed relief, a poem, and an extended footnote documenting the historical, legalistic, and/or religious hypocrisy inherent in slavery.

3. The format presented here does not reflect the original, in which the alphabet letter spanned the stanza length. Two letters and their corresponding poems appeared per page.

4. Xerxes I was a Persian king famous for his invasion of Greece in 480 B.C. and subsequent occupation of Athens.

ANNE WALES ABBOT[1]

(BIOGRAPHY AND DEFINITIVE DATES UNKNOWN)

A MASSACHUSETTS SLAVE (1847)

I suppose many of you, little readers, will stare, and think I have given a strange title to my story. A Massachusetts slave! You can hardly believe that slavery once existed here, where you see no trace of it, and where you hear so much said in reproach of those States which are still disgraced by it. It cannot be denied, however little it is to their credit, that my great-grandfather, and many other good and well meaning men of his day, were possessors of slaves. Their fathers had set them the example, and they had not thought much about it, at the time when my story begins.

Dinah was but seven years old, I believe, when she was bought by my great-grandfather, a good old farmer in Andover, and brought to the homestead to be taught to be useful. She was kindly received, and well fed and clothed; her mistress was a reasonable and gentle woman, who endeavored to make a good girl of her, in every sense of the word. She had very little success; Dinah was seldom much ashamed when she was told how wicked it was to strike the children, to lie, steal, and neglect her work. She would sometimes do well a little while, but in general was a perfect pest and torment in the family. The older she grew, the more violent and unmanageable she became, working only occasionally, unless by compulsion, and doing mischief as her regular and voluntary business.

"Dinah, I will sell you if you do not behave yourself better," was the daily threat. Dinah only laughed at that. She knew there was no one in the family who would consent to see her, who had grown up among them, sold to be perhaps cruelly beaten for her bad temper.

"Dinah, you are ungrateful," said her master and mistress. So said the men on the farm, the women in the dairy, and the neighbors, and everybody.

"My owners have to take care of me; they *must* feed and clothe me, by law," said Dinah, "and what have I to be grateful for? I have no pay, nothing really my own."

"Dinah, you are wicked!"

Dinah would not listen when they talked to her of God and duty. She thought a slave might do as she pleased; right and wrong belong only to the white and the free.

In short there was no motive which would act upon Dinah's mind long at a time. There was neither love, nor hope, nor fear, nor desire of improvement, or a wish to be approved. So she grew up, stout and healthy, but mischievous and capricious, making her owners see and feel the evil effects of hopeless servitude, no doubt, and willing to try the effect of paying her regular wages, when she should arrive at the age of eighteen. About this time the force of public opinion and popular feeling was silently dissolving the bonds of the slave, and it be came generally understood throughout Massachusetts that all might be free who chose to undertake their own support. Masters and mistresses began to feel that neither law nor custom would bear them out in longer requiring unpaid service after the usual age of freedom. Let us hope that the same silent agency is at work at the South, acting like rust upon those fetters which pride, passion, and fear are wishing to bind more firmly than ever upon the colored laborer, even at this late day.

Dinah's owners never had an opportunity of comparing slavery with free labor, in her case. In consequence of some willfulness of her own, I believe it was taking a nap in the wet grass, she was attacked by a rheumatic complaint which deprived her of the use of her limbs. She was helpless, to the day of her death, and she lived to be very old. She could not feed herself, nor leave her chair, or her bed, unassisted. The good people among whom it was her happy lot to have fallen, did not send her away to be taken care of at the almshouse, as they might have done, at the age of eighteen. They were Christian and God-fearing people, and they felt that she had come to them in a way which made it their duty to take care of her. They would not show their conviction of the injustice of slavery by casting off poor Dinah, as if she had no claim upon them. She had a comfortable little room of her own, and every necessary attention, as long as she lived. The house is still standing in Andover, and I myself have visited the little apartment, where my father and his brothers and sisters used to resort to hear old Dinah's stories; they were always ready to fill or light her pipe, or do any other little kind office for her. When they brought her apples, she could cut them up, but could raise the pieces to her mouth only by means of a staff, with a sharp point fixed upon the top. The children all loved Dinah, for her disposition had changed. She knew what it was to be grateful, now. Her sufferings had made her mild and affectionate. For many years she had ceased to bear the name of slave, or to call her protectors her masters. She was a great reader, and had a variety of stories, with which to amuse the children who came to see her. The following story of the Bag of Nails, was one of them. She told it to my father, he remembered and told it to his "little moon faced girl," as he called me, and (though that was a great while ago,) I have remembered it for *you*, and here, is in print. I wish I could give you the very words in which Dinah told it. It would be much more amusing, no doubt.

NOTE

1. From 1857 to 1858, Abbot edited *The Child's Friend*, in which she published "A Massachusetts Slave."

S.C.C.

(Pseudonym. Biography and definitive dates unknown)

S.C.C.'s identity remains a quandary.[1] She authored the abolitionist text, *Louisa in Her New Home* (1854), and cross references on title pages reveal that she also published "The Wishing-Cap" (1847), *The Wonderful Mirror* (1855), and *A Visit to the Country* (1839). S.C.C. "is most likely a woman since this text reflects the characteristic domestic abolitionist text, especially with the inclusion of a feminist mother-figure" (De Rosa 160n. 23). She speaks poignantly and directly about slavery and women's activism, yet she conceals her identity, which suggests the tightrope that domestic abolitionist walked to express their views in the public arena.

S.C.C.'s abolitionist juvenile fiction tests the boundaries of "appropriate" female political discourse through her image of the abolitionist mother-historian.[2] "The Wishing-Cap" includes two sisters (Fanny and Mary) and two brothers (William and Harry) who want to make a wishing cap like Fortunatus's hat so that they can eradicate slavery. In this story, the mother encourages the children to help the disempowered (she does not designate slaves in particular) and assures them that many (she does not mention abolitionists) have already initiated those efforts. Published in 1847, this reserved mother figure may suggest S.C.C.'s struggle with women supporting "radical" abolitionist principles.

S.C.C.'s reluctance clearly dissipated by 1854 since *Louisa in Her New Home* depicts a fascinating mother-daughter dynamic that gives voice to abolitionist and feminist ideals. In *Louisa*, the family's need to sell their luxurious home and dismiss their servants because of debt results in Louisa's awakening from childhood innocence to consciousness of familial, economic, and racial crises. Louisa suddenly learns that her parents have housed a fugitive slave, Mary, for several years. Louisa's discussions with her mother and Mary about Mary's wretched experience as a slave, and the need to send her to Canada because the Fugitive Slave Law endangers her freedom on American soil, initiates Louisa into a world of political consciousness and social activism. Moreover, S.C.C. embeds in this narrative of childhood awakening the image of an abolitionist mother-historian and feminist who responds to Louisa's questions with quasi-seditious answers. Like Mrs. Selden in *The Young Abolitionists*, this mother condemns Southern mistresses who violate slave family bonds, Northerners who support slavery when they do not fight against it, and, most fervently, the Fugitive Slave Law. Rejecting Louisa's belief that gender disempowers women, this politically conscious mother encourages her child to reject slavery using any form of private or public activism and civil disobedience. Ultimately, the mother and daughter's decision to help Mary escape and do whatever possible for her and other slaves resembles a women's coalition combating patriarchal laws and economics, as well as racial inequality.[3]

THE WISHING-CAP[4] (1847)

It was the month of November, the first snow had fallen, and the little folks were all gay at the sight, that is to say all the young people who had comfortable homes and kind friends to take care of, and love them.

It is a very sad thing, but true, that there are many little children who have no comfortable homes and do not know the joy there may be in a family circle where all have enough to eat and to drink and to put on; where tears are wiped away by loving hands; where laughing, and frolicking, and reading, and studying, make the days pass happily by, and where a comfortable bed is always ready to receive the tired body at night.

The little family that I am going to speak of now, had been taught by their parents to remember in the midst of their pleasure that there were other children who had not the pleasures they were enjoying, because they were too poor, and that it was one of their duties to do all that they could to help such children.

On the evening of this white day when the first snow had fallen, two little sisters had been employed by their mother in assisting her to make some warm petticoats for the poor, in case there should any be wanted in the neighborhood; and the two brothers had been in like manner helping their father saw and pile wood where it was stowed away in the charity, or rather, I should say, justice corner of the wood-house. These occupations had filled up all odd minutes and made the day pass happily; there was no desire to quarrel, or do any disagreeable thing when the time from schooling was so employed, and they all gathered round the fire in the evening just at dusk to chat together, and beg father and mother to join them in their amusements. Miss Pussy, too, was also invited; she sat by the youngest boy, (whose name was Harry,) purring with great complacency and looking at the fire so steadily that one would have thought she was trying to find out what sort of a thing it was that made her feel so comfortably. Harry also looked into the fire as if he expected to find something there, strange or wonderful. He presently turned his head from the fire to his mother's face, and said, "I wish I had a wishing-cap, mother."

"What do you want of a wishing-cap, Harry?"

"O, I don't know exactly, but I guess if I had one I should find enough things to wish for. There is one thing I would wish for, that there should be no poor people."

"I know what I would wish for," said his brother William, "I would wish that there should be no slaves in the world."

"And I would wish," said Fanny, "that there should be no people so wicked as to want to have slaves."

"And I," said Mary, "wish that I had money enough to buy the freedom of all the slaves, and enough left to help all the poor people there."

"Those are good wishes, children, and though you can never have the famous cap of Fortunatus to cover your heads, I don't know that you have not something as good, something out of which a cap may at least be begun to be made."

"I don't see how we any of us could ever make such a cap as was given to Fortunatus, mother," said Harry, "I would go to work pretty soon, if I thought I could make such a cap."

"We have never learnt how long this said cap was in the making, but I believe it was a great while before it could be made to do the wonders it did; there is no history of its beginning, nor of who it was that first thought of it, but I should not be surprised if I were to discover that you and William had already begun upon one, and that your two sisters had been helping you; it may be that you will spoil it, or leave it half done when it becomes an old story, and so never have any of the good wishes you have expressed, accomplished."

"I don't understand what you mean, mother," said Harry, "I am sure I have not been making a cap, nor anything like a cap."

"Well, Harry, I will explain to you what I mean. This famous cap that you have been wishing for, I do not suppose was a real cap, like the one you wear to school, but it was a something that had so much power as to do whatever the person who was supposed to wear it, should earnestly wish to do. Now if you really wish there should be no poor person in the world, you will, whenever you have an opportunity, do all you can to prevent it, and if every one were to do the same there would be no poor people in the world. You and William have this afternoon been helping father prepare wood for the poor who want it, and in this way you will help to make them less poor; so have your sisters been at work with me to help cover the naked, and in this way we have begun to make the wishing-cap; and if everybody would take hold and do the same thing, a wishing-cap would be made, a pretty large one, to be sure, that should cover all heads and so do what all heads wished."

"But every body won't take hold, mother, and so there will never be a wishing-cap except in the story."

"We do not know, Harry, how this will be, it no doubt will be a great many years before such a thing is done, long after you and I are gone from this world, I fear, but that is no reason why we should not do what we can to help it on, at least begin one. There are a great many people who have begun this work, and they do it because they believe that such work is the work that God meant they should do.

While you all have such good wishes in your hearts he will help you, but you must not be discouraged because you do not see the cap; you know Fortunatus' cap was invisible, still it worked wonders. Tomorrow we will perhaps talk more of this; it is now time for tea, and as I wished you should have a good supper, I think we shall find one."

S.C.C.

LOUISA IN HER NEW HOME (1854)

"Mother, you do not appear to care much about our new house. Every thing is so new and beautiful I should think you would be delighted with it. I am; I wish you liked it as much as I do."

"I do like it, my dear, and think it very pretty and convenient."

"I think it something more than pretty and convenient; I think it elegant and stylish. Mother, I like style, don't you?"

"What do you mean by style, my daughter?"

"Why, I mean that things should look grand, and as if people knew how to arrange them, and had always been used to them, and were not afraid of their being hurt."

"I like beautiful things, and I like ease and grace wherever they may be, and I like to see one thing suited to another, and that every body should have dress and furniture tasteful and beautiful."

"I see, mother, that you don't think or care any thing about our new house or furniture, or any thing."

"Yes, I do, but at present my thoughts are upon other things; and now, my dear, go and play with your cousins; they will help you to enjoy the new house and all that makes you so happy."

"But, mother, I should be happier if you did not look so troubled, now that we have moved here where there are so many beautiful things, and where we can go to the Concerts and to the Museum, and where I can see my cousins every day. You know I used to have no companions."

"I am glad, my dear, that you look forward to so much pleasure; it makes you happy now, and I will try not to look so sad."

"If you are really sad, mother, I don't care about your looking so; the thing is I don't want you to *be* so."

A month had passed after this conversation between Louisa and her mother. During that month Louisa had made many acquaintances. With health and spirits she enjoyed life to the full. Every thing was beautiful to her. The days were only too short for the accomplishment of all her innocent wishes. It was a bright, cheerful morning when with her usual gaiety she entered the breakfast room. Giving her father and mother the good-morning kiss, she observed by the expression of their faces that something was the matter. She went to her mother, and putting her head upon her shoulder, asked in a whisper if Lucy were more ill?

"No, my dear, little Lucy is much better." Louisa's face brightened as she heard the answer, and she began to talk freely, for she was with her dear father and mother, her little sister was getting well, and the nice breakfast was before her; the sun was shining, her head was full of pleasant thoughts, and her mind interested on many subjects. What was there more for her young heart to wish for or imagine? She thought of nothing painful, and believed she was mistaken about her parents' sadness. Her father and mother looked so lovingly upon her, and spoke so kindly to her, that she felt more than usually happy.

When breakfast was finished Louisa rose to go out of the room. Her mother asked her to stop a little while, as she had something she wished to say to her.

"What I am going to tell you will, I am afraid, pain you very much; we are going to leave this house."

"What, mother! leave this house?"

"Yes, we must leave this beautiful house."

"Why, mother! did not father buy it for us to live in?"

"He did, but he finds that he cannot afford to do so. A person who owes him a great deal of money cannot pay it, as he promised to do, and if father keeps this house he will not be able to pay all the money he himself owes, and so we must give it up, or live upon other people's money."

"I think that must be a bad man that promised to pay father and then did not do it. Well, I am glad father is not going to do so. But, mother, it is too bad that we should have to leave this beautiful house, and when it is not our fault."

"It is very hard, Louisa, but you would not have us remain in it, would you?"

"No, mother, but it don't seem fair."

"It is not fair; but that is no reason why we should not act honestly, because another person has not done so. We shall not only be obliged to give up our new house, Louisa, but many other things that we have been accustomed to, for we have lost nearly all our property. We can keep but one girl now, and you will be obliged to help me in the housekeeping."

"I shall not mind that, mother, but I do mind leaving our beautiful house; it vexes me very much, and I cannot think of any thing else, and I don't care for any thing now; it seems very cruel, and you are not well, mother."

"It would make me better, Louisa, if you were to try to make the best of what cannot be helped. What we have now to do is to bear patiently our loss; and the best way to do this is to busy ourselves with some useful employment; so you may go into the kitchen and ask Mary to give you some hot water, and we together will wash the breakfast cups."

With a heavy heart and slow step Louisa went to the kitchen to ask Mary for the hot water.

"And please, Miss Louisa, what does mistress want of hot water?" asked Mary.

"Mother and I are going to wash the cups and saucers."

"And why are you and your mother going to wash up the things? Does she think I don't wash them clean?"

"Oh, no! Mary, that is not the reason. You don't know what has happened."

"But suppose I do know."

"You can't know, Mary. Mother has but just told me."

"But I do know all about it, and so, my dear Miss Louisa, don't look so sorrowful; there are worse things in the world than losing a little money."

"But it is a great deal of money!"

"Well let it be a great deal; I tell you there are worse things than that."

"Yes, perhaps there are. But, Mary, what should we do if mother had to part with you, that's what I'm thinking of?"

"You need not think about that, Miss Louisa, for I don't mean to part with her. No! while I have a pair of hands they are hers; and couldn't I do all the work in the family? yes, and another beside, and not feel it. I know how it is, master has lost all his money and can't afford to pay wages; but what do I want of wages? Let Betsey leave, she can easily find a place, and I'll be cook and chambermaid and all, for my dear mistress. Did she not tend me when I was sick? and have you not been like a child to me? and am I going to leave you when you want me the most? No; and, God willing, I'll stick to you to the last, and think I'm well off."

"But, Mary, you could not do all the work and have no wages for it; it would not be fair, mother would not let you."

"Do you think, Miss Louisa, that I have never worked without wages; yes, indeed; I know well enough what that is."

"Did you ever work without wages, Mary?"

"Yes, indeed."

"Then you lived with somebody that you loved as well as you do mother?"

"Did I though? it was more like hate than love."

"Why, Mary, did you ever hate anybody?"

"I did *then*, Miss Louisa, the Lord forgive me for it. I did not know any better; how should I? I was nothing better than a beast. I could not read nor write; work, work, work all the day, and no heart to ease it off; all up hill, and no one to smile upon me as you do. Ah me! but that's over, and I don't want to trouble you about by-gones. We must look forward, Miss Louisa, and be ready to see the bright spots; and is it not a bright one for me to be here talking with you, as if I were your equal? Yes, no looking back. Lot's wife, you know, looked back, and what did she gain by it? Isn't that a good lesson? and can't I read now all about such things? and didn't the angel appear after the men that walked through the fiery furnace? and is not your mother the angel that came to me? But I must not run on so. Only don't be down-hearted. I am so happy to think that I can help you."

"I don't feel down-hearted now, Mary, only I am so sorry that you have not always been happy. I don't know what has been the matter."

"Best you should not, my dear; think no more about it. Let me take the hot water into mistress, you will burn your fingers, and then you cannot play the pretty tunes on the piano."

"But, Mary, I am afraid that I shan't have my piano."

"Well, well, we'll make music for ourselves. I always work better when I sing with it; it seems somehow to get on better, and keeps bad thoughts out of my head."

"I don't believe you have any bad thoughts, Mary, and I love you better than anybody next to father and mother."

"Oh, no, Miss Louisa, you have forgotten little Lucy!"

"Oh! I love her because she is little and pretty."

"It's pretty clear that isn't your reason for loving me."

"You are not very little, that is true, but you are pretty enough for me, Mary,—you are so good to me."

"Why have you been so long away, Louisa? this is not the way for us to begin our work."

"Mother, I staid to hear Mary talk; she did not like that you should wash the breakfast things, and I find she knows all about every thing; and, mother, she says she means to stay with you and do all the work, and not take any wages. What has been the matter with Mary, mother? something has, I am sure. I want you to tell me, mother. You know I am going to help keep house, and I think I am old enough now for you to tell me every thing. I am sure there is something you have not told me about Mary."

"My dear child, I was, this very day, going to tell you about Mary, but now that you are so anxious to hear, I will not put off what I dreaded to tell you, for it will make your heart ache when you know all."

"I see now, mother, what it is that has made you sad; it is something about Mary."

"Yes, it is."

"Mother, dear, I would rather have my heart ache than not know what makes you so unhappy. Do sit down, mother, and I will finish these things."

"Our good Mary, Louisa, is a *runaway slave!*"

"What, mother! a runaway slave, did you say?"

"Yes, she is a slave who ran away from her mistress."

"But, mother, Mary is just like other folks. I thought slaves were different from anybody else."

"Mary is not black like some slaves; there are a great many different shades of color, and she happens to be light."

"But, mother, I thought they were not the least like other folks in any thing."

"The great difference is that they have a dark or black skin, and you and I have lighter."

"I don't see what great difference that makes, mother; there's aunt Sarah, she is very dark, and you and I are very light. I don't know anybody that is better than Mary; and is it not very kind in her to say she will stay with you and do all your work, and not take any wages, because she thinks you cannot afford it? You would not let her work for you though without paying her, would you, mother?"

"Yes, I might for a time, for I consider Mary a friend, and her feelings would be hurt if I did not allow her to have the pleasure that friends take in serving one another. The reason Mary is so anxious to serve me is, that I took her in and gave her a home when she had none. You were only a year old, Louisa, when Mary came to me after her escape from slavery. I knew nothing more about her than that she had been a slave, and had escaped to what she believed to be a land of freedom. She had lived with her mistress from a child; had been married under her roof and lived happily with her husband; but her mistress died, and Mary was sold with the house and furniture. Her new mistress did not want the baby, and sold it to another. Poor Mary was miserable, and so angry with the woman who could do such a cruelly wicked thing, that she determined to run away from her, even though she knew that she might starve before she found any one to give her shelter or help her on her long and perilous journey; for after her baby was taken from her she did not care to live, and would have been glad to die at any moment. She hated the woman who could do so wicked a thing as to take her baby from her arms and sell it to another person. She knew the baby came from God, and that it was hers, and no one had a right to it but herself and its father, her husband. After going through great perils, with the agonizing fear that she might be caught and carried back to her cruel mistress, she arrived, almost starved, weary and with sore feet from her long travel, in this city. I happened to see her and to hear her sad story. I longed to comfort her; took her home with me and nursed her till she was well. In time she became strong and able to work, and has lived with me ever since."

"Oh! mother, how glad I am that you heard about her."

"Yes, it was a happy day for me. When I heard her speak of her baby who was just your age, and saw the flash of anger in her eye, and remembered how happy I was when you first opened your eyes upon me, and then thought of what I should feel were you taken from my arms, I prayed God to help me in comforting the poor mother, who had neither child, nor husband, nor friend that she knew of in the world, and had never been told that there is one Friend that is always with us and ready to help us when we seem most alone. Mary had never been taught to read; she knew nothing but how to work. It was some time before I could make her care about learning any thing out of a book; she however took pains to learn that she might please me, and now there are few who take more pleasure in reading the Bible than Mary. She no longer looks angry when she speaks of her mistress. I do not often talk with her of what has passed, but try to make her interested in what is about her. The love she would have bestowed upon her own child she has poured out upon you and dear little Lucy."

"Dear mother, how glad I am that she is living with us. I don't wonder she did not care about the work and about our leaving the new house. Wherever we go she will go with us, won't she mother?"

"My dear child, if you think you can bear to hear it, I have something more to tell you about Mary."

"I don't see how there can be any thing so bad as what you have already told me. Do you think that she is going to die?"

"No, my child; and you know I have told you death is not a bad thing, though it makes us weep when we lose a friend. I am now preparing to send Mary away."

"Why, mother? you must not say so. Mother, don't do such a cruel thing as to send Mary away. She won't go, mother; you can't make her, I know, and I shall beg her not to go."

"When I tell you all, my dear child, you will wish her to go."

"I shan't, I know I shan't."

"Would you not rather have me send her away to a safe place than have any one come after her and carry her away by main force back into slavery?"

"What do you mean, mother? Nobody can take her from your house, out of your kitchen, and carry her off."

"Yes, they can; your father told me this morning that a law has been made that allows masters to send or come here after their slaves."

"Do you mean that Mary can be taken back to that wicked woman who sold her? How can it be that she *owns* her? How can you buy a person, mother? I don't understand. Is every body bought, mother?"

"No, my dear; you and I happen to be born in a country where, if persons are *white*, it is against the law to buy and sell them, but if they are *black* they may be bought and sold. If we had not been born white I might have been sold to one master and you to another a thousand miles off, so that we would never see each other more."

"Dear mother, do wait a little. I feel so in my throat that I can hardly breathe."

"My dear child, it has been very hard to tell you all this about poor Mary; I did not like to give you so much pain, but it was necessary, unless I had been willing to deceive you. This I could not and ought not to do. You must try, my daughter, to forget your own sufferings in hearing about others. When we know the truth we are better able to act, better able to decide what we ought to do. Now, if you think you can't bear to hear and know about this slavery which is in your own country, you can turn away from it and try to forget it by amusing yourself and taking up other subjects that are not so painful."

"Oh! mother, how can I ever amuse myself? How can I ever forget about Mary? Could I forget if little Lucy had been sold to somebody, and we should never see each other again? No, I can never think of any thing else, mother, so don't ask me to."

"My dear child, I do not wonder that you feel so badly. I should be sorry if you did not; but we must act as well as feel; and as soon as you begin to do something you will bear better the knowledge of this painful truth."

"What can I do, mother? I can't prevent Mary's going away from us."

"No, you cannot; but you can help her to bear the pain by showing kind thought for her, and you can make some pretty things for her, as a keepsake, and tell her she must write to you and tell you all about her new home."

"But, mother, where is she going? you did not tell me."

"No, I could not, while your feelings were so much excited,—and I wish first to talk with Mary about it."

"O, mother! I don't see how you can tell her!"

"We can always do what we know it is right to do, provided we care more for the right than for anything else."

"I shall never be as good as you are, mother."

"If you simply do what you know to be right, without thinking whether you are good or not, your mind will become strong, and you will grow up to be what God meant you should be, one of his children, who is to find her happiness in loving and serving all she can in his great family."

"Mother, I hope you mean to tell Mary all about it as soon as you can, for I don't want to see her again till she knows what is going to happen."

"I am going now to do so, meanwhile you can employ yourself in making the parlor neat."

Louisa's heart beat quickly as her mother left the room, and while busy at her work, tried to keep up a strong heart for herself and Mary too. She did not yet know what was to become of Mary, and she was doing all she could to forget the loss it would be to herself, and to imagine how Mary would live in the future. She knew that she was fond of reading the Bible, and she decided that she would give all her pocket money to buy her a new one; and that she would make her a nice useful needle case. Intent upon these plans the time passed for her mother's absence sooner than she expected.

Her mother returned, and, kissing her daughter, said, "Mary is quite reconciled, my dear, and you had better go and speak to her about it."

"O, mother! I don't feel as if I could."

"Only think of her and you will be able to do it."

Louisa went bravely into the kitchen; as soon as she entered Mary said to her, "So, Miss Louisa, my plans have come to the ground, and I'm to leave them that are all the world to me."

She wiped her eyes with the corner of her apron and went on to say: "Them that's made that wicked law are worse off than I am. It isn't much to me now, since I must leave you, where I go, so long as they don't take me back into slavery. No, your ma, Miss Louisa, angel as she is, has put all to rights. Ha'n't I got her and you, and all of you for friends, if I go to Canada? It is not far enough off to make me forget you. No; I guess it would take a bigger world than this to do that. Yes, I've got you all here;" and she placed her hand on her heart, as she raised her eyes and added, "yes, He'll take care of you and of me, poor creature that I am. There's no slavery there, Miss Louisa, and it won't be long before we shall be standing before Him to give an account of what we've done. He'll take care of even poor me. He is the Father of us all, and loves us in one place as well as another, and we are as near to Him in Canada as here, and so I'll be thankful that he has raised me up such friends as you all have been to me. You don't want my thanks; they are too poor for that, but He'll do all."

"Dear Mary," said Louisa, "you have done far more for us than we have done for you," and she threw her arms about her.

"Ah, Miss Louisa, you'll break my heart if you talk so. I can't talk about it, but my dear mistress has done all for me, and I'm going day after tomorrow, and so I've no time to think about it; I've too much to do for that. Thank the Lord for all his mercies. Did I not tell you there was always a bright spot, if we would only look for it? Can there be anything brighter than to have such friends as you all are to me, to have my heart full of their goodness, and to get up in the morning and to go to bed every night thinking of it? It has pleased God to let me escape from slavery, and shall I complain at all else that may come? No, that I won't. So, Miss Louisa, we'll put a bright face upon it and set to work."

Mary then turned to her duties, wiping away the tears gathering in her eyes, that Louisa need not see them.

Louisa's heart was heavy, and she went back to her mother. She was hardly old enough to understand how the greater suffering had strengthened Mary to bear an evil that was so much less.

Louisa's mother approved of her getting the Bible for Mary, and soon she provided her with materials for making the needle case.

"It is not only parting with Mary that troubles me, my dear child, for I have been able to find an excellent way for her to go to your uncle, in Canada. He will be glad to take her into his family, and will treat her with all possible kindness. But there are many other poor runaway slaves besides Mary, who have no friends to think and act for them, as we have been able to do for Mary. When I think of this terrible law I dread the suffering that is before us."

"Can nothing be done, mother to prevent such wicked things from happening?"

"The only thing to be done, at present, is for those who disapprove of them to say so everywhere, and not to obey a wicked law made to please the powerful, without a desire to protect the weak and helpless."

"I wish I was a man, mother, and I would do nothing else but show how wicked and mean I thought it was."

"It is not necessary to be a man for this."

"But women and girls can't do anything about making laws, mother, and if men choose to make such laws I don't see how we can help it."

"We can show what we feel and think about it. All of us have either fathers, or husbands, or brothers, or cousins, or friends that we may try to lead to do right. If a young girl is going to engage herself to be married, she can let her lover know that if he thinks nothing about such a great sin as slavery is, and cares nothing about it, she can't continue to care much about him. Such a girl may well fear, when she is married, her husband may wish to make a slave of her, and she may be sure there can be no love that will last if people are thinking more of each other than of what is right. Such love is always sure to find an end, and that, too, very soon."

"But, mother, are there no people who care anything about the slaves?"

"Yes, there are many good men and women who write against slavery, and some who devote much time and money to show the evils of slavery, and that it is opposed to that law which God has planted in the heart of every one to make him feel about it, as you do Louisa; and that when men for selfish purposes make such a law as forces Mary to leave us, that it is a wicked law, which must not be obeyed; and that you, and every body, whether man, woman, or child, should do all that is possible against it. A strong desire to do right shows a way to everybody, whether man or woman, boy or girl. So don't think anything about whether you are a man or woman, but, whether you are to take sides with the right or the wrong, whatever it may be about."

"Mother, it seems as if this morning has been the longest of my life. I don't care now about our new house; I wish we were out of it; and I wish we were in a country where there was no slavery."

"That would not help the matter, Louisa. It is better to wish you could do something to abolish it; that you could take your share of the pain and the labor it is to make people think about it and be willing to make some sacrifices for the poor slaves. It is selfish to wish to be away when there is disagreeable work to be done."

"Well, mother, I do wish it."

"It is very natural, but you must try to overcome this feeling. The reason that there is such a thing as slavery is because people care too much for their own comfort; they cannot bear to give up their slaves, because they would lose money and power; they care more for these than for obeying the law which bids us "Do unto others as we would they should do unto us." They have been very anxious to obey the Fugitive Slave Law and have thought nothing of breaking the Golden Rule. Jesus did not run away from sinners; and we must not run away from them because it makes us feel unhappy to be with them. We all have faults, and must try to be patient with the faults of others, and do what we can to help to cure them. It is selfishness, and cowardice, and laziness that has made slavery. Whoever is unjust, or tries to get labor from others without paying them justly for it, is a slaveholder in heart. Were such a person in a slaveholding country he would soon like to hold slaves."

"What is the reason we don't have slaves here, mother? We are not any better than other people, or we should not have such a law."

"Very true, Louisa. If we were better at the North than at the South, where they own slaves, we should never have made a law to help them get back their slaves that had escaped to us. No, I am afraid the reason many do not hold slaves here is, that at the present time the laws of the Northern States forbid their doing it. There are some, I know, who would not

'have a slave to till their ground,
To carry them, to fan them while they sleep,
And tremble when they wake, for all the wealth
That sinews bought and sold have ever earned;'

and I wish all were such."

"Do you think *I* could ever be a slaveholder, mother?"

"Not if you think daily of what is just and right, and act accordingly, without asking whether it will bring you pleasure or pain."

"That is very hard, mother."

"I know it is. But it is because so many persons think more of themselves than of others that we are obliged to part with Mary; that she must ever have a pain burning in her heart to know what has become of her child, and whether she will ever again see it or its father. What you know is but a small part of the evils of slavery. As you grow older I hope you will feel it a duty to learn what slavery is, and thus be able to help in removing this wickedness from the earth. At present we will say no more on the subject. We have much to do to help poor Mary. We must do all we can to keep up her spirits."

"Mother, I am so glad you taught Mary to read and write. I shall put her name in the Bible I am going to give her, and copy the hymn she likes so much, and whenever she looks at them she will think of us, won't she, mother?"

"Yes, my dear, and we will often think of her, and try to imitate her patience and quiet endurance; and continually bear in mind that there are millions who are needing our sympathy and help; who have no kind friends to whom they can pour out their griefs, and to whom this beautiful world has been made dark by the injustice and cruelty of their brother man."

"THINK OF THE SLAVE"

By E. M. Chandler[5]

Think of the Slave, in your hours of glee,
  Ye who are treading life's flowery way;
Nought but its rankling thorns has he,
  Nought but the gloom of its wintry day.

Think of the Slave, in your hours of wo!—
  What are your sorrows to that he bears?
Quenching the light of his bosom's glow
  With a life-long stain of gushing tears.

Think of the Slave, in your hours of prayer,
  When worldly thoughts in your hearts are dim;
Offer your thanks for the bliss ye share,
  But pray for a brighter lot for him.

"A TRUE BALIJAD"

By E. M. Chandler

It was a mournful mother, sat
  Within the prison walls;
And bitterly adown her cheek
  The scalding tear-drop falls.

She sat within the prison walls,
  Amidst her infants three;
The bars were strong, the bolts well drawn,
  She might not hope to flee.

And still the tears fell down her cheek,
  And when a footstep came,
A shudder of convulsive fear
  Went o'er her quivering frame.

It was not for the dungeon's chill,
  Nor for the gloom it wore,

Nor that the pangs of conscious guilt
  Her frightened bosom tore—

For though in prison cell she lay,
  In freedom's happy clime,
Her hand was innocent of wrong,
  They charged her not with crime;

'Twas that she wore a dusky brow,
  She lay within that hold,
Until her human limbs and heart
  Were chaffer'd off for gold.

Sold with her babes—all, one by one,
  Forever torn apart—
And not one faint hope left to cling
  Around her broken heart.

Her husband was a freeman good,
  He lived in Maryland;
Where now in bootless grief he wept
  His broken marriage band.

He loved her when they both were young,
  And though she was a slave,
He wedded her, and with his hand,
  Changeless affection gave.

And when their prattling infants smiled
  Upon his cottage floor,
For them and her, with cheerful heart,
  His daily toil he bore.

But woe for him, and woe for her!
  Her children all were slaves;
Less grief their parents' hearts had borne,
  To weep above their graves.

For still as one by one they grew
  To childhood's franksome years,
They one by one were torn away
  To bondage and to tears.

Torn far away to distant scenes,
  Like green leaves from their stem
And never to their home, bereaved,
  Came tidings more of them.

Now all were wrench'd apart—there was
  No deeper grief to bear;
And they might calmly sit them down
  In agonized despair.

For though our land is proudly free,
  All other lands above,
There's none may dare to knit again,
  Those sacred cords of love.

NOTES

1. The Cornell University online catalogue attributes *Louisa in Her New Home* to Sarah C. Carter. However, discussions with the rare books librarian could not confirm how the cataloguer drew this conclusion.

2. See the discussion of the mother-historian and this text in De Rosa, 79–106.

3. See the complete discussion of *Louisa in Her New Home* in De Rosa, 103–6.

4. This edition adopts the traditional line-by-line dialogue format.

5. S.C.C. appended these two poems by E. M. Chandler to *Louisa*. See chapter on Elizabeth Margaret Chandler in this book.

JANE ELIZABETH (HITCHCOCK) JONES

(MARCH 13, 1813–JANUARY 13, 1896)

Abolitionist and women's rights activist, Jane Elizabeth Jones no longer remains "The Forgotten Activist," as I. Kathleen Moser so calls her. Jones's articles for *The Anti-Slavery Bugle* were unsigned; therefore, her abolitionist children's text, *The Young Abolitionists; or Conversations on Slavery* (1848),[1] remains the only identifiable work to document her fervent abolitionism.

Born to Reuben and Electra (Spaulding) Hitchcock, Jones lived in Vernon, New York, (Melder 285). According to I. Kathleen Moser,

> The area of New York where she was born and raised is called "the burned over district" and the nickname means that it was a hotbed of many religious movements, both reformist and revivalist. The broth of ideologies and ideas implicit in such a milieu could account for Hitchcock/Jones' attraction to reformist moral and political activism. (8)

Jones's highly public activism in support of Garrisonian abolitionism took her through New England, Pennsylvania, and Ohio until the 1860s, when upon her husband's death she returned to Vernon, New York (8).

Several domestic abolitionists included in this anthology preserve their anonymity and others carefully encode their abolitionist views to maintain their status as "true women." Jane Elizabeth Jones, however, speaks publicly against slavery despite the risks. Moser states,

> By the age of thirty, [Jones] appears to have initiated the most politically active period of her life when she became a pioneer Abolitionist lecturer in New England and eastern Pennsylvania. She first visited Ohio, accompanying another controversial abolitionist lecturer, Abbey Kelley. In 1845 the two women arrive in Salem, Ohio, a center of fervent aboli-

tionism, and Hitchock / Jones quickly became involved; she helped to organize antislavery activists and co-edited *The Anti-Slavery Bugle*, official voice of William Lloyd Garrison's Western Anti-Slavery Society. Hitchcock [i.e., Jones] and fellow Abolitionist lecturer, Benjamin S. Jones, shared editorial duties from June of 1845 to June of 1849. (3)

However, the seemingly "radical" abolitionists often encountered much opposition. Jones encountered several mob attacks and when she and her husband, Benjamin, learned that "The Butternuts" (an Ohio gang) planned to tar and feather them for their abolitionist involvement, they quickly departed for West Chester, Pennsylvania (Moser 6).

In *The Young Abolitionists; or Conversations on Slavery*, Jones celebrates giving women a political voice despite the trend to silence them. In the text, Mr. Selden (the father) does not want his children to learn about slavery because he "could not bear the thought that the joyousness of their young spirits should be checked by the contemplation of such terrible cruelties" (see 111). However, he succumbs to his wife, who asserts parental responsibility by insisting on presenting their children—especially the eldest, Charlie—with accurate information about the peculiar institution so "that they might have a just abhorence [sic] of wrong, and enlightened views of the course to be pursued toward the wrong-doer" (see 111). As a seditious abolitionist mother-historian, Mrs. Selden candidly tells the children about slavery's evils.

Unlike Sarah Josepha Hale, who spoke indirectly about slavery to children (see 111). Mrs. Selden presents Charlie (and young readers like him) with a revisionist approach to a silenced chapter of American history. Each "conversation" documents increasingly severe statements, evident when Charlie states, "Every time we talk about the slaves, mother, you make their case worse and worse" (see 150). Mrs. Selden's escalating denunciation includes explaining the differences between plantation and house servants; documenting the physical and emotional abuse slaves endure from both male and female slave owners; exposing forefathers like George Washington who owned slaves; condemning Northerners who openly support slavery or those who perpetuate it by not speaking against it; praising men like Elijah P. Lovejoy, Charles T. Torrey, William Lloyd Garrison, Calvin Fairbanks, and Jonathan Walker for speaking against slavery despite the hostilities they encountered; and rejecting the Fugitive Slave Law and other laws passed to support slavery.

Jones intersperses the "conversations" between mother and child with two tactics to support Mrs. Selden's revisionist history and subversive abolitionist voice: including the Irish servant and giving Mrs. Selden the opportunity to enact her abolitionist principles. First, Biddy O'Flanna-gan, the family's Irish servant, intensifies Mrs. Selden's critique of slav-ery. Biddy's commentary repeatedly contrasts the conditions of American slavery to the oppression she and other Irish immigrants experienced due to greedy landlords and poverty. She considers American slavery so much more violent, morally degrading, hypocritical, and barbaric and applauds slaves who rebel against the physically and emotionally oppressive sys-tem. Second, Jones creates the image of an abolitionist mother-historian turned activist because Mrs. Selden "acts on her moral principles, theo-retical abolitionism, and civil disobedience" (De Rosa 102) when she shelters fugitive slaves and denounces the slave catchers who come to her home to seize them (see 138–143). Thus, through Mrs. Selden, Jones gives voice to a distorted history in which women are part of the aboli-tionist efforts, evermore important since neither the protagonist nor Jones ever cite examples of women abolitionists.[2]

THE YOUNG ABOLITIONISTS; OR
CONVERSATIONS ON SLAVERY (1848)

CHAPTER I

"Mother! let me go to meeting too," said young Charlie Selden, who was anxious to know all that was going on.

"No, my child, you must stay at home with Phil and Jenie, and keep Biddy company."

"But I want to go and hear that man that was here to-day. You said he was going to lecture. I like *him*. We chased each other all round the old pasture, he helped me sail my boat, he played with old Tig, and it was rare sport we had. Mother, he asked me if I were an abolitionist. What did he mean? What is an abolitionist?"

"It is one who is endeavoring to liberate the slaves, my dear."

"The slaves! I heard you talking about the slaves the other day. What is a slave, Mother?"

"A slave is one who is deprived of his freedom—one who is obliged to do the bidding of a master," said the parent.

"Is Biddy a slave then? She does just what you and father tell her. She never goes out without your consent, and in every thing waits for your orders. Does this make her a slave?"

"Oh, no! Biddy, it is true, always obeys our orders, but we pay her well for her services. Every Saturday night she receives her wages, and does what she pleases with them. Then Biddy is free to leave us and seek another home whenever she likes; and besides, she spends a great deal of time in reading, and writes to all her friends in old Ireland."

"Don't the slaves read and write too?" inquired Charlie.

"No, they are not permitted to learn. Their masters are afraid to have them taught, and in some States it is prohibited by law, in Louisiana, for instance."

"I know where Louisiana is very well, and on my chart I can tell by the light and dark shading which are the barbarous and which are the enlightened portions of the globe. Now I remember that the United States are all shaded very light, meaning, as my teacher says, that the people are educated. I should think Louisiana ought to be shaded very dark if they won't let the people learn. The slaves are people, mother, are they not?"

"Yes, they are men and women."

"Are the slave women just like Biddy, and the slave men like Cæsar?"

"Yes, some of them are black as Cæsar is, and some are white like

Biddy," replied his mother. "Cæsar, you know, has been so unfortunate as to lose one of his ears, and several of his fingers. Sometimes the slave-holders, that is the masters, are so cruel as to cut off the ears of their slaves as a punishment for some fault; sometimes they whip them very hard and make the blood run freely; and sometimes they heat irons red hot and burn letters in their faces. Sometimes they make heavy iron collars and compel the slaves to wear them, and some have even been burned alive!"

"Oh, how horrible that is!" cried Charlie. "The slaveholders must be very cruel. Why, in the Indian wars I've read about, they didn't do worse than that! Mother, did I ever see a slave?"

"Yes, my child, you saw one the other day. Do you remember the colored man whom we met at Mrs. Walker's?"

"Why! is *he* a slave? Do tell me all about him. How did he get away from his master? I guess *he* never was whipped; he looks too bold and too strong for that."

"My dear child, the boldest and the strongest are alike powerless in the hands of a master! They dare not resist the most severe punishment! They have no protection from the worst of injuries!"

"But I cannot talk more with you now; I must go to the meeting. At some future time I will tell you all you want to know about the slaves."

"Let Jenie and Phil hear too, mother. Phil is a little boy, but I'm sure he would know it was wrong to have slaves. Will Mr. Wright come here tomorrow? He said when he came here again he would mend the mast of my boat, and I guess he could teach me to fly my kite. Mother, we never had such a visitor as Mr. Wright before."

"No, Charlie, you are quite correct in this, and at some convenient time I will tell you all about this visiter [sic]; how he loves little children, and is always teaching them to be good, and to follow peace principles."

"Does he answer all the questions children ask him? If he does, I wish we could have him for our teacher. I don't think Mr. Gardner loves children very much. He don't like to answer our questions. The other day when Jenie was reading her Bible, she asked him what it meant to 'Hide the outcast.' I suppose she was thinking something about Hide and Seek. He told her she asked quite too many questions. Mother, will you tell Jenie some time what it means to 'Hide the outcast?'"

"Yes, my dear, I shall be very happy to." With that the mother departed, and Charlie ran away to the nursery to tell Jenie and Phil what he had learned about the slaves. Jenie was a gentle little girl, very kind to her brothers, and always ready to listen to Charlie's stories. Phil was the youngest, about three years old, and a noble boy he was. He had a great head and a great heart, and his beautiful blue eyes beamed with intense interest at the simple story of the wrongs and sufferings of the slaves. He was besides a droll little fellow. All the odd expressions he heard Biddy, or Cæsar, or anybody else use, he remembered and frequently repeated. More than once while Charlie was talking he exclaimed, "Oh, my stars!" "Gracious me!" "Saints preserve us!" and "Charlie, if I were there, wouldn't I set Tig on the naughty men that do such naughty things?"

Charlie had been better instructed than to suppose that would be right, and he endeavored to make his brother understand the same; still he felt that something ought to be done.

But Phil was decided in regard to the matter. He thought the masters ought to be punished, and he wished a good many times that he was a man, and if he could see the slaves he would tell them all to knock their masters down and then run away.

In this opinion he was greatly strengthened by Biddy, who had considerable of the war spirit in her, and overhearing their conversation, exclaimed—

"And sure, master Phil, ye'd be in the right of it, the ould thieves of the world, to be after trating a nager in that way, who is just as good as the best of them, and a great dale better, bad luck to them! I heard the blessed mister O'Connell, who is now a saint in glory, tell about the murderin [sic] villians before I left swate [sweet] Ireland."

This conversation continued some time, and even after they retired to bed they talked about the poor slaves. They all went to sleep with the expectation that their mother would renew her account of these unfortunate people, which she did at no distant period, as my little readers will learn by the next chapter.

CHAPTER II

The next evening, the children having finished their tasks, and being left alone with their mother and Biddy, their thoughts naturally turned to the subject that had so deeply engrossed their attention the night before.

"Mother!" said Jenie, "Charlie says that in this country there are slave men and slave women; they don't make slaves of little children, do they, and burn *their* faces, and whip *them* till the blood runs?"

"Yes, my daughter, the slaveholders make slaves of just such little girls as you are. Sometimes they sell them away from their mothers so they can never see them again. Then they force the mothers to work very hard and leave them no time to take care of their children; and sometimes these children go nearly naked—have scarcely anything to wear, and not enough to eat."

"Why don't their mothers get them something?" said Jenie.

"All the money their fathers and mothers get they are compelled to give their masters, so that they can get neither suitable food nor clothing, and they are obliged to leave their little boys and girls to take care of themselves, like the pigs; and I have heard it said that they are sometimes fed in a trough as the pigs are, and on food almost as coarse. I think this is not often done, however."

"If they will come here, I'll give them some of my bread and milk," said Phil, who stood leaning on his mother, his chin on her knee, and eyes and ears both wide open to catch every word that was said about the little slaves.

"These people," continued Mrs. Selden, "do almost all the work that is done in the States in which they live. They raise nearly all the cotton that is used in this country, and most of the rice, and make a great deal of the sugar. Yet they don't get enough of this cotton for their own use, nor of the rice or sugar either.

"The slaves sometimes wear what is called *negro cloth*, which is made of very poor, coarse wool, with some cotton perhaps, and I have seen the hair of cattle mixed in it. This makes a pretty warm dress, but we should think it very rough and ugly if we were obliged to wear it. The women in some cases wear a dress or tow cloth made of a single piece, and sewed up like a bag, with a string in one end to draw it around the neck; and many are seen with a few rags only tied above the hips and hanging midway to the ancle [*sic*].

"I do not wish, dear children, to represent slavery to you worse than it really is. Some slaves are well clothed and have a plenty to eat, but as a general thing, very little attention is paid to their comfort. You know horses are treated very differently here. Some are well cared for—always have fine blankets and plenty of oats, while others are half-starved and are very poor and spiritless. It is so with these people; some are treated better than others; but all are regarded as inferior beings, and kept only for the master's use."

"Do they make slaves of little babies?" asked Jenie, "such tiny little babies as Mrs. Walker's? Mother, I love Mrs. Walker's baby dearly—it is a *dear* little thing. They don't call such babies slaves, do they?"

"Yes, Jenie, the wicked men who make the laws in the States where the slaves are, have made one that says, all the children of slave mothers shall be slaves for life. A great many of the mothers work in the cotton fields and in the rice swamps, and they bind their infants on their backs and carry them in that way while they are hoeing and planting. They use very heavy hoes, and the labor is very hard. Sometimes they lay their infants down in a corner of the fence, but generally they are afraid to do this because of snakes and other reptiles. Very often they are left in a cabin alone, or with some old woman who is not capable of taking care of them, and the poor little things cry very hard and suffer very much."

"The babies can't work any for their masters," said Jenie, "and what do they want of them?"

"That is very true," replied Mrs. Selden; "they cannot work when they are small, but when they grow to be large boys and girls, and men and women, their services will be very valuable. If the masters did not keep these children till they were grown up, they would have to buy those already grown, and that is very expensive. Sometimes they think it cheaper to buy infants and raise them. The other day when your father sold some pigs to Mr. Miller, you remember that he weighed them, and perhaps you know that he got four cents a pound. In the same way, infants are sometimes weighed and sold by the pound! American slave-traders, however, regard them as *rather* more valuable than pigs."

"Saint Patrick keep us!" cried Biddy, who catching up Phil and pressing him to her bosom seemed seized with an apprehension that in some way or other *he* might be taken away and sold with the pigs.

"Saint Patrit keep us!" responded Phil, whose attention was diverted by this new expression, with which he seemed right well pleased.

"Its a purty land of liberty I've come to!" resumed Biddy. "Who would iver drame that they sell babies here as they sell pigs! Sure, but the landlords are cruel in Ireland; they're ready to take the last pratie [Irish, potato] a man has, but they'd niver be thinkin of taking away the darlint babe from the mother of it, at all at all."

Perhaps some of my little readers never saw such a person as Biddy. She was a warm-hearted Irish girl, and like most of the Irish was a Roman Catholic. You have all heard the expressions "God bless you!" "Heaven be merciful!" and the like. These are short prayers; and the Catholics in *their* prayers instead of always addressing God, sometimes address the mother of Jesus, and the Apostles, and others who were regarded as holy people that have lived in different ages of the world.

Charlie, who had been an attentive listener all this time, inquired if an abolitionist, then, was a person who was trying to get these people free, so that the mothers could take care of their children.

"Certainly," replied Mrs. Selden.

"Well, mother," said Charlie, "Ned Miller says *he* is no abolitionist. Should'nt [*sic*] you thing [*sic*] every body would be an abolitionist?"

"Every body ought to be, my child."

"I am one," said Jenie. "I don't want them to treat little girls in that way."

"And so am I," said Phil.

"And sure ye'd be a disgrace to the mother that bore ye, if ye were not," responded Biddy.

"Do they often sell children by the pound?" inquired Charlie, very thoughtfully.

"I think it is not a common practice, though it has been done in many instances," said the mother. It *is* very common, however, to sell children, and men and women too, as horses and cattle are sold. They are often put up at auction with mules and other animals, and sold to the highest bidder. Sometimes the man who buys the husband will not purchase the wife, although he implores him to do so with tears in his eyes. The husband is taken away, and sometimes placed in what is termed a coffle—a long row or gang of slaves all fastened together—and then they are driven through the streets as Cæsar drives the oxen. The husband and wife never see each other again. The driver carries a long whip, and pistols and bowie knife besides."

"What does he carry those for?" asked Charlie.

"These slaves," said the mother, "must necessarily be very unhappy and discontented, having been torn away from their friends and their homes. Not unfrequently do they prefer death to this situation. This renders them disobedient, for which the driver whips them; and if they refuse to submit or attempt to escape they are shot! The body of a slave thus killed is thrown aside and left to be buried by some chance hand, or to be devoured by dogs!"

"Sure, mistress," exclaimed Biddy, "if iver I heard the like of that! They shoot a man down like a dog in this country, because he loves liberty, and then lave him for the dogs to ate! Oh, shame on them!"

"Speaking of the separation of families," resumed Mrs. Selden, "reminds me of an incident I heard related not many days since.

"A slaveholder owned a woman who had two fine children, one of which he sold. At this the mother mourned exceedingly—she wept loud and long, for which the master ordered her to be flogged. Soon after, the remaining child was sold; this made the mother distracted. She wept all day, and even in the night her dismal wailing filled the air. She ran up and down the streets—pulled out her hair, and tore up the very earth in her madness. Her constant cry was, 'Me have no children! Will no good massa pity me? Wicked massa sell me child.' Then running up to the passers-by she would exclaim, 'Me go into massa's house, and into massa's yard, and into me hut, and me no see 'em!' Then shaking herself violently, she would say, 'Me heart go so, for wicked massa sell me children. Oh, dear! what shall me do?'"

"Mother, would it make you crazy if they should sell me, and Phil, and Charlie away from you?" asked Jenie.

"Oh, my child! I dare not think of it. I fear I should bear it no better than the slave mother."

"But I won't be sold," cried Phil.

"Nor I neither," responded Jenie.

"That ye shan't," said Biddy, "and evil would come upon them that would take the like of ye."

"THE SLAVE BABY'S COMPLAINT"

Oh mother! dear mother! why leave me alone
    From the dawn of the morning till night?
Your poor little girl is so sad when you're gone
    And she suffers with hunger and fright.

There's no one comes near me when sick and in pain
    But a woman that's crabbed and old,
And though she's so deaf she can't hear me complain,
    She does nothing but punish and scold.

The baby at master's is bigger than I.
    And could wait on itself if they'd let it;
They go to it quick if it happens to cry,
    And there's nothing it wants, but they get it.

Then what is the reason they drive *you* away,
    When I want you should always be here
To feed me when hungry and help me to play,
    And to call me your own little dear?

B.S.J.

CHAPTER III

One day Mr. and Mrs. Selden were sitting in the parlor discussing the propriety of telling children of the suffering and wrong that exist in the world—of the inhumanity that man practices towards his fellow man.

It was rarely that Mr. Selden and his wife differed in regard to the management of their children; but in this matter of telling them about the slaves, they did not altogether agree. He could not bear the thought that the joyousness of their young spirits should be checked by the contemplation of such terrible cruelties. Coming home one day, he had found Jenie engaged in examining very intently a picture of a slave tied to a post and being whipped very cruelly, with this inscription:

"Oh, don't, massa! Don't!"

He leaned over her, and as she tossed the golden ringlets from her eyes, he saw they were filled with tears. She threw her little arms around his neck as he took her to his embrace. Neither father nor child spoke, but the gentle heavings of her bosom made him fear that at too early an age she was becoming acquainted with the history of crime.

Mrs. Selden reminded her husband that their children would be learning these sad stories from one and another, and it was best for parents to instruct them in regard to slavery and other evils, that a proper impression might be made—that they might have a just abhorance [sic] of wrong, and enlightened views of the course to be pursued toward the wrong-doer.

"And besides," said she, "benevolent enterprises have received great advantage from the moral influence of children. Nobody hesitates to instruct them in temperance principles, or to portray the evils of their violation; and many a poor drunkard has been raised from the gutter, and baptised into newness of life, through the saving power of his little child! How many a poor mother, reduced to want and starvation, has had reason to bless the influence of her young boy! They are effective preachers of righteousness; and their freedom from guile, and clearness of vision, render them powerful agents for good when properly instructed."

At this moment Charlie entered the room, and with a countenance all animation and delight said:—

"Father! did you know that Mr. Wright gave me this book the other day? It is called "A Kiss for a Blow," and it shows how we ought never to injure those who injure us, but that we should always return good for evil. I've been reading this morning how he visited the schools and asylums in Boston and Philadelphia, and always taught the children to be very kind and obliging to each other. Then he plays with them a great deal. In one place he tells of a royal old Elm that stands on Boston Common under which children have played for two hundred years. There, he says, he often assembles with fifty or a hundred, and they frolic, and laugh, and have glorious times. He plays tag, and ball and battledore, and runs races with them; and sometimes they all take hold of hands and form a great long row and march across the Common. It must look queer. How I wish I could be with Mr. Wright and those children under that royal old Elm. Father! when you go to Boston again, I hope you'll take me. He tells stories too. I've been reading of one he told them about two boys who pretended they had been fighting in love; and as I read how they stood before their father with black eyes and bloody noses, and told him they had been fighting because they loved each other, I laughed outright. People don't fight when they love each other, and so the children said— they thought the boys told a falsehood. I guess the boys and girls he talked with, that seemed so good and kind, and understood peace principles so well, are all abolitionists—don't you, mother?"

"I hope they are," replied Mrs. Selden. Mr. Selden saw that the logic of his wife was altogether sound in reference to what she had been telling her children; still he loved them so well, and was so desirous to make them happy, that he shrunk from the thought of having a single shadow fall on the sunlight of their young existence. But he saw that even if it were best, and he desired ever so much to keep the evils of the world from their view, it could not now be done. They were getting too old, and had become too deeply interested in what they had heard, not to desire to hear more. So he concluded that his wife might as well make thorough work of it, at least so far as Charlie was concerned, and tell him as much about the system of slavery as he was able to understand.

Mr. Selden went to his counting house, and the conversation between the mother and child was soon resumed. But they had not proceeded far before Charlie proposed to go for Phil and Jenie, thinking they would want to hear too.

"Never mind Phil," said the mother; "you may bring Jenie."

The little girl followed her brother into the parlor, and much to the surprise of the parent, brought in her hand a beautiful embroidered apron. It had been purchased for her but a few days before, and was an article she valued very highly. Looking up with the greatest earnestness she said—

"Mother! will you send this to the little slave girl?"

Mrs. Selden was deeply moved by this instance of generosity and pity on the part of her little daughter, and in her heart she prayed God she might ever be thus, so that in after life her self-sacrificing and compassionate spirit might serve to bless and purify the world.

To make the child understand that the apron could not well be sent, and even if it could, would not be very useful, and that she had better take her pennies and buy tracts and send them to the slaveholders, that they might be convinced that slavery was wrong, was a work that required some time.

So fearful was the mother that she should not sufficiently encourage the beautiful spirit of the child, that she allowed her to sell the apron and purchase an anti-slavery book, which she sent to a distant relative residing at the south, and which Jenie fondly hoped would show him that slavery was wicked, and would induce him to give up all the little boys and girls that he held.

"I've been thinking a great deal," said Charlie, "about the prisoners we saw the other day. You said they were kept in prison as a punishment for crime. I should think the slaves did not fare much better, and I suppose they are not criminals. You said they worked out doors raising cotton, and rice, and making sugar; and the prisoners I know have to work in their cells and be shut up all the time, and that must be *very* bad. Do they build such great houses for the slaves to live in as that prison, and have such little cells, and do they have their food cooked for them as the prisoners do?"

"No, dear. I wish they had food as good as the prisoners have, and houses as comfortable as their cells. Their huts or cabins are very rude and cheerless. Sometimes they are made of clay—generally of logs, and often in the far south, of stakes and the leaves of the palmetto. These huts are very open, frequently having neither door, nor floor, nor chimney. Only think how uncomfortable it must be to live on the cold, damp ground, and in a place so open that it would not protect you from the tempest. Some of these poor beings are sometimes driven from their rude dwellings by the pitiless storm, the rain coming in from every quarter till there is no dry place even for the sole of the foot. They seek shelter in the huts of others, but oh, how glad would they be to find so warm and dry a spot as the prisoner's cell!"

CHAPTER IV

"As you have mentioned the convicts in the State's Prison," said Mrs. Selden to her son, "I would like to show you how much more regard is paid to *their* wants, than to those of the slaves. I have already told you of their miserable huts, and you know there can be none of the comforts of home in such a wretched place."

"When the rain comes in and drives them out," said Charlie, "don't their beds and everything get wet?"

"They have nothing that can properly be called a bed, so many persons say, who have lived in the south, and are well acquainted with their situation. They are generally furnished with one old blanket, and sometimes two. Some have a bundle of straw or a few old rags to lie on, while others sleep on the cold ground. They would consider themselves fortunate indeed could they have such nice beds as the prisoners have.

"I do not wish you to think the situation of the prisoner by any means a pleasant one. Oh! it is dreadful to be shut out from the beautiful world, from all the sources of happiness, almost from the sunlight and the refreshing air of heaven; to be confined in a narrow cell, and never hear the sound of a human voice—as is the case of some prisoners—or be allowed to look upon a human face, save that of the grim keeper who controls the heavy bolt that confines the sufferers in that solitary abode. Oh! the very thought of it makes my blood run cold, and I wonder how human beings ever could have devised such a mode of torture. But when I think of the slave, I see that he is the victim of a system that far exceeds in cruelty any form of punishment ever invented."

"Do tell me how it is, mother; I cannot see," said Charlie, "how slavery can be worse than that."

"Criminals are generally imprisoned," she replied, "for a few years only—the period of the slaves' bondage in the great prison house of oppression ends but with death. The convict, when his term expires, goes out a *free* man. He can return to his home and his friends, if he have [sic] any; he can choose his own employment, and pursue his own happiness as it pleases him best. If he has truly repented of his crime, he will, in a great measure, be restored to society, and can enjoy life as well as before. The slave looks forward to no time when *he* shall go out a free man. If he has been separated from his wife and children, he indulges in no pleasing expectation that in a few years or a few months he may return to those he loved so well. There are prisoners who know, that although *they* are shut up in a gloomy cell, their children are enjoying freedom, the care of friends and the comforts of life. The slave feels that *his* children are smarting under the lash, and that they have no kind friend to protect them, and that they are doomed to the deepest degradation and misery. The prisoner is sustained by the expectation of having his freedom again—of being the master of himself. The slave pines under his affliction, his heart fails him, his spirit is broken by the crushing power of slavery, and he lies down in despair, feeling that a night of endless bondage has closed in upon the hopes, the happiness and the liberty of himself and three millions of his race."

"Three millions! mother?" said the astonished boy. "Mr. Gardner told us yesterday there were only about twenty millions of people in the United States;—are three millions of them slaves?"

"It is a mortifying thought, my child, yet it is nevertheless true. When we were in Philadelphia last summer, you were astonished at the multitude of people that were passing up and down the streets and crowding the shops. Had you gone from the Navy Yard to Kensington, from the Delaware to the Schuylkill, and counted all the inhabitants of that great city, you would have had but a small part of the number of slaves. Indeed there are more than twelve times as many of these oppressed and suffering people as you would have found persons in that place. And I believe you could hardly go to anyone of these three millions, and ask him if he would be willing to exchange his situation for that of the convict, endure for a few years confinement in a close cell, and then forever after have his freedom, but he would be rejoiced to make the exchange. But let any man go to the convict, and tell him that instead of remaining in the solitary cell a few years, he can be made a slave for life, and then ask him if he would choose the latter: the convict would think him a madman for putting the question."

"But, mother, you said some men were imprisoned for life. Would not such rather be slaves than live always in their cells?"

"I cannot tell how a man would feel under such circumstances; still, I believe even then he would much prefer the prison," said the mother. "In the prison he is sure of comfortable food and clothing, and of not being greatly over-worked. In slavery he is liable to be starved, to go nearly naked, to be compelled to work sixteen or eighteen hours a day. Although a prisoner in close confinement, he is regarded as a man; by the law, he is recognised as a human being; by the people he is spoken of as member of the human family. In slavery he is looked upon as a brute; he becomes a piece of property; he has an owner who may inflict untold wrongs upon him, and no voice will be raised in opposition. This consideration alone, my child, would induce every man who has any appreciation of his manhood, who has any sense of the dignity of his position as a member of the human race, to choose the convict's cell for life rather than the lot of the American slave!"

"Were I to choose, mistress, I'm sure *I'd* niver be a slave," said Biddy, who had entered the room and heard the foregoing conversation. She had brought with her Phil, her darling pet, whose attention was attracted from his play by the rising spirit of Biddy, which was manifested by her earnest tone. When *she* expressed an opinion, Phil always felt called upon to sustain her. Consequently he informed his mother that he never would be a slave either.

"And," said he, "if the naughty men should come here, Charlie, would'nt [sic] I shoot them with my bow and arrow?"

"Phil don't understand peace principles very well, does he, mother?" asked Charlie.

"No, my dear, he is a little boy and don't know much about any kind of principles. He must not talk of shooting people though, even with his bow and arrow."

"You asked me, Charlie, the other day, if food were cooked for the slaves. Generally it is not, though sometimes one of their number prepares it, but it is always coarse and poor. On many plantations, or farms, as you would call them, they gave each full grown slave a peck of corn a week. After working in the hot sun all day, they go home at dark very sad and very weary, thinking how their poor little children have wanted them when they were away; and instead of sitting down to rest and finding a comfortable supper, they have to grind or pound their corn, and bake their hoe-cake, and 'tis often past midnight before this and their other work is done."

"What is hoe-cake?" asked Jenie.

"It is bread made of corn meal and water, and baked before the fire on an old hoe," said the mother, "and quite well satisfied would many of the slaves be with this if they could only get enough of it. It is the testimony of many who have lived in the South, that 'thousands of slaves are pressed with the gnawings of cruel hunger during their whole lives.' Boats on the Mississippi River, when stopping over night, are often boarded by slaves begging for a bone or a bit of bread to satisfy their hunger. They always seem very thankful for these favors, and often a poor crust will call forth a strong expression of gratitude.

"In a conversation I lately had with a friend who had seen much of slavery in his trading voyages on that river, he said, that on one occasion when he was stopping at a plantation landing, a bright little slave boy came on to his boat and begged for something to eat. He gave him some bread and butter. The poor child, delighted with the bountiful gift, looked at him, and with gratitude beaming from his face, said, in his own uneducated dialect, 'When I dies and goes to God, I'll tell him that you gib me dis.' Happy, my dear children, will it be for us all, if, when the poor slave goes into the presence of its Father-God, it shall tell of acts of kindness *we* have done!"

"But, mistress," said Biddy, "the slave sure can't suffer from the hunger-pain as I've seen my own people do at home. Oh! but the like of that I hope niver to see again."

"But then," rejoined Charlie, "they are not hungry all their lives, as some of the slaves are."

"That's true for ye. I've seen many a man who had been well to do, and had always a bit and a sup to give the stranger, who was left without a morsel in his cabin, and, God help him! his children crying for bread, and the darlint wife looking so sad and so sorrowful like, and all bekase the crops failed them, and the praties [Irish, potato] they did raise were not fit even for the pig to ate. Sure, I've seen many a sight there that made my heart sore, and at this blessed minit I'm a fearing that hundreds haven't a handful of male [meal] in their cabin.

"Ye've a kind heart, master Charles, and I love ye for it, and if ye had seen what I did before I left the ould country, 'twould be after melting itself into tears. The poor little childer were nothing but skin and bone, and went about so silent and so strange like, that it hurt me heart to look at them. They had done crying, and had done asking for bread, for they knew there was none. And oh, but it was hard on the mothers, for the laugh of their darlints that was like a song to them was gone! and they knew that they all must die, and not have even a friend perhaps to carry them to the churchyard. And the fathers too, who had kept up brave hearts as long as they could, when they saw the dead eyes of them they loved, and saw their beautiful boys and girls become so ghostlike they hardly knew them, and they not able to beg a bite for them, or get a stroke of work to do themselves; God save them! but it was hard."

"Biddy!" said Charlie, whose eyes were swimming in tears, "wouldn't these people rather be slaves?"

"That I can't say," replied Biddy, "for when the head is distracted-like, it's hard saying what a man would do if only himself was concerned; but there's not one of them, that I saw, would have been willing to have had a childer made a slave to save *it* from starvation. Sure, but the curse of

God would have followed them if they would. And as for meself, I'd rather starve a thousand times, if it be God's will, than to be made a slave by the will of man."

"Biddy is right," said Mrs. Selden, turning to her children; "it is far better to die of starvation than to live in slavery. Besides, if you are in slavery you are liable to die of want as many a poor slave has done. Then you would be as badly off as the Irish in that respect, and subject to a multitude of other evils to which they are strangers."

"THE HUNGRY SLAVE BOY"

Oh, will not some massa take pity on me?
   I often am hungry from morning till night,
A bit of good food do I scarce ever see,
   And many a day I get hardly a bite.

What harm can so little a slave boy have done,
   That so sad and so hungry I always must go?
When master calls for me, I'm ready to run
   And do what he bids me as well as I know.

I wish I could get just as much bread and meat
   As the free little boys and the girls that I see!
Oh, how good it would be to have plenty to eat,
   And how strange it would seem for a slave boy like me!

And mother, she tells me that if when I die,
   I have done as I ought, and have always been good,
I shall live where the folks are all free in the sky,
   And where every body has plenty of food.

B.S.J.

CHAPTER V

"I was telling you, my son," said Mrs. Selden to Charlie, "that some of the slaves did not get their corn pounded, and baked and eaten till nearly midnight. You know when your father is obliged to be up late at night, he does not rise early the next morning; but I often get breakfast for him after the rest have eaten. The slaves cannot do so. No matter how late they are up at night, they must be up early in the morning also. On many plantations they are required to be ready to go into the field at break of day. At the sound of the driver's horn all must hasten to their unpaid toil.

"That driver's horn!" said Mrs. Selden; "many a sweet vision of peace and comfort is destroyed by its unwelcome sound. The old slave, who has numbered his seventy winters, is dreaming perhaps of liberty—of the realization of his fondest hopes. He thinks his master has given him his freedom; that he has a little patch of ground he can call his own; that his wife, who was torn from him long, long ago, has been restored to his bosom; and his children, who were sold, some to go in one direction and some in another, have all obtained their freedom and returned to him. Oh, how happy he feels in the free family group and by his own free hearth-stone. I say, he is dreaming this, perhaps, and the sound of the driver's horn dispels the illusion and he awakes to find that he is yet a slave! that no tidings have been received of those he loves, that no prospect of liberty awaits him till he falls into the grave!"

"Oh, mother," said Charlie, "it seems to me that I can see the old man now rising from his poor bed and getting ready to go to his work."

"And if you could see him, my son, you would see one with a heavy heart. You would behold such an expression of despair as you never saw on the human face before."

"I was thinking," said Charlie, "that the slaves lived so badly and had so little to eat that they could not work. I know I could not work if I were treated so."

"I'm sure I *would* not," said Biddy. "I'd not lift a finger. Stalk still I'd stand, and they might do their own work for all of me."

"There are many slaves," rejoined Mrs. Selden, "who would like to say what Biddy does but they dare not. There are many who would refuse to work, if by so doing they would not be great losers rather than gainers."

"Gainers or losers, I'd not work without enough to eat and with nothing but rags to wear. I'd die first!"

"The slaves are generally accompanied by an overseer or driver," continued Mrs. Selden, "whose business it is to see that each performs his alloted task. If one from sickness or inability lags behind, he is urged on by the cutting lash. There is no way of escape—they must work or be beaten, perhaps to death. If they turn either to the right or to the left, and refuse to pursue the beaten track, they do it at the peril of their lives. Whipping is almost universal; indeed, a slave who has never been whipped is a wonder in the country all around. These overseers are notorious for their inhumanity; for their shameless disregard of the common decencies of life; for their utter abandonment of all moral principle, and their entire destitution of every good and generous feeling. Even the masters, as unkind and inhuman as they are, in their souls abhor the overseer. Still he is a necessary appendage to the plantation; for if they keep slaves, they must keep somebody to whip them."

"But, mother, it is not necessary to whip them," interposed Charlie.

"Yes, my dear, it is," replied Mrs. Selden. "It may not appear so at first thought, but when we consider that the slave has no motive for action, that he may work ever so hard and earn ever so much, yet neither he, nor his wife, nor his children will be any better off: he will have, no property, none of the comforts of life; he will gain no consideration in the eyes of the world, but will still be looked upon as a brute, unworthy a place among men; will still be obliged to endure poverty, perhaps actual starvation; we know that his heart must sicken within him and that he cannot work; consequently all that is got out of him must be obtained by the power of the lash. If slavery be right, my child, the whipping is right also, for the former cannot be maintained without the latter.

"I have spoken principally of the plantation slaves, or field hands, as they are sometimes called. Besides these, there are many house servants, including cooks, table-waiters, chamber maids, nurses, seamstresses, and body servants.

"No more regard is paid to the wants or the comfort of these, than to those of the field hands, though the differance [sic] in their situation may give them some advantages. Many who are familiar with southern life have stated that these servants have neither beds, nor chairs, nor tables in their own apartments, indeed none of the conveniences of life so indispensable to home enjoyments. While they are likely to get better food and clothing than the field slaves, on the other hand, instead of having one overseer to please, they have many. They are at the mercy of master, mistress, children, and indeed the whole household, who are each and all liable to fall into fits of passion and inflict upon them the most terrible cruelties. Not unfrequently [sic] does the mistress herself ply the bloody lash, and the abhorred paddle, and sometimes in the heat of her fury will she seize the poker, or tongs, or broom, and fall upon the poor wretched slave with all the ferocity of a tiger.

"I am sorry, my son, to state this dreadful fact about women, who are supposed to be more gentle and kind than men; but slavery renders all hearts hard and flinty that have anything to do with it; it transforms them into unfeeling tyrants, and makes them commit deeds we blush to think of.

"Mr. Calvin H. Tate, of Missouri, relates a case of cruelty that occured [sic] on a plantation adjoining his father's, who was also a slaveholder. A young woman had her back so unmercifully cut by the lash that the garment next to her skin was stiff from the running of the sores. This, with other things, made her so sick that she was obliged to leave the field. As soon as she reached the house she fell upon the floor entirely exhausted. Her mistress asked her what the matter was, but she gave no answer. She asked again, but there was no reply. 'I'll see,' she said, 'if I can't make you speak.' So taking the tongs she heated them red hot and seized hold of her feet, and then her legs and body, and at last in a rage took hold of her throat. The poor girl faintly whispered, 'Oh! Misse, don't—I'm most dead;' and presently the suffering creature expired."

"Oh, mother! I never heard of anything so unfeeling," said Charlie. "I did not know there were such women in the world. I hope there are not many who do such wicked things."

"Should a woman fly at me with the poker or tongs, I guess it's the last time she'd do the like of it," said Biddy, and her eyes flashed fire as she spoke. "It's meself that'd show every one of them, they'd better not be after trying to trate me in that way. Sure, but I'd give them as good as they brought, and may be a little bit better," and in her excitement she began to roll up her sleeves and display a great pair of brawny arms which seemed to bid the offender beware! "They're a burnin disgrace to their sex, so they are, and if they'd dare to lay the weight of their little finger on me, I'd warrant me they'd niver forget Biddy O'Flannagan!"

"I doubt not you would do as you say," observed Mrs. Selden, "but your course would not be christian, or prudent either, if you valued your own life. In some states, Georgia, for instance, if a slave strikes a white person, he must suffer such punishment, not extending to life or limb, as the court may see fit to prescribe; and for the second offence—the second blow—*he must suffer* DEATH! There would be no alternative in your case, Biddy; you would soon lose your life, for I know by your spirit that you *would* fight."

"Well, mistress, and would'nt [sic] I be quite as well off to be killed by the law, as to be killed by a brute of a woman? It's a purty law though you've made in this *free* country," continued Biddy, in the most contemptuous tone, "to kill one bekase he wo'nt paceably submit to be beaten to death with a poker! A purty law surely, and its [sic] a purty country I've come to!"

"Mother, do tell me," said Charlie, "why these people don't run away. What do they stay with the slaveholders for? Why don't they go and live in some other place?"

"Charlie, why does Mr. Willet's horse stay with him? You say he treats him very badly, he don't give him enough to eat, or take any care of him, makes him draw such heavy loads that you sometimes think the horse will be drawn in two; and when he is tired, you say he beats him, and makes him work until he is ready to fall down. You remember he ran away last summer, and Mr. Willet went after him. Perhaps you heard that some man took up the horse and kept him till the owner came. The horse stays with his master because he can't help it, don't he? He submits to the treatment of which you complain because he can do no better. All the men about the country have horses as well as Mr. Willet, and when their's escape, they want assistance to retake them; consequently they will render all the aid necessary to enable Mr. Willet to keep *his* horse. It is just so with the slaves. The most of them remain where they are because they can't help it—because they can do no better. Their rights as human beings are utterly denied them, and the right of the master to hold them for his own use as horses are held, fully acknowledged by the community in which they live, by the law and the public sentiment of the entire South. Every man's hand is against them; every face they meet is the face of a foe. All the people around them have conspired together to keep them in bondage. They feel that the curse of slavery has pierced them to the soul; despair has settled down upon them; they are in the power of an oppressor from whom there is no escape; and like the prisoner in the Iron Shroud, of whom you were reading yesterday, they see the cold, heavy walls of slavery gradually closing in upon them, and they know they must finally be crushed to death beneath their ponderous weight."

CHAPTER VI

Mrs. Selden generally allowed several days to intervene between their conversations on the subject of slavery. She wished to make a lasting impression upon the minds of her children, and she thought this could be done better by giving them a few facts only at a time. When the subject was resumed again, she said,—

"Charlie, perhaps I should have told you the other day, that many slaves have attempted, and succeeded too, in escaping from their masters. I was speaking then of the mass, of the great majority, who see no way of escape. It is not uncommon among the more daring spirits to watch for a favorable opportunity, and in the silence and darkness of midnight steal away and secrete themselves in a neighboring swamp, or make a bold push for a land of freedom. Their absence is quickly noted, and arrangements make [sic] for speedy pursuit. It is not unusual for several planters to join in a Slave Hunt—as such an expedition is called—and this Slave Hunt is one of the most brutal features of the system. The party are always well armed, for they expect the slaves to make resistance, and they prepare themselves to shoot them down if they refuse to surrender. They are generally accompanied by bloodhounds that have been trained to the service of tracking fugitives, and very often they lead the party directly to the place where the poor slaves have taken refuge, or follow on until they overtake them in their flight.

"Perhaps these poor victims of oppression are pressing onward, and onward, and their fear of pursuit begins to subside; when lo! they hear the deep baying of the hounds in the distance, and as the sound draws nearer, and nearer, they hear mingled with it the yells and execrations of the pursuers. Alas! what can the poor fugitives do? They make one desperate struggle to escape—one frenzied rush for life and liberty! They plunge into the dense forest; they seek the most intricate way; they strain every nerve, and summon all the energies of their wearied nature for this last effort. But it is all unavailing. The hounds are upon them! The masters demand a surrender.

"The slaves spurn the command with all the indignation of outraged men, and still attempt to pursue their way. They are fired upon, at first for the purpose of disabling them, and although many a shot is lodged in their limbs and shoulders, and their flesh is torn and mangled by the savage dogs, yet in the madness of their despair they rush on, and on! At length one or two are brought to the ground by the deadly rifle. The fatal work is done! the rest give up.

"The hunters glory in the triumph and exult over the conquest of a few stricken and famishing men and women who desire to be free. They mutter a few curses over the dead bodies of the fallen, and as they gaze upon the yet warm and quivering flesh of their victims, and see to what fearful lengths the love of liberty carried them, apparently no feeling of remorse is awakened in their bosoms, no regret that such is the unhappy condition of a fellow man. They talk only of the loss of property, then bind fast their captives and prepare to return.

"The punishments inflicted upon these runaways," continued Mrs. Selden, "are almost incredible. They receive sometimes one, two, three, and even five hundred lashes on the bare back—it's a strong man, though, who can take the latter and live. Sometimes they are compelled to wear heavy iron collars on their necks till the very flesh is worn from the bones; sometimes a chain with a heavy iron ball attached to it is fastened to the ancle [sic], and the poor creature is obliged to drag that about day after day. Sometimes the victim is placed in the stocks—a machine which confines the feet and legs in an immovable position—and nearly starved to death; and sometimes one ear is cut off, and sometime several teeth are knocked out; and very often they are sold to the far South from whence they can never hope to escape. No offence is punished so severely as running away. Love of liberty appears to be regarded as the highest of crimes."

Biddy, Jenie and Phil were all present, and had been listening with the deepest attention. At length the former exclaimed,—

"Holy Mother save us! if what ye've been telling be true. Sure, mistress, I'd not belave [sic] it, had not your own lips been speaking it. I've seen many a fight in me own country at a Wake or a Fair, and the Orange boys and Ribbon men were cruel to each other; but then it's fighting for their religion they were, and that ye know, mistress, often makes a man savage like. But Slave Hunts! Saints preserve us! May the like niver disgrace swate Erin. Ye've men and women in this country then that are free to be hunted with guns and bloodhounds as wild bastes [sic] of prey are hunted. Sure, it's better to be free to die of famine in Ireland, than to have the freedom of a nager slave in Ameriky."

"Mother," said Jenie, "what do the women do with their children when they run away?"

"Many of them have none," replied the parent, "and those that have, sometimes take them also. Sometimes their children have been previously sold; and sometimes they leave them behind, expecting that in some way or other they can be got away afterwards."

"Well, mother," said Jenie, "you wouldn't run away and leave Phil and me with the cruel men, would you?"

"No dear, I should rather stay. The thought that my little children were slaves, would make me very wretched, and destroy all the pleasure of being free myself. Many slave mothers feel in the same way; so long as their children must be slaves they choose to remain slaves also."

"Well," said Phil, who was always seeking ways to punish the tyrant, "I should think the slaves would set the dogs on the masters. I would, and make them tear the ugly men all to pieces."

"I'm sure it ought to be done, master Phil," responded Biddy, "and if the dogs were but sensible-like they'd be after doing it."

"That would be returning evil for evil," said Jenie, "would it not? Mother says that is wrong."

"But the dogs would'nt [sic] bite their masters," observed Charlie. "Nobody could make old Tig do us any harm, and I suppose its [sic] just the same with their dogs. Mother, you said some time ago that some slaves did get away. Do tell us more about *them?*"

"I will; you can hardly imagine though, my child, what difficulties lie in the way of the fugitive. If the slave is valuable and is not found immediately, handbills are circulated in every direction offering a reward of twenty, fifty, and sometimes two hundred dollars for his apprehension. There are men all around the country who would be glad to obtain this reward by seizing and returning him, so he is obliged to keep out of the sight of men, and travel only in the fields and woods, and hide himself in swamps, and dens, and caves. Often for weeks and months the haunt of the wild beast and the poisonous reptile is his only home; yet he had rather risk his life with these than to endure the cruelties of man. He fears less the beast of prey than the power of the oppressor. He lives on nuts, and fruits, and roots, and whatever he can pick up. After long, and lonely, and wearisome travel he succeeds in reaching a land of freedom."

"The slaveholders must be very different from other people, mother?" said Charlie, enquiringly. "I am sure no one that I know would be guilty of doing so wickedly. No one would set a dog upon a poor wretched woman who wanted to be free; no one would whip her for crying because her children were sold."

"Slaveholders are not so different from other people as you might at first suppose," observed Mrs. Selden. "I presume you are not acquainted with any who would *now* in his present situation do such cruel acts as I have been telling you about. But take a person and surround him for awhile with the hardening influences of slavery—let him daily witness extreme sufferings and torture; give him power—let him hold slaves, and feel that it is for his interest to get a great amount of labor out of them; and he would whip, and beat, and brand, and hunt with dogs his wretched victims just as other slaveholders do.

"The exercise of power over a fellow man corrupts the human heart and turns it into a heart of stone. When you become better acquainted with the world, my son, you will find that many who are noted for cruelty, were once kind and compassionate as any of the people about you. The commencement of the reign of some of the Roman Emperors was marked by the greatest lenity and kindness; but so corrupting was irresponsible power—power that none dare attempt to restrain—that at length they seemed to take pleasure in deluging Rome with human blood! Thousands of human beings were sometimes sacrificed in a single hour!

"I greatly desire to impress upon you, my dear boy, the importance of cherishing and cultivating all the good and generous feelings that you have; and of suppressing all selfish and revengeful thoughts. If you feel prompted to speak a kind word to the unfortunate, to lend a helping hand to one in distress, to confer a favor upon the needy, always act out these feelings, and never suffer yourself to be restrained by a laugh or a sneer from your companions, or by the opposite course of those around you."

"Well, mother, "I hope I shall always be a good boy, and I will *try* to act out my good feelings. The other day, Frank Hulton, whose mother has been sick all summer, and who is very poor and never buys anything for her children to play with, wanted my little cart—he said I had a wagon and did not need it. I felt like giving it to him, and almost said he might have it, but a selfish feeling came up that made me change my mind. I think now I will give it to him."

"Yes, dear, I hope you will not let the day pass without making glad the heart of Frank Hulton by the gift he desires."

"THE FUGITIVE"

The night was cold and stormy
  When a dark browed man came forth,
And with quick and eager footstep
  Pressed onward to the north.

The lash that day was buried
  Deep in his quivering flesh,
And the crimson drops came trickling
  From wounds that bled afresh.

What seeks he in the shadow
  Of the deep and tangled wood?
Why lurks he in the forest
  Where wild beasts seek their food?

Why cringes he with terror,
  Why trembles he with fear
At every sound that falleth
  On his quick and listening ear?

Why does the blood-hounds' baying
  That cometh to him now,
His dark cheek blanch with terror
  And with cold sweat bathe his brow?

Why rushes he so madly
  And with fleetest foot away,

As though no human barrier
  His onward course could stay?

He is fleeing from oppression—
  From slavery's deadly ban;
He is seeking for the Freedom
  His Creator gave to man.

God speed him in his efforts!
  May he never be the prey
Of blood-hounds, or of tyrants
  More merciless than they!

B.S.J.

CHAPTER VII

Charlie was a great talker. He had an inquiring mind, and was always seeking the why and wherefore of every thing. Like other boys he often asked his mother to tell him stories, and unlike most boys he never wanted to hear any that were made up. He liked true stories—he asked for facts, for real events—he wanted to know about people and things. He was interested in her slave stories because she assured him that all her statements were literally true. Many a time he wished that these were made up stories, and that there were no slaves in the world.

Charlie talked a great deal with his father, and I think some of my young friends would like to know what their conversations were about; but in this little book I shall tell them, only what his mother said about slavery.

Mr. Selden was always instructing his children, and when he went to town on business, or round the neighborhood in which he lived, he often took Charlie and went with him into all the shops and factories where the people work on wood, iron, tin, brass, stone, clay, cotton, wool, &c., and explained to him every thing connected with their several handicrafts. He frequently asked his father questions about the slaves; but Mr. Selden did not say much to him on this subject, so he generally preferred talking with his mother.

He came home from school one day, evidently somewhat perplexed. He immediately went to his mother that he might tell her what Ned Miller, one of his school-mates, had said about the abolitionists. Charlie had been contending that every one ought to be opposed to slavery, and Ned, on the other hand said, "He didn't care for the old niggers, and whipping was just good enough for them." Charlie said, "We talked about this at recess, and after we went into school, as we sit on the same seat, we continued to talk. At last Mr. Gardner came along and asked us what we were talking about. I told him we were talking about the slaves. He frowned and looked very much displeased; then he said, 'Let me hear no more of that; you'd better be talking about things that concern you—you have no business with *them*.' Mother, I never saw Mr. Gardner look so before. I am sure this *is* a subject that concerns us."

"I was telling you not long since," rejoined Mrs. Selden, "that many people about here are not very different from slaveholders. They know that three millions of their fellow-citizens are wearing chains—that they are enduring a worse form of oppression than ever disgraced any barber-ous [sic] age or nation; yet they raise no voice against it—they utter no protest—but allow the slaveholder to go on and commit his crimes with impunity, and not only that, but strengthen his arm in the performance."

"Why, mother! it seems to me that's the worst part of the story," added Charlie.

"Yes," said Mrs. Selden, "what I have to tell you of the indifferance [sic] of the people of the North to this subject; of their hostility to every movement for the overthrow of slavery; and of their actual support and sanction of the system, will astonish you more, perhaps, than all I have told you of the woes and sufferings of those in bonds.

"It seems almost impossible," continued the parent, "to awaken any-thing like a determined opposition to slavery except on the part of a few; but a strong feeling is daily shown in favor of it, and a determination to maintain it, let the sacrifice be what it may."

"But, mother, the people who live in the Northern States don't want men and women to be robbed of their wages, and compelled to live on corn as the pigs do, and live in such mean huts, and have their children sold away!" urged the enquiring boy.

"They *say* they don't, my child, yet their whole influence is in favor of slavery—both by *word* and by *deed* do they encourage the slaveholder to continue his wicked course."

"Why! don't they think it very wrong," asked Charlie, "to hunt men with dogs and shoot them down because they don't want to be slaves? Perhaps though it's necessary, as you said the other day if men kept slaves they must keep somebody to whip them, or do it themselves, as they could not be made to work without. Are all the cruelties you have men-tioned necessary to keep them on the plantations?"

"Slaves are sometimes punished, doubtless, to gratify the rage of a master," said Mrs. Selden, "and to make them *feel* they are in the power of one they must not disobey; still I think a great amount of cruelty is actually necessary in order to bring down the spirit of a man and make him grovel in the dust like a base reptile at the feet of a master. Man was never made for that condition; he has within him a proud spirit that naturally spurns the restraints imposed upon him. Implanted in his bosom is a love of freedom; it is part of his very being; he has a desire to advance—to rise higher and higher; and it takes strong cords and prisons, heavy boats and bars, much scourging and beating, to break his spirit and confine it in the narrow dungeon of slavery.

"There is not an animal in creation that loves not its liberty, and it is only in strong iron cages that some can be confined; it is only by great watchfulness, and long training, and much force that our horses and oxen even can be made to endure the bit and the yoke; and just in proportion as a man is more intelligent, more noble and exalted in his nature than the animals around him, in that same proportion must the power of those who claim dominion be increased to keep him in bondage.

"Yes, my child, much power and cruelty too are necessary to make and keep a man a slave. The foot of the oppressor must be on his neck *continually*, or he'll be up and away!

"And here let me observe that it is not the cruelties so much, that the abolitionists complain of and wish to abolish, as the principle of holding men in slavery—it is treating men as property against which they protest. Most men claim the right to do what they please with their property, therefore it is not right to buy and sell men and women and call them property, and *then* they will not be subject to this abuse."

"I see now how it is," said Charlie; "if these people were not slaves they would not be treated so badly, so we should try to make them free, and not expect they will be much better off while they remain where they are."

"Yes, my dear, you understood me aright," replied Mrs. Selden.

"Mother, at one time when you were talking, you said the slaves that run away, sometimes got to a land of freedom. I suppose you meant they were free when they came into the Northern States. This is the land of freedom you spoke of, is it not?"

"No, my son, there is no freedom *here* for the slave. Would to heaven there was! If old Tig should run away, though he might go ever so far, even to Georgia, he would be your dog still, would he not? and you could go and bring him back."

"Yes, I understand that."

"Well," said the mother, "it is just so with the master and the slave. The former can get the latter if he can find him, and bring him back from any part of the United States where he may take refuge."

"Why, mother, is there no spot where the slave would be free? That's bad enough! Why what a dreadful condition he is in! A slave everywhere! Suppose he should come and live with us, would'nt [sic] he be free then?"

"No, even at our own fireside he would still be a slave—the master would claim him as *his* property, and bring him back again if he could."

"Do tell," said Charlie, somewhat impatiently, "where this land of freedom is! I suppose it's somewhere on the earth."

"Yes, there are many places where he would be free. Canada is the place I referred to; that is where fugitives generally go."

"I know where it is, right north of us; but what makes them free when they get there?" asked Charlie.

"Canada is under the government of Great Britian [sic], and that has declared that one man shall not hold another man as property and compel him to work as he does his cattle without pay. The slaveholder might go there and demand the fugitive, but the English government would scout his claim to his fellow man, and laugh him in the face; and at the same time would declare the poor slave free, and make him as safe as any of its own citizens."

"Do many slaves go there, mother?"

"It is said some twenty thousand have settled there within a few years past."

"Well," said the boy, who had a very retentive memory, and could call up all he ever heard as occasion demanded, "I remember that Mr. Gardner told us once that the government of the United States was the best government in the world. I should think the government of Canada was better, as it does not let one man hold another man in bondage."

"So far as slavery is concerned, it is far better," replied the parent; "still I do not suppose Mr. Gardner meant to tell you an untruth. No people have ever laid down such broad principles or freedom and equality as we have, and none have ever so shamefully trampled these principles in the dust."

"But he told us," returned Charlie, "that the English government was *very* oppressive."

"And so it is," added the mother. "You have heard Biddy talk of the poverty of the Irish—their extreme destitution is owing mostly to the oppressive acts of the British government. And when you go to England you will find a state of things but little better. In the cities you will see the most costly edifices in the neighborhood of the most miserable hovels; the titled nobleman rolls through the streets in his luxurious coach, while the beggar searches for kitchen offals [*sic*] in the filthiest of gutters! In the country, too, you find the same extreme of poverty and wealth;— on the one hand stands the lordly mansion, with beautiful gardens, extensive parks and magnificent forests, while all around it, men are crushed and degraded, compelled to incessant toil, and in their extreme destitution craving the very food upon which the hounds of the nobility are fed! Americans sometimes go there and talk against this inequality and oppression, but they are always met with the indignant reply, 'We don't hold SLAVES, as *you* do.'

"One of our good abolitionists, who was in England a year or two since, was deeply moved by the extreme destitution and suffering of the poorer classes—it made his heart ache to witness the oppression there.

"One day he obtained permission of the keeper of Her Majesty's jewels to examine the crown of the young queen, which is worth three millions of pounds sterling. Having learned its immense value, his mind reverted to the fact that thousands of the poor and needy had been robbed in order to sustain the monarch with her royal insignia, and feeling too that a great amount of suffering might be alleviated by applying the wealth thus lying useless to feed those who were starving at the gates of her palace, he involuntarily exclaimed, 'Thank God, I don't live in a country where one woman wears jewels worth millions of pounds, while others are dying for want of food!' A gentleman present hearing his remark, sarcastically replied, 'Thank God, *I* don't live in a country that holds SLAVES!' And 'tis ever thus. When an American abroad speaks of the oppression he sees around him, he is tauntingly told,

'Go, loose your fettered slaves *at home!*'"

"Well, mother," said Charlie, "if I understand you, the English government will not give up slaves to their masters, because the people do not make slaves of each other; and they will not acknowledge that one man has a right to another man. Now the people here in the North do not make slaves of each other, and I suppose if one of our neighbors, Mr. Parker for instance, should try to make slaves of any of us, the people would deny that he had a right to do so."

"They certainly would," returned Mrs. Selden.

"Why then," inquired Charlie, "do they give up the southern slaves, if they do not acknowledge that a man here has a right to make slaves of his neighbors?"

"They surrender them," said the parent, "because they have agreed to do so, or they do it voluntarily because they wish to keep them in bondage."

"How have they agreed to? Do tell me something about that."

"I will, my child; but in order to do it, I must go somewhat into the nature of our government, which I cannot do at this time. When a convenient opportunity offers, I will tell you as much about it as I think you can understand."

CHAPTER VIII

"You have learned from your school books," said Mrs. Selden to her son, "that the United States were once colonies of Great Britain."

"Yes," interposed Charlie, "I know all about *that*. George the 3rd taxed their tea, and glass, and paper very unjustly, and slighted their petitions, and kept soldiers here that burnt some of their towns and killed the people. The colonists refused to submit to this, and declared themselves independent; but they had to fight a seven years' war before they got their independence."

"I see you have learned the story," remarked the mother smilingly. "I wish the injustice of America as well as that of England had been taught you also. Have you learned, my child, that when the colonists separated themselves from the mother country, they issued a Declaration of sentiment in which they said, God gave to all men, that is to every man, a right to liberty?"

"No, I don't know much about that, but if they said all men had a right to liberty, I suppose the people of the present time think they were greatly mistaken, as they take away the liberty of three millions, and hunt them with dogs and guns if they attempt to obtain it. The people who wrote that must be a great deal better than the people who live now. But, mother, I don't understand this matter. You say when we became an independent nation the people declared that all were free; how did we happen to have slaves in this country then?"

"Alas! my child, that Declaration did not make all men free. We had slaves here at that time; and the very men who said to all the world, every man has a right to liberty, and appealed to the Supreme Judge of the Universe to witness their sincerity, at the same time held their fellow men in slavery! Their own plantations were watered with the sweat and tears of suffering bondmen!"

"Why, how strange that was!" cried Charlie. "Didn't they *mean* what they said?"

"I cannot tell what they meant," added Mrs. Selden, "only as I see their conduct. We must judge them as we do other people. If a man should declare that all men had a right to their own property, and it ought not to be taken from them, and yet should steal it as often as he could get a chance, we should begin to suspect that he was not altogether sincere in his professions; or that he spoke only abstract truth without any design of making a practical application."

"I suppose," said Charlie, "that none of the men that I know anything about held slaves. I've read about many of the brave generals in the war, and they seemed to be very good and sincere. General Washington was a great man, wasn't he, mother? Although you have told me many times that war was wrong—that we ought always to carry out peace principles and forgive our enemies; yet I never could help feeling that I should like to be a brave general like Washington, and have such a gay horse, and fine uniform, and a sword by my side, and a feather in my cap. Mother, I should be *very* great and *very* grand! Wouldn't you be proud of me? I don't know but this is wicked, but I *should* like to be a great general."

"Would you not rather save life than destroy it? Would you not rather be a good man, my child, one whom the poor and needy would remember with gratitude? one who has the satisfaction of feeling that he has delivered the poor stricken slave from the hand of the spoiler? He only is truly great who is a good man. Strive *earnestly* then to be good, if you would be great."

"But, mother you won't let me strive in the right way. I was just telling you I would like to be a general, and if I could be such a general as Washington, I should be both great and good. Every body says *he* was a good man."

"Washington," replied the mother, "doubtless had good traits of character, but he was a *warrior*, and a SLAVEHOLDER, and to be either is inconsistent with christian principles."

"A slaveholder!" cried the astonished boy. "*General Washington a slaveholder!* Why, mother, was he so cruel as to take little children from their mothers, and compel men to work for him without pay?"

"The latter he certainly did, and it is generally reported that he was guilty of the former. Let that be as it may, it is enough to know that he was a slaveholder. I ask not whether these slaves are well or ill treated; indeed I know that no one can be well treated while a slave. The very act of depriving a man of his freedom is an act of unmitigated cruelty."

"Do you know certainly," inquired Charlie, "that he was a slaveholder? I have always heard every body speak well of him, and wherever I have read anything about him it has always been in his praise. Mr. Gardner told us once, too, that the name of Washington would ever be beloved by every true American. I should not think his slaves would love it much. Perhaps Mr. Gardner thinks they are not true Americans. Why do the people call him good if he was a slaveholder? Slaveholders are not good, are they?"

"People have different ideas of goodness. Some think that those who take their neighbor's service without wages and give them naught for their work; who shut out the light of knowledge, and the truths of the Gospel from the human mind; who darken the intellect, break the spirit, beat and brand the bodies of their fellow men, are true christians. And some think that those who go to war and slay their brethren, and trample out their life's blood on the red field of battle as you talk of doing, are good men."

"Oh, no! mother, you misunderstood me. I never wanted to kill any body. I should think I was a very wicked boy if I wanted to do that. I only thought I'd like to be a great general."

"What makes a great general, Charlie? It is laying and executing great plans for the overthrow and destruction of those whom God has told you to forgive and love as brethren. It is skill in the work of human butchery!"

"Well, if that makes a great general, I'll never wish to be one again," rejoined Charlie. "I was'nt [sic] thinking of the dead and the dying: I was thinking only of the grand music that I've heard at trainings, and the prancing horses, and the plumes, and the swords, and handsome dress, and all that. But I know trainings are wrong as well as war. I've read about them in the book Mr. Wright gave me, and so I won't wish to be a trainer even. I think you ought to have let me gone to hear Mr. Wright when he was here; I am afraid I shall never have another chance."

"I hope you will. I would much rather, my son, that you would take a peace man and an abolitionist for your model, than a great general and slaveholder. The influence of the former blesses the world, softens the hearts of men and makes them speak words of love and tenderness—it carries hope and rejoicing to the bosom of the pining, down-trodden slave; while the influence of the latter awakens hatred and the spirit of resistance—it tramples into the dust the hopes and the rights of our equal brethren.

"But we have wandered very far from the subject we began to talk about, which was, the agreement the States made with each other to give up fugitive slaves."

"Yes, mother, I want to hear about that. Last evening, when Mr. Hastings was here, he and father were talking about the government, or Constitution, or something I don't know what being anti-slavery and pro-slavery. I didn't understand them. Can you explain it to me?"

"I will try," returned the parent. "All the states, with the exception of Massachusetts, held slaves at the time the government was formed."

"What! The Northern States?" interrupted Charlie. "I never knew that they held slaves."

"Yes, they did, and I think we may reasonably infer that a slaveholding people would not form a constitution of government opposed to slavery, if they wished to maintain the system; and it certainly is doing them no injustice to suppose they wished to perpetuate it, inasmuch as they did not do it away."

"But, mother, I don't know as I understand what the constitution is. I've often heard father speak of it, and I thought it was some kind of a law every body ought to obey."

"Well, it is—we must obey it or suffer for our disobedience. When the colonies were contending against Great Britain, they thought it very desirable to be united; so they formed a kind of league which served as a government, and their agreement was known as 'The Articles of Confederation.' After peace was made, some of the colonies, or states, as they were then called, wished a stronger bond of Union, something that should fully protect the interest of all and unite them more closely together. After much consultation they adopted in 1789 another form of government called the Constitution of the United States. Each State has its own laws, and Governor and other officers; but the Constitution is above them all, being the highest law in the land. What *it* requires is superior to all other legal obligations."

"What does it say about the slaves?" asked Charlie.

"It describes a class of persons like the slaves, and makes provision in regard to them, saying they shall be given up to the claimant, &c. It matters very little, however, about the way it reads; the people have always understood it to be in favor of slavery. Both States and individuals have always surrendered fugitives under it. Though some have acknowledged that it was a sin and a shame to do so, yet they said the law required it."

"How did the slaveholders get back their runaway slaves before they had a constitution?" inquired Charlie. "Didn't the articles of confederation say that the masters might take them wherever they could find them?"

"No, my child. If a State chose to give them up, it did so, but there was no compulsion in the case—no Constitution to require it—no general understanding to demand it; and the fact that they were not more frequently given up, was a cause of sore complaint on the part of the slaveholder. Since 1789, the slavecatcher has felt that he had a legal right to hunt out his fugitives and drag them back from any part of the Union where they had taken shelter; and the people do not question his right to do it, and very many stand ready to help him.

"And the men all around us, Charlie," continued Mrs. Selden, "our very neighbors and friends, join with the slaveholders in sustaining this wicked Constitution and all the laws that are made under it, even those which justify the master in all the terrible cruelties I have mentioned. They sustain a government under which the poor mother is robbed of all her little ones, and left with nothing to love, nothing to hope for. Her very existence becomes a burden and she longs to die! They sustain a government under which man is robbed of all the joys and hopes and objects of life; robbed even of the right to the heart that beats in his bosom and the immortal soul that God gave him!

"The free men of the north sit down to make laws with those who rifle their neighbors' pockets and steal away all their living; and not content with that, rob them of their wives and daughters, whom they subject to outrages of the most brutal character.

"Slavery, my child, is the highest kind of crime! It is a far greater sin than was ever committed by any of the criminals that you have seen. *They* were guilty of petty thefts and robberies, and now and then one in the heat of excitement had given a blow that destroyed his fellow. These were all wrong, but slavery is a system that embodies all these crimes on a most stupendous scale. It robs millions of *every thing*, and annually murders its thousands! Yet the men who do these things are regarded as men fit to make laws for an enlightened and *christian* nation."

"Well, I'm sure," said Charlie, "that father has nothing to do with such a government."

"No, I hope not," replied the mother. "I trust he will never enter into a government with the oppressors of his race; and that he will give no voluntary support to laws that deny equal liberty to all. I am glad, my son, that you are spared the deep mortification that I once saw a little girl experience."

"Tell me about it, mother."

"One evening at the house of a friend in Penn's Manor, a number of anti-slavery persons had a social meeting, and among them was a very beautiful little girl and her father. Mrs. Foster was also present—she is one who has been devoting many years to the cause of the oppressed. With her life in her hand she has faced all the prejudices of the age; has labored much and suffered much that she might redeem children like you from the curse of slavery.

"The child had been singing, much to the delight of all the company, for she sung very finely. Mrs. Foster saw that she was very fond of her father; and he, of course, was very proud of her, as all fathers are of good children. She called the child to her and engaged her in conversation. She showed her a picture on an anti-slavery paper where a child was being sold, and told her that men made laws in this country which said little children *might* be sold and added, 'I don't know but thy father helps to make these laws.'

"The child looked very indignant and appeared to feel that he had been accused of a very vile act. At length she said,

'No! *my* father *don't* make laws to sell little girls, and he wouldn't let anybody else do it.'

'Go and ask him,' said Mrs. Foster—'ask him if he does not *help* to make laws which allow children to be sold.'

"The child refused. She said she knew her father didn't do it, and she didn't want to ask him. But her father told her to do as the lady wished. She ran to his arms and looking earnestly into his face, said,

[']You don't, papa, I *know* you don't make laws to sell little girls away from their fathers.'

'I suppose I have helped do so,' was the honest confession of the parent.

"The child turned from him in sorrow and humiliation. She was so shocked and so grieved she could make no reply. That father in whose bosom she had ever nestled, and who had always wiped away her tears and made her glad again, was disgraced in her eyes; and for a time she could not feel that he was her father."

"Well," said Charlie, "I guess that father never again helped to make laws to sell children. If our father were so wicked, I don't know what I should do; and Jenie would feel quite as badly as that little girl."

CHAPTER IX

Unfortunately for some poor fugitives who were flying from southern bondage, Mrs. Selden's children had an opportunity of witnessing the pro-slavery spirit of their neighbors.

Early one cold frosty morning, Charlie was out trying his sled on some ice and a little newly fallen snow, when his attention was attracted by Cæsar, who was coming across the lot accompanied by a colored man and his wife. On a nearer approach he saw that the woman had in her arms an infant; but such sorrowful, woebegone countenances he had never seen before. They wore such tattered garments, and had such a weary gait, and such a forlorn appearance, that Charlie concluded they could be none other than slaves; and he was right. They had been directed by a person some miles back to Mr. Selden's, but coming in the evening, and some of the way across the fields, they failed to find his house; and fearing lest they should get among enemies they took refuge under a neighbouring haystack until morning. It was a cold chilly night— a piercing wind and driving sleet had made both man and beast seek their warmest shelter. Think then, my young friends, of the sufferings of these poor creatures, who had no shelter to protect them; and were afraid to enter the abodes of men, lest they should be caught up and thrust back into the prison of southern slavery!

They were warmly welcomed to the fireside of Mr. Selden—parents and children were alike glad to minister to their necessities. It was a long time before feeling was restored to their benumbed limbs and so completely chilled was the child that they feared it might not survive. The mother seemed nearly frantic at this thought. She used all the remedies prescribed and watched it with the closest attention. When she saw there was but little prospect of its recovery, she pressed it to her bosom and sat in silence. At last the big tear began to fall, and turning to Mrs. Selden, she said,—

"Missis, I've carried this child many a mile, Tom and me; and we both love it dearly, for we've nothing else to love. Poor little thing! Missis, I can't have it die now! Oh, its [sic] hard to lose the last!"

After a brief space the expression of her countenance changed, and she continued,—

"Missis, I never could bring up this child for old Massa to have for a slave; and if I had to do that, I'd rather 'twould die now! "Yes, if you knew what it was to be a slave woman in the South, you'd say so too. Let it die if it must, but, oh God! save it from being a slave!"

But the child was not doomed to perish thus. Presently it began to recover its concisousness [sic], and in a few hours appeared to be out of danger. Often, in the course of the day, as it lay on its mother's lap, did little Jenie stroke its face, and lay her cheek to its cheek, and say, "They shan't sell it away from its mother. The dogs shan't bite it, and it never shall go and live with those naughty people again."

During all this time, Phil was by no means an uninterested spectator. He was so familiar with Cæsar that he soon got acquainted with Tom, and if I should record all the questions he asked, my young friends would tire of reading them. His principal object seemed to be to find out, whether there was any way in which the slaves could revenge themselves upon their masters.

"Why couldn't you get their guns and shoot them?" said he. "And couldn't you lock them up in their houses, and let them starve?"

"No, little massa," replied Tom, "we don't want to do it. Our freedom is all we ask. Though they have made us very poor and forced us to work when we were sick, and whipped and beaten us, and sold away our children; yet we wish no harm to come upon *them*. If they will make us free, we will never hurt a hair of their heads, but always stand ready to defend them."

This forgiving spirit of Tom's was quite a check to the vindictive disposition of Biddy, who would have recommended that all the punishments ever inflicted upon the slaves be visited upon the masters with seven fold violence. Phil was such a little boy he had no correct idea of slavery, or of the punishments he talked of, but Biddy thought the masters ought to be severely handled, and consequently he said the same.

"See! see!" cried Jenie, as she returned from her mother's drawers and held up a pair of little shoes that Phil had outgrown, "can't the baby wear these? And here is Phil's little wrapper; do put that on the baby, mother, so it never shall get so cold again."

Not many days had elapsed before it was noised abroad that these fugitives were staying at Mr. Selden's, and as it was uncommon for fugitives to pass that way, it produced considerable excitement. Some pitied the poor creatures and wished them a happier lot; others manifested no sympathy, and when they heard the slavehunter was on their track, they entertained no fears for their safety; but on the contrary were quite willing, not to say anxious, that he should secure his victims.

These hunters had been prowling about the neighborhood for a day or two, and one afternoon they were seen at a public house very near Mr. Selden's.

Tom and his wife were all unconscious of their danger; but Cæsar discovered the kidnappers and hastening into the house exclaimed,—

"Run, run, Tom! for God's sake run! Woman, take the child and go! Through the garden—across the creek—over into the woods. Away! away!" he cried, and he swung his arms and tore around with all the wildness of a maniac.

"The Lord save us! ejaculated Biddy, "but what's the matter with ye, man; are ye mad?"

"Here, here!" said Cæsar, "put on this overcoat of mine, and button it up tight, and this hat too, and hold up your head and walk strait like a man, and never let them know you're a crouching slave."

Mrs. Selden taking the hint, flew to her wardrobe, and brought a good cloak and bonnet for the woman. Tom and his wife were soon ready, and walked off through the garden with all the dignity of a lord and lady.

"But, surely, the terrible man-hunters are not a comin," cried Biddy. "It's meself that would break every bone in their skins, should they harm the woman that's laving us, and the darlint [sic] babe she carries. What an iligant country this is!" said she scornfully. "What quare freedom they have in Ameriky! Niver did I see the likes."

Every inmate of Mr. Selden's house was filled with great anxiety for the fate of the poor wanderers. It was feared that the persons who walked off so leisurely might be suspected of being the slaves in disguise and would be pursued; but they were shortly relieved of this apprehension by the approach of the kidnappers. With the air or desperadoes they entered the back yard and swaggered around the premises muttering curses and threats, and ever and anon casting looks of vengeance at the house. So fierce and savage did they appear, that even Biddy was awed into silence; and little Jenie actually shrieked with fear. At the suggestion of Mrs. Selden, they both retired to the nursery.

Phil stood on a chair at the window, and his great blue eyes grew larger and shone more brightly at every move of the intruders.

"I hope they won't get that baby," said he; "but, mother, where's my dog?" and he began to call, "Here Tig! here Tig! here Tig!"

Presently the more daring of the two came to the door and gave a violent rap. Phil scampered off into an adjoining room, but was sure to leave the door ajar so that he could see with one eye all that was going on. Mrs. Selden was slightly startled at the bold summons, which was immediately succeeded by a rude push that sent the door back against the wall with a slam. This warned her to collect all her energies.

On the threshold stood a coarse, brutal looking fellow; his hat cocked on one side, and his overcoat buttoned up, but stretched back in front so as to allow him to thrust both hands into the depths of his pockets. With a savage leer, he said,—

"I'm told my slaves are here."

"You have been misinformed," replied Mrs. Selden, with quiet dignity.

"But, woman, your neighbors have seen them here. Come! show me where the skulking devils are hid," said he, somewhat in a coaxing way.

Mrs. Selden, feeling indignant at the manner and the request, replied—

"I told you they were not here; but if they were, do you think I would lead a rapacious man-hunter to their hiding place! Do you think I would betray them into the hands of the base miscreant before me! Go home, and seek some more honorable employment than hunting out the stricken and famishing children of oppression, and dragging them back into the vile den of slavery. Begone! unmerciful wretch! let not my threshold be disgraced by contact with such pollution."

The man cowered before the stately bearing and contemptuous tone of Mrs. Selden. He had been accustomed to measure arms with men who gave him offence, but there was something in her earnest rebuke and firm purpose that made him forget his weapons of death; and feeling assured by her manner that the slaves were not there, he and his companion sneaked away to the bar-room from whence they came, and where they found congenial company.

"And where was Cæsar all this time?" my little readers will ask. Gathered up into the smallest possible compass, and trembling from head to foot like an aspen leaf, he stood in a remote corner of the cellar—a place as dark as midnight. He too had been a slave, altho' he kept it a secret; and he feared that somebody besides Tom and his wife would be seized as a runaway.

An hour or two after this occurence [sic], Mr. Selden returned, having been necessarily absent the last two days. Learning the foregoing facts, he immediately sent Cæsar to find the fugitives, and directed him to keep them in the woods and take them on to a road some two miles distant, where he would meet them with his carriage. Night had set in and the evening was nearly spent before he was joined by Tom and his wife. He drove on, and on, at a rapid rate: midnight came and passed, and still they pursued their Northern course. The stars began to fade, and ruddy light streak the east; still they went on.

Quite early in the morning, however, they called at the house of a friend of Mr. Selden. As they drove up, the owner stood in the door. His face beamed with benevolence; time had silvered his locks, and his once tall and noble form began to feel the weight of years. After a few brief words with Mr. Selden, he told his son George to hitch the horses to the covered dearborn, instead of taking them into the field as he was ready to do.

"But, father, that work *must* be done," observed George.

"Let the plow ever stand in the furrow, and the corn rot on the ear, rather than I should fail in my duty to God's suffering poor!" replied the parent.

George did as ordered. The slaves got into the dearborn; the old man taking the reins followed, and after a breakfast was handed in to Tom and his wife, they departed.

This kind friend took them on some fifteen or twenty miles, and placed them in charge of another, who continued the same course northward, and by changing hands a good many times and walking a long distance, they at length reached Canada in safety.

"THE FUGITIVE'S SONG"

We're away, we're away, and bend gladly the oar
To the heart-cheering sound of Niagara's roar;
For a fate worse than death would be ours should we stay;
So to Canada's borders we hasten away.

We come from the plains of the sunny South-west,
Where the Earth in her beautiful garment is drest;
And where all would be fair, did not slavery's hand
Scatter mildew, and blighting, and wo o'er the land.

Then away, then away o'er the foam-crested wave
To Britannia's home for the fugitive slave;
Where the Lion of England keeps ever at bay
The prowling man hunter who seeks for his prey.

And though long have our spirits been weary and sad,
Thy anthem, Niagara, maketh us glad:
And we read in the beautiful bow on thy spray,
A promise of safety and freedom to-day.

Then away, then away, and ply cheerly the oar,
Each stroke brings us nearer to Canada's shore.
We are there! we are there! our boat touches the strand,
And the bow of our vessel is high on the land.

Unship every oar, for our labor is done,
Our freedom is gained, and our manhood is won!

The toils we endured, and the dangers, are past!
We are *free*! we are FREE, we are FREE then at last!

B.S.J.

CHAPTER X

In the course of a few days the excitement attendant upon the events mentioned in the last chapter subsided; but they left a lasting impression upon the minds of the young Seldens. The appearance of the fugitives among them deepened their interest in the condition of the bondman; and made them hate slavery more than they had ever done before. They tired not in hearing of the slave, and the mother ceased not to instruct them.

"I have many things yet, my dear children, to tell you," said she; "indeed I have but just begun to expose the horrors of the great prison house. The workings of slavery, however, in all their details you could not comprehend; and I suppose you could form no correct idea of the amount of vice, and the deep degradation produced by this system.

"I have spoken to you of cruelties, the thought of which seems to make you shudder; yet these same cruelties, the whipping and branding, the starving and burning, are the least objectionable part of slavery. Probably you will not be able to understand this now; but when you grow older you will know better what I mean. The human mind, that part of man that thinks, and reasons, and plans, and embraces truth, and struggles to rise above the earthly things that surround it, is of far more worth than the body that is doomed to perish. But in slavery the mind fares worse even than the body. It cannot rise—it is kept in darkness—it is forbidden to expand, or catch a glimpse of the light and knowledge that prevail. I remember, Charlie, that you felt very badly last summer when you found out that Wm. O'Rafferty could not read."

"Well, mother, I like so well to have new books, and know how to read them, and to study geography, and history, and to learn something about the world and the people who live in it, I pity one so ignorant as William was."

"He was ignorant," replied the mother, "because his parents did not send him to school. They could have done so had they wished, but every school in the land is closed against three millions of American slaves! They are spurned from the threshold of every institution of learning; and an attempt even to learn to read the name of God is punished as a crime! If books had never been made, and the art of printing was unknown, the slave would be just as wise as he is now. Oh! it is dreadful to keep a man in such darkness and blindness—to hide from his view all knowledge and science, the discoveries of present and past ages—to shut out the beautiful truths of the gospel, and keep him as ignorant as the beasts of the field. This is far, far worse than to have the body beaten and bruised."

"Why do they keep them in ignorance?" inquired, Charlie. "They could work just as well if they knew more."

"If they did not keep them in ignorance they could not keep them in slavery—people who are enlightened can't be enslaved."

"Well," said Jenie, "if I was there I'd teach the little girls their A B C's."

"My dear one!" replied the parent, "they would punish my little daughter very severely for this kind act, if they thought she was old enough to understand the law against it."

"But I would teach them when nobody saw me—after the folks had all gone to bed."

"The overseer might be up though," returned her mother. "He is often sneaking about the negro quarters in the night, and peeking into the cabins to see if anything is going on contrary to plantation rules. The slaves, and all who are supposed to be their friends, are watched in all their movements, and every offence promptly punished. The slaveholders will allow no information to be given, nor anything said to make the slaves discontented.

"Should I go to Louisiana and tell the poor creatures that they ought not to be compelled to work without wages, and that they have as good a right to liberty as their masters, although they knew this before, yet my words would doubtless make them more dissatisfied, and for that offence I thould [sic] be thrown into a prison. I should be separated from my family and shut up with pickpockets and murderers. My heart, I think, would be very sad; perhaps I should grow pale and poor, and be so worn and wasted that when I came out my dear children would not know me.

"Or should I carry there," she continued, "any papers or pamphlets against slavery, and distribute them among the people; if calculated to produced [sic] disobedience among the slaves—and all such papers would if the slaves knew what they contained—I should be sentenced to imprisonment at hard labor for life, or suffer death at the discretion of the court. Yes, if I was not hung at once or killed in some other way, so long as I lived my only home would be within the cold walls of a prison; and I should have to labor daily under the eye of a taskmaster."

The thought of their mother being treated thus, made the children look sorrowful; but Charlie bethought him of the instruction she had given, and said—

"But that wouldn't be equal to what the slaves have to suffer."

"That's very true," she replied, "and I am glad that you understand that imprisonment for life is better than slavery."

"But it's quare enough, mistress," cried Biddy, "to bring such a black trouble upon a body, and shut him up like a thief, or break his neck as if he had done murder, when he's guilty of nothin at all, at all. For sure, mistress, it's no crime to talk or write agin slavery; the Holy Mother would niver smile upon him that should hould his pace [*sic*]."

"It *is* strange, Biddy, and very wicked too, but the slaveholders are determined to maintain their system; and therefore they threaten; and treat with the greatest severity all the abolitionists they can get hold of. They used to say that slavery should not be talked about among them; and a South Carolina paper once declared that the man who should attempt to speak of its evils with a view to its overthrow, in that same moment should have his tongue cut out and cast away.

"A Georgia paper, speaking of an abolitionist once, said, 'He ought to have been hung as high as Haman, and left to rot on the gibbet until the wind whistled through his bones! The cry of the whole South should be *death*, INSTANT DEATH to the abolitionist wherever he is caught!'

"The general sentiment of southern papers has been, that slavery is deep rooted among them, and *shall* remain forever; and he who speaks against it is fit only for the halter. The acts of violence committed upon abolitionists by slaveholders and their abettors would fill many a volume.

"It is not two years, since Charles T. Torrey died in a prison for no act but that of delivering the oppressed from the hand of their tyrant masters. He went where slavery existed and witnessed the hopeless condition of its victims. He saw then truly that they had fallen among thieves—they were stripped and wounded—they were bleeding and groaning under the weight of the burdens imposed upon them. They cried for deliverance but there was none to help! The people all around were enemies and determined to prolong their captivity. They were bowed down under a load of sorrow—affliction such as seldom falls to the lot of man, was theirs. The worst forms of heathenism, the deepest ignorance had settled down upon their moral being—the world was to them a vast desert, lighted up by scarcely a ray of joy, or hope, or comfort.

"Mr. Torrey was moved with pity, as every body would be who had a heart to feel. He had read in his Bible these commandments, 'Open the prison doors to them that are bound,' 'Break every yoke and let the oppressed go free,' 'Deliver him that is spoiled from the hands of the spoiler.' He endeavored to obey these precepts by assisting slaves to escape from the power of the oppressor. He succeeded in a great many cases; and the name of Charles T. Torrey will ever be remembered with the deepest gratitude, by many an emancipated slave who now treads the free soil of Canada, happy in the consciousness of his liberty, and in the possession of his wife and little ones.

"But at length he was detected in his work of mercy and confined in a loathesome jail. After two years of suffering—and years are very long in a prison where one is shut out from all who love or care for him—he attempted to escape. For this he was loaded with heavy irons and placed in a cold cell. His fate then was hard indeed—severe pain and sickness came upon him and he got neither rest, nor sleep, nor comfort. The long days passed slowly away, and it seemed to him that the nights would never end. Oh! how he needed the kindness and care of his family; but they could not be with him to minister to his wants. He desired to see the faces of those he loved; he longed to hear the voice of some kind friend; but the stillness of his gloomy cell was broken only by his groans and the clanking of the chain that bound him."

"But, mother, didn't his little children want to see him?" asked Jenie.

"Yes, dear. His little Charles and Mary greatly desired his return. They felt, I suppose, just as you would feel should your father be taken away and shut up in jail. They missed him every where; they felt that the family circle was broken. When they came to the table, they saw his vacant place; when they kneeled with their mother at morning and evening prayer, the absent father ever came up before them. The voice of him they loved was heard no more in their midst; and they anxiously inquired, 'When will father come?'"

"*Did* he never come again?" inquired Jenie.

"No, my child, he was sentenced to six years hard labor in a penitentiary. Many efforts were made to clear him at his trial, and also to secure a pardon after his sentence, but they were all in vain. He was doomed to fall a victim to that law which forbids man to obey God; for six years, or two years even, of confinement and labor, added to what he had already suffered, were more than he could endure. Oh! it was hard to die in that cheerless abode far away from home and friends, and have none save an officer of the law to listen to his last words and smoothe his dying pillow.

"Less than eighteen months after this sentence, word went abroad that Charles T. Torrey was no more; and when his children asked again 'When will father come?' the reply was, *Never!* NEVER! His eyes are closed in death, and his voice silenced in the stillness of the tomb."

"Then the little children have no father," said Jenie, thoughtfully.

"No," returned the mother, "slaveholders have robbed them of their father, and left their mother very sad and sorrowful."

"Did they ever try to treat others in that way?" inquired Charlie.

"Yes, a great many have suffered at their hands. Wm. Lloyd Garrison, the man who first roused this guilty nation by declaring that the slave ought to have his liberty immediately and unconditionally, was once imprisoned in the same jail where Mr. Torrey suffered so much; and the great State of Georgia has, for the last fifteen years, been offering a reward of FIVE THOUSAND DOLLARS to any person who would place him in the power of the slaveholders, that he might be murdered as Charles T. Torrey was murdered.

"Very many have been imprisoned," continued Mrs. Selden. "Calvin Fairbanks is now in a Kentucky penitentiary; and he has got to live and labor there fifteen long years from the time he was put in, unless death comes to his relief, and all because he was merciful to the slave.

"Jonathan Walker, of Massachusetts, was imprisoned in Florida— placed in a pillory, and had the letters S. S. burned into the palm of his right hand with a red hot branding iron, and all because he turned not a deaf ear to the cry of the perishing bondman."

"What were the letters S. S. for?" inquired the boy.

"Slave Stealer, they were designed for."

"But he didn't steal slaves, did he?" rejoined Charlie.

"Just as much as your father stole Tom and his wife the other day— they both helped slaves to escape from their masters.

"The Southerners are roused to fury at the least movement on the part of any to destroy slavery. So angry do they become, that their ravings are like the ravings of madmen. A Southern woman once said of Arthur Tappan of New York, 'I could cut his throat from ear to ear.'"

"Niver did I hear the like," cried Biddy. "Bould work that for a woman to be after doing. I'd like to show her the strength that's in me. I'd teach her better manners than to talk of cutting a man's throat bekase he spake agin slavery."

"I am sorry to hear you talk so much about fighting, Biddy," said Mrs. Selden; "a fighting spirit is no better than the spirit of slavery. You must try to be more gentle and forgiving. I am afraid my children will catch your warlike disposition, and forget the peace principles I have taught them."

"Well, mistress, I beg pardon if what I've been spaking be wrong. But what ye've been telling us is enough to stir the heart that's in a body, and make every drop of blood spake out. The blessed St. Patrick himself, although he was a saint, would have been as full of fight as meself maybe; and there's not an Irish lad of spirit but would be ready to give the ould thieves a taste of his shillalah.[3] Though 'taint very pacable like, the feelin would come up in me that I'd like to try them a bit myself."

CHAPTER XI

Charlie did not often wait for his mother to commence the conversation about the slaves and their friends; but he generally opened the subject himself by asking questions.

"I was thinking," said he, "from what you told us the other day, that some abolitionists had, after all, been treated almost as badly as the slaves."

"Slaveholders," replied the mother, "are as cruel to them as they well can be, but it is not in their power to injure them so deeply as they injure the slaves."

"Well, I shouldn't like to live in the South. I don't suppose any body would care what such a young boy as I am would say; but when I grow to be a man, I shall do all I can for the slaves, and if I lived there they might put me in prison or kill me. Mother, I *am* glad that we live here in the North where we can say what we please about slavery, and do as much as we like to help fugitives."

"But are you quite sure, Charlie, that we *can* say what we please, and do what we like?"

"Why, can't we?" said he.

"No! Should any one choose to prosecute your father for harboring Tom and his wife who were here last week, and for carrying them off beyond the reach of the hunters, they could fine him FIVE HUNDRED DOLLARS; and should he refuse to pay it, he might be imprisoned."

"Why, mother! I did not think there *was* such a law. How did father dare to do it?"

"He dares to disregard all laws that interfere with our duty toward our fellow men," observed the parent. "It is our duty to feed the hungry— Tom and his wife were nearly starved. It is our duty to clothe the naked— Tom and his wife were covered only with rags, and any laws which forbid us to do these things, we should no more be forced to obey than our hands could be bound with a spider's web. If men choose to punish us for

such acts, we are ready to suffer. It is our duty to 'Hide the outcast'; therefore did we secrete Tom and his wife, and convey them away from their
enemies."

"Oh! that's what it means to 'Hide the outcast,' is it?" cried Charlie.
"Then the slaves are outcast, are they?"

"Yes, child, there are no people to whom the word would better apply,
for there are none so poor—none so afflicted—none so cruelly cast out
from the regard and fellowship of men and the joys of life as the slave."

"Now I can tell Jenie what it means to 'Hide the outcast.' You needn't
do it, mother; let me. You remember she wanted to know once. But I
guess this law against hiding the outcast is only just to frighten people—
nobody ever was taken up for doing such a thing?" said he inquiringly.

"Yes, it has been done many times; and so far from being free to speak
as we please against slavery, the greatest violence has been used upon the
abolitionists—their property has been destroyed—their meetings broken
up—their persons injured, and life has been sacrificed."

"What! not by northern men, mother?"

"Yes, and by men who call themselves gentlemen and christians. I have
already told you that the people of the North are no better than slaveholders; indeed they *are* the slaveholders. They don't claim the slaves as
their property, and get the benefit of their labor, it is true; but they uphold the master in his wickedness, and stand ready to aid him to retain
his victims whenever their services are needed.

"Let me make it plain to you. Supposing Edward Miller should take
away all your books, and playthings, and good clothes, and make you
work very hard and earn money so that he could have it to spend; and
suppose his father, who is a very large, strong man, should stand by and
see his son's conduct, and if you attempted to escape should seize you,
and put you back again into the power of Edward; and if you refused to
submit to his authority, the father should threaten to shoot you; whom
would you blame most, Mr. Miller or Edward?"

"I should blame Mr. Miller most," was the prompt reply, "for Ned
couldn't treat me in that way without help. We often wrestle at school,
and I am always an overmatch for him."

"Very well. Now Mr. Miller would stand in the same relation to you,
that the North stands to the slaves. *They* are an overmatch for their masters; and were it not for the aid of northern men they would get their
freedom tomorrow. Many a slave have I heard say, 'Leave us alone with
our masters, and we'll take care of them! It is the interference of the
North we dread—it is the northern people that keep us in our chains."

"But, mother, the northern men don't threaten to shoot the slaves if they don't obey their masters."

"Certainly they do. It is but a short time since that Mr. Wilmot, a distinguished member of Congress from Pennsylvania, declared in a great convention, that should the slaves rise up and resist the outrages committed upon them, he would go down to the South and shed the last drop of his blood, if necessary, to put them down and bring them into subjection again. He said he would sacrifice his life in order to maintain the system.

"So you see, Charlie, if the slaves *should* make an effort to throw off the oppression they are laboring under—should they say, God gave us a right to liberty and we will maintain it—we will be free—we will no longer suffer violence upon our wives and daughters—our little children shall never be torn from our arms and sold away—we will work no longer without just compensation; should the slaves rise up and say *these* things, the military force of the South would be called out, and with musket and cannon they would threaten to shoot every man who would not surrender. But if the slaves still maintained their ground, and were determined to be free; if the threats and curses; the smoke and blaze, and roar of guns, and the groans of their dying companions who were falling all around them did not induce them to yield; if they still said, we *will* have liberty or death, then Mr. Wilmot, and those who feel like him, would go down and compel the famishing and wretched victims of American despotism to submit their necks again to the yoke of slavery. He might be gratified by bathing his glittering bayonet in the heart's blood of men who were struggling to be free—whose only crime was that of endeavoring to break the chain of tyranny."

"I hope there are not many men like Mr. Wilmot," observed Charlie.

"There are not many who would *say* what Mr. Wilmot has said, but there are very many who would do what he said he would do. Indeed, it is required by the supreme law of the land that they shall do it; and northern men have entered into an agreement with southern men that they will do it; and every year they renew the promise they have made."

"Every time we talk about the slaves, mother, you make their case worse and worse. Why, what a condition they *are* in! The very thought of it makes me shudder. They are treated so cruelly where they are; and when they try to get away they are often caught and carried back; and when they rise up and try to be free, men all over the country stand ready to shoot them. I don't believe any poor creatures ever *were* treated so badly before. Why don't the folks talk about it, and try to do something for them? I should think ministers would preach on the subject."

"Some of them do. Now and then one preaches the doctrines of liberty, and brings up the wrongs and sufferings of the oppressed before the people, and rebukes them for their indifference and their support of the system; but generally they talk only in favor of slavery. They are as much interested in sustaining it as any other class of persons; and a great many actually hold slaves, and beat, and drive, and starve, and hunt them, just as the worst of slaveholders do."

"What! ministers, mother! Do ministers hold slaves? I shouldn't think anybody would want to hear them preach. Why I thought *they* were all christians. You never told me much about them, but, I've heard the boys say that their mothers told *them* they must remember what the ministers said, for they were good men; and little Mary Fisher, when she was here yesterday, said when her mother put her to bed, she often asked her to repeat what she could that the minister said the Sunday before, and told her she must always remember it, for he was a man of God."

"I suppose she had reference to Mr. Perkins," returned the mother, "and he does say a great many things that ought to be remembered; but so far from doing his duty to the slaves, he is one of the most violent opposers the abolitionists have. He says that slavery is *right* and ought to exist; and that they who talk against it are fools, fantatics, and infidels. There is not a tyrant on a southern plantation that has more of the spirit of slavery than he; and there are scores of others, both ministers and church members, who are just like him. They profess to do as they would be done by, then bind, or help to bind their own brethren and sisters in the church with the strong cord of slavery—strike down all their rights, and turn their sources of happiness into fountains of grief and misery. The society and affection of my dear husband and children make *me* very joyous; but these professed christians make the slave woman mourn that she ever had a husband; they make her regret the day her children were born. Instead of taking pleasure in loving her friends, they make her wish that she had no love, and that all the sources of her tenderness were dried up; then would she be saved the extreme agony of separation from the objects of her affection. After her husband is torn away she is forced to live with another; and thus at the will of the master she is married and unmarried as many times as he chooses. The exceeding sinfulness of this you will understand better as you grow older. It destroys the pure and holy relation of husband and wife, for he whom the slave woman calls her husband to-day may be the husband of another tomorrow, so there is no lawful marriage among them; and this is the cause of untold vice and immorality. This, you understand, is the fault of the system and those who sustain it, and not the fault of the slaves.

"The most horrible treatment I ever read of, has been that received by these oppressed people at the hands of professors of religion. Frederick Douglass, who was once a slave, says he 'ever found *them* the meanest and the basest, the most cowardly and cruel of all masters.' Any crime that other slaveholders are guilty of, they certainly do not hesitate to commit."

"Then they are not christians, are they?" inquired Charlie. "You have taught me that a christian was one who spent his life in doing good—in trying to make the people around him better and happier. A christian, you said, always loved his fellow men, and never meant to do them any injury—he looked upon them all as his brothers and sisters, so he could not harm them. You have often said we all had one Father who was called God, who made us all, and this beautiful world too, and every thing that exists, and that we could best show our love and gratitude to this Father by loving each other. I remember that, for you told me also there was no way in which I could please *my* father so well as in loving and being very kind to my little brother and my dear sister Jenie."

"I am glad you remember the lesson so well," replied the mother; "and in regard to slaveholders being christians, I think you can judge for yourself. Mrs. Weld, who was a native and for a long time a resident of South Carolina, knew a presbyterian woman in the city of Charleston, who had a young girl so unmercifully whipped that large pieces of flesh were actually cut out of her back. Mrs. Weld saw the girl, and she said she could have laid her whole finger in the gashes. Did that woman love the girl, Charlie, and had she the spirit of a christian?"

"No, mother, she hated her, and I should think she was more of a Turk than a Christian."

"The Rev. Francis Hawley tells us of a presbyterian minister who whipped a slave very cruelly, and then nearly drowned him, and finally fastened him into a corner of a fence between the rails, and kept him there so long that he died a few days after. He tells also of a methodist minister who had a slave that was suspected of knowing that some others were going to rise and try to get their liberty; and on that suspicion merely, he was hung up like a dog and left to die. Mr. Hawley states that he himself, although a baptist minister, had been out with rifle and dogs to hunt down flying fugitives. I might mention hundreds of similar cases.

Did those ministers treat their fellow men kindly, and try to do them good, my son?"

"Why, no! of course not; they tried to do them all the harm they could. They did not treat them as though they were their brothers at all. But, mother, do these ministers preach, and pray, and sing like other ministers?"

"Yes, and those who whip hardest, and whose lash cuts deepest, are often those who sing and shout the loudest and pray the longest. That Charleston woman I spoke of, used to pray three times a day; and once every day, and often three times, did some one of the servants of her house receive a scourging. Sometimes they were beaten, as in one case Mrs. Weld mentioned, till the blood gushed from the mouth and nose and ears of the sufferer."

"Why are they whipped so much? I am sure they must do wrong in some way."

"Sometimes there would seem to be a pretty good reason for punishment, if punishments are ever justifiable; but often the slightest mistake, such as spilling a cup of tea, or burning a piece of toast, causes the offender to be treated in the most brutal manner. John Graham, of Massachusetts, describes a scene that he witnessed at a breakfast table in South Carolina, or rather on an island near by.

"The servant happened to pour a little more molasses on the plate of a child than it usually had. Her master was angry, rose from the table, and took both of her hands in one of his, and with the other, beat her first on one side of the head, and then on the other as long as his hand could endure it. Then he took off his shoe and with the heel began in the same manner as with his hand. Finally the woman raised her elbow to ward off the blows; for which he called a stout negro to hold her hands behind her. This being done, he renewed his blows until they became intolerable, and she fell upon the floor and screamed for help and mercy. After she fell he continued to beat her, and Mr. Graham thought she would die in his hands. She got up, however, went out and washed off the blood, and came in again before they arose from the table. Then she was a pitiable object indeed. Her ears were three or four times as thick as usual, her eyes awfully blood-shotten, her lips, nose, chin, and whole head so swollen that no one would have known her; and for all this she had to say 'Thank you, massa.'"

"What a shocking story!" cried Charlie. Why, mother, you will make me feel that every body is bad, and that there are no good people in the world. The people in the south are slaveholders and friends of slavery;

and the people of the North, although they don't own slaves, help to hold them, which is just as bad; so I am sure there can't be any good folks in this country at least."

"Oh, yes, Charlie, there are many good people. All ministers and church members are not like those I have spoken of, though there are a multitude who are no better and many who are worse; yet there are some good people among them who are doing what they can for the poor and the distressed, and for the cause of human liberty. There are a great many abolitionists who are laboring faithfully and earnestly for the redemption of the bondman."

"Are all abolitionists christians?" asked Charlie.

"No, I do not call them so. They are good as far as their hatred for slavery goes, but some of them do not seem inclined to carry out the principles of love and kindness toward those around them, as well as toward the slave. Such do not appear to me to be christians altogether."

CHAPTER XII

"You said the other day," observed Mrs. Selden to Charlie, "that a slaveholding woman we were speaking of, was more of a Turk than a christian. The religion of the Turks, which is Mahomedan, does not allow them to hold in bondage one who is a Mahomedan also. The moment he professes to believe in that religion, he is no longer a slave; but in this country slaves join the same churches with their masters, and they are slaves still. The yoke of bondage is made no lighter, the scourging no less, the years of suffering no fewer. It was once well said by Wendell Phillips, of Boston, 'It would be better for the slaves of America if we should all wake up Turks tomorrow morning, instead or professed christians.'"

"Do *tell* me," said Charlie, "how these slaves are ever going to get their liberty. I don't see that they ever can be free."

"I trust they will," replied the mother. "I feel assured that the progress of human liberty in the world, and the agitation of the slavery question in this country, will at length effect their deliverance. We cannot tell how soon this time will come—it may be nearer than we think for; and it may be very distant. Great progress toward their liberation has already been made. Slavery is far less defended now than formerly. 'Tis but a few years since that abolitionists could hardly have a peaceable meeting. Their assembling was a signal for all the rowdies in the country round about to collect clubs, and stones, and brickbats, and eggs, and burst in upon the meeting and hurl these missiles at the speaker and his friends."

"What! people here in the North do that? Well, they were only rowdies, and rowdies are always ready for anything," observed Charlie.

"There were many, my son, engaged in these mobs that would not like to be called rowdies. There were merchants and doctors, lawyers and ministers, deacons and elders that gave countenance to, and assisted in these disgraceful scenes. Those were not the most guilty who threw the stones and the eggs, for they would not have done it had not others, calling themselves gentlemen, urged them on; had not ministers justified slavery, and talked and preached against the abolitionists; and had not professing christians said the abolitionists ought to be put down. It was these who were most to blame."

"Was anybody ever injured or killed at these times, mother?"

"Yes, a great many have been seriously injured, and some have lost their lives. Many have been severely beaten—stones and brickbats thrown by madmen are very apt to hurt. Abolitionists have been taken off at night into the woods, covered with tar and feathers, and otherwise treated in a most brutal manner, and then left there in an exhausted and suffering condition. Anti-slavery printing presses have been seized, dragged away and thrown into a neighboring river, there to rust beneath its waters. Private houses have been forced open and their furniture brought out and burned in the public street. Elijah P. Lovejoy was pursued many a time by a ruthless mob and finally murdered. Five rifle balls were lodged in his body, and he fell a bleeding corpse. His enemies, who were the friends of slavery, rejoiced that the voice of one more defender of liberty was hushed forever.

"Meeting houses have been burned, and temples dedicated to liberty reduced to ashes. When we go to Philadelphia again, I will show you the spot where stood Pennsylvania Hall, one of the most beautiful public buildings in that city. It was erected by the friends of the slave, and was the first hall in the country ever dedicated to free discussion. When the building was completed, the advocates of liberty assembled from all parts or the northern States to consecrate it to the God of Freedom. But the spirit of slavery was roused. On the first and second days of the meeting threats of violence were boldly uttered, and ere the third had closed, the Hall was surrounded by a mob who yelled, and hooted, and hissed, and broke in the windows and committed acts of personal outrage. On the evening of the fourth day they set it on fire. Dense volumes or smoke burst from the doors and windows, the red flames lighted up the dark sky, and in a few hours only the crumbling and blackened walls remained to tell of the vile deed that slavery's defenders had done."

"It seems to me there is no safety in this country for anybody who tries to do right," observed Charlie. "For keeping fugitives they can be fined or imprisoned, when holding meetings they are mobbed, their property destroyed, their public houses burned, and they themselves beaten, and tarred, and killed, and all because they want to make the slaves free, and stop men from robbing them and selling away their children. Why, mother, it is horrible! I should think that such things would not be allowed, even among savages, who are very ignorant and wicked."

"Such things," replied the mother, "would disgrace savages, and how much more disgraceful are they in this nation which claims to be the only free nation on earth, and professes to be better, more enlightened, more truly christian than any other. The fact that the United States hold three millions of slaves, proves that the people are neither christians nor lovers of liberty. Their professions are a hollow mockery, and render them subject to the disgust, and censure, and ridicule of the whole world. Those who make the highest professions of good-will to all, are the very persons who rivet the chains of slavery upon the necks of starving, heart-broken, and sorrowing men and women. Many who stand up in the pulpit and say God ordained *them* to preach, say also that slavery is not sinful, and ought not to be overthrown. It is the influence of such men, added to the power of guns and bayonets, that keeps the slaves where they are. Indeed, I doubt whether guns and bayonets would be used, were not their use sanctioned by the ministers and the church. They say that it is right—they themselves use them; and thus, by the words and example of those who profess to be christians, are the people made easy in their sins, and continue to hold in bondage those whom they ought to love, and labor to benefit. Nothing stands so much in the way of giving freedom to those in bonds, as the churches which defend slavery, and oppose all the efforts of the abolitionists."

"I suppose abolitionists have nothing to do with such churches," returned Charlie. "But tell me, mother, if there are such bloody mobs now-a-days as there used to be?"

"No! I was going to say that there are a great many encouraging things at the present time. Meetings are not often broken up now, and slavery is talked about every where—in the North, at least—in public and in private, in churches, in political meetings, and in social gatherings. You can scarcely take up a newspaper but has something in it against slavery; it is to be regretted, however, that so much is published in favor of it; still the tone of the press is very different from what it was. For sixteen years have the abolitionists been scattering their papers, and tracts and pamphlets throughout the land; they have sent abroad their speakers, both men and women, who have gone to and fro among the people telling of the wrongs and oppressions of the slave, and calling upon those who loved justice and mercy to aid in his deliverance. The happy results of this agitation are now seen; the rebukes, the reasonings, the appeals of these laborers have been abundantly prospered. Thousands and tens of thousands have been led to see that slavery is a sin; political parties have been distracted and weakened by the discussion of this question; many have withdrawn from them, and their leaders begin to see that it is necessary to do, or pretend to do something in favor of liberty.

"This agitation has affected the churches in a still greater degree— their holiness has been shown to be mere pretence, and their love of self and sect greater than their love of truth and righteousness. Those who really desire to do right, have been made to feel, that that is not a christian church whose members bind, and rob, and bruise their equal brethren. Thousands have left these churches as well as the parties, and proclaimed to the world that they will no longer remain with those who support slavery.

"Even a change has been effected in the South, which was formerly so bitter, and so determined not to hear. The truth has been forced upon the slaveholders, and here and there one has given freedom to all those he held in captivity. A willingness to hear this subject discussed has gradually increased among them, and especially is this true of Western Virginia and Kentucky. In the latter State an anti-slavery paper has been established which is read with interest by hundreds of slaveholders, and tells mightily on the cause of human freedom.

"Prejudice against a colored skin, which has so deeply injured the black man both at the South and at the North, is giving way before a more enlightened and christian feeling. It has excluded colored children from our schools and colleges, it has driven men and women from the cabins of our steamboats, and thrust them upon the deck, no matter how cold or unpleasant the weather."

"But, mother, I don't understand you; did'nt [sic] the white people want them to sit in the cabin?"

"No, they said they couldn't bear the presence of a negro. I knew one woman who was traveling on a boat, who sickened and died in consequence of being turned out of the cabin and being exposed to the night air on the deck of a steamer. This prejudice has compelled colored people to ride in an inferior car on railroads, and entirely excluded them from stage coaches in various places. It has set apart for them an obscure corner of the church, called the 'Negro Pew'; for the religion of this land is so full of hatred to the colored man, that it will not permit him to sit with his white brother, even in the house of prayer. The abolitionists have succeeded to some extent in convincing the people that this prejudice is anti-christian, and they have themselves set the example of treating the colored man as an equal. The result has been, that many of the schools in the North admit colored children the same as white; colored people are much less frequently driven from the cabins of our steam-boats and excluded from railroad cars; the churches are beginning to be ashamed of their 'Negro Pews', and to admit that all men are brethren and should treat each other as such. These things encourage us to believe that the cruel reign of slavery is drawing to a close.

"We should think the slave's deliverance close at hand, were not his oppressors adding extensive territory to their domains, and waging an infamous war with Mexico in order to extend and perpetuate the system."

"What territory have they added, mother, and why can they hold on to their slaves any longer by fighting the Mexicans?"

"The masters were afraid their slaves would escape into Texas, a province belonging to Mexico, and adjoining our southern border; consequently they seized upon it, and re-established slavery, which Mexico had abolished nearly twenty years ago, and finally added it to the United States. You know that men who take children from their mothers, would not hesitate to steal land from their neighbors. As might be supposed, many difficulties grew out of this, and as the Mexicans do not so well understand the art of war and are a much less powerful people than those of the United States, the latter sent down their soldiers, who destroyed their forts, captured their cities, murdered their men and women, and even killed little children who could do them no harm. Thousands have been murdered and wounded in this war, and hundreds of bodies have been left to rot, and taint the air; and all because the slaveholder wanted more power and more territory in order that slavery might live forever."

"The abolitionists certainly have a great work before them yet—very much remains to be done, although a great deal has been accomplished. Many have united in the work which was commenced by a very few. Where there was one in former days to labor for the slave there are now hundreds, and a great many little boys and girls like you and Jenie are helping in the work. If we all do what we can, and try to get others to do what they can, I think it will not be many years before slavery shall be no more; and the happy faces of the slave children, and their gay and joyous laugh, will be a pleasant sight and sweet music to those who aided in making them and their parents free."

"FREEDOM'S GATHERING"

A summons is spoken, the land is awake
And free hearts have gathered from ocean to lake.
The cause we engage in is spotless and pure,
And the triumph we seek shall forever endure.

Though tyrants denounce, and pursue us with ill,
Our hearts shall be faithful to liberty still.
Then rally, then rally, come one and come all;
'Tis for Truth and for Freedom we echo the call.

Thy hill-tops, New England, have leaped at the cry,
And the far spreading West and the South give reply;
It has rolled o'er the land till the farthermost glen
Re-echoes the summons again and again.

Oppression has heard in his temple of blood,
And reads on its wall the handwriting of God;
Niagara's torrent has thundered it forth,
And it burns in the sentinel star of the North.

It is seen in the lightning, it speaks in the thunder,
And slavery's fetters are breaking asunder;
Ere long will the captive's deliverance be won,
And our country her beautiful garments put on.

Then on to the conflict of Freedom and Truth!
Come Matron, come Maiden, come Manhood and Youth!
Come gather, come gather, come one, and come all!
And soon shall the altar of slavery fall.

The forests shall know it, and lift up their voice
To bid the green prairies and vallies [sic] rejoice;
And the "Father of Waters" join Mexico's sea,
In the anthem of Nature for millions set free.

B.S.J.

NOTES

1. Jones extends the idea of women's activism in *The Wrongs of Women: An Address Delivered before the Ohio Women's Convention* (1850) and *Address to the Women's Rights Committee of the Ohio Legislature* (1861).

2. Stephen Foster encouraged her to write *The Young Abolitionists* (Melder 285).

3. A shillalah is a club or cudgel.

ANN PRESTON

(Pseudonym: Cousin Ann,
December 1, 1813–April 18, 1872)

Dr. Ann Preston was the first of five Quaker women to enroll in the Female Medical College of Pennsylvania when it opened in October 1850 (Bacon 20). Having watched her mother and sisters suffer from illnesses that led to their deaths, Preston grew interested in women's health (Fullard 9). After serving a two-year apprenticeship under Dr. Nathaniel R. Moseley, she applied to medical school in 1849, but was rejected because she was a woman (Bacon 21; Stille 22). The following year the Quakers opened the Female Medical College of Pennsylvania and Preston enrolled. By 1853, she became professor of hygiene and physiology, and in 1866 she became the college's dean, which allowed her to champion women becoming physicians despite staunch opposition (Bacon 20; Fullard 9; Wells, "Women" 179). Interestingly, this woman who spent her life advocating for women wrote a children's book, *Cousin Ann's Stories for Children* (1849), which includes poems defending African Americans' right to freedom.

Preston's abolitionist views most likely stemmed from her upbringing and affiliations with the Society of Friends in Chester County, Pennsylvania. Born in West Grove, Pennsylvania, Preston was the daughter of Margaret Smith Preston and Amos Preston, a Quaker minister. Both of her parents supported the abolitionist and women's rights movements (Bacon 21). According to Joyce Fullard, "Her father's farm adjoined that of his brother, Mahlon Preston, a Quaker minister, and both men frequently helped fugitive slaves, using their homes as supplementary stations [on the Underground Railroad]" (9). Following in her parents' footsteps, Preston "acquired a belief in the need for social action to alleviate the misfortunes of others" (Fullard 9). She is "famous for disguising an escaped slave as a Quaker grandmother and driving her past patrollers"

(Wells, "Women" 183; see also Fullard 10; Stille 21). Later Preston became secretary for the Clarkson Anti-Slavery Society and "thus obtained a detailed knowledge of the problems caused by bounty hunters from the slave states and by local supporters of slavery" (Fullard 10). She also read William Lloyd Garrison's speeches about immediate abolitionism (Jensen 17). In addition, she was a friend of Lucretia Mott, a Quaker abolitionist and feminist, and she met James Russell Lowell and John Greenleaf Whittier, who spoke at the local literary society (Bacon 21).

The intersection of her affiliation with abolitionists and poets may have inspired her abolitionist writings. Preston wrote a poem in "commemoration of the burning of the Pennsylvania Hall by a proslavery mob in 1837" (Wells, Out 57) and published "Woman's Rights and Wrongs" in the National Anti-Slavery Standard on June 17, 1852. She also published Cousin Ann's Stories for Children through J. M. McKim, a Pennsylvania abolitionist who supported William Lloyd Garrison's abolitionist views. Although only three of the seven works in the collection address slavery, McKim advertised the collection in the National Anti-Slavery Standard (New York) for nine years after its original publication date (De Rosa 24).

Cousin Ann's Stories for Children offers young readers glimpses of slavery's horrors amidst traditional, sentimental, didactic, and moral poems and stories about white children. For example, Preston includes stories about "Mary May," who welcomes new classmates and never cheats; "Charles Clear," who resists peer pressure and therefore does not suffer the shame of deceit; "Johnny Valine," who dies by the roadside because of his alcoholism; and "Basil Brown," a selfish and abusive child who kicks his brother so hard that he dies. Reflecting the tradition of children's literature that women authors helped to create, each story or poem teaches young readers about the threats to character and morality.

Cleverly, as Cousin Ann, Preston suggests that supporting slavery also threatens American children's character formation. Her abolitionist juvenile texts challenge white children's views of slavery to foster increasing compassion for and an understanding of "the corrosive effects of slavery on human nature [white and African American] and to demonstrate the complete social disenfranchisement of slaves" (Hoganson 561). For example, Preston voices her critique of slavery's violation of familial bonds in "Tom and Lucy," a narrative poem that reflects the tradition of sentimental, pseudo slave-narratives for children (De Rosa 48–50). The young white listener, Little Lizzie, hears the story of two slave children who experience lost innocence and grief when violently separated from their mother and ultimately from each other. Lizzie responds with tears, a reaction Preston may have designed to inspire her young readers to compassion and then to activism that would counteract the destruction of the mother-child bond and the violation of childhood innocence. Another pseudo slave-narrative, "Henry Box Brown," narrates the experiences of Henry, a slave, who encloses himself in a box—with his friends' help—and stows away on a ship for a three-hundred mile journey to Philadelphia in March 1849. This brief biography contains elements found in authentic slave narratives, namely the recognition of enslavement, the struggle for and flight for freedom, and the assimilation into a free society. However, Preston does not leave her young readers with a "happily ever after" ending in that even though Henry Box Brown resides in the "city of brotherly love," he nonetheless grieves for his violated family bonds. Thus, she presents children with the Garrisonian belief that "slavery did more than undermine male rights; it prevented men from fulfilling the male responsibilities of supporting and protecting their families" (Hoganson 564). While Tom and Lucy cannot escape their enslavement and Henry Box Brown uses deceit to escape his, "Howard and His Squirrel" represents an encoded, abolitionist poem that celebrates Howard, a child slave owner turned liberator, when he frees his enslaved squirrel. Through this image of liberating a squirrel, Preston subversively advocates that Southern masters liberate their slaves (De Rosa 120). Children who read these abolitionist texts would, hopefully, recognize that violating the rights of African Americans was just as wrong as cheating, deceiving, and abusing their white peers.

That Preston cloaks herself as Cousin Ann to support Garrisonian politics and to advocate social reform may suggest her strategy for surviving the walk across the tightrope of women's gender codes. From the late 1850s until her death, Preston walked a similar tightrope while writing about women in the medical field. In *Out of the Dead Horse*, Susan Wells,

When there was nothing to do but to fight . . . Preston made a case [for women practicing medicine] with the materials at hand and transformed those materials in the process. Her organizational contributions to women's work in the medical profession were substantial, but not least among them was the construction of a rhetoric that allowed women to avoid or enter controversy, to claim and enact their gender or to bracket it, to locate themselves within the medical profession or to project its progressive transformation. This *fluid, combative, achingly anonymous and adroitly cross-dressed rhetoric gave women a voice with*

which to be doctors, a voice that later women physicians would elab-
orate, complicate, and contradict. (79, emphasis added)

Likewise, years earlier, Preston created an abolitionist voice for herself
through the friendly, didactic persona of Cousin Ann because she knew
she must. Concerning women's abolitionist rhetoric, Kristin Hoganson
writes,

> The unwritten rules of political participation stipulated that only
> "manly" men had the authority needed to speak in public debate. . . .
> The women who were active within Garrisonian ranks never had this
> legitimacy to begin with. Nonetheless, their activities lost them the
> amorphous moral power wielded by politically transcendent "true
> women." (559)

As Cousin Ann, the activist Preston could conceal her identity, but by
using a female pseudonym she could contest the culture against women's
political rhetoric. In so doing, Preston could maintain her status as a
"true" woman as well as wield moral and political power by making antislavery behavior just as important for children to learn as the lessons of
respect, temperance, and honesty that *Cousin Ann's Stories for Children*
praises.

FROM *COUSIN ANN'S STORIES FOR CHILDREN*
(1849)

"HOWARD AND HIS SQUIRREL"

Our Howard had a little squirrel,
  It's tail was long and gray,
He put it in a wiry cage,
  And there it had to stay.

Its hickory nuts and corn it ate
  From out its little paw,
And such a funny, active thing,
  I think, I never saw.

But Howard thought he should not like
  A little slave to be;
And God had made the nimble squirrel,
  To run, and climb the tree.

And so he opened Bunny's door,
  And laughed to see it run
And spring right up the leafy tree,
  As if 't was only fun.

A bird or squirrel in a cage
  It makes me sad to see;
It seems so cruel to confine
  The creatures made so free.

"TOM AND LUCY: A TALE FOR LITTLE LIZZIE"

Come Lizzie, and I'll tell that tale
  Of Tom and Lucy Lee,
Two little slaves, no bigger, dear,
  Than cousin Charles and thee.

They lived in Carolina state,
  Beside the great, deep sea;
Their mother was a weary slave
  And wanted to be free.

She only came to them at dark,
  For she must work all day,
And with her, on the cabin floor,
  They slept the night away.

Long sunny days they played alone,
　　As little children play,
But never hurt the butterflies,
　　Nor pelted frogs away.

Sometimes they rambled in the wood,
　　Where moss and flowers grew,
And little birds sang them to sleep,
　　As birds will often do.

But one dark night their mother dear
　　Stayed all the night away,
And long they cried, and waited there;
　　Until the break of day;

And then their master came, and bade
　　Them to his house repair,
For they were old enough, he said,
　　To earn their victuals there:

They met their mother in a drove
　　Of slaves, upon their way;
Her heart was broke, for she was sold
　　To go to Florida.

She gazed on them and cried "my God"!
　　She stopped, and begged to stay:
The driver fiercely called "move on,"
　　And drove her fast away.

Through dreary days and dreary years
　　Toiled Tom and Lucy there,
And when they stopped, the great whip cracked
　　Upon their shoulders bare.

But though they'd none to pity them,
　　They loved each other well,
And love will always bring some joy,
　　Wherever it may dwell.

They said when they grew big and strong
　　They both would run away,
And, up in Pennsylvania, learn
　　To read and write, each day.

But once, I think it was May morn,
　　A stranger came along,

While Lucy milked, and sadly sung
  Her mother's little song.

He called her master to the road,
  And told him he would pay
Six hundred dollars for that girl,
  And take her right away.

Her master took the trader's gold;—
  Such wicked things they do;
Just like a calf was Lucy sold,
  Though she was good as you.

Tom heard her scream, and ran to her;—
  To part they could not bear;
He held her fast, and cursed the men,
  Who stood in wonder there.

They knocked him down, and roughly took
  Poor Lucy far away;
And toiling in some cotton field
  She weeps, perhaps, today.

Tom ran away, but dogs and men
  Were set upon his track,
And broken-hearted from the swamp
  They brought him quickly back.

And then, 'twas said, they sold him off,
  All chained, to Georgia men;
He may be dead, I never heard
  From that poor boy again.

"HENRY BOX BROWN"

I will tell you the story of Henry Box Brown. It is a strange tale, and it is all true. Henry was a slave in Richmond, Virginia, and then his name was Henry Brown. He had a wife and four little children whom he loved very much.

One night when he went home to his little hut, his children and their mother, were gone, and poor Henry found they had been sold to a trader, and were taken away to Carolina. It made him almost crazy to hear this dreadful news. He felt sure he should never see them again, for he was a slave, and would not be allowed to go after them. He had to work away for his master, just as if nothing had happened. But he thought every day about his family, and he was very sad. He thought what hard times they would have when the overseer, with his whip, drove them to work in the cotton field. He feared they would have none to be kind to them, and love them; for the traders often sell the mother to one master, and the little children to others, and they never meet again. At last, Henry thought he would try to get to a free state. He resolved that, live or die, he would not be a slave much longer. So he set to thinking how he should get off. He was afraid to run away, lest he should be caught and sent back. A slave is not allowed to travel without his master's leave. But he hit upon a lucky thought. He got a box just large enough to hold him when he was sitting down, with his head a little bent. The box was three feet long, two feet eight inches deep, and twenty-three and a half inches wide. Then, he got a kind man to send word to a trusty friend in Philadelphia, that the box would be sent on the cars to Philadelphia, on a certain day. On the top of the box was written in large black letters, "this side up with care." When it was nearly time for the cars to start, Henry took a bladder of water, some biscuit, and a large gimlet,[1] and got into his box. Then a man nailed down the top, and porters took the box to the cars, thinking, I suppose, that it was a box of goods. It was very hot in the box, and Henry could hardly breathe, there was so little air. But he had made up his mind to die rather than make a noise, for then he would be found out, and sent back into slavery. Part of the way, he travelled by water, and when the box was put on the steamboat, it was placed so that Henry's head and back were down; but he heard people moving about, and he feared they would hear him if he turned; so he kept quite still. He lay in this way, while the boat went twenty miles, and it nearly killed him; he said the veins in his temples were great ridges that felt as big as his finger. While Henry was lying with his head down, some men came and sat on the box, and he thought he heard one of them wonder what was in it. He staid in his little box-house twenty-six hours; but he could not eat any of his biscuit, and instead of drinking the water, he used it to bathe his hot face. Most likely, he would have died if he had not bathed his face with the water. There he sat in the dark, sometimes fanning himself with his hat; and four times he bored a hole with the gimlet, to let in a little fresh air. At last, on nearly the last day of March, 1849, the cars stopped in Philadelphia, and soon Henry felt the porters carrying him to the house of the kind man who was to receive him. The man shut the street door when the porters were gone, but he was afraid Henry was smothered, so he tapped with his fingers on the top of the box and asked, "all right?" "All right, sir," said a voice in the box. Quickly the top of the box was knocked off, and Henry stood up. He shook hands with his new friend, and he was so happy that he hardly knew what to do. After he had bathed himself and ate breakfast, he sang a hymn of praise, which he had kept in his mind to sing if he should ever get to a land of freedom in safety. The first lines were,

"I waited patiently for the Lord
And He inclined and heard me."

Henry was a strong, fine looking man. He was named Henry Box Brown, because he came nearly three hundred miles in a box. We call people heroes who do something that is brave and great, and Henry is a hero. Every body but the slaveholders seems glad of his escape from slavery. Henry will be well off in the free states, but his heart will always ache when he thinks of his wife and dear children. No one in Carolina is allowed to teach a slave to read or write; so he will never get a letter from any of his family, and it is not likely they will hear from him, or ever know that he is free.

NOTE

1. A gimlet is a small boring tool with a pointy spiral tip.

HARRIET BEECHER STOWE

(June 14, 1811–July 1, 1896)

Harriet Beecher Stowe's publication of *Uncle Tom's Cabin* in 1852 met unprecedented worldwide response, negative and positive, and prompted Abraham Lincoln to call Stowe the little woman who started the great war. Many Americans read the last chapter of the serialized version of the novel in the April 1, 1852, edition of *The National Era* ([Bailey] 54). Having gained permission from the newspaper, publisher John P. Jewett embraced his wife's advice to publish it as *Uncle Tom's Cabin* after Phillips, Sampson, & Co. considered it too risky a venture. Jewett struck a nerve in the American reading public. He sold an unprecedented 10,000 copies within a few days of the March 1852 issue and 300,000 copies by December 1852 (Shackelford and Wilkie 226; Lenz 345). According to Sidney Howard Gay, Stowe earned royalties of "*Ten Thousand Three Hundred Dollars*, as her copyright permission on the sale of 'Uncle Tom's Cabin' for three months. It is stated that this is the largest sum ever received by any author, either English or American, from the sale of a single work in so short a period" (31). The novel also gained unprecedented popularity in Canada, England, France, Germany, and Italy, among others. The *Uncle Tom's Cabin* craze spawned fictional proslavery responses in music,[1] theater productions,[2] art,[3] games and toys,[4] and (of course) adaptations for children.

The novel's popularity quickly led Jewett and others to adapt the novel for juvenile audiences, even though Stowe considered the original appropriate for children. Millicent Lenz reveals that Stowe "read [the original version] to her own children as she wrote it and shared the first Little Eva episode with her class of school children in September 1851" (345). Furthermore, in the final installment in *The National Era*, Stowe states,

> Dear children, you will soon be men and women, and I hope that you
> will learn from this story always to remember and pity the poor and op-
> pressed. When you grow up, show your pity by doing all you can for
> them. Never, if you can help it, let a colored child be shut out from
> school or treated with neglect or contempt on account of his color. Re-
> member the sweet example of little Eva. . . . Then, when you grow up,
> I hope the foolish and unchristian prejudice against people merely on
> account of their complexion will be done away with. (qtd. in Lenz 345)

Notwithstanding Stowe's view, publishers adapted the novel for children.
For example, securely tucked in the temperature-controlled vault in the
William B. Cairns Collection of American Women Writers at the Uni-
versity of Wisconsin, Madison, the avid *Uncle Tom's Cabin* bibliophile
would revel in the more than two-dozen copies of children's adaptations
in all languages (from English to Yiddish) published from 1852 until the
1960s. The endeavor to adapt the novel began when Jewett as well as
Sampson, Low and Sons (London) published *A Peep into Uncle Tom's
Cabin* (1853), an abridged version of *Uncle Tom's Cabin*. Although "Aunt
Mary" (Mary Low, Sampson Low's daughter) edited *A Peep* ("Harriet,"
BAL), Stowe included a prefatory address "to the children of England
and America" (front cover [?]). As part of his Juvenile Anti-Slavery Toy
Books series, Jewett published *Pictures and Stories from Uncle Tom's Cabin*
(1853?) to "adapt [the novel] for the juvenile family circle" (Preface [2]).
The Preface states,

> The verses have accordingly been written by the authoress for the ca-
> pacity of the youngest readers, and have been printed in a larger font
> type. The prose parts of the book, which are well suited for being read
> aloud in the family circle, are printed in a smaller type. ([2])

"Jewett's decision to use two font sizes to accommodate family readings
and independent youngsters reveals his conscious marketing to a dual audience. Stressing the text's appropriateness for the 'family circle' rein-
scribed this political narrative into a gender appropriate sphere" (De Rosa
28–29). In addition, Vincent Dill, a publisher from New York, published
Little Eva: The Flower of the South and *Little Eva's First Book for Good Children*. In 1860, Darton and Co., a London publisher, printed *True Stories
from Uncle Tom's Cabin*. Dill and Darton's editions also made slavery a
topic of family discussion and, in particular, elevated Little Eva into a
young abolitionist heroine.

In *Domestic Abolitionism and Juvenile Literature*, I argue that Eva (in the novel and in the children's adaptations) represents "the first female who takes center stage, talks, and tries to abolish slavery. While I acknowledge Eva's evangelical nature, critics who limit her character to an evangelical figure, a saintly child, a sentimental victim, or an image of female purity have 'silenced' Eva's abolitionist voice" (De Rosa 120–133), which she expresses in her repeated attempts to change her family members' proslavery views and behavior as well as to educate and free the slaves.[5]

In the same vein, the children's adaptations are important in several ways. First, each presents young readers with the image of an abolitionist child. As in Stowe's original novel, each adaptation, in different degrees, depicts Eva as an educator of slaves, a very subversive act considering the slave codes that made such behavior illegal. Second, except for Elizabeth Margaret Chandler's female figures in "The Sugar-Plums" and "Oh Press Me Not to Taste Again," abolitionist girls did not appear in any recovered text by domestic abolitionists before 1852. Third, Stowe's young abolitionist female set a new precedent for the portrayal of white girls in subsequent juvenile abolitionist works. The works of Aunt Mary, *The Edinburgh Doll* (1854); M.A.F., *Gertrude Lee, or, the Northern Cousin* (1856); Maria Goodell, Frost *Gospel Fruits* (1856); and Anne Richardson, *Little Laura, the Kentucky Abolitionist* (1859) contain fictional girls who combat silence and oppose slavery. These domestic abolitionists do not depict the girls negatively as nonconformists, but approvingly as heroines, who, except for Mary in *The Edinburgh Doll*, survive to see the fruits of their activism.

Front page from *Pictures and Stories from Uncle Tom's Cabin*
Courtesy, American Antiquarian Society.

PICTURES AND STORIES FROM UNCLE TOM'S CABIN (1853)

"UNCLE TOM'S PICTURE BOOK"

"THE SALE OF LITTLE HARRY"

Come read my book good boys and girls
That live on freedom's ground,
With pleasant homes, and parents dear,
And blithesome playmates round;
And you will learn a woeful tale,
Which a good woman told,
About the poor black negro race,
How they are bought and sold.

Within our own America
Where these bad deeds are done,
A father and a mother lived
Who had a little son;
As slaves, they worked for two rich men,
Whose fields were fair and wide—
But Harry was their only joy,
They had no child beside.

Now Harry's hair was thick with curls
And softly bright his eyes,
And he could play such funny tricks
And look so wondrous wise,
That all about the rich man's house
Were pleased to see him play,
Till a wicked trader buying slaves
Came there one winter day.

The trader and the rich man sat
Together, at their wine,
When in poor simple Harry slipped
In hopes of something fine.
He shewed [sic] them how the dandy danced,
And how old Cudjoe walked,
Till loud they laughed and gave him grapes,
And then in whispers talked.

The young child knew not what they said,
But at the open door

Eliza, his poor mother, stood,
With heart all sick and sore.
Oh children dear, 'twas sad to hear,
That for the trader's gold,
To that hard-hearted evil man
Her own sweet boy was sold.

And he would take him far away,
To where the cotton grew,
And sell him for a slave to men
More hard and wicked too.
She knew that none would heed his woe,
His want, or sickness there,
Nor ever would she see his face,
Or hear his evening prayer.

So when the house was all asleep,
And when the stars were bright,
She took her Harry in her arms,
And fled through that cold night:—
Away through bitter frost and snow
Did that poor mother flee;
And how she fared, and what befell,
Read on, and you shall see.

Before setting out, Eliza took a piece of paper and a pencil, and wrote hastily the following note her kind mistress, who had tried in vain to save little Harry from being sold:—

"Oh missus! dear missus! don't think me ungrateful; don't think hard of me. I am going to try to save my boy; you will not blame me! God bless and reward you for all your kindness!"

Hastily folding and directing this, she went to a drawer and made up a little package of clothing for her boy, which she tied firmly round her waist; and so fond is a mother's remembrance, that even in the terrors of that hour she did not forget to put up in the little package one or two of his favourite toys.

On the bed lay her slumbering boy, his long curls falling negligently around his unconscious face, his rosy mouth half open, his little fat hands thrown out over the bed-clothes, and a smile spread like a sunbeam over his whole face. "Poor boy! poor fellow!" said Eliza, "they have sold you, but your mother will save you yet."

It was some trouble to arouse the little sleeper; but after some effort he sat up, and began playing with his wooden bird, while his mother was putting on her bonnet and shawl.

THE SALE OF LITTLE HARRY.

Oh children dear, 'twas sad to hear,
That for the trader's gold,
To that hard-hearted evil man
Her own sweet boy was sold.

"The Sale of Little Harry"
Courtesy, American Antiquarian Society.

"Where are you going, mother?" said he, as she drew near the bed with his little coat and cap.

His mother drew near, and looked so earnestly into his eyes, that he at once divined that something unusual was the matter.

"Hush, Harry," she said; "mustn't speak aloud, or they will hear us. A wicked man was coming to take little Harry away from his mother, and carry him 'way off in the dark; but mother won't let him—she's going to put on her little boy's cap and coat, and run off with him, so the ugly man can't catch him."

Saying these words, she had tied and buttoned on the child's simple outfit, and taking him in her arms, she whispered to him to be very still; and, opening the door, she glided noiselessly out.

It was a sparkling, frosty, starlight night, and the mother wrapped the shawl close round her child, as, perfectly quiet with terror, he clung round her neck.

At first the novelty and alarm kept him waking; but after they had gone a considerable way, poor Harry said, as he found himself sinking to sleep—

"Mother, I don't need to keep awake, do I?"

"No, my darling; sleep now, if you want to."

"But, mother, if I do get asleep, you won't let him get me?"

"No! so may God help me!" said his mother with a paler cheek, and a brighter light in her large dark eyes.

"You're *sure*, an't [*sic*] you, mother?"

"Yes, *sure*!" said the mother, in a voice that startled herself; for it seemed to her to come from a spirit within, that was no part of her; and the boy dropped his little weary head on her shoulder, and was soon asleep.

When morning came, as poor Harry complained of hunger and thirst, she sat down behind a large rock, which hid them from the road, and gave him a breakfast out of her little package. The boy wondered and grieved that she could not eat, and when putting his arms round her neck[,] he tried to force some of his cake into her mouth, it seemed to her that the rising in her throat would choke her.

"No, no, Harry, darling! mother can't eat till you are safe! We must go on—on—till we come to the river." And she hurried again into the road and proceeded on her journey.

When the trader came to take away Harry, he was in a great rage, because neither the boy nor his mother could be found. The master who sold him was also very angry, and ordered two of his negroes, called Andy and Sam, to bring out two of the swiftest horses, and help the trader to pursue Eliza, and take Harry from her. Andy and Sam did not like that work, but being slaves, they dare not disobey. However, they did what they could to detain the trader; for, pretending to be in great haste, they squalled for this and that, and frightened the horses, till they ran off over hedges and ditches, with Andy and Sam after them, laughing till their sides ached as soon as they got out of sight. The trader all the while stood cursing and swearing, like a wicked man as he was.

When the horses were caught, they were so tired with their race, that he was fain to let them stay and rest till dinner-time. But when dinner-time came, Chloe the cook, of whom you will hear more in the course of the story, spilled one dish, kept another long in baking; and so the trader did not get his dinner till it was late in the afternoon.

The horses were brought out at last, and he set off with Sam and Andy in pursuit of poor Harry and his mother. They had gone a great way by this time, and Eliza's feet were sore with walking all the night and day, and Harry was ready to lie down and sleep on the snow. As the sun was setting, they came in sight of the great river Ohio. There was no bridge over it. People crossed in boats in the summer time, and in winter on the thick ice, with which it was always covered. Now it was the month of February. The ice had broken, because spring was near. The river was swollen over all its banks, and no boatman would venture on it. There was a little inn hard by, and there poor Eliza hoped to get a little rest for herself and Harry, who was now fast asleep in her arms. She had just sat down by the fire, when, who should ride into the yard but the trader and his guides. The swift horses had brought them much quicker than she and Harry could walk, but the weary mother would not lose her child. She darted out with him that moment, and the verses will tell you by what means she escaped.

"ELIZA CROSSING THE RIVER"

From her resting-place by the trader chased,
Through the winter evening cold,
Eliza came with her boy at last,
Where a broad deep river rolled.

Great blocks of the floating ice were there,
And the water's roar was wild,
But the cruel trader's step was near,
Who would take her only child.

Poor Harry clung around her neck,
But a word he could not say,

For his very heart was faint with fear,
And with flying all that day.

Her arms about the boy grew tight,
With a loving clasp, and brave;
"Hold fast! Hold fast, now, Harry dear,
And it may be God will save."

From the river's bank to the floating ice
She took a sudden bound,
And the great block swayed beneath her feet
With a dull and heavy sound.

So over the roaring rushing flood,
From block to block she sprang,
And ever her cry for God's good help
Above the waters rang.

And God did hear that mother's cry,
For never an ice-block sank;
While the cruel trader and his men
Stood wondering on the bank.

A good man saw on the further side,
And gave her his helping hand;
So poor Eliza, with her boy,
Stood safe upon the land.

A blessing on that good man's arm,
On his house, and field, and store;
May he never want a friendly hand
To help him to the shore!

A blessing on all that make such haste,
Whatever their hands can do!
For they that succour the sore distressed,
Our Lord will help them too.

When the two negroes saw Eliza's escape, they began to laugh and cheer; on which the trader chased them with his horsewhip, cursing and swearing as usual. But he could not get over the river, and went in very bad temper to spend that night at the little inn, determined to get a boat, if possible, and catch Harry in the morning. The man who had helped Eliza up the river's bank, showed her a pretty white house at some distance, where a kind gentleman and his wife lived. The dark night had fallen, the tea-cups were on the table, and the fires were bright in kitchen and parlour, when the poor mother, all wet and weary, her feet cut by the sharp ice (for she had lost her shoes in the river), walked in, with Harry still in her arms. Before she could ask for shelter, she dropped down fainting on the floor. The good people of the house thought she was dead, and raised a terrible alarm. Mr. and Mrs. Bird ran into the kitchen to see what had happened. They were good, kind people, and great in that place, for Mr. Bird was a member of the American Parliament. He kept slaves himself, and tried to think it was no sin. He had even been trying that very night, in conversation with his wife, to defend a law lately passed, which forbade any one to give shelter to poor runaway slaves. But Mrs. Bird would listen to no defence of such a law, and said, "It is a shameful, wicked, and abominable law, and I'll break it for one the first time I have a chance, and I hope I shall have a chance too. I know nothing about politics, but I can read my Bible, and there I see that I must feed the hungry, clothe the naked, and comfort the desolate; and that Bible I mean to follow. No, no, John, said she, you may talk all night, but you would not do what you say. Would you now turn away a poor, shivering, hungry creature from your door because he was a runaway? Would you, now?"

Now, if the truth must be told, Mr. Bird was a very kind man, and could not in his heart give a very decided reply to his wife; and it was just at this moment that poor Eliza and little Harry came to his door. As we said, Mr. and Mrs. Bird ran to the kitchen to see what had happened. They found poor Eliza just recovering from her faint. She stared wildly round her for a moment, and then sprang to her feet, saying, "Oh! my Harry! have you got him?" The boy at this ran to her, and put his arms round her neck. "Oh! he's here, he's here!" she exclaimed. And then she cried wildly to Mrs. Bird, "O, ma'am, do protect us, don't let them get him!"

"Nobody shall hurt you here, poor woman," said Mrs. Bird. "You are safe; don't be afraid."

"God bless you," said the woman, covering her face and sobbing, while poor little Harry, seeing her crying, tried to get into her lap.

With many gentle and womanly offices which no one knew better how to render than Mrs. Bird, the poor woman was rendered more calm. A temporary bed was provided for her near the fire; and after a short time, Eliza, faint and weary with her long journey, fell into a heavy slumber, with little Harry soundly sleeping on her arm.

"I wonder who and what she is," said Mr. Bird, when he had gone back to the parlour with his wife.

"When she wakes and feels a little rested, we shall see," said Mrs. Bird, who began to busy herself with her knitting.

Mr. Bird took up a newspaper, and pretended to be reading it, but it was not long before he turned to his wife and said, "I say, wife, couldn't she wear one of your gowns; and there's that old cloak that you keep on purpose to put over me when I take my afternoon's nap, you might give her that; she needs clothes.

Mrs. Bird simply replied, "We'll see;" but a quiet smile passed over her face as she remembered the conversation they had had together that very night before Eliza and little Harry came to their door.

After an hour or two, Eliza awoke, and Mr. and Mrs. Bird again went to the kitchen. As they entered, poor Eliza lifted her dark eyes, and fixed them on Mrs. Bird, with such a forlorn and imploring expression, that the tears came into the kindhearted woman's eyes.

"You need not be afraid of anything; we are friends here, poor woman! Tell me where you came from, and what you want?" said she.

"I came from Kentucky," said poor Eliza.

"And what induced you to run away?" said Mrs. Bird.

The woman looked up with a keen, scrutinising glance, and it did not escape her that Mrs. Bird was dressed in deep mourning.

"Ma'am," she said, suddenly, "have you ever lost a child?"

The question was unexpected, and it was a thrust on a new wound; for it was only a month since a darling child of the family had been laid in the grave.

Mr. Bird turned round and walked to the window, and Mrs. Bird burst into tears; but, recovering her voice, she said—

"Why do you ask that? I have lost a little one."

"Then you will feel for me. I have lost two, one after another—left them buried there when I came away; and I had only this one left. I never slept a night without him; he was all I had. He was my comfort and pride day and night; and, ma'am, they were going to take him away from me—to *sell* him—a baby that had never been away from his mother in his life! I couldn't stand it, ma'am. I knew I never should be good for anything if they did; and when I knew the papers were signed and he was sold, I took him and came off in the night, and they chased me—the man that bought him and some of master's folks, and they were coming down right behind me, and I heard them—I jumped right on to the ice, and how I got across I don't know, but first I knew a man was helping me up the bank."

"Crossed on the ice?" cried every one present.

"Yes," said poor Eliza, slowly. "I did, God helping me. I crossed on the ice, for they were behind me—right behind—and there was no other way!"

All around were affected to tears by Eliza's story.

Mr. Bird himself, to hide his feelings, had to turn away, and became particularly busy in wiping his spectacle-glasses and blowing his nose.

After a short pause, Mrs. Bird asked:—

"And where do you mean to go to, my poor woman?"

"To Canada if I only knew where that was. Is it very far off ma'am?" said she, looking up with a simple and confiding air to Mrs. Bird's face.

"Poor woman," said Mrs. Bird, "it is much further off than you think; but we will try to think what can be done for you. Here Dinah," said she to one of the servants, "make her up a bed in your own room close by the kitchen, and I'll think what to do for her in the morning. Meanwhile, never fear poor woman, put your trust in God, He will protect you."

Mrs. Bird and her husband re-entered the parlour. She sat down in her little rocking chair before the fire, swinging it thoughtfully to and fro. Mr. Bird strode up and down the room, grumbling to himself. At length, striding up to his wife, he said:—

"I say, wife, she'll have to get away from here this very night. That trader fellow will be down after her early to-morrow morning."

"To-night," said Mrs. Bird, "how is it possible—and where to?"

"Well, I know pretty well where to," said Mr. Bird, beginning to put on his boots. "I know a place where she would be safe enough, but the plague of the thing is, nobody could drive a carriage there to-night but me. The creek has to be crossed twice, and the second crossing is quite dangerous, unless one know it as I do. But never mind. I'll take her over myself. There is no help for it. I could not bear to see the poor woman caught."

"Thank you, thank you, dear John," said the wife, laying her white hand on his—"Could I ever have loved you had I not known you better than you do yourself?"

Off Mr. Bird set to see about the carriage, but at the door he stopped for a moment, and then coming back, he said, with a quivering voice,—

"Mary, I don't know how you'd feel about it, but there's the drawer full of things—of—of—poor little Henry's clothes." So saying, he turned quickly on his heel, and shut the door after him.

His wife opened the little bedroom door adjoining her room, and taking the candle, set it down on the top of a bureau there; then from a small recess she took a key, and put it thoughtfully in the lock of a drawer, and made a sudden pause, while two boys, who, boy-like, had followed close on her heels, stood looking, with silent, significant glances, at their mother. And oh! mother that reads this, has there never been in your house a drawer, or a closet, the opening of which has been to you like the opening again of a little grave? Ah! happy mother that you are, if it has not been so!

Mrs. Bird slowly opened the drawer. There were little coats of many a form and pattern, piles of aprons, and rows of small stockings; and even a pair of little shoes, worn and rubbed at the toes, were peeping from the folds of a paper. There was a toy horse and waggon [sic], a top, a ball— memorials gathered with many a tear and many a heartbreak! She sat down by the drawer, and leaning her head on her hands over it, wept till the tears fell through her fingers into the drawer; then suddenly raising her head, she began, with nervous haste, selecting the plainest and most substantial articles, and gathering them into a bundle.

"Mamma," said one of the boys, gently touching her arm, "are you going to give away those things?"

"My dear boys," she said, softly and earnestly, "if our dear, loving, little Henry looks down from heaven, he would be glad to have us do this. I could not find it in my heart to give them away to any common person— to anybody that was happy; but I give them to a mother more heart-broken and sorrowful than I am; and I hope God will send his blessings with them!"

Mr. Bird returned about twelve o'clock with the carriage. "Mary," said he, coming in with his overcoat in his hand, "you must wake her up now. We must be off." Soon arrayed in a cloak, bonnet, and shawl that had belonged to her benefactress, poor Eliza appeared at the door with her child in her arms. When she got seated in the carriage, she fixed her large dark eyes on Mrs. Bird's face, and seemed going to speak. Her lips moved, but there was no sound; pointing upward with a look never to be for-gotten, she fell back in her seat and covered her face. The door was shut, and the carriage drove on.

It was not long before they arrived at the place where Mr. Bird thought they would be safe from the cruel trader. It was a village about seven miles off, consisting of neat houses, with orchards and meadows about them.

They all belonged to Quakers, a sect of Christians whom foolish people laugh at, because they think it right to wear broad-brimmed hats, and odd old-fashioned bonnets; but they do many good and charitable things, espe-cially for the poor negroes, and one of them took Harry and his mother in.

I cannot tell all the kindness the Quaker and his family did to them, giving Harry such good things, and watching lest the trader should come that way; but the greatest joy of all was, one evening, when a tall strong man, called Phineas Fletcher, who was a Quaker, and a great traveller, guided to the village Harry's poor father, George. His master was going to sell him too, and he had run away, and searched everywhere for his wife and child, to take them with him to Canada, which you know belongs to England. Oh what a happy meeting that was between George, Eliza and little Harry.

But they could not remain long with the kind Quakers. Their cruel pursuers had found out where they were hid, so they had all to set out again together. This time they were guided by the brave-hearted Phineas Fletcher, and hoped to reach Canada in safety. But their pursuers overtook them, and they had to run to the rocks to defend themselves, as the verses will tell.

"THE DEFENCE"

See Harry's poor father, with pistol in hand,
How bravely he takes on the steep rock his stand,
Over rivers, and forests, and towns he has passed,
And found his Eliza and Harry at last.

The kind Quaker folks that wear drab, brown, and gray,
To the wanderers gave shelter and bread on their way,
Their warm clothes were given them, their waggon [sic] was lent
And the strong-armed Phineas along with them went.

Their hope was to journey to Canada's shore,
Where the trader or master could reach them no more;
For the English flag floats there, o'er land and o'er sea,
And they knew in its shadow the negro was free.

But far is their way through the slave-dealing land,
And now on their track comes the trader's fierce band;
So for refuge and rest to the rocks they have run,
And the father will fight for his wife and his son.

He fires on the first up the steep rock that springs,
But the trader comes on, shouting all wicked things,
Till Phineas right over the crag flings him clear,
Saying, "Friend, in my mind thou hast no business here."

Then off go the traders to find them more men,
And off go the friends in their waggon [sic] again;

THE DEFENCE.

But far is their way through the slave-dealing land,
And now on their track comes the trader's fierce band
So for refuge and rest to the rocks they have run,
And the father will fight for his wife and his son.

"The Defence"
Courtesy, American Antiquarian Society.

But don't you wish well to the good man for life,
Who would fight for his freedom, his child, and his wife?

After this, George and Eliza, with their little Harry, journeyed on, never stopping, except at the house of another kind friend, to disguise themselves before going on board the steamboat, which at last brought them safe to Canada.

"ARRIVAL IN THE LAND OF FREEDOM"

Look on the travellers kneeling,
    In thankful gladness, here,
As the boat that brought them o'er the lake,
    Goes steaming from the pier.

'Tis Harry, like a girl disguised,
    His mother, like a boy,
But the father kneels beside them,
    And their hearts are full of joy.

No man can buy or sell them,
    No trader chase them more,
The land of freedom has been gained,
    The good Canadian shore.

And they are strangers on the soil,
    As poor as poor can be,
But the English flag above them floats,
    They know that they are free.

George got employment in a factory, and as he was active and clever in his work, he soon earned enough to take a pretty little house, where they all lived together. Harry grew older, and went to school, where he was a good boy, and never forgot how God had preserved him from the wicked trader, and what his poor mother had suffered to bring him away. His father, George, though he worked all day, was learning too from all sorts of good books, which he used to read by the fire in the evenings. He was ever thinking of the poor heathen kings in Africa, and the negroes they sold for slaves. So at last, when he had learned a great deal, he determined to become a missionary; and, with his wife and family, he embarked for Africa, where he still labours, teaching the poor negroes the glad tidings of the gospel.

ARRIVAL IN THE LAND OF FREEDOM.

No man can buy or sell them,
No trader chase them more,
The land of freedom has been gained,
The good Canadian shore.

"Arrival in the Land of Freedom"
Courtesy, American Antiquarian Society.

WHO UNCLE TOM WAS

Now I must tell you something about Uncle Tom, from whom this
book is named. He was a negro man, as black as jet, and a slave, belonging to Mr. Shelby, the rich man who at first owned Eliza and Harry.
Mr. Shelby had a great estate, and many slaves to cultivate it, but they
all loved and respected Tom, for he was a good Christian, and kind to
everybody, on which account they used all to call him Uncle. Tom's master was kind to his slaves, and especially to Tom, because he was honest
and careful with his property. Tom had a cabin or cottage hard by the
rich man's house; it was built of logs cut from great trees; there was a garden in front, with beautiful flowers and strawberries in it; and climbing
plants, so common in our country, twined along the walls. Tom had also
a wife as black as himself; her name was Chloe, and she cooked for the
Shelbys. You will remember how late she kept the trader's dinner when
he wanted to pursue Eliza. They had two little sons, with very black faces
and curly heads, and a little black baby just beginning to walk. Tom and
his family were very happy in that cabin; the poor negroes used to gather
there to hear Tom sing hymns and pray, for, as I said, he was a pious man,
and the slaves had no other church to go to, for many people in America will not let negroes worship God with them. Mr. Shelby's son, a very
clever boy, who had gained many prizes at school, liked Tom too, and
used to come to teach him to read and write in the evenings, and Tom
had great hopes of being able to read the Bible at last. As Chloe was a
cook she always contrived to have ready something very nice for Mr.
George when he came to teach her goodman, and George would stand
with one eye on Tom's copy, and another on the cake she prepared, while
the boys and the baby played about them.

But all these pleasant days came to an end. Mr. Shelby lost his money,
and got in debt to a man who dealt in slaves; for that debt he sold little
Harry to him, and the rest of it was paid with poor Tom. Think what sad
news that was for the cabin!

"TOM AND HIS WIFE HAVE HEARD THAT HE IS SOLD"

The work of the winter day is o'er,
But Tom and his wife are weeping sore
Beside the hearth, where you can't forget
How the cakes were baked, and the copy set.

Oh, never again will Tom be taught!
From his master, by wicked trader bought;
And he will carry poor Tom next day,
From children, and wife, and home away.

His home—It was low of roof and wall,
But there had been room and love for all,
The peace that waits on contented days,
The voice of prayer and the hymn of praise.

And Tom himself, he is black of skin,
But, children, his soul is fair within,
His life is good and his heart is brave,
And yet they have sold him as a slave.

The fire light shows on the lowly bed,
Each dusky face, and each curly head
Of his little children, sound asleep;
Oh well may their poor tired mother weep!

Now Tom is trying to soothe her woe:
"Dear Chloe 'tis best that I should go,
Our babes and you will live safely here,
And I may be far, but God is near."

"Yet think of me, love, when I am gone,
And the days of the pleasant spring come on.
Don't grieve, dear wife"—and his tears fell fast.
"You know we will meet in heaven at last."

Tom might have fled away, as Eliza did with Harry, but he took pity on Mr. Shelby for being in debt to the trader, and also feared that if he fled, his wife and children would be sold to pay it. Poor Chloe wept sore, and so did the boys, and all the negroes on the estate were very sorry to part with him. George Shelby was from home when Tom was sold, and knew nothing about the matter. But he returned that very day, and the moment he learned that Tom was gone, he saddled his horse and rode after him. When he came up to the waggon [sic] he sprang into it, and throwing his arms round Tom's neck, began sobbing and scolding most violently.

"I declare it's a shame! I don't care what they say, any of them. It's a nasty mean shame! If I was a man, they shouldn't do it," said George.

"Oh, Mas'r George! this does me good!" said Tom. "I couldn't bear to go off without seein' ye! It does me real good, ye can't tell!" Here Tom made some movement of his feet, and George's eyes fell on the fetters.

TOM AND HIS WIFE HAVE HEARD THAT
HE IS SOLD.

The fire-light shows on the lowly bed,
Each dusky face, and each curly head
Of his little children, sound asleep;
Oh well may their poor tired mother weep!

"Tom and His Wife Have Heard That He Is Sold"
Courtesy, American Antiquarian Society.

"What a shame!" he exclaimed, lifting his hands. "I'll knock that old fellow down—I will!"

"No, you won't, Mas'r George; and you must not talk so loud. It won't help me any, to anger him."

"Well, I won't, then, for your sake; but only to think of it—isn't it a shame? They never sent for me, nor sent me any word, and, if it hadn't been for Tom Lincoln, I shouldn't have heard it. I tell you, I blew them up well, all of them, at home."

"That wasn't right, I'm feared, Mas'r George."

"Can't help it! I say it's a shame! Look here, Uncle Tom," said he, turning his back to the rest of the party, and speaking in a mysterious tone, *"I've brought you my dollar!"*

"Oh, I couldn't think o' takin' it, Mas'r George, no ways in the world," said Tom, quite moved.

"But you shall take it," said George. "Look here; I told Aunt Chloe I'd do it, and she advised me just to make a hole in it, and put a string through, so you could hang it round your neck, and keep it out of sight, else this mean scamp would take it away. I tell ye, Tom, I want to blow him up! it would do me good."

"No, don't, Mas'r George, for it won't do *me* any good."

"Well, I won't, for your sake," said George, busily tying his dollar round Tom's neck; "but there, now, button your coat tight over it, and keep it, and remember, every time you see it, that I'll come down after you, and bring you back. Aunt Chloe and I have been talking about it. I told her not to fear; I'll see to it, and I'll tease father's life out if he don't do it."

"O, Mas'r George, ye mustn't talk so about your father! You must be a good boy; remember how many hearts is set on ye. Always keep close to yer mother. Don't be gettin' into them foolish ways boys has of gettin' too big to mind their mothers. Tell ye what, Mas'r George, the Lord gives good many things twice over; but he don't give ye a mother but once. Ye'll never see sich another woman, Mas'r George, if ye live to be a hundred years old. So, now, you hold on to her, and grow up, and be a comfort to her, thar's my own good boy—you will, now, won't ye?"

"Yes, I will, Uncle Tom," said George, seriously.

"And be careful of yer speaking, Mas'r George. Young boys, when they come to your age, is wilful, sometimes—it's natur [sic] they should be. But real gentlemen, such as I hopes you'll be, never lets fall no words that isn't respectful to thar parents. Ye an't [sic] offended, Mas'r George?"

"No indeed, Uncle Tom; you always did give me good advice."

"I's older, ye know," said Tom, stroking the boy's fine curly head with his large, strong hand, but speaking in a voice as tender as a woman's—"and I sees all that's bound up in you. O, Mas'r George, you has everything—larnin', privileges, readin', writin'—and you'll grow up to be a great, learned, good man, and all the people on the place, and your mother and father, 'll [sic] be so proud on ye! Be a good mas'r, like yer father; and be a Christian, like yer mother. Remember yer Creator in the days o' yer youth, Mas'r George. And now, Good-bye, Mas'r George," said Tom, looking fondly and admiringly at him. "God Almighty bless you!" Away George went, and Tom looked, till the clatter of his horse's heels died away, the last sound or sight of his home.

When the trader was disappointed in catching Harry, he put handcuffs on poor Tom to prevent his escape, and took him away in a waggon to a town, where he bought more slaves—children from their mothers, and husbands from their wives—some of them as black as Tom, and some nearly white, like Harry and his mother. Then he put them all on board of a steamboat going down the great river Mississippi. You will see on the map that it is one of the largest rivers in America. There are many towns on its banks, and steamboats go from one to another carrying goods and passengers; and the trader seeing that Tom was quiet and peaceable, took off the handcuffs, and allowed him to go about the steamboat helping the sailors, for Tom would help anybody. There were many people on board besides the negroes, and among them a rich gentleman called Mr. St. Clair. He was returning home from a visit to his relations, who lived in New England, and had with him his little daughter Eva, and his cousin Miss Feely. Eva had long yellow curls, and a fair, pretty face; better than that, she had the fear of God and the love of all goodness in her heart. Always cheerful, meek, and kindly, everybody loved Eva St. Clair, especially her father, for she was his only daughter. Tom saw her play about the steamboat, for they were days and nights on the voyage. Eva used to come close and look at him, when he sat thinking of Chloe and the children. The little one was shy, notwithstanding all her busy interest in everything going on, and it was not easy to tame her. But at last Tom and she got on quite confidential terms.

"What' little missy's name?" said Tom at last, when he thought matters were ripe to push such an inquiry.

"Evangeline St. Clair," said the little one, though papa and everybody else call me Eva. Now, what's your name?"

"My name's Tom; the little children used to call me Uncle Tom, away back thar in Kentucky."

"Then, I mean to call you Uncle Tom, because, you see, I like you," said Eva. "So, Uncle Tom, where are you going?"

"I don't know, Miss Eva."

"Don't know?" said Eva.

"No. I am going to be sold to somebody. I don't know who."

"My papa can buy you," said Eva, quickly; "and if he buys you, you will have good times. I mean to ask him to, this very day."

"Thank you, my little lady," said Tom.

The boat here stopped at a small landing to take in wood, and Eva, hearing her father's voice, bounded nimbly away. Tom rose up, and went forward to offer his service in wooding, and soon was busy among the hands.

Eva and her father were standing together by the railings to see the boat start from the landing-place; the wheel had made two or three revolutions in the water, when, by some sudden movement, the little one suddenly lost her balance, and fell sheer over the side of the boat, into the water. Her father, scarce knowing what he did, was plunging in after her, but was held back by some behind him, who saw that more efficient aid had followed his child.

Tom was standing just under her on the lower deck as she fell. He saw her strike the water and sink, and was after her in a moment. A broad-chested, strong-armed fellow, it was nothing for him to keep afloat in the water, till, in a moment or two, the child rose to the surface, and he caught her in his arms, and, swimming with her to the boat-side, handed her up, all dripping, to the grasp of hundreds of hands, which, as if they had all belonged to one man, were stretched eagerly out to receive her. A few moments more, and her father bore her, dripping and senseless, to the ladies' cabin, where she soon recovered.

Her father was much rejoiced, and Eva took such a liking for Tom, that she would not rest till the rich Mr. St. Clair had bought him from the trader; and the girl hoped that she would one day get her father coaxed to set him free. From that day Tom and Eva were great friends. The steamer brought them safely to New Orleans. The trader took all his slaves away to sell them in that town; and Tom was taken to Mr. St. Clair's fine house, where you see him and Eva. You may also see the doings of little Topsy, a poor negro child, whom Mr. St Clair bought, and made a present of to his cousin Miss Feely.

"EVA PUTTING A WREATH OF FLOWERS ROUND TOM'S NECK"

Poor Tom is far from his cottage now,
From his own good wife, and children three,
Where coffee, and rice, and cedars grow,
By a wide old river like the sea.

And he has a master rich and kind,
With all that his heart can well desire,
But homeward still goes the negro's mind,
To the curly heads by his cottage fire.

He the gentle Eva's life did save,
When over the great ship's side she fell,
And brought her up from the drowning wave,—
So Eva had grown to love him well.

She will read to Tom for hours on hours,
And sit with him on the grass all day;
You see she is wreathing pretty flowers,
About his neck, in her pleasant play.

Different in colour and in years
Are the negro man and that fair child's face;
But a likeness in God's sight appears,
For both are the children of his grace.

"TOPSY AT THE LOOKING-GLASS"

See little Topsy at the glass quite gay,
Her mistress has forgot the keys to-day,
So she has rummaged every drawer, and dressed
Herself out in Miss Feely's very best.

Mark where she stands! the shawl of gorgeous red
Wound like a Turk's great turban round her head;
A finer shawl far trailing on the floor,
Just shews her bare black elbows, and no more.

With what an air she flaunts the ivory fan,
And tries to step as stately as she can,
Mincing fine words to her own shadow, "Dear!
How very ungenteel the folks are here!"

EVA PUTTING A WREATH OF FLOWERS
ROUND TOM'S NECK.

She will read to Tom for hours on hours,
And sit with him on the grass all day;
You see she is wreathing pretty flowers
About his neck, in her pleasant play.

"Eva Putting a Wreath of Flowers Round Tom's Neck"
Courtesy, American Antiquarian Society.

TOPSY AT THE LOOKING-GLASS.

Mark where she stands! the shawl of gorgeous red
Wound like a Turk's great turban round her head,
A finer shawl for trailing on the floor,
Just shows her bare black elbows, and no more.

"Topsy at the Looking-Glass"
Courtesy, American Antiquarian Society.

197

But while that shadow only Topsy sees,
Back comes the careful lady for her keys,
And finds her in the grandeur all arrayed—
Poor Topsy will be punished, I'm afraid.

Now it is wrong, as every reader knows,
To rummage people's drawers, and wear their clothes;
But Topsy is a negro child, you see,
Who never learned to read like you and me.

A child whom bad men from her mother sold,
Whom a harsh mistress used to cuff and scold,
Whom no one taught or cared for all her days,
No wonder that the girl had naughty ways.

No home, no school, no Bible she had seen,
How bless'd besides poor Topsy we have been!
Yet boys and girls among ourselves, I've known
Puffed up with praise for merits not their own.

The copy by some clever school-mate penned,
The witty saying picked up from a friend,
Makes many a miss and master look as fine,
As if they coined the words or penned the line.

But none can keep such borrowed plumes as these,
For some one still comes back to find the keys,
And so they are found out, it comes to pass,
Just like poor Topsy at the looking-glass

"TOPSY BRINGING FLOWERS TO EVA"

Poor Topsy, trying to be kind,
Has brought a bunch of garden flowers
To Eva, when she lies reclined
Through the bright summer's sultry hours.

For sickness hangs on Eva now,
She can no longer run or play,
Her cheek is pale, her voice is low,
And there she lies the livelong day.

Yet Eva does not fear to die,
She knows a better home remains
For her, beyond the great blue sky,
Where comes no sickness, tears, or pains.

TOPSY BRINGING FLOWERS TO EVA.

"Oh mother dear, let Topsy stay,"
Says Eva in her gentle mood,
"She brought such pretty flowers to-day,
Indeed she's trying to be good."

"Topsy Bringing Flowers to Eva"
Courtesy, American Antiquarian Society.

For in her happier days of health
She read and prized her Bible true,
Above this poor world's pride or wealth,
And loved her blessed Saviour too.

And she like him was kind to all,
And pity on poor Topsy had,
Because the rest would scold and call
Her names, for being black and bad.

So Eva strove to make her good,
And told her, of all tales the best,
How Christ came down to shed his blood,
That sinners might be saved and blest.

Poor Topsy tried to understand—
None ever taught her so before—
And brought the sweet flowers in her hand,—
The negro girl could do no more.

But Eva's proud mamma comes in
With scornful look and frown severe,
She cries, "begone, you nasty thing!
In all the world what brings you here?"

"Oh mother dear, let Topsy stay,"
Says Eva in her gentle mood,
"She brought such pretty flowers to-day,
Indeed she's trying to be good."

"I'm going fast, where there will be
No difference, but in sins forgiven,
And mother it might chance that we
Would bring poor Topsy flowers in heaven."

"DEATH OF EVA"

There is peace on Eva's wasted brow,
And a soft light in her eye;
But her father's heart grows hopeless now,
For he knows that she must die.

Yet the thought is kind and the trust is true,
As she takes him by the hand,—
"Dear father I will look for you
In the light of God's own land.

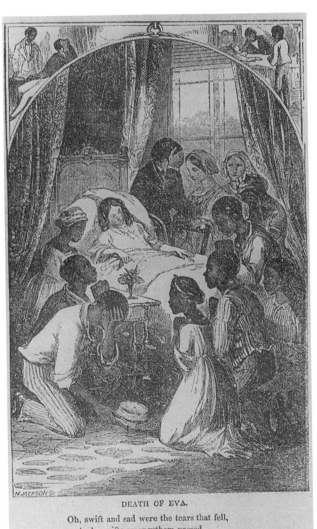

DEATH OF EVA.

Oh, swift and sad were the tears that fell,
As her gifts among them passed,
And Tom, he got the first fair curl,
And Topsy got the last.

"Death of Eva"
Courtesy, American Antiquarian Society.

"Oh let them cut the long, long curls
That flow about my head,
And let our poor kind negroes come
For a moment round my bed.

"They have smoothed and stroked it many a day
In their kindly sport, and care,
And it may be they will think of me
When they see that curling hair."

The negroes loved her, young and old,
With a fond and deep regard,
For Eva's look was never sour,
And her words were never hard.

And her old nurse by the bedside stood,
Sore sobbing in her woe,
That so many sinners here should stay,
And the good and young should go.

"Dear nurse" said Eva "I go home
To the happiest home of all;
Where never an evil thing will come,
And never a tear will fall.

And I will hope each one to see,
That blessed home within;
Where Christ himself will set us free
From the bonds of death and sin."

Oh, swift and sad were the tears that fell,
As her gifts among them passed,
And Tom, he got the first fair curl,
And Topsy got the last.

But first and last alike were given,
With some words of love and prayer;
And it may be, hearts were helped to heaven,
By the links of that soft hair.

When Eva was dead and buried, Tom missed her sore, but he knew it was the will of God, and tried to comfort his master. Mr. St. Clair intended to set him free for Eva's sake. He was a kind man, but given to delay, and one day a wicked man stabbed him in a coffee-house, when he was trying to settle a quarrel. Mrs. St. Clair was a proud, hard-hearted woman, who cared for nobody but herself. She sold all the negroes, and

Tom among them, to a cruel cotton planter, called Legree, and you shall see how he behaved.

"LEGREE STRIKING TOM"

Tom's good wife Chloe, far at home,
  And his boys so blythe and black,
Are all working hard, in hopes to win
  The dollars, to buy him back.

And George, who taught him long ago,
  Has many a pleasant plan,
To pay his price, and set him free,
  When he comes to be a man.

But little does that wicked man,
  In his angry madness, know,
That God himself will take account
  Of each cruel word and blow.

And children dear, who see him here,
  At night and morning pray,
That you may never have aught like this
  Laid up for the judgment day!

By the time all these things happened George Shelby had grown up; but when he came to buy back Tom, the pious, kindly negro, had been so ill-treated by that cruel planter, because he tried to save the other slaves from his evil temper, that he lay dying in an old shed; and there was no law to punish the wicked planter, because Tom was black.

When George entered the shed where Tom lay, he felt his head giddy and his heart sick.

"Is it possible?" said he, kneeling down by him. "Uncle Tom, my poor, poor old friend!"

Something in the voice penetrated to the ear of the dying. He smiled, and said—

"Jesus can make a dying bed
Feel soft as downy pillows are."

Tears fell from the young man's eyes as he bent over his poor friend.

"O, dear Uncle Tom! do wake—do speak once more! Look up. Here's Mas'r George—your own little Mas'r George. Don't you know me?"

LEGREE STRIKING TOM.

But little does that wicked man,
In his angry madness, know,
That God himself will take account
Of each cruel word and blow.

"Legree Striking Tom"
Courtesy, American Antiquarian Society.

"Mas'r George!" said Tom, opening his eyes, and speaking in a feeble voice—"Mas'r George!" He looked bewildered.

Slowly the idea seemed to fill his soul; and the vacant eye became fixed and brightened, the whole face lighted up, the hard hands clasped, and tears ran down the cheeks.

"Bless the Lord! it is—it is—it's all I wanted! They haven't forgot me. It warms my soul; it does my old heart good! Now I shall die content! Bless the Lord, O my soul!"

He began to draw his breath with long, deep aspirations; and his broad chest rose and fell heavily. The expression of his face was that of a conqueror.

"Who—who shall separate us from the love of Christ?" he said, in a voice that contended with mortal weakness; and with a smile he fell asleep.

Beyond the boundaries of the plantation George had noticed a dry, sandy knoll, shaded by a few trees; there they made a grave for poor Tom.

"Shall we take off the cloak, mas'r?" said the negroes, when the grave was ready.

"No, no; bury it with him. It's all I can give you now, poor Tom, and you shall have it."

They laid him in; and the men shovelled away silently. They banked it up, and laid green turf over it.

"You may go, boys," said George, slipping a quarter dollar into the hand of each. They lingered about, however.

"If young mas'r would please buy us," said one.

"We'd serve him so faithful!" said the other. "Do, mas'r, buy us, please!"

"I can't—I can't," said George, with difficulty, motioning them off; "it's impossible!"

The poor fellows looked dejected, and walked off in silence.

"Witness, eternal God," said George, kneeling on the grave of his poor friend—"O witness that, from this hour, I will do *what one man can* to drive out this curse of slavery from my land!"

There is no monument to mark the last resting-place of poor Tom. He needs none. His Lord knows where he lies, and will raise him up immortal, to appear with Him when He shall appear in his glory.

LITTLE EVA SONG.

UNCLE TOM'S GUARDIAN ANGEL.

WORDS BY JOHN G. WHITTIER. . . . . . MUSIC BY MANUEL EMILIO.

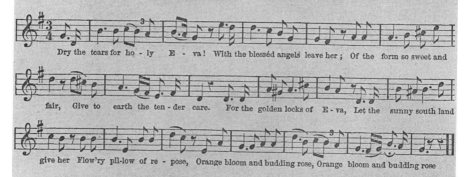

Dry the tears for ho - ly E - va! With the blesséd angels leave her; Of the form so sweet and fair, Give to earth the ten - der care. For the golden locks of E - va, Let the sunny south land give her Flow'ry pil-low of re - pose, Orange bloom and budding rose, Orange bloom and budding rose

All is light and peace with Eva;
There the darkness cometh never;
Tears are wiped, and fetters fall,
And the Lord is all in all.
Weep no more for happy Eva;
Wrong and sin no more shall grieve her,
Care, and pain, and weariness,
Lost in love so measureless!

Gentle Eva, loving Eva,
Child confessor, true believer,
Listener at the Master's knee,
" Suffer such to come to me."
O for faith like thine, sweet Eva,
Lighting all the solemn river,
And the blessing of the poor,
Wafting to the heavenly shore.

THE END.

"Little Eva Song: Uncle Tom's Guardian Angel"
Courtesy, American Antiquarian Society.

From *Little Eva's First Book for Good Children* (ca. 1855)

"Uncle Tom and Little Eva"

Uncle Tom was a slave belonging to a Mr. Shelby, who was compelled to sell poor Tom to pay off his creditors—otherwise he must have been ruined. His cabin was a small cottage built of logs; and in the evening when work was over, Master George Shelby would come and teach him to read and write. A religious meeting of the slaves took place every week in Tom's cabin, where they prayed, they sung [sic]—and happy hours they were, for negroes love music, and have wild airs of their own. Master George would sometimes read a chapter of the bible to them, and they declared it was "reely 'mazin to hear him lay it off, that a minister couldn't do it better." On board the steamer, on the river, in which Tom was being conveyed down south, (the best market for negroes, because they are all slave states,) little Eva was observed flitting about like a sunbeam hovering around the poor fettered negroes. She would look at them in sorrow, lift their chains with her slender hands, and sigh heavily. She had violet blue eyes and golden brown hair, and was dressed in white. Tom had noticed her a long time before he could prevail upon the shy little girl to speak, at last Tom and Eva grew quite familiar. "What's little Missy's name?" said Tom. "Evangeline St. Clare," replied the little one, "but papa and everybody else call me Eva. Now, what's your name?" "My name's Tom, the little children call me Uncle Tom." "Then I shall call you Uncle Tom, because you see I like you," said Eva. "So, Uncle Tom, where are you going?" "I don't know, Miss Eva." "Don't know!" said Eva. "No, I am going to be sold to somebody—I don't know who." "My papa can buy you," said Eva, quickly, "and if he buys you, you will have good times; and I mean to ask him to do so this very day." "Thank you, my little lady," said Tom. That very day, Eva by some accident fell over the side of the steamer into the water. Tom happened to be just at hand, and plunging in brought her safely up. This made Eva still more attached to him, and she begged her kind papa so much to buy him, that he did so and took him home to their house in New Orleans, where he became coachman, and had a very happy home, and a most indulgent good master.

Eva loved the negroes, she loved everybody; but for the black people she felt the most tender pity and she never treated them as slaves, but as fellow creatures. One day her papa brought home a little wild girl about ten years old, who had lived with cruel masters, and never yet heard the voice of love. Hearing herself forever abused and called wicked, she had left off trying to be good, and even when in the same house with Eva, she was at first very naughty. One day, when this was the case, Eva called the child to her and said, "What makes you so bad, Topsy? Don't you love anybody?" "Don't know nothin 'bout love," said Topsy, "I likes candy and such." "Don't you love your father and mother?" "Never had none, I told ye that, Miss Eva." "Oh, yes, I know," said Eva, sadly; "but, Topsy, if you'd only try to be good you might." "Couldn't never be nothing but a nigger if I was ever so good," said Topsy. "But people can love you if you are black, Topsy." "No, there can't nobody love niggers, and niggers can't do nothing," said Topsy; "I don't care," and she began to whistle. "O, Topsy," said Eva, laying her little white hand on Topsy's shoulder, "I love you because you've been a poor abused child. I love you, and want you to be good. And you can be one of those 'spirits bright' that Uncle Tom sings about." Then the black child felt love melt into her darkened soul, and she bowed down her head and wept. "Oh dear, Miss Eva, I will try, I will try. I didn't care before." "Ah," said Eva's papa, who had watched this scene, to her aunt, "It reminds me of what my mother used to tell me, as a child, of Jesus. If we want to do good to the poor, we must call them to us, and put our hands on them."

This example of little Eva all children should follow; and, like Topsy, try to be good.

Little Eva, The Flower of the South (185?)

LITTLE EVA, THE FLOWER OF THE SOUTH

Little Eva lived in the bright sunny South, in the State of Alabama. She was the only daughter of a wealthy planter, who owned many slaves, and a large plantation. Eva was the joy and pride of her parents, she obeyed them in everything; she had a smile or a kind word for all; she is called the Flower of the South.

EVA, TEACHING THE ALPHABET

Here you see, is little Eva teaching the little colored boys and girls the alphabet. See how pleased they are, for they all love Eva, and would do anything to please her; and Eva takes a great deal of pleasure in teaching them and making them happy. She is teaching them the letters one by one, which she marks on the black-board.

EVA VISITING HER OLD NURSE

Eva does not forget her friends, for she calls on her old nurse every day to give her comfort and bring her all the news that is going about, for her nurse is very old and sick. Eva has just brought her some chicken broth; the nurse is always glad to see Eva, and she loves to talk of the time when Eva was a dear little baby.

EVA READING THE BIBLE

It is Sabbath morning, and Eva as usual, is reading the Bible to the colored people; she has learned some of them to read, but they would rather hear Eva read than read themselves, for they say her voice is so sweet; and she always explains all the questions they ask her so pleasantly, that it is a greater pleasure to hear her.

EVA, TAKING A MORNING RIDE

Eva rises early like all good children. Sometimes, when the weather is clear and beautiful, she takes a walk, and gathers a pretty bunch of flowers for her dear mother, who is very fond of them. Eva is riding a pony

"Little Eva, the Flower of the South"
Courtesy, American Antiquarian Society.

"Eva, Teaching the Alphabet"
Courtesy, American Antiquarian Society.

"Eva Visiting Her Old Nurse"
Courtesy, American Antiquarian Society.

this morning; she is not afraid of him, for he is a very kind and gentle animal; he sometimes follows her like a dog.

SAM, SAVING LITTLE EVA FROM DROWNING

Eva has fallen into the water. See how the poor dog is swimming to save her, but he is too late, for Sam is taking her safely out. Poor Eva, she was reaching to catch hold of some grass which grew in the water, when she lost her balance and fell; but she is safe now. She will remember not to play again near the water.

LITTLE EVA'S BIRTH-DAY

This is Eva's birth-day. She is just nine years old; there is double rejoicing, both because Eva was saved from drowning, and because it is her birth-day. See, she is presenting Sam with a beautiful Bible, as a token of her esteem. Eva's parents were so pleased with Sam for saving Eva that they gave him his freedom; but he never left them, he loved them all too well.

"Eva Reading the Bible"
Courtesy, American Antiquarian Society.

"Eva, Taking a Morning Ride"
Courtesy, American Antiquarian Society.

"Sam, Saving Little Eva from Drowning"
Courtesy, American Antiquarian Society.

"Little Eva's Birth-day"
Courtesy, American Antiquarian Society.

NOTES

1. John G. Whittier composed "Little Eva Song. Uncle Tom's Guardian Angel" ([Garrison, William Lloyd]); Mary A. Collier composed "Eva's Parting Word" ([Dwight, J. S.?]); J. E. Carpenter created "The Little Evangelist" ([Uncle Tom's Companions]); and Linley wrote the ballad, "A Tear for Poor Tom" ([Uncle Tom's Companions]).

2. Between 1852 and 1863 stage adaptations and minstrel shows appeared in several theaters, including performances at the National Theater in New York and the Washington Theater (see *The Daily Tribune*, *The Philadelphia Press*, and *The New York Herald*).

3. According to C.W.K.,

> "The people of Boston, and of large towns generally, have long been accustomed to see Uncle Toms, Evas, and Topsys without number, in engravings of various degrees of merit and price. Lately, they have been represented in beautiful and spirited engravings printed in oil colors, by Baxter, or some of his imitators; and now I find not only large engraved heads, in the finest style of Parisian mezzotint, one of Uncle Tom, life-size, and another of Eva and Topsy, but a group in real bronze, showing Eva putting the wreath of jessamines around Tom's neck, and separate statuettes of George Harris, and Eliza and her child. I infer, from seeing these elegant and expensive works in the shop windows with Paul and Virginia, Little Nell and Undine, not only that the general heart of humanity has been touched by them as by their predecessors, but that they have an established market value, and that people of wealth and taste now begin to seek such works as the ornaments of their parlors and chambers" (203).

4. According to an unsigned article in *The Independent*, "V.S.W. Parkhurst, Providence, has published a box of cards called "The New and Interesting Game of Uncle Tom and Little Eva," the interest of which consists in the continual separation and reunion of families. Sold [for 25 cents] by Leavitt & Allen" ([Uncle Tom's Companions] 207).

5. For a complete analysis of Eva acting as an abolitionist in *Uncle Tom's Cabin*, see De Rosa 120–133.

AUNT MARY

(PSEUDONYM. BIOGRAPHY AND DATES UNKNOWN)

In *The Edinburgh Doll and Other Tales for Children* (1853; text reprinted here represents 1854 Jewett edition), Aunt Mary overtly challenges Stowe's story of Little Eva; however, Aunt Mary's life story remains an enigma. Archival research suggests that the Aunt Mary pseudonym *may* belong to a Mrs. Hughs, the author of *Aunt Mary's Tales for the Entertainment and Improvement of Little Girls, Addressed to Her Nieces* (1817), *Aunt Mary's Stories for Children Chiefly Confined to Words of Two Syllables* (1823), *Aunt Mary's Stories for Children* (1850), *Aunt Mary's Multiplication* (1850–1859?) and several other children's books published in New York, Boston, and Philadelphia. However, attributing Aunt Mary's *The Edinburgh Doll and Other Tales for Children* (1853) to Mrs. Hughs would be a conjecture because of the inability to confirm a definitive "Mrs. Hughs"; the geographic and chronological variance in publication history for "Mrs. Hughs"; and the possibility of other women using "Aunt Mary" as a pseudonym. Consequently, we can only speculate about the domestic abolitionist who protected her identity when she submitted *The Edinburgh Doll and Other Tales for Children* to John P. Jewett, to publish from his Boston and Ohio offices.

The Edinburgh Doll[1] encourages children, especially girls, to celebrate abolitionism. In this narrative poem, Mary and her doll embody heroic nonconformists who participate in a public forum to advance abolitionism. As a first-person narrator, the doll recalls her journey from Scotia to the antislavery fair and auction at Boston's Horticultural Hall. The doll offers young readers a glimpse into the international and national efforts to use antislavery fairs as a means to abolish American slavery. She also documents the range of products, such as needlework, "books [specifically *Uncle Tom's Cabin*], portraits, puzzles, medals, games" (see line 25) and so forth, that were sold at these fairs. More important, she remembers her owner, Mary, as a heroic female whose abhorrence of slavery's violation of Christian principles of brotherhood and love motivates her to donate her doll at the Boston Anti-Slavery Fair. Like Little Eva from Harriet Beecher Stowe's novel, Mary dies in the midst of her abolitionist efforts; consequently, Mary's mother carries out her daughter's work.

Interestingly, while Aunt Mary may have used *Uncle Tom's Cabin* (to which she makes an intertextual reference), as a model, her juvenile text empowers females—Mary, her mother, and her doll—not only to voice their political views but also to participate as successful public, abolitionist activists.

THE EDINBURGH DOLL
AND OTHER TALES FOR CHILDREN (1854)

Dedicated by Little Mary to All the Children Who Read it.

"THE STORY OF THE EDINBURGH DOLL"

On ocean wide I tossed about,
   'Mid stormy waves, full many a day,
And glad was I to hear the cry
   That we were safe in Boston's bay.

For I had come from Scotia's land;
   And if you'll read my simple rhyme,
Who sent me here, and why I came,
   You'll know it all, dear child, in time.

When first in Horticultural Hall
   I was uncased and brought to light,
Such brilliant things around me shone,
   My eyes were dazzled at the sight.

For busy hands in other lands
   Had worked and toiled for many a day,
And sent most rare and costly gifts
   To add to all this rich display.

I could not ever hope to tell
   Of all the treasures rich and gay,
Which from your own and other climes
   Were gathered in the hall that day.

The tables rare, the flowers fair,
   The needle-work so gay and bright—
Statues and toys for girls and boys—
   I could not tell you all till night.

Books, portraits, puzzles, medals, games,
   Sweet-scented fans from climes afar,
Glass, china, bronze, of thousand names,
   Had come to grace the great bazaar.

And useful things of various kinds,
   Many from here, and some from home;
And pictures rare—I saw one there
   Of Eva and poor Uncle Tom.

Girl holding doll
Courtesy, American Antiquarian Society.

I thought *I* should a stranger be,
   When brought to this far-distant shore;
Yet many in that hall, it seemed,
   Had heard of humble me before.

And heeding not the riches rare,
   Gathered with pains from land and sea,
Passing the thousand treasures there,
   They came and stood to gaze on me.

Adults and children at an anti-slavery booth
Courtesy, American Antiquarian Society.

And as they gazed, I saw the tears
    Slowly beneath the eyelids fall,
As sadly, tenderly they said,
    "So this is *little Mary's doll*."

And many sought the doll to buy,
    (Only because I once was *hers*,)

So many wished for me that I
    Might have found fifty purchasers.

And why are all these precious things
    Gathered from places near and far,
And why have those in other lands
    Helped to enrich the great bazaar?

Ah, they have heard a cry of woe
    From thousands in this same fair land,
And while their tears of pity flow,
    They stretch to them a helping hand.

They've heard of those in southern climes,
    Who 'neath a cruel bondage groan,
And they have felt that these are *men*,
    Though with a skin unlike their own.

Men for whom Jesus Christ hath died,
    On whom he looks with eyes of love,
And who, though chained and fettered here,
    May conquerors reign with him above.

And they would aid to speed the day
    When every yoke shall broken be;
When chains shall fall which bind the slave,
    And "every bondman shall be free."

And this is why they've worked and toiled,
    And sent their precious gifts so far;
This is why Mary begged that I
    Might come for sale to the bazaar.

I once was little Mary's doll—
    In Edinborough [sic] town she dwelt;
And when a Christmas gift I came,
    How happy little Mary felt.

But she had heard the story too
    Of those who in sad bondage wail;
She scarce could think such things were true—
    It made her lovely cheek turn pale.

She had seen one in her own land,
    Who his escape from bondage made;
She heard that he could not return,
    Until his ransom had been paid.

"And is it so indeed!" she cried;
  "Have those oppressors ever read
Of the good Jesus—he who died
  For all the souls his hands have made?

"And have they heard that he hath said
  Of every man, 'he is thy brother?'
And do they know that sweet command,
  'My children, love ye one another?'"

She scarcely could believe that those
  Who knew their Master's will so well,
Should slight it thus, and, sighing, said,
  "Then Satan in their hearts must dwell."

And when she heard of efforts made
  For freedom's cause in lands afar,
With eager look she begged and prayed
  To send her doll to the bazaar.

"I'll make her pretty clothes myself,
  Dear mother, if you'll let me try;"
But ere her work of love was done,
  Sweet Mary laid her down to die.

They laid her gently on her bed,
  From which she never more might rise;
The rosy cheek now lost its bloom,
  The brightness faded from her eyes.

When she was told that she must die,
  And leave her loving friends so dear,
Calmly she heard without a sigh—
  Her heart was fixed—she felt no fear.

Nor did she seem to feel regret,
  For Heaven was present to her view;
But once she gently whispered low,
  "My poor mamma, I'll pray for you!"

Calm, gentle, patient, Mary lay,
  Through sleepless nights of pain severe;
And much she feared that others might
  Suffer neglect because of her.

And when the wintry morning dawned,
  She often to her nurse would say,

Mother, daughter, and doll
Courtesy, American Antiquarian Society.

"Don't let the cinder gatherer old
    Wait for her crusts this cold, dark day.

"And pray don't let poor Mrs. A—
    Wait for her breakfast, nursey dear,
She works so very hard all day—
    I will not miss you, never fear."

A poor old bird, now blind with age,
   Which carefully she used to tend,
Hung in the nursery, in his cage—
   "He'll miss," said she, "his little friend."

"Poor lonely thing, how dull he'll feel,
   So old he is, and lame and blind;
Dear mother, when you go from town,
   Pray do not leave my bird behind[.]

"But take him in the coach with you,
   And in the long, bright summer day,
Take care of him, as I have done;
   Mary will then be far away."

And just before her eyelids closed,
   To ope in yonder heavenly clime,
She raised her head and said, "Mamma,
   Pray tell me, if you please, the time."

And then she asked, "Now what's the time
   In states where slaves in bondage are?
Do tell me, if you can, mamma—
   Tell me if it is nighttime there."

It was; and laying back her head,
   With peaceful look on lip and brow,
"I'm glad it's night with them," she said;
   "No toil, no sorrow there, just now."

Then starting suddenly, again—
   "But those in other lands afar,
The children in the Kaffir tribes,
   May have sore frightened hearts, Mamma."

"But Mary, dear, don't you forget
   What you've so often said to me,
That the good God is every where,
   Here and in lands beyond the sea,

"Watching the creatures He has made—
   No place, no clime where He is not?"
"O, ay!" dear little Mary said,
   "I *had* almost forgotten that!"

And then she murmured to herself,
   "There's Jesus, Peter, James, and John,
And all the holy angels there
   Are ever singing round the throne.

Death-bed scene
Courtesy, American Antiquarian Society.

"O, sweetly, sweetly now they sing,
　　But we can't hear them yet, mamma;"
Then quickly, hastily she cried,
　　"I'm going, mother—call papa!"

"Dear, good papa, good bye," she said;
　　"Now, don't for little Mary fret;
Nursey, my little sister bring—
　　The dear wee darling, dear wee pet."

"The baby's sleeping, Mary, dear"—
　　"Then don't disturb her from her rest;

But kiss her soft, wee cheek for me,
  And tell her Mary's with the blest.

"Good by, once more"—death's icy chill
  Was on her brow as cold as stone;
That loving little heart was still—
  Sweet Mary stood before the throne.

They gently kissed her marble brow,
  And laid the loved one 'neath the sod—
Her *body only*. Mary, now
  A little saint, is with her God.

And every thing she loved in life,
  And all who did her kindness share,
By Mary's friends are minded still—
  Watched over with a tenfold care.

The old blind bird she loved so well
  Has not been left her loss to feel;
And none for whom she would have cared
  Now to her friends in vain appeal.

And I was taken from her drawer,
  And all my clothes, so nicely made,
Were from her little workbox brought,
  Where they were all so neatly laid.

The work begun by Mary's hands,
  Those hands now moldering in the grave,
By others now has finished been,
  And sent to aid the suffering slave.

And in the last great gathering day,
  Will not dear Mary's blessing be—
"Ye did it to the least of these,
  And thus ye did it unto me"?

And to the children I would say,
  Whate'er your hands may find to do,
O, do it quickly now, I pray,
  For short may be the time for you.

The taper which a little child
  Carried a short time in her hand
Shines brightly now above her grave—
  Shines e'en to this far distant land.

O, may it beam upon the heart
  Of every sister, every brother;

Like Mary's may your motto be,
  "Dear little children, love each other."

"THE STORY OF HELEN, GEORGE, AND LUCY"

"O Mother, I am so glad you have got home!" said Lucy. "I have been studying very hard, and have learned eight lines of poetry to say to you, besides my lesson. Are you ready to hear me say them?"

"In a few minutes; let me see what they are," said her mother.

"I think they are very pretty," said Lucy. "Do not you?"

"Yes; I have always liked those lines exceedingly, and now I shall be glad to hear you repeat them."

Lucy began:—

" 'I would not have a slave to till my ground,
To carry me, to fan me while I sleep,
And tremble when I wake, for all the wealth
Which sinews, bought and sold, have ever earned.
No, dear as freedom is, and in my heart's
Just estimation prized above all price,
I had much rather be myself the slave,
And wear the chains, than fasten them on him.' "

"Did you select this passage yourself, my dear?" said her mother.

"No, mother; brother George chose it for me."

"I like them better than any lines I know," said George. "It is so noble to be willing to be a slave, and to suffer the hardships of a slave, rather than to make anyone else suffer them."

"What is a slave?" said little Helen. "Is it any body that works very hard?"

"No," said her father. "I have been working very hard at my office to-day, and John Wilson has worked very hard sawing wood for us, and he works very hard every day; but we are neither of us slaves. But if I were forced to work for some other person, and to do whatever he told me to do, without my having agreed with him to work for him, and if this man could beat me and punish me if I did not do what he liked, and could sell me to somebody else, and could do almost any thing he chose to me, then I should be his slave. Do you understand me, Helen?"

"Yes," said Helen. "But I should not think you ought to have to work

Death-bed scene, 2
Courtesy, American Antiquarian Society.

for the man, unless you told him you were willing to work for him if he would give you some money. That's the way John Wilson does when he comes to work here, is it not?"

"Yes, certainly it is," said her father.

"And would the man sell you if you were his slave?" said Helen.

"Yes, masters very often sell their slaves."

"And what," said Helen, "would the person that bought you do with you?"

"Perhaps," said her father, "he would carry me away to some other place, and make me work for him."

"I should not like to have him carry you away from all of us. Father, how could you come to be any body's slave?"

"My dear little girl," said her father, "I believe I am in no danger of being made any body's slave, and carried away from you. But I can tell you about the poor people who are slaves, if you would like to hear about them."

Ships
Courtesy, American Antiquarian Society.

"O, yes," said Helen, "do tell me."

"Begin about their being brought from Africa," said George.

"In Africa," said their father, "is the country where the negroes or black people live. People used to go there in ships, and take the negroes away, and then sell them for slaves. The people of some countries do so still."

"What did they do so for?" said Helen.

"The people who bought them wanted to have slaves to work for them, and the people who carried them away from Africa wanted to get money by selling them," said her father.

"I think," said Lucy, "they had better been poor all their lives, than to have got money by being so wicked."

"Was it wicked?" said Helen.

"Why, Helen!" said Lucy, in a tone of great astonishment and indignation, "don't you think it would be wicked for any body to come and steal you away, and carry you off where you would never see papa, or mamma, or me, or brother George, or any body who cared any thing about you again, and then sell you to be somebody's slave as long as you lived, who would make you work very hard, and whip you with a great horsewhip if he was angry with you?"

"O, it would be very, very wicked!" said Helen, almost crying.

"My dear Lucy," said her father, "you have quite frightened your little sister. Helen, you are in no danger of being carried off; but some of the little black children were carried away from their homes, in this way, and sometimes the fathers and mothers were carried away, and the poor little children left without any body to take care of them."

"I don't know," said Lucy, "how they could get such a great number of black people as have been brought to America and the West Indies."

"The slave traders," said her father, "either stole the negroes, or bought them of any body who would sell them. Then these poor people, Helen, were put on board the ships which sailed away with them across the ocean. When they got to the country they were going to, the masters who bought the poor slaves set them to work, and these people and their children are the slaves spoken of in the poetry Lucy has been saying:—

'I would not have a slave to till my ground,
To carry me, to fan me while I sleep.'

"These were things the slaves were employed to do. When it was very hot, the masters and mistresses sometimes made their slaves fan them while they were asleep. But Mr. Cowper, who wrote these lines, thought it was very wicked to keep people slaves, and says he would not have a slave to do these things for him."

"'And tremble when I wake,'" said Lucy. "I suppose he thought the poor slaves must be very much afraid of their masters. I do not wonder he did not want to have any body so afraid of him as to hate to have him wake up. There is one line I do not quite understand, mother. Why does he say 'sinews bought and sold'? I know the sinews are some part of the body, but the slave's sinews are not bought and sold any more than the rest of him."

"The sinews," said her mother, "are what give men strength; and it is by using their strength and sinews in labor that slaves make their masters rich. But Cowper would not have had one of his fellow-creatures for a slave for all the riches which all the men who have ever been bought and sold for slaves in the world could gain for their masters."

"I should think," said Lucy, "that Mr. Cowper must have been a very good man, if he really felt just as he says in these lines—if he really would have preferred to be a slave himself, which must be such a dreadful thing, rather than make any body else a slave."

"Why, Lucy," said George, "what should make you think of doubting that Cowper really meant what he said?"

"I don't know," said Lucy; "sometimes things in books are not real things."

"Cowper *was* a very good man," said her mother, "and, I have no doubt, felt all that he expresses, that he would much more willingly have *worn the chains himself* than have fastened them on another."

"Were the slaves really chained?" said Lucy, "or does he only say chains *figuratively*, because they were not free?"

"They are often really chained," said her mother, "but perhaps he meant it both ways. You seemed to doubt, Lucy, whether the poet really felt as he says; but should not you rather be the person who was hurt, than knowingly to hurt any body yourself?"

"To be sure!" said George.

"I don't know," said Lucy.

"Well, you may sleep upon it," said their mother, "and consider the question to-morrow, for it is time to go to bed."

NOTE

1. For a complete discussion of *The Edinburgh Doll*, see De Rosa, 134–135.

GRANDMOTHER

(BIOGRAPHY AND DATES UNKNOWN)

Published as part of John P. Jewett's Juvenile Anti-Slavery Toy Books series, *Grandmother's Stories for Little Children*[1] (1854) cleverly depicts girls and women giving voice to an abolitionist agenda. In "Grandmother's Story," Lizzy Howard and her brothers, Charlie and Willie, live with their maternal grandmother in the North because on her deathbed, their dying mother requested that her children not grow up in the South, where their experience with slavery would most likely lead to their support for the institution and the ownership of slaves. Despite their geographical separation from Southern slavery, the children still come to learn about slavery from "Grandmother's Story" and "Aunt Nelly," the African American servant whom grandmother conceals from slave-catchers. Although it grieves Lizzie to hear these stories, she *must* listen. Her own mother's act of intercession serves as a model for a series of rebellious women (Nelly, Mrs. Walberg, and Grandmother) who tactfully subvert men and their laws that support slavery so as to restore a semblance of American familial and political ideals (De Rosa 66).

Grandmother's collection also includes two pseudo-slave narratives that give a fictional child first-hand knowledge of slavery. In "Aunt Nelly," the former slave gives Lizzie a detailed narrative that adds to the information the child learns from her grandmother. Similarly, in "Old Cæsar" a young white child (perhaps Lizzie?) asks a former slave to narrate his life history. In the *only* recovered work from a slave father's perspective, Cæsar's narrative follows the pattern of an authentic slave narrative in that he reveals the sorrow that ensued from being torn from his family, his new consciousness about his powerlessness as a slave father and husband, which in turn motivates his escape. Like Henry Box Brown (see 167–169), Cæsar secures his freedom (though he does not reveal how he did so, as is the case in many authentic slave narratives), but notes his unhappiness. For Cæsar, freedom heightens the memory of his lost family and his inability to restore his violated domestic realm.

The stories in Grandmother's collection raise important questions about the power of sentimentality.[2] Can tears effect change? Scholars of nineteenth-century American literature disagree. Philip Fisher and Ann Douglas suggest the very limited power of sentimental literature to effect change. In contrast, Nina Baym, Catherine E. O'Connell, Helen Waite Papashvily, and Jane Tompkins argue that women authors employed sentimental literature to arouse sympathy that would in turn raise consciousness and effect change. By literally including the fictional white listener (Lizzie and other children) in the collection, Grandmother highlights the importance of listening to stories of the slaves' plight because knowledge arouses sympathy and a desire to respond, if only with a child's prayers of intercession at first. Domestic in its emphasis on the ruptured family and sentimental in its preponderance of tears, Grandmother's collection derives its political nature by insinuating that prayer serves as an intermediary form of intervention until the child can exert public, political influence (De Rosa 55).

From *Grandmother's Stories for Little Children* (1854)

"GRANDMOTHER'S STORY"

It wanted but a few days to Lizzie Howard's birthday, and she was very busy planning how she should spend it: she knew her kind grandmamma would let her have her choice. "How very pleasant it will be, grandmamma," said Lizzie, "having my birthday come on Saturday; for the boys will be at home, and you will let me ride on Charlie's pony, and he or Willie can ride grandpapa's old Buck! It will be so nice!" And the little girl skipped about with delight.

"Well, after the ride, grandmamma, what shall we do?"

"I advise you to wait, my dear, until Saturday comes, and see what kind of weather it will bring; then you can determine what you will do: there is not much dependence on April sunshine."

My little readers may wish to know why Lizzie lived with her grandparents. Her mother was their only child. At an early age she married her cousin, Mr. Charles Howard, of Georgia, and accompanied him immediately to his southern home. The second year of her marriage she had twins, little sons, Charlie and Willie, as they were called. Mrs. Howard was so delicate after the birth of her children, that, as soon as she was able to travel, her husband brought her north to her anxious parents and the home of her childhood.

She never returned south. Mr. Howard spent his summers with her, but was obliged to return every winter to see after his large plantation.

When Charlie and Willie were two years old Mrs. Howard had a little girl, born at her grandfather's: the mother lived only a few days, leaving her little orphans to the care of her deeply-afflicted parents, and committing them to a covenant-keeping God, praying fervently that he would so order their lives that they might be kept from ever being slaveholders, and brought up and educated at the north.

Their father was perfectly willing to yield to his wife's dying requests; and the children had never known any other home than Maple Grove, and desired no other. Their grandparents were very indulgent to them; and their father, marrying again after a few years, did not give himself any anxiety about them, occasionally making them a short summer's visit, leaving them to the entire control of their grandparents, knowing that they would inherit their large estate.

The boys had been for two years at an excellent boarding school, only three miles from Maple Grove, their grandfather's residence, and came home every Saturday and remained until Monday; but Lizzie could not be parted with even to attend a day school, and her grandmamma, so far, had educated her herself.

When Lizzie opened her eyes, Saturday morning, the rain was beating against her window, and every thing out looked dismal enough. She could scarcely keep from crying; but she did not fret; for she knew that God sent the rain, and her grandmamma had taught her it was very wicked to find fault with what God did, and very silly too; for it could do no good, and he did every thing right; and, when any thing worried or troubled her, that she might go to God and tell him of it.

Lizzie struggled hard to keep back the tears, and her eyes looked very watery; but, washing and dressing herself, she knelt down by her little bed and said her morning prayer, "Our Father who art in heaven:" then she prayed that God would keep her from fretting about the rain, and make her patient all the day, though she should not be able to go out; and asked him, in her own simple language, if "he would please to make the sun shine, and let her dear brothers come."

When Lizzie rose from her knees she felt a great deal happier; and, when she met her grandmamma in the breakfast room, she looked so bright, grandmamma kissed her, and called her her "sweet little daughter," and told her "how glad she was to see her bear a disappointment so well;" and "she need not ask her if she had said her prayers, for she was sure she had sought for strength from her heavenly Father."

Mrs. Howard determined to make it a happy day to Lizzie in the house; and, after breakfast and prayers, she took her into the library. In the bow window stood Lizzie's "own little table," as she called it, full of parcels, with her name written on. She did not know which to open first.

There was a beautiful "workbox from grandmamma;" a "portfolio from grandpapa," filled with writing materials and many very pretty books; for every servant in the family had placed a gift there for "Miss Lizzie." She was a great darling with them all. After she had admired them again and again, grandmamma took from the window seat a little flower pot, over which was a coffee cup. On removing the cup, she displayed the tiniest rosebush, with the tiniest rosebud, just beginning to unfold its perfect little leaves. Lizzie's joy and wonder were unbounded.

"O grandmamma, how beautiful! Did you ever see any thing so perfect? Where did it come from? And is it mine?" exclaimed Lizzie, without waiting for a reply.

"Yes, dear; it is aunt Nelly's present to you. A lady, knowing her fondness for plants, sent her two last fall from the city, and she has been nursing this all winter very secretly for you: last evening she gave it to Robert for 'young missis.'"

"How good she is to me," said Lizzie, when it was sent to her! "Does it seem possible, grandmamma, that it can be a real rosebush? I never saw one before."

"They are very rare," said Mrs. Howard. "I do not recollect their botanical name, but have heard them called the 'miniature rose.'"

The morning passed so quickly with Lizzie, in arranging her presents, admiring her rosebud, and talking with grandmamma, that she was quite astonished when the dinner bell rang.

"Can it be two o'clock, grandmamma?"

"No, dear; only one o'clock. Your grandpapa wished an early dinner, that he might ride into town when Robert goes for your brothers."

"Then they will not be here to dine with us, grandmamma?"

"No, Lizzie; we shall look for them at three o'clock."

She was much disappointed; but, when they went down to the dining room, the sun came out from under a cloud and sent its beams dancing through the windows, promising a lovely afternoon. All dark shadows fled from Lizzie's face; and she seemed like a sunbeam herself, sent to gladden the hearts of her dear grandparents.

"Well, my little daughter," said Mr. Howard, "you see the sun, after all, will do his part towards brightening your birthday; though he was sulky this morning, and would not show his face to greet you."

"Yes, grandpapa. I asked God, this morning, if he would not please to make the sun shine; and he heard me. I ought to be very good, I am sure."

"We should be thankful for all the mercies he bestows on us, my child. Well, what will grandmamma and you do, to get clear of the two hours, before I can return with the boys. Time drags heavily when we are waiting."

"O, grandmamma will tell me a long-promised story."

After dinner, Lizzie stood at the window to watch her grandpapa's setting off. When he was fairly out of sight she followed her grandmamma to her room, and begged her to tell her how Nelly came to live with her, and how she got away from her "mas'r Dick."

"I am afraid, my dear," said Mrs. Howard, "it is too sad a tale for a birthday. You know that you were so excited when she only related to you the beginning of her troubles that I feared it would make you sick."

"I think, grandmamma, I shall not feel as bad to hear you relate it as I did when aunt Nelly's sorrowful face was before me."

"Her history, my love, is only that of hundreds of her unfortunate race, whose sufferings have had no alleviation, who have only found rest in their graves. Aunt Nelly's old age is one of comparative comfort. But I will give you her sad life of bondage as she has told it to me at different times. I shall relate it in as brief a manner as possible. She endured every cruelty that a passionate, unfeeling master could inflict. He permitted her to marry a young slave of his to whom she was much attached; then in a few years sold him, and thus separated them forever. She had two children at the time—one an infant, the other three years old. It was not long before her eldest child sickened and died; and 'she rejoiced,' she says, 'when she followed him to his quiet little grave.'"

"Rejoiced when her own child died, grandmamma!" exclaimed Lizzie.

"Yes, my dear; its death was preferable to the service of a cruel master."

"How dreadful, grandmamma!"

"Well, her 'mas'r Dick' married a very fine woman, who tried, though frequently in vain, to relieve her poor slaves and lighten their yoke of bondage."

"What was her master's name?" said Lizzie.

"Walberg; he was a relative of your father's."

"I am sorry to hear that he was a relation of ours, grandmamma."

"To return to my story," said Mrs. Howard. "Mrs. Walberg took a great fancy to Nelly and her child, and persuaded Mr. Walberg to let her have Nelly as her maid, one summer, when she was coming north. She knew that he thought of selling her, and very probably would separate her from her child, and urged him to defer it, at last, until their return in the fall. The Walbergs brought letters of introduction to your grandpapa from some very dear friends in Georgia; and we were so much pleased with Mrs. W. that we invited her to remain with us whilst her husband went farther north. She had a lovely little girl of two years old, and Nelly her maid; and, what for some time seemed very unaccountable to us, Nelly's child came too. One day I remarked to Nelly that she was blessed with a good master and mistress, to allow her to bring on her own child.

"'Tis all missis, ma'am; Mas'r Dick no let her come. Missis get her mother send one of her niggers to her, and she mak him tak Juley down to ship, tell captain keep her till we cum; so mas'r never know Juley there for three days; then he swear and rave, say 'he throw her overboard;' but missis she let him go on, say nothin', till he talk out. She manage him such a quiet way. O, Nelly serve her all her life."

"We regretted much parting with our new friends. They promised to write as soon as they reached their home. But months passed, and we did not hear of them. A terrible epidemic had been raging in Philadelphia,—some said it was typhoid, some yellow fever,—and it spread into some of the neighboring villages, cutting off our communication with the city. As the Walbergs were to spend some time there on their way home, we had felt considerable anxiety about them. It was a dismal, stormy evening, early in December: your grandpapa was absent from home. I was sitting alone in the parlor, when Willis, then quite a lad, put his head in the door, saying, 'Mistress, poor creature in the kitchen, most froze, and little girl too.' I hurried out and found poor Nelly almost speechless and stiff with cold. I recognized her at once as Mrs. Walberg's maid. Little Juley was not in as bad a condition as her mother: to screen her, Nelly had taken off her own shawl and wrapped her in it. She could not speak to be understood. I gave them warm tea and had a bed prepared for them: gradually they began to revive. Nelly's feet were so frozen I thought that she would lose them entirely; but good nursing for a few days restored them. When the poor creature was sufficiently recovered to talk, she told me, in her simple language, how they had traveled about after they left us and reached Philadelphia, supposing the fever had gone, when Mrs. Walberg's little girl was attacked with it and died: then Mrs. Walberg was taken down, and lingered for weeks. Having a strong constitution, it triumphed over the disease, and she got able to sit up. Her physicians said it would be some time before she would be able to travel. Mr. Walberg felt that it was necessary for him to return south immediately; and he left his wife, designing to come back for her or send her brother. Nelly had proved herself such a faithful nurse that even her master's heart was softened towards her. Not many days after Mr. Walberg's departure, Mrs. Walberg felt so much improved that she sent for a carriage; and, contrary to the remonstrance of her devoted attendant, she would visit the grave of her darling child. The effort and the renewal of her grief caused a relapse, and she sunk rapidly. Aware of her situation, she told Nelly as soon as she was gone to escape with her child before her master was summoned back, and directed her to me for succor and protection. The faithful creature closed her mistress's eyes, and then watched by her lifeless remains until they were borne by her physicians to a vault, to await the arrival of Mr. Walberg, who had been summoned immediately. Nelly then put all her mistress's clothes and jewelry into her trunks, locked them, and gave the keys to Dr. R. He insisted upon Nelly's going to his house and remaining until her master came for her. Poor Nelly had no desire to return south to her former state of servitude, and determined to follow her mistress's dying command; but how to find us she did not know. She did not dare ask any questions that might excite suspicion. She knew that we lived somewhere on the river that they traveled on to get to the city. She did not even burden herself with her clothes and Juley's any more than they could wear. The evening before the doctor was to have them removed to his house, Nelly, with Juley in her arms, left the boarding house. Wandering from one street to another, occasionally sitting down on the steps of a house to rest, before morning she had got down to the river. God alone guided her; for earthly guidance she had not. The Delaware was frozen over; and, thinking she should be more safe from pursuit on the opposite side, she crossed it. She met kind persons, who gave her milk for her child and food for herself, but asked her no questions. She ventured to inquire for our residence, and finally reached us in the condition I told you."

Lizzie, who had scarce taken her eyes from her grandmother's face, and had listened with almost breathless attention, burst forth,—

"O grandmamma, she was safe when she had got to you! How glad I am! I was afraid you would say, the doctor followed and overtook her."

"I don't know what he did," said Mrs. Howard; "but I was very sure that her master would be after her, and I was determined to save her if I could. As I told you, your grandpapa was very fortunately away from home, attending the legislature, and I had Nelly boarded in the country for several weeks in a farmer's family. Mr. Walberg wrote to your grandpapa informing us of his trials, of Nelly's escape, and wished to know if he had seen any thing of her. I had prepared for all this by keeping your grandpapa in ignorance of Nelly's arrival, that he could reply, with perfect truth, that 'he knew nothing about her.'"

"O, that was good, grandmamma!"

"There is little else to add. We hired Nelly for many years, and a more faithful servant I never had; but she had been so broken down by the cruel treatment she had received in her youth that she became prematurely old. I taught her about her Savior. God blessed my efforts; and I believe that she is a true follower of our blessed Master."

"Thank you, dear grandmamma, for telling me. I hope that none of father's slaves will ever suffer. I mean to beg him, when he comes again, to set them all free."

"I wish you could, my dear," said Mrs. Howard."

"Here, here are the boys, grandmamma!" exclaimed Lizzie. "I had really forgotten that we were waiting for them." And away she ran to meet them.

"AUNT NELLY"

"O Grandmamma, do you know aunt Nelly is sick?" said Lizzie Howard, as soon as she saw grandmamma in the morning.

"Yes, my dear; I heard it last evening, and sent Rachel down to stay with her. She has just been up to my room to say it was only a turn of cramp and she is much better; and you may go and sit with her to-day if you please, as you have no school, and she loves to have you read to her."

"Thank you, thank you, grandmamma!" And she jumped about with delight; for Lizzie was only ten years old, and a joyous little girl. "Minnie White wanted me to spend the afternoon with her; but I would rather go and see aunt Nelly, as she is sick. Perhaps she will tell me what makes her so sad sometimes; while she says God is so good to her, and you and grandpapa are so good to her, that she never wants any thing."

"You must not tease her, Lizzie," said Mrs. Howard; "for poor Nelly has had a great deal of trouble in her life; and when she feels like it, I dare say that she will tell you all about it."

"Don't you think she will to-day, grandmamma?"

"I cannot say, my impatient little girl: it is a long story and a sad one. You know that she was born a slave."

"Slaves are not always unhappy, are they, grandmamma?"

"That depends upon their masters and mistresses: but I suspect that they would all tell you that they would be much happier free."

Soon as Lizzie finished her breakfast, she could scarcely wait for her grandmamma to finish hers and fix a basket of nice things for aunt Nelly, she was so anxious to be off. It was a lovely spring morning: the crocuses were peeping up their bright yellow heads, and the robins had just come from their wintering in the south, and were hopping from bush to bush, singing so sweetly, when Lizzie started for her walk. She was as happy as her little favorites, and would like to have stopped and told them how glad she was to see them, and how she hoped that they would make their nests again in the large apple tree by her bed-room window. But her grandmamma had always told her never to stop and talk or play when she sent her with any thing; and the little basket on her arm, laden from grandmamma's pantry, hurried her on.

It was some distance to aunt Nelly's, down in the back street, quite out of the bustle of the town, where old Mr. Howard owned a little cottage, and Nelly had lived in it for several years; but Lizzie's heart was so light she tripped along very fast, and soon reached the wicker gate, and feared that she had come so early her old friend would not be ready to receive a visitor. A tap at the door, and it was opened by an old woman that the children said was "black as a crow," but with such a good-natured face, and such a warm greeting for Lizzie, that she thought she was handsome. Aunt Nelly—for it was she—made a low courtesy [sic], and bade Miss Lizzie walk in.

"I am so glad to see you up, aunt Nelly!" said the little girl. "Grandmamma will let me stay with you and read and talk till I am tired, if you would like to have me!"

"O, yes; so good in old missis, and so good in young missis too! Nelly can no work to-day; she only think—think—and that make her worse; she love to hear Miss Lizzie so well."

Nelly's cottage was no new place to Lizzie; many an hour she had spent in it. But it is to my young readers; and we will take a look round whilst she is enjoying a frolic with Rover, who is giving her a very warm greeting in his expressive dog way, and aunt Nelly has disappeared in a closet to empty the basket, and perhaps refresh herself with some of Mrs. Howard's nice biscuit and ham.

The front door opened into a small sitting room. On the floor is a nice rag carpet: it does not quite cover it, leaving just board enough for aunt Nelly to show how neat she is by keeping it scoured so white that it could be used for a table. Between the two windows, which have very nice white cotton curtains, is a small looking glass; and under it a small stand, with a white cloth upon it and a large book. You know that it is the Bible. Nelly cannot read in it, though Lizzie has tried to teach her; but she loves to look at it and hear "little missis" read it.

Some plain wooden chairs, with two that are cushioned with gay pieces of cloth sewed in stripes, and a little bureau, complete aunt Nelly's parlor furniture: but peep through that partly opened door, and you will see her snug bed room, with a strip of rag carpet before the bed, and a bright calico spread upon it and her snow-white pillow cases; and you wonder where aunt Nelly works.

She has a little shed out of her back door, where she has just moved her stove, and uses it for her summer kitchen; and you conclude that she is very comfortable, and may say, as Lizzie did, "Why does aunt Nelly ever feel bad?"

Aunt Nelly had emptied and washed the plates and put them with the napkin in Lizzie's basket, ready for her to take, and she had said, again and again, "God bless my good missis; too kind to old Nelly;" and then she put a clean white apron on and sat down on her low chair in the corner. Lizzie was very glad to rest too, for she had had such a frolic with Rover; and he laid down at her feet, weary as herself.

"Now, aunt Nelly, what shall I read to you?" said Lizzie.

"Out of God's book, missis, how Jesus Christ died for Nelly and gone to prepare a home for such poor sinner. O, it goes right down into Nelly's poor sinful heart, such great love."

Lizzie got the Bible and read several chapters from the Gospel of John, Nelly often interrupting her with her exclamations. "That's good! Good Savior come to save poor slave! He love Nelly and die for her! O, it give Nelly strength! Young missis love Jesus too."

Lizzie read until she was tired and hoarse: when she stopped she wanted to ask Nelly why she often looked at her so sad and would shake her head; but, recollecting that her grandmamma said she must not tease her, she did not.

"Now young missis tired, Nelly talk to her—she want to tell her many things before she go home. Last night Nelly think she go; had no tell Miss Lizzie all she want to many a long day."

Lizzie wondered what aunt Nelly meant by "going home;" for she often spoke of it, and she knew Nelly had no other home on earth.

"Well, missis, you often think queer me look sad when you come so happy; but me think of Miss Rosey and old missis. They war very kind too; and Nelly play all day long with Miss Rosey and love her so much."

"Were you unhappy then, aunt Nelly? for grandmamma says you were a slave."

"Not then, Miss Lizzie; I no think 'bout any thing but play. My mammy Kate was Miss Rosey's mammy; and Miss Rosey let no one scold Nelly. We play on veranda all day long—then all sunshine—good mas'r and missis. Miss Rosey give Nelly pretty ribbons and nice frocks. Sometimes old missis say, 'Rosey, I must send you away, or else sell Nelly.' She cry; say 'No, no, mamma! I love Nelly!,' and then she put arms round my neck; she no feared black skin. But Mas'r Dick, he no bear me. He very proud, cross, and be angry wid Miss Rosey 'cause she have me on veranda all time. He say he no have black nigger under his foot: then he pinch and strike me when no missis there; but I hollow and run; he hate me more; but Nelly no mind when Miss Rosey come, she so happy; for Miss Rosey always good. Bam by [by and by] Miss Rosey getting big girl, and

missis say she must go to school; but she say she no go without me; but
missis say she must. It was black day when she go; no more sunshine for
poor Nelly. Me see her now: how she cry when she call all servants and
say 'Good by!' say, too, she soon come back; no forget Nelly, but bring
her lots of pretty things; send some by old missis and mammy Kate when
they come. How we all cry too, and 'God bless Miss Rosey!' and carriage
drove off; but she never come back; then come trouble; Nelly happy no
more. Old mas'r went down wid them to Savannah, put them in big ship
to go north to great city: he come home agen. Then times changed; mas'r
kind, but he so easy like, let Mas'r Dick have his own way; he give word,
then blow, sometime blow first; he say I fat, lazy nigger; he make lazy nigger know what work is now my silly young missis gone; should pick cotton. O, how my blood boil when he tell me I be field hand! I know only
play. I tell him me no belong to him; me Miss Rosey's. Then he cuff me;
old mas'r tell him stop for Miss Rosey's sake. Many days pass, no hear
from the missis; then come story big ship lost, and missis both gone;
mammy Kate too. Mas'r tell Jim get up horses, set right off for Savannah.
He and Mas'r Dick go; no sorry he go; but Nelly's heart brak when she
think of them all. She hope it not be true; aunt Elsie say it be, for she
hear owl hooting round house all night, and see ghosts too; she shake
her head—all believe aunt Elsie. Two weeks, then come mas'rs, all dress
black; servants all know then no good news. How they all scream, wring
hands! No more see good missis, Miss Rosey, and my own mammy. Nelly's
heart brak. O, trouble then: old mas'r he no care for any thing."

Tears trickled down old Nelly's cheeks as she recalled all the sorrows
of her childhood, and Lizzie wept with her.

"Don't talk any more now," said the feeling little girl; "it will make you
worse, aunt Nelly."

"Me want to tell you all now, Miss Lizzy [sic]; for God may call Nelly
to come home, and you not know what poor slave suffer, and when Miss
Lizzy [sic] go south have slaves."

"I will never have them!" exclaimed Lizzie, interrupting Nelly.

"Well, Miss Lizzie, me hope so too; but me finish soon. Then Nelly's
troubles only begin. Mas'r Dick now take 'thority; little while he so so;
but soon he 'gin to say niggers nohow impose on him; he have them
whipped. Nelly have no friend left; cry, cry, and no eat. He say eat, or
whip. Nelly have no Savior then; think all her friends gone; she no care
to live. Then Mas'r Dick have her tied up, whipped, whipped; hope now
God forgive him."

"I can't hear any more, Nelly; it makes me sick: some other time," said Lizzie.

"Good grandmamma can tell you rest, Miss Lizzie. Lor' bless her! She make old Nelly full of comfort now."

Lizzie felt that she must get into the air: it was her first lesson in the horrors of slavery, and sickened her young heart.

"Aunt Nelly, it is quite noon; and I will go, and come again."

Putting on her bonnet, and taking her little basket in her hand, she bade aunt Nelly good by with more kindness and tenderness than she had ever done. Rover escorted her some distance; but she could only pat his head in silence. The birds sang as sweetly, the sun shone as brightly, as when she tripped along so happy a few hours before, wondering then that any one could be sad in such a bright, beautiful world. Now every thing seemed changed; her young heart felt ready to burst with sorrow and sympathy for her poor old friend.

When Lizzie reached her grandfather's she ran into her grandmother's room; and, throwing herself into her arms, she burst into tears and wept unrestrained.

"O grandmamma," she exclaimed, "I wish I had never heard about it! Why does God let people be so cruel and wicked? I am sure father does not treat his slaves so. I never, never want to go south, grandmamma."

"Perhaps you never will, my dear," said Mrs. Howard. "We will talk about that another time, and you shall hear how aunt Nelly got her freedom and is now so comfortable."

"OLD CÆSAR"[3]

"Come, now, old Cæsar, sit you down
　In this cool spot of ours,
And let me crown your dear old head
　With this sweet wreath of flowers.

Now leave your work a little while
　And take me on your knee;
And, while I crown you with a wreath,
　A story tell to me.

I like your stories better far
　Than any in my book.
O, how I wish that you could see
　How beautiful you look!

You've told me many a pretty tale
    When we've sat here alone;
But they were all of other men:
    Now tell me, please, your own.

I know that you were once a slave
    And toiled beneath the sun:
But now; old Cæsar, tell to me
    How you your freedom won.

I often see the great tears steal
    Over your cheeks so black:
Is it because you wish to go
    To chains and slavery back?"

"No, missy: no. I pray that I
    May never be a slave again;
For slavery's a bitter thing—
    A life of anguish, tears, and pain.

Yet once I had a happy home;
    A good, kind wife and children dear;
A master good, and kind, and true
    As any I could meet with here.

Yet, then, what was I but a slave?
    Though 'neath the lash I did not groan;
I did not own myself or wife;
    My children,—they were not my own.

I knew that, should old master die,
    We must be scattered far and wide;
And every night, in dreams, I saw
    My loved ones severed from my side.

O, bitter, bitter tears I shed;
    I raised to heaven my hopeless cry:
'O, ere that day, my God, my God,
    Pray let me lay me down to die!'

Vain were my prayers: that wretched day
    Came all too soon: old master died.
Another came his place to take,
    And we were scattered far and wide.

That sad time I remember well
    When we all left our cabin door;

My mistress dear shed many a tear
   And bade us farewell o'er and o'er.

O, who can tell how sad our hearts,
   With bitter grief and anguish torn?
O woe the day!—the dreadful day!
   I wished that I had ne'er been born.

I had short time to say farewell
   To children dear and wife so true:
I loved my children, missy, dear,
   Just as your own papa loves you.

Yet then, alas! I knew I should
   Their faces nevermore behold:
One and another left my side,
   To a more cruel bondage sold.

Unheeded were their anguished prayers;
   Unpitied fell their bitter tears:
I seem to hear their pleadings now;
   I've heard them every day for years:—

'O, starve and beat us as you will,
   And let us nothing know but pain;
Yet grant but this, O master, pray—
   That we *together* may remain.'

With cruel blows their cries were hushed;
   They dragged them from us one by one;
With aching hearts we saw them sold,
   Until at last we stood alone.

Yes, e'en the little one, whose smiles
   Had ever served our hearts to cheer,
Was dragged from its fond mother's arms,
   And taken off we knew not where.

My poor, sad, trembling wife and I
   Drew closer to each other then;
But all in vain. We too, alas!
   Were parted by these cruel men.

Frenzied at heart, yet mute and still,
   In dumb despair I saw her go;
That arm—so strong to work for them,—
   For her it must not strike a blow.

I cared not now what might become
   Of such a wretched thing as me;
For all I loved were scattered now;
   Their forms I nevermore might see.

Yet years of slavery and toil
   Gave me a longing to be free:
My fellow-slaves and I oft talked
   Of the delights of liberty.

Three of us then arranged a plan;
   And one dark night we sallied forth:
We knew not where we were to go,
   But only turned our faces north.

Yet, e'er we many miles had gone,
   Pursuers came upon our track:
Their shouts and cries we plainly heard.
   'O, must we go to bondage back?

'Far rather death!' we cried; and on
   Through bush and brake we bounded;
While now, on our affrighted ears,
   The bay of the bloodhounds sounded.

One poor wretch faltered in the race,
   Weary, and faint, and worn:
They've got him now; alas! he's done,
   By the fierce bloodhounds torn!

On, on they came: with frantic haste
   We dashed the swamps and marshes through;
Until at last the hounds were foiled
   In passing through a deep bayou.

We now laid still till darkness came,
   Then took again our toilsome way;
And so we travelled every night,
   And hid like felons through the day.

God guided us, and guarded us,
   And raised up friends both true and kind;
Yet still my heart, sweet missy, turns
   To those dear ones I left behind.

And this is why the scalding tears
   Roll down my withered cheeks like rain;

I weep for those I dearly love
    Yet never shall behold again."

"Now, Cæsar, say no more to-day;
    Your story makes me cry:
O, what a wicked, wicked thing
    Is human slavery!

I wish I was a woman grown
    And had great heaps of gold;
I'd travel to the south and buy
    Each slave that could be sold.

And then I'd free them all at once
    And make them happy too;
I'd buy your wife and children all
    And bring them back to you."

"No, missy; that can never be;
    I'll never see them here below;
But if we all our Savior love,
    Why, then we all to heaven will go.

He's paid a price, more precious far
    Than all the wealth this earth can give,
To buy his children, white and black,
    And take them up with him to live.

And all I ask or hope for now
    Is, that our sins may be forgiven;
That we may serve him here below,
    And all may see his face in heaven."

"Then, Cæsar, I will meet you here
    At this same hour each day,
And for your wife and children dear
    We will together kneel and pray."

It was a holy thing to see
    That lovely face, so young and fair,
Beside old Cæsar's sable brow
    While they together knelt in prayer.

And he who hears the feeblest cry
    Of all the lowly and the meek
Will never turn his face from one
    Who does his blessing humbly seek.

No matter what their clime or race,
    Their sins, through Christ, may be forgiven;
And thus his children all will meet,
    To praise him evermore, in heaven.

NOTES

1. For a detailed analysis of these texts, see De Rosa 29, 53–55, and 65–67.

2. See chapter 2 in *Domestic Abolitionism and Juvenile Literature* for a discussion of sentimental literature.

3. Interestingly, one of the images included in this original text, "The Fugitive Caught," also appears with a different caption in Julia Colman and Matilda Thompson, *The Child's Anti-Slavery Book: Containing a Few Words about American Slave Children. And Stories of-Slave Life* (1859). See "Aunt Judy's Husband Captured" (p. 350 in this anthology).

HARRIET NEWELL GREENE BUTTS

(PSEUDONYM: LIDA, 1819–1881)

Harriet Newell Greene Butts (Lida) authored a variety of children's books: *Thwing Family Thanksgiving: at The House of Almon Thwing* (1854), *Little Harry's Wish, or, "Playing Soldier"* (1868), *Plouf, Canard Sauvage* (1935), and *Chancun Son Nid: Jue du Père Castor* (1936). However, *Ralph: or, I Wish He Wasn't Black* (1855), part of a series entitled *Lida's Tales of Rural Home*, addresses the issue of American slavery.

In *Ralph: or, I Wish He Wasn't Black*,[1] Harriet Butts offers a unique perspective on slavery when compared to other domestic abolitionists in this anthology. Two mother figures, the white Mrs. Medford *and* the African American Mrs. Willard, employ seemingly nonsubversive religious rhetoric to document and counteract a hypocritical community's racism. When Ralph Medford almost succumbs to the sneers from peers who call him a "little abolitionist" for befriending Mrs. Willard and her son (Tommy), Mrs. Medford calmly and lovingly reinforces Biblical principles that counteract racial prejudice. Similarly, when Tommy tells his mother that he dislikes his dark skin and cannot understand why he cannot live with his father, Mrs. Willard does not denounce the racist white boys or the Fugitive Slave Law; instead, she reminds Tommy of God's color-blind love and His promise of a family reunion in Heaven. In contrast to the openly critical abolitionist mother-historians in Chandler's "What is a Slave, Mother?" Follen's "Dialogue," S.C.C.'s *Louisa in Her New Home*, Matilda Thompson's "Aunt Judy's Story: A Story from Real Life," and Jones's *The Young Abolitionists*, Mrs. Medford and Mrs. Willard appear rather nonthreatening. However, Butts could not resist making her mother figure betray a glimmer of defiance, evident when Mrs. Medford defends nonconformity and critiques, in a seemingly tangential remark, the religious hypocrites who uphold the Fugitive Slave Law. In a narrative lacking effective Sunday School teachers and adult male characters, Butts charges mothers to document the tensions between religion and proslavery politics so as to expose racially inspired religious corruption. Thus, although these mother figures appear devout and pacifying, they are, in their own way, outspoken abolitionist women.

RALPH: OR, I WISH HE WASN'T BLACK (1855)

"RALPH"

"Mother, why is it that Tommy Willard and his mother sit in our pew every Sunday? I do wish you would tell them to sit somewhere else. I don't see why they can't."

"And why, dear Ralph, do you desire them to sit somewhere else? How do they trouble you? Haven't you room enough? or what is the matter?"

"Yes, I have room enough; but you know they are colored, and people think it very strange that you should notice *them* so much."

"Is this all the charge you have to bring against poor Aunt Molly (as we call her) and her poor little Tommy. If so, I do not consider it a very serious charge."

"I guess, Mother, *you* would think it a very serious thing if *I* was as black as Tommy Willard!"

"I would like to ask my little son who made Tommy so black?"

"I suppose, Mother, you would say God made him so. But it does seem strange to me, why God could not have made him white just as well; then I should not feel towards him as I now do. I know he is a good boy but I cannot feel just as I should towards him if he were a white boy like *me*." And Ralph drew himself up before the mirror with a self-satisfied air, as much as to say, "Am I not a very good looking fellow?" His mother saw the look, and knew full well what thoughts were passing through her son's brain. She drew a deep sigh, for she felt that prejudice had already been sown in his young heart, and she knew how hard a thing it was to be rooted out, when it had once obtained root in the plastic soil of the soul.

Ralph noticed that his mother sighed deeply but knew not that his words had called forth that sigh. Mrs. Medford called Ralph to her side, and tenderly smoothing back his brown curls which hung carelessly over his high and intellectual forehead she said, "Ralph do you really think it is because Tommy is black, that you desire I should have him remove his seat in church? Or is it because you are afraid people will laugh at you, and you have not the courage to stand the ridicule? My son, how is it?"

"Dear Mother, it seems to me it is because he is black. But I don't know as it is all that, either; for I did feel really ashamed last Sabbath, when Mrs. Pride looked over to our pew, and then turned around to Mrs. Scornful and whispered. I know they were talking about you, and I know they thought it strange you should allow Aunt Molly and Tommy to sit with us. And then George Pride told me the other day that his mother thought it very strange you should allow Aunt Molly to come to the table and eat with us. He said his mother did not allow their servant to come to the table at all, only to wait on them; and their servant is an Irish[2] girl, and white of course; and he said his mother had talked a good deal about it, and thought it so strange when you was [sic] so ladylike, and had such an influence in society. He said a great deal more which I can't remember."

"I think, dear Ralph, you have remembered *too much*, if it is going to cause you to be so unhappy, and I feel very sorry my son should allow himself to be disturbed about so trifling a thing as this. But dear Ralph, you say Mrs. Pride's servant is white—certainly she ought to be allowed a seat at the table. It is only those that have a darker skin who should be excluded from our pews and our tables, or that should only come near at our bidding, to do for us what we could do for ourselves. So you see, my son, that you must explain to me a little, for I want to know why Mrs. Pride's servant is not allowed a place at the table, and I also want to know how my dear Ralph would like to have me exchange our faithful and well experienced domestic, for one like Bridget McDonald."

"Mother, do you think I would have you turn Aunt Molly and little Tommy out of doors because they are black? or do you think I would have you exchange Aunt Molly for a strapping Irish girl like Bridget? Why, Aunt Molly is one of the best housekeepers in the world! She is so kind to me, too, why, mother, I really love her; and Tommy would run all day long for me. He is a good boy and I like him."

"But they are black, Ralph, and ought not to sit in our pew, nor have a place at the table. They do very well to do all our hard work, and we have no scruples about their being near us when we need their assistance. Suppose, Ralph, Mrs. Pride had called on me this morning[;] she would have found me in the parlor assisting Aunt Molly about some work which was actually necessary to be done at that time and which was impossible for Aunt Molly to do alone. Well, I receive Mrs. Pride's call. I state to her the circumstances, and she thinks it all well enough in this case. But suppose she should call this afternoon, and find Aunt Molly and myself sitting quietly together, talking socially, and I treating her with the same respect, and courtesy that I would a lady of high rank, one that moved in the best circles, and was by all admired much for her wit, talents and intellectual endowments; do you not think this same Mrs. Pride would be utterly astonished at my course of conduct? Well, now, where is the difference? Aunt Molly is just as black in the morning as in the afternoon. Her features are the same also. But these are not objectionable if

the wearer acts as a servant. If we make her inferior to ourselves, all is
well in the eyes of society. But when we act upon the principle which
Christ taught us we should ever use, and treat all as equals—all as brothers and sisters, children of the Great and Good Father, then the whole
fashionable world are [sic] against us, and they raise the aristocratic cry,
"Servants, be obedient to your masters," forgetting that all are servants
of God in one sense, and, in another, all are His children without regard
to color, caste or clime. My son, try, and from this hour discard the feeling which is already so common, that the colored people are only fit to
do our drudgery. Try, too, and rise above the false theories which men in
their blindness have set as parting walls between the laboring classes and
those who think themselves too good to labor. And, Ralph, I want to impress upon your mind the dignity of labor; never despise it. But I will not
say much more on the subject now, for I think you understand me, and
my reason for allowing Aunt Molly and her little boy seats in our pew."

"Dear mother, I thank you for what you have said to me, and I wish I
could always feel on this subject, as I now do. But I do get so vexed sometimes. It was but yesterday, at school, that one of the boys called me a
"little abolitionist," and asked me when I was going out lecturing, just
because I said Tommy was a good boy, and knew a great deal more than
some white boys I could tell of. I do wish God had made Tommy white,
then everybody would love him, and I think I should love him quite as
well."

"Do you think you should love your little black pony any better if God
had made him white?" asked Mrs. Medford.

"Why, mother, I should not like a white pony half so well! I am glad
Billy is black; he is the prettiest pony in the world."

"I readily perceive my son is not very much prejudiced against color,
and if it was customary to take ponies to church, I think Billy would have
the best seat in the pew; or, perhaps he would be allowed to stand on all
fours on the nice velvet cushion."

Ralph now laughed heartily at the picture his mother had drawn, and
he could almost see in imagination his favorite pony standing reverently
on the soft cushioned seat, listening with gravity and concealed delight
to that passage of Scripture, which might perhaps be read on the occasion, relating to the impropriety of using cattle, and ponies perhaps, on
the holy Sabbath. Ralph was so intent upon this picture, he almost fan-
cied he heard the pony say "Amen!" to this passage, which, of course,
was a favorite with animals of every description, that had to labor the six
appointed days.

But his reverie is broken by Tommy, whose merry voice is now heard under the window talking to some canary birds which seemed to understand the colored boy as well as their little master Ralph, for birds have no prejudice against color, but sing as sweetly to the delighted Tommy, as they could have done to the bright and beautiful Ralph.

I must say in justice to Ralph, that he was a very beautiful child. He had a fine organization, and his education had been well cared for. He was not only taught book science, but was also taught goodness. His mother took every opportunity to impress upon his young and tender mind the truth and beauty of religion. Not that religion which clothes itself in gloom, and causes a somber cloud to rest pall like, on the free, glad spirit. No, this was not the religion which Mrs. Medford possessed. Her's [sic] was a joyous piety, a piety which could see God in everything,—in the little flower that bloomed so carelessly at her feet—in the song of birds—in gentle, running brooks—in the starry heavens—all, all proclaimed to her the God of love. In the human soul, also, she saw the divine as well as the human; and no soul, however lost in guilt and folly, did she pass by. Her religion was a hopeful one, and she believed that God kindly cared for all, and would never forget a soul which He had formed. The dark Theology of the past with its blighting influence found no resting place in her benevolent soul; and while she saw God in everything that lived and moved, and dwelt with joy and sweet satisfaction upon all his beautiful works, she forgot not the meek and lowly Jesus. She felt that His life was a pattern, and she humbly tried to follow in his footsteps.

Perhaps we can better make our young readers acquainted with Mrs. Medford's idea of Jesus by relating part of a conversation which she held with Ralph a few evenings after the commencement of this chapter. Ralph asks of his mother the following question:

"Mother, do you think the Savior was ever naughty, when he was a little boy like me?"

Mrs. Medford replied thus: "I think, Ralph, when Jesus was a very little boy, he was very superior to any child I ever heard of. He was kind and affectionate, loving and docile, every ready to do his parent's [sic] bidding. I love to think of Jesus as a little child mingling with his playmates. I fancy I see his mild eye lit up with kindness and affection. I seem to hear his gentle words and behold his countenance beaming with innocent pleasure and delight; and I mark how cautiously he treads, lest he should trample upon the smallest flower or cause one bud to wither, that had joyously greeted the morning sunbeams; and I would have my Ralph as kind, as tender-hearted, as pure, as gentle, as with this child of

Nazareth. Never hurt or destroy anything that lives; for all life is for some purpose. Never tread upon an insect, even, which basks in the warm and gentle sunbeams which our dear Father has caused to shine upon the evil as well as the good; and if you are kind and gentle now, and strive to cultivate those finer qualities of the soul, you will, on arriving at manhood, be true to what is most pure and beautiful,—you will love the truth and seek after those hidden treasures that purify and elevate the soul above the earthly, the sensual." Thus did Mrs. Medford early impress on the plastic mind of her little boy, truths lofty and pure, simplified to his youthful comprehension.—The religion that she taught him was void of that mysticism, which so often confounds the childish head. It was a natural as well as revealed religion, and so loving did God appear in the character with which she clothed Him, that Ralph early learned to associate everything that was pure with the "Good Father" as he very appropriately called Him. Often, when a very little boy, he would exclaim, as he stood gazing up into the starry heavens: "O, Mother, come and look out; the Good Father has lit up all the stars tonight; and I believe some of His angel children are peeping through the stars to look at me. Mother, what makes the minister call this a wicked world? How can it be a wicked world, when God made it all? He did not then understand how man had marred and defaced many of the works of God, and how he had departed from that straight and narrow way which leads to virtue, peace and happiness."

But we will return to our friends, Aunt Molly and Tommy. Perhaps my young readers would like to know if they have always lived with the kind and gentle Mrs. Medford. No! they have been with this lady about two years. Aunt Molly had once lived with Mrs. Medford's father. She spent many years in his family and was universally beloved by all its members. She lived there until she was married. She found in Thomas Willard a kind and affectionate husband. They lived happily together several years, and might have lived so for years to come, enjoying each other's companionship, had it not been the blighting curse of Slavery. O, Slavery, Slavery! what hast thou not done? Thou hast caused the holiest and best affections of the soul to die out by thy power. Yes, many a heart which has pulsated with affections as warm, as pure, as ever beat in the human soul has by thy hellish power been prostrated in the dust—its fairest, sweetest flowers trampled upon by those who called themselves "Christians."

It seems Thomas had once been a *slave*, and feeling that he had a better right to himself—to those powers which God had endowed him with—than his master could possibly have, he one night took the liberty to bid adieu to the sunny south, with its smiling groves and chattel slaves, its flowering lawns and cotton plantations, where the overseer's lash is heard above the music of the feathered songsters who sing their free songs regardless of the tyranny that reigns so rife in the isles of the south. He bids adieu to all, nor lingers to drop a tear upon the graves of those loved ones that have been freed by the kind angel Death. No! he lingers not, but with his eye fixed steadily upon the north star he travels by night and hides himself by day. At last he reaches our northern shores, and is kindly cared for by those who feel for the oppressed and down-trodden. He is ambitious and quite a genius. This man who had been deemed a thing, to be bought and sold like cattle, evinces genius for inventing. He is encouraged by kind friends and succeeds well. He soon gathers together a small amount of this world's goods, is assisted by Mrs. Medford's father, gains a good situation, takes our good Aunt Molly for his companion, and begins life anew. I would that we could leave our friends here, happy in the society of loved ones; but alas! we must, with tearful eyes, speak of hearts wrung with anguish because they are rudely torn asunder. Yes, the Fugitive Slave Law, more infamous than any law ever framed in *heathen* lands, is the law of our "*Christian* America," and is sanctioned by those who profess to love liberty and equality—ah, more than this, even those who profess to love and follow the liberty-loving Savior. Yes! the Fugitive Slave Law has reached our worthy friend Thomas. It found him happy in his own home surrounded with peace and plenty, together with love pure as an angel's breath! O, ye who coldly and deliberately stood up in our Congress halls using all the eloquence which wit and intellect could possibly call to your aid, could you but look upon this heart-stricken family and see that strong man bowed in sorrow,—yes, more than sorrow, intense *anguish* such as ye have never known, (for it is those who have *souls* that suffer most deeply)—could ye have *seen* all this, methinks the love of fame, ambition, power, would have sunk into nothingness, and ye would have spurned the idea of adding another fetter to the bond-man's limbs, or causing another sigh, another groan to be wrung from the bosom of the enslaved. Ye cannot form the *faintest* idea of the anguish which has come like a thunderbolt from a clear sky. See that wife cling-ing with devotion to him she loved, as well perhaps, as those who have skins a few shades whiter than her own. See our little Tommy with his arms fondly entwined about his father's neck, begging the officers of (*in*)justice, not to take away his dear papa. But tears and lamentations are of no avail; affection, devotion, parental love, and connubial happiness are trampled low in the dust, and made subservient to tyranny, ambition and power. The colored man is now powerless in the hands of his tormentors. He is taken, bound hand and foot, and driven away from his own peaceful home to return no more. We will not follow our afflicted friend and brother through all the scenes which he passed, but will only say that the change was too great for a soul like his. His was a crushed spirit; he sickened and died. Death was far more welcome to him than life, and so this angel of mercy came one calm, still night and took our friend Thomas, led him safely through the cold valley to those spheres of light and love, where the glad free songs of equality and love are chanted by angels of the higher life. In that pure celestial home, where the soul cannot be fettered, will we leave our brother, for we know it will be well with him there. The incongruities which so often puzzled his brain will not now disturb him, for the light there is not all darkness. But the sunlight of freedom, justice, and equality is so clear and transparent that he is not bewildered by its glow, but can bask serene and tranquil in its softened beauty.

We will now return to the desolate wife. But we will not try to delineate her sufferings. Words are not feelings, and her sorrows must be felt to be understood. There were feelings in her soul that took no form. She sat like one petrified, for hours and days after her husband was torn from her. At length for the sake of her little Tommy she aroused herself, and the kindness of Mr. Medford and his excellent wife soothed, in a measure, her intense grief. They insisted on her making their house her home. At first she thought it impossible for her to leave her own dear home. She clung with tenacity to everything that reminded her of her husband. Ye who think the colored race are devoid of feeling, go and visit Aunt Molly the night before she leaves the spot dearest to her on earth; dearest because of the associations which bound her to the blissful memories of the past, together with its painful realities. But we will hastily draw a veil over this troubled heart, and silently weep with her, while we wash our hands clean from this blighting mildew—this curse of slavery—this moral cancer which is eating out the highest and noblest faculties of the soul, and causing man to act the demon towards his brother man.

It was long after Aunt Molly took up her residence with Mrs. Medford ere she seemed to have any interest in life. Her little son engrossed her time and attention somewhat; aside from him she had no interest in life. But time, that friend of all the sorrowful, brought resignation. The kind and gentle spirit which Mrs. Medford ever manifested for her, soon called forth her gratitude, and she caught the inspiration which seemed to attend this excellent woman wherever her influence was felt. But not to dwell too long, lest I should weary the youthful mind, I will take my readers to a Sunday School scene. Ralph has kindly persuaded Tommy to attend school this day with him. This was about a year and a half before the commencement of our story. Ralph walks boldly into the vestry leading Tommy by the hand, to the consternation of all the bright eyes present on that occasion. He lifts Tommy's cap from his head, for our little fellow was at that time quite young and had not yet learned the rules of etiquette. They are at last seated quietly in one of the front seats, and Ralph seemed quite proud of his young charge. He did not feel this morning just as he did when he asked his mother if she would not provide another seat for this same Tommy. He had not then been laughed at, because he played with a "little nigger," as the rude uncivil boys termed our little friend. But to return. Tommy was there with his eyes wandering from one face to another, his own expressing pleasure not unmixed with wonder. Soon the teacher commences catechising the scholars, and when she came to Tommy, he being a new scholar, she asked him the oft repeated question, "Can you tell me who made you?" Tommy hung his head a moment after the question was repeated, for he had not expected to be catechised, and was not prepared to give an answer. In a moment, however, he recovered himself, and looking square into the teacher's face said, "I expect God makes all the white folks, but don't know 'zactly who makes the black ones, 'less as Topsy says they all growed; but I don't b'leve this for I b'leve some would grow white as well as black. I can't tell how it is if God did make the black boy as well as the white boys, why He lets wicked men sell little black boys' fathers, when he always lets the white boys' fathers stay at home. I can't tell—I don't know; I wish you would tell." But the teacher is as much puzzled now as was Tommy a moment before. This was a harder question than she had ever found in any catechism and she was at a loss what to say. So she very quietly told Tommy she would explain this matter to him when he was "old enough to understand it." This is the way many of our Reverends keep the laity waiting till they are wise enough to understand what they fail to understand themselves. But Ralph was not so easily satisfied, and on returning home he interrogated his mother on the subject. His mother gave him her views of God as being a loving Father and that it was his will all should be free and happy. It was man's wickedness which caused this misery in our world. But we have related a conversation between Ralph and his mother, giving the reader an insight into her soul which was one of gentleness and love.

When Tommy returned home he went directly to his mother, his little brain filled with new ideas. He was wondering why God should love the white people better than he did little colored boys. He expressed this thought to his mother and said: "I wish I was a little white boy, like Ralph. Everybody seems to love him; all the boys run up to him after school, and I know they would not have done so if he had been black like me. Mother, can't you wash off the black nohow? Take some strong soap suds and scour my face, mother, and see if I look any whiter. When I was coming from school one of the boys ran up to me and put his finger on my face and rubbed hard, and then he looked to see if the black did not rub off at all. Do you see any white mark off my face, mother?"

His mother drew a deep sigh, and taking her boy on her lap said:

"God who gave your friend Ralph such beautiful skin, and formed his features so regularly, also gave my little Tommy the skin which he is destined to wear. God does not look at the *skin*, my son, but at the *heart*. If you try to do well, and love to be a good boy, God will love you as well as He possibly can the most beautiful child, graced with the fairest features and vieing [sic] with the lily in whiteness."

Tommy's tender heart was touched with his mother's impressive words; winding his arm gently round her neck, he said: "Mother, if you think God will love me as well as he does beautiful white children, I will not care so much if I am black, for I do want God to love me. But why did God take away my dear father? He lets Ralph's father live here with him!" This question coming so unexpectedly from her little boy for a moment caused the tears to flow afresh, but hastily wiping them away, she explained to him how man had framed laws, in opposition to God's laws, and how selfish man had become; and then she talked with him about the beautiful spirit land—told him his father had gone to live where color ceases to be a crime; that in a little while they would all be in Heaven. "What," interrupted Tommy, "do you say I shall see my father in heaven? I wish God would let me go there now, for it has been a great long while since papa took me in his arms as he used to do. I wish I could go now?"

"What! and leave me all alone, Tommy?"

The little boy looked thoughtful a moment, and then said: "O, I would ask God to let me come back after you. I would tell Him how you had cried ever since that wicked man carried away my father. O, mother, don't you think God would let father come with me after you, and when you see us coming out from the stars wouldn't you be glad?"

Aunt Molly was at a loss how to reply to this, and what seemed to her strange questionings, and a superstitious fear came over her. She feared lest this last earthly treasure should be torn from her also. She finally evaded answering him, and told him he had better lie down on the sofa and rest. She watched beside him till she saw his eyes close, and knew by his breathing that he had fallen asleep. With tearful eyes she sought Mrs. Medford and told her fears concerning Tommy. Mrs. Medford soon quieted her fears—told her it was probably nothing more than the excited state of his mind, caused by going to the Sabbath School and then she said, "Aunt Molly, children have many beautiful thoughts which when breathed into our ears, seem almost like the voice of God speaking to our hearts. Ralph often utters sentiments which surprise me much. But hark, Aunt Molly! Tommy has forgotten his thought concerning heaven, for there he is in the garden trying to sing 'O Susannah, don't you cry for me.'"

Aunt Molly looked a little confused and seemed to feel somewhat sorry that he should so soon go from the "sublime" to the "ridiculous." Mrs. Medford saw this expression of Aunt Molly's face, and with her usual ingenuity said, "This is just like our little boys, for a moment causing us mothers to feel that there never were such precocious children; and the next moment we have to confess that after all they are very much like other children." Aunt Molly seemed very well satisfied with this conclusion, and went to her own room exclaiming: "If there are other children equal to Ralph, there never was another woman half so good and kind as Ralph's mother."

Ralph has now joined Tommy in the garden, and you would not suppose, to see him now, that he had any prejudice against color. They are both reclining on a seat in the arbor, Ralph's head resting in Tommy's lap; and I will say here, that since the opening of this story Ralph has not been heard to ask his mother if Tommy cannot sit in another pew.

"HAVE WE NOT ALL ONE FATHER?"

O, is it so! and have we all
  One Father and one God?
Then why should man his brother man
  Rule with oppression's rod?

"Our Father," oft the white man cries
  "Forgive as we forgive"—

Then takes his brother, binds him fast
   In hopeless chains to live.

"Our Father," now the black man cries,
   "Forgive our erring brother,
For we have all one Father, God,—
   Teach us to love each other."

NOTES

1. For a complete analysis of this text, see De Rosa 92–96.

2. See Jones, *The Young Abolitionists* for an Irish, antislavery female character, Biddy.

KATE BARCLAY

(BIOGRAPHY AND DATES UNKNOWN)

Biographical information about Kate Barclay has not surfaced. However, evidence reveals that before publishing children's abolitionist literature, Barclay authored *The Odd Fellow's Token: Devoted to Friendship, Love and Truth* (1846), *The Temperance Token, or, Crystal Drops from the Old Oaken Bucket* (1846), and "The Lost Child" (1856), which reflect her humanitarian interests. She published these works in Geneva and Auburn, New York, which may suggest that she resided in upstate New York. In 1854, however, Barclay apparently transcended geographical boundaries when she sent *Minnie May: With Other Rhymes and Stories*—her antislavery juvenile collection of illustrations, poems, and short stories—to John P. Jewett in Boston, perhaps because she knew of his success with *Uncle Tom's Cabin* and his antislavery collection for children. *Minnie May's* reprinting in 1856 suggests the marketability and acceptability of Barclay's abolitionist sentiments for children.

A significant portion of *Minnie May* presents first- and third-person slave narratives that capture the slave's experience for the young, white reader. Of the ten titles in the collection, four focus exclusively on slaves' experiences. In "Little Nell," the narrator encourages Nell, a slave child, to stay close to her mother, since this bond was so frequently violated. Slavery's threat to family bonds reappears in "Sambo's Toast," which contrasts the bountiful but very materialistic nature of a "white Christmas" (with its focus on tangible gifts received) to the slave family that celebrates, with quiet fear, their gift: that the master has not sold their family members to separate plantations. While "Little Nell" and "Sambo's Toast" give third-person accounts of slave experiences, "Crispy's Story" most resembles the first-person narrator typical in "authentic" slave narratives. Two white children, Eddie and Tommy, listen to Crispy tell of his shattered family unit, his sale to increasingly cruel and violent masters, his awakening to his condition, his subsequent escape (the details about which he remains silent, as many ex-slaves did in their narratives), and his life as a freeman. Like narrators from traditional slave narratives, Crispy corrects the white children's misunderstandings about his experiences as a slave; however, unlike the traditional narratives, he does not propose a call to action, evident when he simply ends his story by encouraging the children to go play. In "Cuffee," Barclay adds a more blatant critical current as an adult documents Cuffee's biography for a young listener, Anna. Like Crispy, Cuffee awakens to his right to freedom, stating, "*I will be free!* It is my right, and I will have it" (see 273). Unfortunately, Cuffee claims his freedom for three years but the Fugitive Slave Law permits his recapture and sale into slavery. Barclay's pseudo slave-narratives repeatedly focus on the slave's emotional suffering under slavery, but her condemnation of the law that allows recapture represents a blatant critique of the American legal system that supports slavery.

In addition to the pseudo slave-narratives that posit a level of "remove" between narrator and reader, a second pattern emerges in Barclay's narratives: white children who witness slavery's cruelties. "Minnie May," "The Ride," and "The Sale"[1] depict children who experience a life-changing moment as each witnesses slavery firsthand. In "Minnie May," Barclay captures the sudden, shocking knowledge an innocent white child feels upon learning from her mother that her nurse, Aunt Ruth, is sold. The child's inability to dissuade the slave trader from purchasing Aunt Ruth leads to Minnie May's lost innocence. "The Ride" also includes the image of a daughter's sudden recognition of the paradox inherent in American democratic principles that permit slavery. Barclay depicts a mother disturbed by her innocent daughter's sadness upon witnessing a slave auction. Unlike Henry, her companion, who has grown accustomed to the sales, the daughter confides that the distressing experience has awakened her opposition to slavery, if only to escape it and return to her seemingly utopian Northern home. Finally, in "The Sale," Johnny learns about slavery when he witnesses a slave auction. This poem also includes a mother figure to whom Johnny poses questions; however, in this case, the mother asserts the reality of the slave auction and this awakens a new consciousness about slavery and sympathy for its victims. Barclay suggests that such sentimental stories that arouse tears and sympathy can ultimately lead to insights that support the abolitionist campaign.

In *Minnie May*'s final text, "The Slave," the narrator forcefully calls young readers to action through various rhetorical strategies. "The Slave" narrates the life of a slave woman, who, though liberated with the help of the underground railroad, returns to her former plantation to be reunited with her family. Ironically, her act of self-sacrifice and familial love results in her punishment and sale to a North Carolina slave trader. Through this narrative, Barclay petitions young readers to imagine the horror of slavery and to take pity on its victims, stating, "O, I do want you to feel for their condition, and, when you pray, ask God to bless *them*" (see 281). Thus, "Barclay's emotional didacticism socializes readers . . . by imparting specific images, words, and actions to arouse "right feelings" of compassion that reform the reader's conception of the "other" as human being rather than as object" (De Rosa 56).

MINNIE MAY: WITH OTHER RHYMES AND STORIES (1854)

"MINNIE MAY"

The flower of Savannah was sweet Minnie May,
With soft eyes of blue and brow open as day,
With lips ever ready to wreathe in a smile,
And wee merry dimples to dance round the while.

A sunbeam of summer was sweet Minnie May;
Her heart was so light and her spirit so gay,
Her friends were so true, so loving and fond,
She seemed to possess some bright fairy's kind wand.

But the sceptre of love in sweet Minnie May
Was the sceptre that ruled where'er it held sway;
And fairies might poise on invisible wing
To catch the joy notes as from her they would spring.

No cloud had e'er darkened o'er sweet Minnie May,
And life seemed to her but a bright summer day;
'Twas good just to live; and she lived but to love
And rejoice in the gifts of the Father above.

But trouble at length came to sweet Minnie May—
A shadow fell darkly across her smooth way.
"Aunt Ruth" was her nurse, and she loved her full well;
But now she was missing—where, no one would tell.

All over the premises searched Minnie May,
High and low, in and out, and every way;
She inquired of all, but not any would tell;
Though where "aunt Ruth" was they knew perfectly well.

Suspicion at last rose in sweet Minnie May;
She had heard there were slaves to be sold that day;
Could it be that this was the fate of "aunt Ruth"?
She ran to her mother and learned the sad truth.

Then fast fell the teardrops of sweet Minnie May;
The cloud was a dark one that shadowed her way;
She sought her lone room, and there fervently prayed
On Jesus the heart of "aunt Ruth" might be stayed.

Down she took then her Bible, and sweet Minnie May
Ran bounding along, stopping not by the way,

"Ware room for slaves—Minnie Mae and Aunt Ruth"
Courtesy, American Antiquarian Society.

Till her hand tightly clasped "aunt Ruth's" dear old hand;
She heeded not then any master's command.

She leaned on her bosom there, sweet Minnie May,
For there those soft curls in her infancy lay;
She gave her the Bible with many a tear,
And bade her look upward in each trying fear.

There she sits on that slave block, sweet Minnie May,
And tries to shed light on "aunt Ruth's" darkened way;
She pleads with that master so stern and severe
To be kind to old nurse, to her ever dear.

Alas for your pleading now, sweet Minnie May;
His heart is of stone, and he lists not your lay;
Already he's angry, and threatens, e'en now,
To cause her to know at *his will* she must bow.

Bid adieu and return now, sweet Minnie May;
Dark shadows have fallen across your light way;
No life is all sunshine, no pathway so bright,
But sin clouds it over with mildew and blight.

"CRISPY'S STORY"

"Crispy, I wish you would tell us now all that long story about your being a slave. You promised it a great while ago; and now it rains so hard we can't go out to play, and you have hurt you so you can't work, and I don't believe we shall ever have a better time. Won't you tell it now, Crispy?"

"Yes, Eddie, I will. You and Tommy shall hear dat story now. I guess after dis you no say you don't belieb I eber was slabe. It is a good many years since I run away and cum north to lib free; but I 'member bery well all 'bout it when I was a slabe. Now I'll tell it. Where shall I begin? I don't know what to tell first."

"O, begin at the very beginning of it, when you were a little boy like us. Were you ever a little boy, Crispy? You are such a great big black man, I can't think of you a little boy."

"Well, Tommy, ebery body was little once, and I 'member when I was not so big as you and Eddie. I had one little brudder and tree sisters. My massa he die, and den missis hab all de rule; and she always cross as fury, always when I seed her. De first 'ting I 'member much 'bout was dis. One day mammy was gettin' tings ready for de dinner. We young uns were all in de house, playin' 'round; so she told us we must help. She set down wid her pipe in her mouth, and we all 'round her. De girls helped pick de chickens, and Jim and Crispy dey shell peas. Just when we got a-goin' and was feelin' bery nice 'bout helpin', den Dinah open de door, and missis she walk in. She look crosser dan eber as she shook out a table spread to show it to mammy wid a spot on it of somethin'. She say it ruined, but mammy must clean it carefully—make it good as new. Den she look 'round; she shake her head and say, 'I won't hab so many dirty brats 'round. Dare be Jim and Crispy 'specially, dey always in de way. Dey shall be sold; I hab more niggers dan I want; I sell 'em—good-for-nothin' little brats.' Dat's de way she talk; and den she go back. Den mammy she lay down her pipe; and O, how she cry! We don't know what she cry 'bout. But Crispy know well 'nough now; she cry 'cause we be sold away from her, she don't know where—to bad massa, likely. Well, she didn't hab me great while longer. One day dare come 'long a man buyin' up niggers; missis sent for me to come to de veranda; she be more cleber to me dan eber before. She make me jump 'round, and dance, and sing; and dey both laugh. Den de man tell me to run down to de gate, get into dat big wagon, stay till he come, and he gib me a ride. Dat was a long ride. I neber see mammy, nor Jim, nor my sisters any more."

"Why, Crispy, did your missis sell you to that man, then?"

"Yes, she sell me to him den."

"What did she want you to jump and dance for, and sing?"

"O, to show me off, as dey do a horse when dey wants to sell him. Missis showed me off to let de man see what smart nigger I be: so he tell how much he gib missis for me, and den he pay her de price she ask."

"What did you do then, Crispy?"

"Well, my new massa take me home wid him, and dare I 'gin to work. He say I big 'nough to work; so dey keep me runnin' and doin' so many tings you call 'chores' all de time. When I get tired and don't want to work, den dey cuff me 'round and flog 'de little black nigger' till me glad to do all me can. But my new missis, she so pleasant like; I tink I like her. I tink when I grow big and strong I please her; den she hab Crispy for her waiter, or some such like; so I work on and try to please her. I cry great many times when nobody see me, 'cause I tink 'bout mammy and my tree sisters and Jim, and want to see 'em bery much. But dey all great way off, wonderin' where Crispy be, knowin' he sold. It all go on 'bout so some time. De bigger I grow, de harder I hab to work. When I be ten or 'leben years old, den massa he lose money, and den he sell some of his niggers. I hear 'em talkin' 'bout it, and wonderin' which he sell. I tink I keep out ob massa's sight, den he no tink to sell me; for I like better to stay dare dan to try new place. But Crispy couldn't stay. He sent to de auction wid four more niggers. Poor old Phillis, she feel de worst of all of us; she bery old, 'most worn out. She lib once wid bery bad massa, and she 'fraid some bery bad one buy her now. Den dey were sellin' her, and leabin' her da'ter Sukey wid massa. Poor Phillis, she feel bery bad indeed. Old Nero, he feel bad too. But Denny and Jake, dey no mind it."[2]

"Who bought you this time, Crispy?"

"Well, Crispy tell you 'bout it. Me de bery first one dey look at. While dey openin' and shuttin' my hands and mouth, and liftin' up my feet to see how heaby and strong I be, den Crispy lookin' 'round to tell which massa cross and who cleber. But Crispy couldn't hab pick. Dey begin to bid for me, and dey bid, bid; and de bery crossest, wo'st-lookin' one, he bid de highest, and me knocked off to him. Den he march me to his home and wid a sorrowin' heart me 'gin de world anew. O boys, such a sorry time poor Crispy hab he know how 'gin to tell. He no make your little hearts so ache by stories of such cruel deeds. Me bery young; but dey send me to de cotton field, and make me pick wid all my might, or lay de heaby whip 'cross my poor back. Dare, sick or well, alibe or dead, dey whip poor Crispy to he daily work. One night me lay upon de ground, and could no sleep at all. Me keep tinkin' and tinkin' all de night, 'Why can't Crispy run away, go to de north, where de niggers all run free, work for de pay, and not be slabe and bear de whip and chain?' Me 'tink all 'bout it, and plan it out well as me could how me get dare. But you see, boys, me didn't know much 'bout de roads and de way. At last me made up mind *to start.*"

"Good! good! I'm glad you did that, Crispy. I wouldn't stay there to be a slave; I know I wouldn't."

"Well, next day me settle how Crispy get out. Massa hab comp'ny, and dare was great fuss stirrin' 'round. Me watch chance and crawl out, and after a bery great deal trouble and fear me get a good start. Me can't tell you all 'bout dat, nor all 'bout my journey. Dat's a long, dark story. Me 'most starbed, and have many troubles. After seberal days and nights ob slow trabel, me tink now Crispy far 'nough away to go to public house. It be a bery little village. Me go in, and dare sit a fat, good-natured white massa readin' a newspaper. Me ask him to gib me drink ob water. Just as me took de cup from his hand me hear men comin' in. Dey swearin' and talkin' loud. Me 'fraid bery much, and slip into de bar wid de massa, beg- gin' him hide me quick. He push me under a shelf, and I keep still, trem- blin' wid fear."

"O Crispy, I'm afraid they caught you there."

"No, dey didn't, for dat was good massa, and help de poor nigger dis time. One big, bushy, ugly-lookin' man, he come in fust, and, trowin' down a whip, swore he hab a drink if de nigger nebber was found. He name Keelout, and he after me. Den two more come; and dey all take brandy and talk and swear 'bout 'de runaway little nigger.' O boys, den didn't Crispy feel bad! Me no tell how me feel den, and you neber know. Poor Crispy, he 'most die right away. Dey stay but little while; den dey start off, 'most drunk, to look somewhere else for 'de runaway little nig- ger.' O, I 'fraid to come out. But dat good cleber massa, he keep me till night. He feed me; den he put bread and meat in bundle, and he say, 'Now go, Crispy, fast as you can go.' It take me many days and nights to get dare; and ebery day as I come north it grow colder and colder, for de winter had come. Sometimes me 'most starbe and freeze, 'cause me 'fraid to stop much. One day poor Crispy he grow bery sick. He lay down by big log. It was just at de edge of de forest; and dare me lay shiverin' some time, 'fraid me goin' to die. After while me hear wagon rattlin' 'long and men talkin' loud. Den me try to go on; but me so sick me couldn't walk. De wagon come 'long; and dare was in it white woman and black one, and white man. Dey stop and take me in. Me lay down in de wagon. De

men talkin' so loud come shoutin' 'long. Me tink one be Keelout. Den
Crispy heart shake wid fear. But de man whip up his horses, and den we
soon leabe 'em way behind. Boys, dat wagon brought Crispy to free country. When dey tell me dat, den how my poor sick heart leap right up wid
joy! Den me feel safe; den me cry and laugh, cry and laugh, and don't
know any way how to act."

"Then, Crispy, was that the end of your being a slave? Did you come
to live with us then?"

"Dat was de end ob me bein' a slabe. But me no come to lib here den.
Me hab great many fears dat somehow bad massa find me yet. So me keep
comin' north more and more till me get here. Dat was when Crispy only
a boy; now he an old man, you see. Me guess dey won't eber find me and
want me now. Me don't tink me shall eber be slabe any more. Me hope
to die free man, and be buried like free people, where dey be buried. Me
wish mammy and Jim and my tree sisters, if dey be alibe, was free too,
and ebery body else. Dey ought to be. Dare, boys, I guess you'll 'member
Crispy's story a good while. You sit bery still. But see how de sun shine!
Now you run and play. Dis is free country, and Crispy free as you now."

"THE RIDE"

Here they come! They're sending the horses away;
    On the steps they still linger a while;
They are fanning their brows in the gentle breeze
    And awaiting the sun's last smile.

What a glow they are in! How the roses bloom
    Once again on the cheek of my child!
Ah, this sweet southern home is the place for her,
    Where the sunbeams dance and the air is mild.

But how earnest she grows! Now her face is sad
    As she talks with that proud, gifted boy:
I'll go down to her aid; she's weary, I know—
    My frail flower, my lily, my joy.

"What is it, my darling? No cloud should now rest
    On your brow or your heart, I am sure:
Did you find some dark path in your lengthened route
    Too stony and rough to endure?

"Such a beautiful day, such a balmy breeze,
    Such a gallant young friend at your side,

A surefooted pony, both gentle and swift,—
   Was it not a most elegant ride?"

"Yes, mother, it was; I enjoyed it so much
   While we cantered so gayly along,
With gladness and life welling up in our souls
   As the hills echoed back each wild song,—

"That I almost forgot I was far from my home,
   Seeking health in these bright blooming vales:
But, mother, we came to a drove of poor slaves,
   Chained together, handcuffed—for the sales;—

"And my heart grew sore at the sight of them there,
   So weary, and wayworn, and faint;
While the stern driver's lash around them was cast
   If they moaned or made slightest complaint.

"Henry says I am foolish, and chides me now
   For distressing myself at such things;
Says these scenes are often and often seen here:
   Then he laughingly whistles and sings.

"But, mother, that sight from my mind ne'er will pass;
   And my free spirit droops 'neath the power
Of slavery's deeds, which appear to me now
   To deepen and darken each hour.

"Let us not live here, though the bright flowers bloom,
   The sun never clouds, and the air chills not;
Though the sweet sunny south an Eden might be
   If it were not for slavery's blot.

"Let's return, mother dear, to our own sweet home,
   Love-hallowed spot, where free banners wave;
Where no chains, no handcuffs, and no driver's lash
   Are e'er laid on a poor helpless slave."

"CUFFEE"

"When those ladies called here this afternoon, who was it they were talking about? Who was put in chains?"

"It was poor Cuffee, a colored man, who had once been a slave."

"Will you tell me the story now? I did not understand much of it, but I was sorry for poor Cuffee."

"Yes Anna, I will tell you. Cuffee had lived away at the south, where the oranges grow, you know. He was a slave there, and I suppose served his master, or his massa, as he called him, very faithfully; for one summer he was brought as far north as the State of Maryland by some of his master's family, who came there and wanted Cuffee to wait on them. As they were travelling from place to place, Cuffee heard about negroes a little farther to the north being free and living by themselves, or working for white people and being paid for it; and if they were not well treated at one place and did not wish to stay, they could leave and go to another; and as long as they were industrious and behaved well they could make a good living and be happy. Cuffee began to wonder why he couldn't live in this way as well as any of them, and not go back to the south and be always a slave, toiling for nothing and having few comforts. Besides this, he was likely to be sold at any time to a bad massa who would treat him very cruelly. He had often seen those on a neighboring plantation beaten for almost nothing. They themselves often could hardly tell why the whip was laid over their shoulders. He could by some means get away from the family who owned him and go to the free states where they could not find him. Then they would go back without him, and then he would be free, and he would get work as others did and be paid for it. He thought it all over and over again, and every time he wished more and more to be free, until one day he said to himself, 'I *will* *be free!* It is my right, and I will have it.'

After a time he had a good opportunity to get away, and he left his master's family and travelled off farther and farther north. He could work, and had no trouble in finding good places where he was well treated and well paid. So he worked his way along, learned how people live at the north, and bought him some clothes, and did just as other free people do. He kept himself very quiet and out of the way for a long while. But when he thought there was no danger of being found out and taken back to the south to be a slave again, he became a waiter at a hotel in the city. He pleased the landlord, and all liked him very much. He lived there three or four years and felt quite safe. One day there came a gentleman to this hotel who watched Cuffee very closely and asked some questions about him of those in the bar room. The landlord listened, and began to suspect that this was a southern gentleman. He feared he was a slaveholder on the lookout for some runaway slave, and he determined to send Cuffee out of the way until he left the house. Quite a number were sitting and standing around, smoking, and talking, and taking their ease, when in came Cuffee, bringing a trunk and an umbrella.

He set them down and turned to go out. The landlord stepped to the door to speak with him, and, giving him some general orders, sent him off until he could get an opportunity to tell him what he suspected. The southern gentleman watched the movements, but said nothing, and soon after paid his bill and left the house. The next morning Cuffee was nowhere to be found. No one there knew any thing about him. The landlord hoped he was in some safe place, safe from the slaveholder; but it was not so, as they soon found out. The southern gentleman, who had watched him so closely, had laid claim to him as his slave and had him seized and bound. As soon as it was known there was a great excitement about it, and the friends of freedom tried to rescue him; but they could not do it. The law allowed the man to take him; and nothing could now be done to save him. Poor Cuffee was bound with chains and carried back into slavery again."

"O, that was too bad! I am so sorry for Cuffee! Is that all you know about him?"

"Very nearly all. The last that was known of him by anyone at the north was what a blacksmith told about him. He said a man came into his shop one day to get him to fix a pair of handcuffs which did not exactly fit the wrists they were wanted for. The blacksmith would not touch the handcuffs, and said, with some spirit, that he never did such miserable work as that. He looked out at the door, and there sat Cuffee in a wagon, with heavy chains upon him; and he looked as if all courage and hope had gone out of him."

"Poor Cuffee! I fear he will never be free again. His bonds will seem worse than ever now, I am sure. His heart must be almost broken and life but a burden."

"THE SALE"

"'Sale at twelve o'clock!' Now, what does it mean?
    Dear mother, do just look at that!
See that girl standing there, with her head bent down,
    By that man in a beaver hat!

"And that one behind, with his hand on her arm,
    Seems pushing or pulling her back:
I wonder if that is a slave being sold;
    She don't look to me very black."

"Yes, Johnny; this is a slave auction you see;
    There's the auctioneer standing up there,
With mallet in hand, crying, 'What will you bid?'
    And the purchasers stand down there.

"Sale at 12 O'clock"
Courtesy, American Antiquarian Society.

"How my very heart fills with sadness and grief
    As I think of that poor girl's fate!—
Not a friend to protect or shield her from crime,
    Nor lift from her spirit the weight.

"That vile slavery's curse must evermore bind
    On all who are held in its thrall:
Poor delicate, sensitive, heart-bowed quadroon,
    You must bear the rudeness of all.

"You stand on that block to be sold for a sum
    That to you is nothing at all;
The one who bids highest will claim as his own
    Your body, your spirit, your all.

"How sad and how hopeless your young life must be!
    How hard to endure its rough blast!
O, may you but hear of the Savior's kind power,
    And on Jesus your sorrows all cast.

"Then, when this life is o'er and the soul roams free
    In that blessed home above,
'Twill be sweet to bow down in adoring praise
    To the God of infinite love."

"LITTLE NELL"

Cling tight, little Nelly, clasp fondly now
    That bosom so warm and true:
Too soon all her joy, her comfort, below,
    Alone will be centred [sic] in you.

She's leaving the only place that is dear,
    The only spot she can prize:
Her father and mother are living here;
    And she is the light of their eyes.

Your father has gone to his dreamless rest;
    He's sleeping beneath the sod:
Cling close, little Nell, cling close to her breast;
    She'll have only you and her God.

Her poor old father weeps bitterly now;
    His heart is all full of woe;
He presses his hands on his throbbing brow,
    And a fervent prayer breathes low.

Her mother, the picture of grief, looks up
    And grasps for a ray of hope:
Not a ray is found; they must drain the cup
    As their darkened way they grope.

Cling close, little Nell—ay, closely cling now;
    Too soon, all too soon, may you too
Be torn from those arms, 'neath a stern will to bow,
    And the work of a slave to do.

A slave has no rights. At his master's will
    He must leave all he loves and go:
He is bought and sold, though his spirit fill
    With sorrow or break with woe.

Then closely cling to that grief-stricken breast;
    Cling close, little Nell, while you may;
And O, may you learn on Jesus to rest,
    And then praise him in endless day.

"LITTLE LOO"

Little Loo is a darling. She numbers her years one, two, three, four,
and has soft, blue eyes and a round, fair face. She does not care to run,

and jump, and shout as many little girls do, or to play much out of doors, especially in cold weather, for then she does not seem well and strong. But she plays very happily with the kitty, and dolly, and her dishes, and a variety of playthings such as generally please little girls. Sometimes she washes a part of dolly's clothes, and pieces of calico and muslin, and then irons them up quite nicely with her own little flatiron, which she considers a great treasure. She is learning to sew, and is now making dolly a dress. But, of all the things she owns, she values her books the most. We read little stories to her, which she remembers; and she has learned a great many verses, which she loves to repeat. She is a thoughtful child, and often asks strange questions for one of her years.

A while ago a colored girl came in on some errand. Loo was afraid of her, and went to the other side of the room, and kept quite still all the time she was here. But when the colored girl went away little Loo came with her questions.

"Do you like colored people, aunty? Does God make white skin for some people and black skin for some people? What does he make some black for?"

After we had talked about it a while she went to her play, but she did not stop thinking. She soon came again, asking,—

"When colored people die, will they go to heaven? Then, when they are holy angels, will they be black?"

She often talks about heaven, and about who are there, and what they are doing. Sometimes little Loo sits and thinks and thinks until she grows very sad and tears steal out of those soft, blue eyes, and her little bosom heaves with the quick sob of grief.

Her thoughts then are of her own dear mamma, who many months ago went up to God. Yes, little Loo's mamma is dead. She was sick a long time, and grew pale and thin, and her strength all went away; but her mild, blue eyes grew brighter and brighter, and her love to God grew stronger and purer, as she drooped and faded from the earth. Little Loo remembers her well, and loves to talk about her. She sometimes weeps very much because she has no mamma now to love her and to whom she may give the full, free love of her own warm heart. She often takes her daguerreotype and says,—

"This looks just like my mamma, who is up in heaven now. I want to put my arms around her neck and kiss her. I wish I could go up there where the stars live, and see her just a little while, and hear her sing and make sweet music on that golden harp God gave her when he took her there. O, I wish she hadn't died! But God wanted her."

And then she asks,—

"What do the holy angels do all the time? and what makes it so bright and beautiful up in heaven? Does it never be night there? and does my mamma never be sick any more?"

She has a kind papa, who loves her dearly and does all he can to make her happy; and she sometimes says,—

"Papa is the best man in the world, and he knows every thing."

"I suppose all little boys and girls think just so of theirs; and all who have kind, good mothers think they are the very best that any little children ever had. You think so of yours, don't you? Remember, God gave you such good fathers and mothers; and in the Holy Bible, which is God's own book, he says,—

"Children, obey your parents in the Lord; for this is right."

"You should always do what you know they would wish you to do, whether they are with you or not; for God sees you. As little Loo says,—

"God always knows when we are good and when we are naughty. He can see us just as well when it is night and the stars come as he can when it is all light and the sun shines."

"SAMBO'S TOAST"

'Tis a time of good cheer, a time of good cheer;
   Santa Claus is abroad in the land;
And "A happy New Year!" "A happy New Year!"
   Echoes gayly in every band.

Now the north and the south, the east and the west,
   Are in sympathy full and free;
For in each loved home St. Nick is a guest,
   And scatters his gifts merrily.

Some are costly and fine, some simple and poor,
   Some only a wish or a prayer;
But all are made welcome—all open the door
   To take with good will each a share.

The little girl dances and sings in her joy
   O'er her beautiful doll, all dressed:
"O, look at my rocking horse!" shouts the glad boy;
   "My gift is the best—is the best."

Some other a top has received or a cup;
   Another a drum or a fife;
A new set of china makes Lucy look up
   With smiles and a tear in glad strife.

New skates, or a sled, or a chair, or a book,
    Or a dress, or a coat, or a hat,
Or rabbit, or squirrel, or fish on a hook,
    Or a dear little dog, or a cat.

Fine, nice things, so many, some little ones get,
    Their hearts are quite full of delight;
While others, less favored of good things, have yet
    Been content with even their mite.

It is no matter what; when love's warm and true,
    And the spirit all free from guile,
You remember how happy such gifts make you,
    How they gladden your life a while.

On this happy New Year St. Nick made a call
    Where he never had called before—
'Twas in a slave's cabin, with low, smoky wall,
    And only the earth for a floor.

The negroes were sitting quite sullenly there,
    Heart and soul bound down as with chains;
He left them the gift of a warm, fervent prayer,
    Which filled them with love's purest flames.

They began to rejoice: one good thing was still
    Granted them, though hard was their lot—
Stern, selfish "old massa," with strong iron will,
    Had their family band parted not.

They hoped he ne'er would; and this brightened their eyes
    And made them look up with good cheer:
One blessing was left; this they would not despise;
    So their spirits from gloom rose clear.

Now Chloe prepared them their simple repast;
    On the table she placed just one dish;
It was all that she had, their first course and last;
    But gayly came with it the New Year's wish.

Then Sambo sat down in his rough, wooden chair;
    One hand he hung over the back;
In the other he held, steaming up in the air,
    A potato, taken from Jack.

He stuck up his foot as he laughingly said,
    "Here, Chloe; me just gib a toast;

Cum, Cato, and Susey, and Jack Woolly Head,
  Let tree cheers ring round all de coast."

They eagerly listened: then with a good grace
  Each one with a will did his part:
"Old massa," he cried, "he hab a white face,
  But a bery black heart, black heart."

"THE SLAVE"

Whose heart does not bleed for the wrongs inflicted on Africa's sons? What eye can remain unmoistened at the recital of their woes?

Not a great many years ago, a woman came from one of the Southern States to a town in New England, accompanied by a female slave. She was very ignorant; had never been taught her letters; and was not permitted on the Sabbath to hear the word of God read or explained. A colored man, who heard of her condition, wished very much to set her free; and after one or two ineffectual attempts he succeeded, with the help of a colored woman, in taking her from her cruel mistress. A chaise was in readiness, and the slave was carried about thirty miles from town to an acquaintance of one who had previously engaged the situation. But the poor woman was not contented here: she thought of her husband and children whom she had left at the south, and this made her feel unhappy. Meanwhile her mistress offered individuals fifty dollars and one hundred dollars if they would find and return her: but none made search.

After the slave had been absent two or three weeks, she was so discontented and anxious for her children that she was brought back to town, and, of her own accord, went back to her mistress. "You shall pay dear enough for this when I return," said she; and the poor African was sorry that she had not retained her liberty. But now she could not be set free again; for her mistress watched her very narrowly, and confined her in a chamber a great part of the time she remained in town.

Little children cannot conceive of the wretchedness and the miserable condition of the poor slaves. Many of their owners treat them more like dumb beasts than like human beings. It was so with the mistress of this slave. After she had returned to her with the hope of meeting again her husband and children, even this privilege was denied her; for on the homeward-bound passage *she was sold to a slaveholder in North Carolina.* Ah, then were all her hopes of ever seeing again those whom she loved as life at an end. How must her heart have been rent with agony at the thought! her beloved partner no more to enjoy her company, and her dear children to mourn the loss of a tender and affectionate mother.

Little children, pity the poor slaves—pity them with all your heart. How would you feel to be separated forever from your kind mother—to see her face no more—no more to see her smiling look of approbation— no more to receive the kiss of affection? I ask, how would you feel? Dear reader, you cannot imagine how much suffering is endured by the poor blacks. Husbands are separated from wives, children from parents, brothers from sisters. O, I do want you to feel for their condition, and, when you pray, ask God to bless *them*. Can it be that some of you fret and scold, and disobey your parents and your teachers, when you have so much to enjoy and make you happy? Think of the poor blacks. Do you sometimes say you are cruelly treated when requested to leave your play to do some favor for your parents? Think of the poor blacks. At all times, when you imagine you have reason to be angry, or complain, or disobey your friends, I entreat you to remember the condition of a great many thousands of your fellow beings who are in slavery—ignorant, unhappy, and miserable.

I pity the poor little slave,[3]
  Who labors hard through all the day,
    And has no one,
    When day is done,
  To teach his youthful heart to pray.

No words of love, no fond embrace,
  No smiles from parents kind and dear;
    No tears are shed
    Around his bed
  When fevers rage and death is near.

None feel for him when heavy chains
  Are fastened to his tender limb;
    No pitying eyes,
    No sympathies,
  No prayers are raised to Heaven for him.

But I will pity the poor slave,
  And pray that he may soon be free;
    That he at last,
    When days are past,
  In heaven may have his liberty.

NOTES

1. For more detailed analyses of "The Ride" and "The Sale" see De Rosa, 90–91.

2. One of the images included in this text, "Selling Negroes at Auction," also appears with a different caption in Julia Colman and Matilda G. Thompson, *The Child's Anti-Slavery Book: Containing a Few Words about American Slave Children, And Stories of Slave-Life*. See "Little Lewis Sold," (319).

3. This poem also appears in the Juvenile Department of *The Liberator* on Saturday, December 24, 1831, where it is attributed to D.C.C. It also appears in Garrison's *Juvenile Poems*.

[MADAME]

(BIOGRAPHY AND DATES UNKNOWN)

The American Reform Tract and Book Society (ARTBS) was a Cincinnati-based sectarian reform group established in 1852.[1] In its zealous effort to abolish slavery, the ARTBS published primarily abolitionist books and tracts from which it pledged to "strike no sin from the catalogue of iniquities, because it is popular and powerful. It proposes to deal with slaveholding as with other sins, bestowing upon it attention according to its importance" (*Constitution* 11). Recognizing the need to include materials for children in its efforts, in 1855, the ARTBS sponsored a contest soliciting "the best manuscript for a religious Anti-Slavery Sunday School book, showing [children and youth] that American chattel slaveholding is a sin against God, and a crime against man, and that it ought to be immediately repented of and abolished" (Frost [v]). Maria Goodell Frost's work, *Gospel Fruits; or, Bible Christianity Illustrated: A Premium Essay* (1856), won the one hundred dollar prize; however, one of the forty-seven contestants included the work of the anonymous "Madame,"[2] *Jemmy and His Mother, A Tale for Children* and *Lucy; or, the Slave Girl of Kentucky* (1858). Madame's two narratives arouse sympathy for the slave child's plight and cast both black and white women as rebels who fight, to varying degrees of success, for the child's best interests.

In "Little Lucy; or, The Slave Girl of Kentucky" (1858),[3] Madame depicts how a slave child's anxious response to losing her mother leads a white woman (Aunty) and her nephew (Arthur) to move from ignorance, to compassion, and to a commitment to abolitionism. Madame uses sentimental strategies to document a slave child's emotional distress stemming from her efforts to remain with her mother. Although Lucy temporarily prevents the separation through her voice (tears and screams); she considers starving herself because she realizes she is powerless to thwart further violated bonds. Incapable of alleviating the child's suffering because she cannot purchase Lucy *and* her mother, Aunty tries to reduce Lucy's emotional distress by encouraging the child to find freedom through faith. However, the recurrent, external threats that prevent her from ending Lucy's emotional pain arouse sympathy in Aunty and lead her to criticize Harriet Beecher Stowe for oversimplifying her portrait of the slave's emotional suffering in *Uncle Tom's Cabin*. According to Aunty, sympathy and religion cannot eradicate slavery. Finding herself politically powerless, she hopes that her eyewitness account enables Arthur to recognize slavery's brutal reality so that as an adult he will intervene and adopt an abolitionist agenda.

In contrast to Madame's images of powerless women in "Little Lucy," the pseudo slave-narrative "Little Jemmy and His Mother" (1858)[4] depicts women rebelling against slavery. Susan's, anxiety about the threat to her son Jemmy's innocence arouses her rebellion. Madame casts the slave mother Susan's flight in much the same vein as Stowe's depiction of Eliza's flight to save Harry. However, although Eliza heroically steps across the Ohio River as the slave catchers pursue her, Susan cannot cross the ice and momentarily contemplates suicide. But her rejection of suicide shifts the focus away from tragic sentiment to images of rebellious women. Madame includes a white woman who consciously educates Susan and facilitates her escape. Like Mrs. Walberg and Grandmother in *Grandmother's Stories for Children*, this white woman helps a slave mother to regain the inherent right to raise and nurture her child like other nineteenth-century white mothers.

Madame's two narratives epitomize the tightrope that women had to walk in the abolitionist debate. "Little Lucy" suggests that women must rely on men (symbolic in Arthur) to effect change in that like the fictional characters, they are powerless. However, in "Little Jemmy," she depicts women violating all gender and legal codes (i.e., the law against educating slaves and the Fugitive Slave Law) to free a slave woman and her child.

JEMMY AND HIS MOTHER, A TALE FOR CHILDREN AND LUCY; OR, THE SLAVE GIRL OF KENTUCKY (1858)

"LITTLE JEMMY AND HIS MOTHER"

CHAPTER I
SUSAN'S LOVE FOR JEMMY

Jemmy was a happy little slave boy. Do not be surprised because I tell you he was happy, for he was too young to know what a dreadful thing it is to be a slave. He had never been bought or sold; and he had always lived at one place.

His mother was owned by a wealthy planter in Kentucky, who kept her for a house servant, and treated her, generally, very kindly; but she was not happy, for she knew when her little boy was old enough to work he would be taken away from her, and perhaps be sold and carried away where she could never see him again.

Poor Susan, for that was her name, used to lie awake at night, and think about her precious child, and wonder how she would feel to have him taken away from her, and who would put him to bed, and who would be sorry for him if his master should whip him, and who would take care of him if he was sick; and then she would weep, and weep, and weep over him, sometimes until the sun rose in the morning, and would wish that she could die, and her little boy could die too, that they would not have to be slaves.

The poor, poor slave mother! No one had ever told her there was a God, and that it was sinful to have such thoughts. No one had ever taught her to pray; and there was no one that she knew of, who could help her out of her trouble. The slaves who worked in the field thought she was a great deal better off than they were; and so she was, so far as work was concerned, but she felt that it would be just as easy for her to go out and work under a hard overseer, as it would be to have her boy go; and she knew that he would have to go as soon as he was a little older; and would have to be driven and whipped if he did not do as much work as he was told to do, and that no one would care whether he was tired or not; and if he should cry, as children are apt to do sometimes, she knew that no one would pity him, or say a word of comfort to him.

These thoughts of course made her feel very miserable. She used to go about her work with tears in her eyes; and whenever she heard little

Jemmy playing and singing about the house, or in the yard, it would seem as though her heart would break to think she must part with him.

Her mistress used often to find her crying, and she would give her a new dress, or a new hat or apron for Jemmy, to pacify her, for she knew well enough what made her feel so bad; but such presents did poor Susan no good, so long as the dreadful thought haunted her that they would in a short time take away her dear, dear child. She knew that they often sold bright-looking little children, when they were no more than two years old, and she used to be afraid whenever strangers came to the house, for fear they would see her little boy and want to buy him.

At length her mistress became angry with her, and told her to be more cheerful, or they would sell her to one of those Southern Slave-drivers who treat their slaves very badly, and work them very hard. So she tried to hide her feelings all she could, but she found it very hard to do so.

My dear children, when you hear any one say that the slaveholders treat their slaves well, when they are good and obedient, you kindly ask them if they would think they were well treated if they had all they needed to eat and to wear, but were obliged to see their children one after another sold away from them, or put to work near them, where they could never help them if they saw them tired and sick, and knew that they themselves would be sold to any one who would give a trifling sum for them, when they were too aged to do hard work. Ask them if they could be happy and cheerful with such thoughts in their mind. And if they finally acknowledge that they do feel sorry for the poor slaves, ask them if they are doing any thing for them—if they ever send any thing for the comfort of the poor creatures who are fortunate enough to get away from the Slave States, and who have to flee to Canada, where the climate is cold, and where they suffer much because they are not used to cold weather; though they consider such suffering very small when they can feel that they shall never be bought or sold again, or separated from parents and brothers and sisters, and know that when they labor hard they can receive the pay for it and build their own houses and call them theirs, and have their own things without fear of any one taking them away from them.

Talk to your school-mates about these things, and tell them when you are old enough to vote, you shall vote for no man that thinks such a wicked thing as slavery is right, for fear he will be wicked about other things, and wrong the people who put him in office. I suppose you think you are young now, and can not do much, but you must remember that it will be but a few years before you will be the only ones there are to do, for your fathers and your mothers will be buried and gone; and you should be thinking now what you will do when you are grown up, for the good of the world and the praise of God, and your own happiness after death; for that you know depends upon what you do while in this world. If we do not try to do good while we live, we have no reason to suppose we shall be happy hereafter.

But let us go back again to poor Susan. She found it impossible to appear cheerful, and she was very much distressed, and knew not what to do. If she had known how to pray, or to whom to pray, she would have found some relief for her troubled mind; but, alas! every thing looked dark to her.

CHAPTER II
THE ESCAPE

Susan felt that life would be dreary without her child, and she did not believe she should see him again after death unless they both died together, so she kept wishing and wishing that they might die. She thought sometimes she would go away with her child into the garret, or some lonely place, and stay until they starved to death, and then she supposed they would be buried in one coffin, and so they would not be separated. But God put better thoughts in her mind, and did not let her do such a dreadful thing. She finally concluded she would try and get away from those who pretended to own her as they did their houses and lands, and claimed the right to buy and sell her. She had heard about slaves running away, and going north to be free, and she knew, too, when they were caught and brought back they were severely whipped, sometimes so severely that they died. But yet she thought she had rather run the risk of being caught, than to stay there and be separated from her child.

It did not take her long to get ready after she had made up her mind to go, for she had no friends to bid "good by." She did not dare to tell anyone she was going, for fear her master and mistress would hear of it, and would watch her so that she could not get away.

She started one dark, windy night, when she thought but few would be out. She had gathered up a few things for little Jemmy, and tied them up in a pocket handkerchief, and taking him off his bed where he was fast asleep, she went as quickly as possible out of the house and through the yard into the road. After she had gone a short distance she put her little boy down, and stopped to rest. The little fellow was wide awake by this time, and clinging hold of his mother's clothes, began to cry. Poor

Susan quieted him as well as she could, and told him little stories, until at last he began to laugh and hop along by her side. You know I have told you he was a happy little boy, and I think he was not so much afraid of the dark as some children are; which, by the way, is a very foolish kind of fear, and very wrong too, for children who are taught to trust in God. For He could let you get hurt just as well in the daytime as in the night, and it is distrusting His goodness and care to be always afraid, and is very displeasing to Him. There is no doubt but God often punishes His children, by sending trouble upon them, when they manifest such a want of trust in Him.

I can not tell you how sad poor Susan felt after she had got out of sight of her old home, for she did not know what she could do if she should get where she would be free, or whether any one would give her work and pay her for it, but she thought she would rather die of cold and hunger than to have her child sold away from her. So she walked on as fast as she could toward that wonderful North she had heard of, where loving mothers rock their little ones to sleep, night after night, without fear of any strange men coming and taking them away.

How thankful we should be for the great blessings of liberty which we enjoy, and how earnestly we should try and do something for the poor oppressed ones, if it is only to make some one else pity them, which would be *something*. When we are in trouble, it is a great comfort to know that others are sorry for us.

Perhaps you are wondering where little Jemmy's father was, and why he didn't go with them. Poor Susan did not know much about her husband, for he lived upon another plantation, and was sold a few months after they were married, and taken farther South, so that little Jemmy never saw his father and did not know any thing about him. You would not know how to spare your dear father, and you expect to live with him until you grow up; but if you ever have naughty feelings when he bids you do what you do not want to do, or when he refuses you something you desire, remember those who have no fathers, or whose fathers are slaves, and can not get little presents for their children to make them happy.

After Susan and her little boy had gone a mile or two, she heard wheels approaching. She crept close up to the fence, and crouching down by a little bush, she spread the dark-colored shawl she had on over Jemmy, and telling him to be quiet, she bent down her head and waited for the vehicle to pass. Fortunately, it passed without their being observed, but it frightened her so that she thought it best to get over the fence and go through the fields. She found it more difficult getting along there with her child, for he began to grow very weary, and did not want to go any farther, but she gave him a cake, for she had put a few in her bundle for him, and so encouraged him along until day began to break, and then she began to look for a place to hide through the day, for she knew it would not be safe to travel except in the night.

They came, at last, to a little thicket of trees and bushes, and, tired and almost discouraged, the poor slave mother sat down to rest. "Oh! what a weary, weary life this is," she murmured to herself, as she took her little boy in her arms and looked around to see where she could lay him down when he fell asleep. Poor, poor Susan, if she had only trusted in God, and prayed to Him to give her strength and courage, how comforting it would have been to her. But she had never prayed in her life. The people with whom she lived were not religious people; they seldom went to church, and never sent their slaves, so that she was very ignorant about her Maker and the duties we owe Him.

Perhaps you wonder if any of the slaveholders are religious, and if they dare to pray God to bless them while they are doing so wickedly by their fellow-men. Yes, many of them make professions of piety, and go to church, and let their slaves go too. But we will not judge them, for we are warned in the Bible against judging the sins of others. God will take care of them, and if it is best for them to be punished, He will surely do it. God brings about punishments in very unexpected ways, sometimes so that it is impossible to escape them.

Susan laid little Jemmy down upon the grass after he had gone to sleep in her arms, and then looked around and found some berries for her breakfast, for she would not eat any of the cakes she had taken for Jemmy. She then lay down beside her little boy, but it was a long, long time before she could get to sleep, and when she did, she dreamed strange dreams. She dreamed about lying in a damp bed, and about snakes crawling around her and Jemmy, and then again about dogs chasing them, so that when she awoke, towards noon, she did not feel much refreshed from her sleep, and she began wearily again to pick berries and to look after nuts.

We should think it was rather hard fare to live upon nuts and berries, even for a single day, but that was the least of poor Susan's trouble. She thought if she could only be free, she could live on almost any thing.

Little Jemmy did not awake until late in the afternoon, for he was very tired from the long walk. His mother gave him another cake and some of the berries she had gathered, and then picked flowers to amuse him until it was dark again.

Susan had found so much trouble in getting along through the fields, she thought she would venture to go in the road again, as she thought she was so far away from her master's home, that no one would know her. But she had not gone so far as she imagined, though it no doubt seemed a great way to her; for she had only gone four miles. She had to walk very slow on little Jemmy's account, and sat down often to let him rest.

The stars came out bright that night, and she was glad, for she wanted to see the north star, so as to be sure she was keeping in a northerly direction. It was not so lonely as it was the night before, and they proceeded faster, so that before daylight they came in sight of the Ohio river.

CHAPTER III
THE RETURN

And now what a wonder was opened to poor Susan's eyes. She had heard tell about the Ohio river, and knew that it was about ten miles from where she lived, but she had a very indistinct idea as to what it was. She had seen small streams, and supposed it was something like those, so you can imagine her surprise when she saw so much water, and wondered how she was going to cross it.

There was a ferry-boat there, but she did not know what it was, and would not have dared to go upon it if she had.

She now sat down and wept bitterly, and felt very much like taking her child in her arms and throwing herself into the deep water, where she would sink to rise no more. But little Jemmy, who was delighted with the wonderful sight, put his arms around her neck, and wiped the tears off her face with his little hands.

When Susan saw Jemmy smiling and so pretty, she could not think of doing him any harm, neither could she think of drowning herself and leaving him there alone; so, after thinking a long time, she concluded to go back and try and learn something more about the way the slaves escaped to the north.

But what should she tell her mistress? Where should she tell her she had been so long? After another half hour of sad thinking, she made up her mind to go back and tell her mistress that she went out into the swamp to pick berries and got lost, and could not find her way out! Poor ignorant slave. She did not know that telling an untruth was sinning against a just and good God, or that any but earthly beings would know of it.

Susan had never been in the habit of telling wrong stories, because her mistress had told her she must not, and she had always tried to do as she was told.

This was the first time she had ever undertaken to deceive any one, and she did not feel exactly satisfied with herself. And this proves that God has given us all a knowledge of right and wrong, though education makes that knowledge much clearer, and makes us, too, more responsible for the wrong we do.

Susan did not find much trouble in getting back again; she met but one or two vehicles on the road, as it was a rather unfrequented one; but when she reached the house she felt bad enough. Oh, how *could* she give up the hope of being free and keeping her child, and yet she greatly feared she should never dare to undertake again to get away.

CHAPTER IV
NEW VIEWS—PROGRESS IN KNOWLEDGE

And now we shall see how wisely God orders all things that take place in this world. After Susan had returned, her mistress gave her a new dress, and some old playthings for Jemmy, that her children had become tired of. Among the playthings she gave to Jemmy, were some old books—several picture books, old spelling-book, and a part of an old Testament. Susan looked them over, and the idea came into her mind that perhaps she could learn to read, and possibly she might, some time or other, read of something that would enlighten her as to how she could get to the land of freedom she so longed to see.

Now was not that a very wise thought for a poor ignorant slave? And do you not think a kind and merciful God put the thought into her mind? We have every reason to believe that the Spirit of God speaks comforting words to many a worried mind, and thus soothes many aching hearts.

Susan carefully laid away the old books, and waited for an opportunity to get some one to show her a little about them. There was a young lady in the family, a governess, who taught her mistress' children, and she had often spoken very kindly to Susan and her little boy, and Susan thought, perhaps if she should ask her, she would help her to learn to read.

Susan, Jemmy, and Miss Harris
Courtesy, American Antiquarian Society.

Only think, my dear children, what advantages you have, and how you ought to prize them. You have teachers provided for you, and every inducement to learn; and when you feel indolent again and want to skip over your lessons without learning them well, you must think how many there are that would like to be in your place, and have such kind friends to teach them. I have known some Sabbath School scholars, bright little girls and boys too, who would idle away their time through the week, and then go into their class on Sunday without having learned the short lesson given to them the Sabbath before. And this is very, very wrong. I think if such children were slaves a little while, and had no one to instruct them, they would never want to neglect their lessons again, for there is no little boy or girl that would like the idea of growing up ignorant.

It was a long time before Susan found an opportunity to speak to Miss Harris, the governess, and when she did, she was afraid to tell her what she wanted. Susan was putting the school-room in order one morning, when Miss Harris came in. Little Jemmy was with her as usual, and Miss Harris stepped up to him, and patting his little curly head, said, "I guess you are a nice little fellow." Then she turned round to speak to his mother, and saw her tears falling thick and fast, though she was bending down her head and trying to conceal them.

Miss Harris kindly asked her what troubled her, but poor Susan still felt afraid to tell her. At last, seeing that Miss Harris appeared so very kind, she ventured to tell her what it was that made her feel so sad.

They talked a long time, until the children came in and they were obliged to stop. Susan opened her heart fully to the kind lady, and even ventured to tell her how she had tried to run away, and how much she wanted to get where she could always keep her child with her, and feel as if he were her own.

She was greatly delighted when Miss Harris told her that she would instruct her all she could in her spare moments.

You may be sure the school-room had good care taken of it after that, and almost every day Miss Harris found an opportunity to talk with Susan, and teach her how to read, and to understand what she read. She was very happy in doing it when she thought of pleasing her heavenly Father in this way. She was very glad, too, to see how quick and bright Susan's mind was, and how greatly she was delighted when she found herself really learning to read.

. Susan became very industrious and attentive to her work, and very cheerful too, for now she had such happy thoughts in her mind she could not help being cheerful. Her mistress noticed the change in her, and praised her very much, and gave her a good many new things, until the poor slave began to think it would not be right to go away and leave her; but when she looked at her little boy, and thought that he would probably outlive her present master and mistress, even if they should never sell him, and then perhaps he would have a cruel master, and when she remembered an old slave they had sold not many months ago, because he was of but little use to them, she felt it would be more wrong to stay than it would be to go away where she and her child would be free. So she worked away as fast as she could for them, and learned all she could from Miss Harris, who was pious, and did not forget to tell her about God and Christ and the duties she owed her Heavenly Father, and the comfort she might obtain by trusting in him and asking his guidance in what she did.

When Susan had learned to pray, and began to understand what a wise Being her Heavenly Father was, she felt that it was all right that she failed in getting away from slavery, and was obliged to come back again, for she thought if she had succeeded in getting away then she should have been so overjoyed, that she should never have cared for any greater happiness, and perhaps would have lived in freedom and died a slave to sin, which she now saw would have been far worse than to live in slavery here, and to die and go home to heaven. So she felt glad that God had sent her back again, and she determined never to undertake any thing again without asking His assistance and guidance.

CHAPTER V
SUSAN'S SECOND ESCAPE

It was some time after this, that Susan, thinking she had found a way to escape, and what route to take, determined to try again. She had carefully saved all the little money given to her in presents. She had heard, too, that there were good people on the way who would help her. All this encouraged her to start, and find a land of liberty for herself and child. It was a long and perilous journey for her, but she reached Canada at last in safety.

Do you never wish, my dear children, that the slaves were not obliged to go so far North to find safety from their pursuers? It is very cold there, and being unaccustomed to a cold climate, they often suffer very much. I saw a colored man from there not many months ago, and I observed that he coughed very badly. I felt very sorry for him, and asked him if the fugitives did not suffer from the coldness of the climate in Canada. "Yes, madam," said he, "some keep taking cold after cold, until at last their lungs become affected beyond cure, and they die with consumption. But," he added, smiling very pleasantly, "we don't mind that when we are free."

I have seen another man who lives there, a very good man, and if he was only white, he would be called a very smart man, for he never had all education except what he has picked up here and there as he had opportunity, but he can talk to a house full of people until the tears come into their eyes, and no one dares to move for fear he will make a noise and will not hear every word he is telling them.

His escape from slavery was very remarkable, and I would tell you about it but that he wants to have it all written in a book that he can sell and get money to buy his little daughter, who is still in bondage. He was caught and taken back and put into jail, the first attempt he made to get away, but he trusted in God, and he told me that he felt sure that God would release him, and he did not cease to pray, and his prayer was heard, and he was enabled the second time to elude his pursuers and reach Canada in safety.

He has labored hard, and has now a good home, which proves the saying of slaveholders, that their slaves cannot take care of themselves, very untrue. There is no doubt, many slaveholders honestly believe that their slaves could not take care of themselves if they were to give them their freedom; and we must have charity for them, and pray that they may be convinced of this great error. It is always safer to have too much charity than too little; and those who hold the slaves in bondage are certainly to be pitied as well as the poor slaves.

Some of them are to be pitied for the great punishment that awaits them, and many of them are to be pitied because they cannot see they are doing wrong. They have been brought up to believe that slavery is just and necessary, and early impressions are very difficult to get rid of; so, see to it, my little friends, that your early impressions are such that you will not need to get rid of them when you are grown up, that "they may grow with your growth and strengthen with your strength" until they become mighty, and cast an influence all around. There is scarcely a sentence you utter but that influences some one for either good or evil. Think always more than you speak, and be sure that what you say is right. You have all either brothers, or sisters, or playmates, and you must not let them learn any thing bad from you. And now let me ask, if you have ever done any thing for the poor slave? Have you ever prayed for him or his unwise master, that God would soften his heart to let the bondman go free? And do you ever wish that we might have better rulers—Christian men, who would not allow these things to be? The little girls must talk to their little brothers, and the brothers must talk to other boys of their age, about these matters, and you must form societies among yourselves when you go to school, at recess and at noon-time, and you must pass resolutions condemning such great wickedness; then you will be growing with good impressions upon your minds, and will be prepared to act when you are men and women,—to act in the fear of God and for the good of all who may feel your influence.

"LUCY; OR, THE SLAVE GIRL OF KENTUCKY"

"I've got it!" shouted little Arthur Morton, as he came bounding in from school one day. "Here is my report, that shows I've not missed a question, or got a black mark for any thing for two weeks; and now, aunty, for a story; for you know that you promised when I got this, you would spend two hours telling me stories."

"Very true, Arthur, so I did," said the good aunty, and I am right glad you have been so good a boy. But I hope the promise of the story was not all that induced you to do your best?"

"Oh no, because I found out a good while ago, that the more I tried to be good, the happier I grew, and the easier it grew, too, to learn my lesson, and always be in season; but of course, aunty, I could not help thinking about the fine stories every day that I got no black marks. There could'nt [sic] have been harm in that, could there?"

"To be sure not; I only wanted to know what had been your highest motive; and am more than ever pleased to think you are learning to prize an approving conscience, and to do right simply because or for the sake of right; and now, as you have fairly earned a story, or several of them, I will be very happy to commence the two hours' talk whenever you are ready. But tell me first what it shall be about? Something somebody has *written*, or a true story of what has really happened?"

"Oh, something *true*, aunty, and I do want to hear what you told cousin Ben the other day, that made him say he should lay up all the money he could get, to free little colored boys and girls with. He was going to tell me the story, only he said you could tell it so much better, that I finally chose to wait for it."

"I think it must have been about little Lucy, whom I saw once on my way to New Orleans."

"Yes, that is it, I know," said Arthur, and he drew his chair close up in front of aunty's sofa, where he could watch the expression of her face as she told the following true story:

Just imagine yourself on board one of those enormous Mississippi river steamers, that carry not only hundreds of passengers, but all articles of merchandise, from a Jew's harp to barrels of pork, and of live animals, from a chicken to the largest oxen. You would like to see in reality one of those steamers loaded for the Southern market, though you would be sorry for the poor animals, herded so close that they cannot have any comfort—pigs, sheep, lambs, oxen, and horses, in their different pens on the lower deck. The middle deck is empty, but the upper one is usually covered with long coops filled with hens, chickens, geese, ducks, pigeons, doves, and turkeys. When I first heard these little creatures eating their breakfast above my head, I could not imagine what the noise was—they made such a tapping picking up the corn. They are so crowded together, that sometimes several die in a day, and then again, some of those that are only tied by the legs to the outside of the coops and cages, now and then break their fastenings, and fly or fall off into the river. It was sad enough to see them struggle and drown in the cold muddy water. If you will look upon the map, Arthur, some time, you can find the town of Paducah on the north-western boundary of Kentucky, a place at which our boat stopped late one evening. It was a clear frosty night, and the moon and stars shone almost as bright as suns in the dark sky, and gave a magic beauty to almost every thing beneath them. Your uncle came to my state-room for me to go out upon deck to look at the town. It was a lovely landscape, though I am not sure it would have appeared so charming at midday. Nothing could exceed its serenity and beauty then, as it stretched out before us in the bright moonlight—the town seemingly cradled among the gentler slopes, as I said to brother, "as quiet and still as a sleeping child," that the stars themselves were watching with twinkling pleasure.

"That," said he, "is just a piece of nonsense; for to me those stars seem to blaze with indignation quite as manifestly as to you they twinkle with pleasure, and with far more reason, for I cannot forget that this is slave soil, every inch of it a cradle of tyranny and oppression, and the very beauty of those residences suggests the human miseries which have both directly and indirectly been involved in their construction."

I was unwilling that my enjoyment should be marred by any such reflections, and had turned our conversation to a happier subject, when the air was suddenly rent by the most piercing, distracting shrieks I had ever heard. One after another they followed, unearthly and wild, as though the agony and despair of twenty souls might have been concentrated in that one. Neither of us could speak for a few moments, so fearful and startling were those terrible shrieks, that seemed likely never to stop. They came from the shore near the bow of the boat, but the huge wheelhouses hid the cause from our sight, and the length of the boat prevented us from hearing any *sounds* that could give a clue to the mystery. Still they continued!—what could it mean? We knew it could be no slavewhipping, else we should hear the crack of the terrible whip; but we could not even guess a torture that should wring from any human being shrieks like those. After some little time, they stopped as suddenly as they began, and all was still as before, save the noise of the boat as it was preparing to leave the wharf. Then we heard a different sort of cry just beneath our feet—a poor little lamb, in its careless capers in the moonlight, had fallen overboard into the river. Its little white head was all we could see above the black freezing water, and its piteous bleating made me shiver in sympathy. We knew it must drown, too, for we could hear by its gurgling cry that the pitiless water was filling its little throat, and that each answer it made to its mother's calls was less and less loud. We tried to save it by a lasso, but the swinging about of the boat prevented our success, and drew the poor thing entirely under the water. You may think it strange, but the excitement of the last incident had thrust from my mind the one that went before it, and the boat had not gone far on its way when I returned to my state-room, all unmindful of human sorrow, and little dreaming that there were beings only a few feet beneath me who would gladly have shared the poor lamb's fate, or that there were heartaches there which, if made apparent by a sound proportioned to their intensity, would have brought upon their feet the many sleepers within the boat, and made it seem like a floating volcano.

The next morning, as I was passing through the lower cabin, I saw, sitting on a rug before the grate, a little girl about a dozen years old apparently.

"Just my age," interrupted Arthur.

Yes, but she was not so large as you though, and was withal very slender looking. I never saw such a picture of distress in a child. She sat staring into the fire as though she saw in its bright flames what no one else could see, her hands clenched convulsively upon her sides, and even her little toes, which appeared from under her blue checked frock, were curled up tight as her fingers, and every few minutes her little body shook with convulsive sobs, that were evidently the remains of a tempest of passion. On the floor beside her was a tempting breakfast of chicken, ham and eggs, rolls and coffee; but she gave no signs of caring for it. Neither did she notice me, though I stood quite close to her. After watching the poor creature a few moments I said, "Good morning, Netty dear, how do you do this morning?" She looked up at this with the most hopeless expression imaginable, and answered, "Please, missis, my name ain't Netty, its Lucy; an' I ain't well at all dis yer morning."

"I am sorry if you are sick; what is the matter?" I asked.

"Oh, my head hurts me—I nebber was a well chile, nebber. Granny says as how I'se giben her more trouble dan all de res' de chil'en she eber had. Sometimes I'se a little better, but now I'se wus again. Specs I hurted mysef a-cryin so las' night—did missus hear me? De Cappan said I'd scar all de people to death der was on de boat."

"No, I didn't hear you," I answered, "I have never heard any crying on the boat; what time was it, and what made you cry?"

"Oh, twasn't on de boat at all—'twas back dar at Paducket."

"Why, that could not have been you who screamed so at the wharf where the boat stopped!"

"Oh yes, 'twas, missus. You see dey wouldn't nudder let me come wid mammy, nor take me back to granny, and so I couldn't do nothin' but scream."

"Where *is* your granny?"

"Oh, she's back dar to massa Tom's house—yer see massa Tom got broke de oder day, an had to sell most all his folks; dat is, de young hands an de little folks, but he said he wouldn't sell de ole uns, what his fader had on de place afore him, no-how; an yer see, missus, granny's one o' de ole uns, and stays dar yet; but mammy's 'mong de young hands, and I'se 'mong de little uns, an so we'se done got sold!"

And here the poor child clenched tightly again her little thin fingers that had been gradually loosened during our talk, and turning her face toward the fire, commenced rocking her body to and fro, and talking as if to herself.

"Oh, I wish I'se wid poor granny again; she hain't got no more sick chil'n to take care on now, an' I hasn't got nobody to take care o' me, no more neber."

"Where is your mammy?" I asked.

"Oh, she's forrard dar 'mong dose people, dat missus can see," she answered, pointing to a group which I had not noticed at the other end of the cabin;—such a group as I hope never to see again—men and women of different ages and appearances, some of whom had just been sold from all they loved in the world, to a new master who was again to sell them to another, and probably to a more severe bondage than they had ever known—while others among them had been bought by different individuals then on the boat, who had been up into the country to buy fresh hands for the next cotton crop, to supply the places of those who had died during the harvesting of the last.

"Dat ar is mammy," continued Lucy, "dat ar one dat sits by de man dat takes on so—an' dat's Sam. Dey're de only two what's come from massa Tom's place; an' he don't like, nudder, to go away from aunt Sukey, an' Johnny, an' little Snowball; nor to go down de river at all; an' I specs he'd a drowned hisself in de riber las' night, if dey hadn't tied him so he couldn't.

The poor man sat upon the floor, his head bowed upon his knees, with his hands clasped over his neck, silent as a statue, but his whole appearance bespeaking the most hopeless grief. Mrs. Stowe had not then told us Northerners what a horror the poor negroes have of being sold down the river, and so I supposed that all his grief was occasioned by the separation from his wife and little ones, and I felt that to be a sufficient cause for it. I could not endure to look at them, but went on talking with the child.

"I thought you said, Lucy, that they wouldn't let you and your mammy go together?"

"An' so dey wouldn't," she answered, "for when de massa buyed mammy in Paducah, he wouldn't tink o' me at all, 'cause he said as how

I'se a poor little sick good-for-nothin' lookin' ting, and aint o'no account nohow; an' arter all, said he hadn't got no more money dan jus' enuff to buy mammy; but I cried so, he wasn't goin' for to take her nudder, but de oder massa said he'd sell me for fifty dollars if dey took us togedder, so massa said he'd come aboard de boat to try an' borrow de money. But de Cappan was out dar, an' told him he'd lend de money if I'd stop cryin, an' let go o' mammy, an' so dey took me, an' here I'se be missus!"

"Well, Lucy, now I think you had better eat your breakfast; it will soon be entirely cold, if it is not so already.

"No, missus, I aint a-goin for to eat no more," she said determinedly.

"Why not?"

"'Cause dey want to hab me eat, an' say I'll die if I don't!"

"Why, child, you don't want to starve yourself, I hope!"

"Not 'zac'ly, missus, but I hopes I'll die anyhow afore dey has time to take me from mammy agin; an' if I don't eat, specs I shall, an' den I'll be glad."

"Which would you like best, Lucy, to be free and go and live with me, or go with mammy and be a slave?"

"I'd radder go back to granny dan to go wid eider ob yees—an' yer see, missus, 'taint o' no kind o' use a freeing a little sick nigger child like I'll be, anyhow, cause I'se agwine for to die one o' dese yer days, an' be buried up in de groun', an' go an' lib wid de Lord, an' den I'll be done free for sartain. Ebrybody 'll be free an' equal when dey'se dead! Didn't missus know _dat?_" she said, her face lighting up with something of hope and triumph.

"Yes," I replied, "if we have first been freed from sin by Christ, and unless we have been, I fear none of us will go to live with the Lord."

"Why, how's dat," she said, astonished; "what's bein' freed from sin?"

"Free from the power of our own willful, selfish spirits, made willing to submit to God's will concerning us, and to obey all His commands; to bear patiently and cheerfully all that happens to us. Now, Lucy, are you sure you do all this? White people don't expect, when they are unwilling to live, and try to starve themselves, that the Lord will take them to live with him; and I am afraid he looks into the hearts of little colored children, and wants to see a good spirit in them, just as he does into the hearts of white children, because we suppose they are of equal value in His sight _before_ their bodies are buried in the ground. The heart of a colored child may be free from sin while the body is a slave, and the heart of a white child may be a slave to sin, while its body is free; all hearts must have good spirits in them if they would be taken to live with the Lord when the body is dead."

"Nobody neber told me dat afore; but what can I do, missus?" she said, sorrowfully; "white ladies what neber knowed nottin' at all 'bout sickness an' trouble, don't know how hard 'tis for us colored people to be good an' wan' to lib, when we'se done sold, an' down de riber too! But granny said the Lord knowed."

"Well, Lucy, I will tell you, that first you must try to eat your breakfast, and be thankful it is so nice—try to think how much better your condition is than it would be if God had not put it into the heart of the man to buy you with your mammy. Ask God every day to forgive your wicked wishes, to help you to be patient and cheerful, and to help you to comfort your poor mammy and to make her happier; and ask Him to make you fit to live with Him when you die, and He certainly will hear you, and make you willing to wait here till He call[s] you to a home where you never will be sold again." The poor child stretched out her hand slowly toward the food, but let it fall listlessly by the plate, and though big tears rolled over her little swollen cheeks as I told her of our Savior's love for her, and of His readiness and pleasure in helping her to do all her little duties, it was evident that they were not so bitter as those she had shed during the past few days. Presently a happier expression came over her face, and she looked up almost with a smile as she said, "Oh, I'll try for sartin. And does missus tink He'll call me afore long?"

"I hope so," I answered, "and that He will make you happier till he does." Then after persuading her to commence her breakfast, I left her with a promise to talk with her again the next day.

So on the following morning I went down and found the little thing evidently watching for me, and I had no sooner opened the door than she commenced a sort of pirouetting first upon one foot and then upon the other, looking at me intently at the same time, as much as to say, "Do you see how I try to be happy?" When I inquired how she felt, she said, "I'se 'sidable better dis yer morning, tank yer, missus." Then, as if afraid that I had not noticed the pranks she was really too weak to keep up, continued, "an' I'se a-tryin' to be happy; but mammy took on mighty bad las' night in de night 'bout Dinah an' little Dickey, an' all de res' on 'em, cause as how we're a-goin' furder and furder 'way from 'em, and neber 'll see none on 'em no more, an' she don't know whar dey all is."

The mother came forward while we were talking, and with a very gracious courtesy commenced saying she was much obliged to me for talking to Lucy as I had the previous day, and hoped I would excuse all her bad ways, because she had always been a sick little thing, and lived with her granny, who let her have her own way: and when she went up to the hall to stay, massa Tom always petted her, and would never have her ruled by the servants, or crossed any way, "cause as how (to use her own words) he sot such a heap by her." The poor woman was suffering badly from asthma, with which she had always been so troubled as never to have done much hard work, being only called upon to sew a little, or help in the kitchen, at the hall, when there was extra work to be done. She declared "massa Tom" to be the best kind of a master, and said he made the man who bought her promise that she should not be sold for anything but a house servant, and also that none of the people should be sold down the river. But spite of all that, she had been bought by a cotton planter on Red river, where she would be compelled to work in the field early and late, in the dews and fog and rain, which would probably soon kill her. But worse than all, she said the man had broken another promise, not to separate the families to go in different directions, but that the members of one family should be sold in the same county, or, if possible, in the same town or neighborhood; and now he had scarcely any two members of the same family to go the same way. When I asked her if she had other children than Lucy, she answered, "Oh yes, indeed, missus, only three weeks ago I had a home, a husband, and eight children, and didn't 'spect no kind o' trouble, cause massa Tom was always so good; but all sorts o' trouble comes soon enough arter de officer what come wid de writins, an massa Tom couldn't help us bein' sold, an now I'm goin' down de riber; home, husband, and chil'en all gone different ways, all but dis yer poor little sick thing, an de good Lor only knows what'll become o' *her* when *I'm* gone, as I soon shall be;"—and the poor woman covered her face with her hands, and bursting into a violent fit of weeping, walked hastily away to the other end of the cabin. I am sorry I cannot tell you, Arthur, what became of the poor things after; but that night they were taken off the boat at the mouth of Red river, and I was thankful that it was while I slept, for I wouldn't like to have seen them grieve at bidding good-by to their dear friends going further down the river."

"That's a right sad story, aunty," said Arthur; "and I can't help thinking that they are both dead before this."

"They probably died long ago," said aunty; "but the saddest part of the story is, that it is *less* than what might be told of what passes every day in a slave country."

"Oh aunty, can it be so?"

"Yes, Arthur, I have no doubt that those foul, muddy Mississippi waters bear down on their surface, every day, even worse evidences than this of that more foul and filthy system of slavery, in the shape of manacled limbs, bruised backs, and broken hearts; parents mourning for children, and children for parents, who loved each other as you love your home and parents—brothers and sisters grieving for each other, and husbands and wives who are as much one in the sight of our Heavenly Father as are *your* father and mother, Arthur!"

"Well, I cannot bear to think of it, aunty."

"But I want you to think of it, at least till you sicken and hate it as every Christian ought, so that when you are a man you will resist its aggressions with your whole soul."

"I hate it now, aunty," and he continued to say what I hope all boys and girls who read this will join him in saying; "I'll pray that I may continue to hate the whole thing with all my might, and I'll give thanks, too, every day, that I was not born a colored child, to be sold away from all I love and be taken down the Mississippi river."

NOTES

1. For a history of the ARTBS, see De Rosa, 31–37.

2. Note author's female self-reference ("madam") in "Susan's Second Escape" (chapter 5) in "Little Jemmy and His Mother" (see 294).

3. For a complete analysis of "Little Lucy," see De Rosa, 56–57.

4. For a complete analysis of "Little Jemmy," see De Rosa, 67–69.

ANNA H. RICHARDSON

(DATES UNKNOWN)

Like Amelia Opie, her British foremother who wrote twenty years earlier, Anna Richardson made significant contributions to abolitionist juvenile literature. Little biographical information has surfaced about Anna Richardson except that she lived at 54 Westmoreland Terrace in Newcastle-upon-Tyne in Northeast England. However, *Little Laura, the Kentucky Abolitionist: An Address to the Young Friends of the Slave* (1859) reveals a politically active woman willing to raise funds for American abolitionism.

Addressed to the children of England, Scotland, and Ireland, *Little Laura* documents the true story of a ten-year-old American girl's abolitionist efforts. With her parents and her elder siblings as her role models, Laura B. advocates abolitionism through both written and oral rhetoric. From their Kentucky home, Laura's family publishes an antislavery newspaper, even after a mob burns the press to silence its abolitionist message. Laura "learned to handle type" (308), which symbolizes her role in perpetuating this written, abolitionist rhetoric that situates her in a public, political discourse from which females were often excluded (De Rosa 145–146). When Laura becomes ill and can no longer help at the press, she transforms her written discourse (as an assistant in her father's press) into oral, political discourse when she enrolls in the local school. Laura's classmates (whose parents own slaves) scoff at her abolitionism, but by degrees they accept Laura's ideas and voice compassion for the slaves. Thus, Laura resembles "her foremothers who challenged the ideology of separate spheres by writing for abolitionist newspapers and speaking publicly despite criticism" (De Rosa 146).

Richardson's *Little Laura* not only invites abolitionist consciousness but also requests activism—monetary donations to support the family's continued abolitionist efforts. Like the American juvenile antislavery societies that encouraged children to speak and act against slavery, so too Richardson appeals to English, Scottish, and Irish children to consult with their parents and to collect financial donations—the additional five hundred pounds needed to alleviate the Kentucky family's financial crisis. Most interestingly, written on the eve of the Civil War, Richardson's true story calls children to engage in immediate and tenable action, a realization of the hopes that domestic abolitionists infused in their juvenile fiction. Like her foremothers, Richardson walks the tightrope of political rhetoric and asks seemingly powerless children to engage in the same feat.

LITTLE LAURA, THE KENTUCKY ABOLITIONIST: AN ADDRESS TO THE YOUNG FRIENDS OF THE SLAVE (1859)

To The Young Friends of the Slave

Time was when the late Editors of the "[The] Olive Leaf" had the pleasure of talking from month to month to many of their dear young friends.
From circumstances beyond their reach, it is long since this pleasant intercourse was closed. Perhaps we may be allowed again to address them,
though in another fashion. It is not, however, with the late readers of
"The Olive Leaf" alone that we desire a little intercourse. We want to
have a few minutes' talk with every little boy and girl whom we can reach
throughout the British Islands who feels for the down-trodden American
Slave, and wishes for him to be free.

In a few words we shall tell our young friends why we address ourselves
to them on the present occasion.

A year ago there was a dear little girl named Laura B. living in one of
the Slave States of America, who longed very earnestly for the coloured
people around her to be liberated from their bondage. She had seen them
in chains, and her heart ached very much over their wrongs and sorrows.
Laura was not alone in thinking with tenderness of the afflicted slaves.
Her father was a very brave man, and her mother and eleven brothers and
sisters were warm-hearted people, and for a long time past had been doing
all they could to assist in liberating the poor Negroes. Laura's father has
a printing press; and with this press he prints a newspaper which contains
a great deal about the slaves, and urges the American government and
the American people not to allow the poor blacks to be slaves any longer.
The coloured race (and also many of their white neighbours) are very
grateful to Laura's father for taking up the Negro's cause so boldly; but, as
we may suppose, those who "own" the slaves are *not* glad, for they want
the poor creatures to go on toiling for their employers without pay, and,
two or three years ago, they got so angry as to hire wicked men to tear
and burn down Mr. B.'s premises and printing-office, and tried their utmost, in every way they could, to put an end to his noble efforts.

But Laura's father was not a man to be stopped in his course by this
mean and ungenerous usage, and his wife and children were equally

brave-hearted, and one and all of them determined to press on, and still to publish their anti-slavery newspaper.

Mr. B. was not rich, and to effect all they desired, they had to mortgage their home (a kind of half selling it), and the children were willing to be but poorly clothed and often to have hardly sufficient food; but still they pressed on, and at last a good part of the burned buildings were restored, and the young people continued to labour hard in assisting their parent to carry on his arduous work, and even young Laura, though at that time scarcely ten years of age, learned to handle type, and was as busy as any one in helping her dear father. Time rolled on, and though pressed down by many hardships, one and all of these good people still laboured diligently; but in the spring of this year little Laura's cheek grew pale, and now she is no more, for in the latter end of July she was taken from her loving family.

Mr. B. wrote to us on that touching occasion:—"But first I must tell you of the loss of our youngest daughter Laura, who was between 12 and 13 years old. She died on the 25th inst., and was buried yesterday. She had been ailing for some five or six months, and was the only delicate one of my children, but did not become seriously ill until about three weeks before her death. The day before she died, she sang one verse of the song—

"Do they miss me at home?"

in a tender, weak, and delicate voice, bringing a shower of tears from every eye in the room where she was. So truthful were the words, 'She would be missed at home,' that they, struck every one to the heart. So nimble were her little fingers in picking up type, and so deep was her sympathy for the coloured people, some of whom she had seen in chains, that she worked often with eagerness for their sake. I cannot describe the affecting scenes that occurred within a few days prior to her death."

On receiving this affecting intelligence we asked Mr. B. for a few more particulars respecting his precious child, and we have this day received his reply. On reading it, our thoughts turned to you, beloved young friends, and in a few hours' time we determined not only to tell you about Laura, but also to ask if you cannot assist her worthy family in their efforts to set the Negro free, in at least one of the Slave States.

One hundred pounds have already been sent to them, but it will require five times as much to make all straight, and for them to have their own home, and all that belongs to it, as their own again; for Mr. B. and his family have worn themselves down by their untiring labours, and have left themselves short of the ordinary comforts and necessaries of life.

Before we go on, however, you must hear something more about Laura. Her father wrote to us on the 21st Sept.—"You wish some further particulars of the last few weeks of our departed daughter. During the time of her three weeks' serious illness she had but little to say. She had been in a poorly [sic] state of health for about six months, and we rather feared her confinement in the office at her printing case did not agree with her, although the rest are all hearty children. We therefore sent her to school, in which she took much interest; but her mind seemed to be bent upon the freedom of the poor coloured people, and she talked about it so much to her class-mates, that they also became seriously interested in their freedom.

"There were three or four children who came to her school whose parents had a few slaves, and these children (little girls), told our Laura that their parents did not want them to associate with her because she was an 'Abolitionist,' but this seemed to cause quite a number of children to gather around her at times of recess, both girls and boys, to talk with her and ask her questions; but Laura, God bless her, was so earnest and kind in her responses, touching the rights of the poor coloured people (whose children would often steal into the group under the shade of trees where they sat to hear her answers), that they could not help but love her. They all saw her soul was moved with righteousness—open, clear, and candid. The mark attempted to be put upon her by wealth, to avoid the little 'Abolitionist' had a contrary effect. The children had no interest in the 'peculiar institution,' further than to see and converse with 'the Abolition girl,' in whom they found nothing desperate or wicked, but on the contrary humanity, kindness, and love. She would shake hands with any of the children on leaving the school, that were present when starting. She always told them they must love one another on earth, to be happy in heaven. Indeed, my friend, I am proud to have been the father of so good a child. She caused many of her companions to express the wish that *they* were good 'Abolitionists.' When she became so poorly as to be kept at home, the children came from school at noon to see her. I could see that they all loved her, and so could my wife. We were pleased to see their fond attachment for her. After she was confined to her bed, she seemed to be more concerned about the industry of her brothers and sisters, in getting up the matter for the newspaper in time, and often told them when she got well, she would make their work lighter; but as she grew worse, she inquired for, and requested, her neighbouring friends to come in and pray for her, which they did with true Christian devotion.

"The day before she died, she sang the last verse of the song, which I

send you by this mail. I find that the odium attached to the word 'Abolitionist' has been assuaged in some circles, through the kindness and
earnestness of Laura's pleading, and from believing, as I think all her acquaintances do, that she is now a loving angel in the arms of a blessed
Redeemer."

Precious little Laura! How sweet is the thought of her standing under
the shade of the green trees of Kentucky in the heat of the summer sun,
and of her pleading with her school-fellows in the spirit of that Savior,
who came "to comfort all that mourn," "to heal the broken-hearted," and
"to preach deliverance to the captives." It is very interesting also to know
that even the coloured children were often amongst Laura's hearers. How
their hearts would be gladdened by hearing her speak of these blessed
truths! We fancy we hear her telling them that our Heavenly Father is
"no respecter of persons" and that the hue of the skin does not in any
way lessen His loving kindness and tender mercy towards those that fear
Him—telling them also that Jesus is equally a Savior *to them*, and will
take ALL little children as lambs into His arms if they only come to Him
as their Lord and Shepherd.

We feel quite sure, beloved children, that by this time you also love
little Laura. Would you not like to assist her in her work of love and
mercy? "Though dead she yet speaketh;" and we think if you try, though
she is gone, very many of you might learn to walk in her footsteps.

Our particular business, however, just now is with the poor coloured
people of Kentucky, and in assisting Laura's father to labour for their freedom. We want him and his family to have their "homestead" as their
own again; for, as we said before, they mortgaged it to pay the debts in-
curred by the destruction of their property, and for provisions, clothing,
&c., when the riotous mob burned down Mr. B.'s machine shop and
printing office two or three years since.

We should like you, dear young friends, to talk over this matter with
your parents and teachers, and if they *quite* approve of your collecting
small sums on the slave's behalf, it would give us very great pleasure to
forward these to Mr. B. as "collected by the children of England, Scotland, and Ireland, in remembrance of his departed daughter." A great
many little sums put together would form a large one, and we are much
inclined to believe that in making this kind effort, you will be led to
think more and more of the suffering slave. Thirty years ago (as many of
you are aware), Great Britain had slaves of her own in the West Indian
Islands.

Happily, these have been set free. With God's blessing, this was chiefly brought about by the lovers of freedom in this country striving very, very earnestly for the Negroes' emancipation. We want the same efforts to be made for the American slaves; and being now in close correspondence with some of those who live and labour amongst them, we fully believe that by strengthening *their* hands, *we* also may aid the good work. Mr. B. lately remarked that it was not his own family alone that would be grateful for sympathy and aid from this country, but that the friends of freedom "throughout Kentucky" would thankfully rejoice at this kind help being extended.

We now leave that matter in the hands of those interested, simply supplying them with little forms for putting down subscriptions, and assuring them that if these are sent (when more or less filled up) to

Anna H. Richardson, 54, *Westmoreland Terrace,*
Newcastle-upon-Tyne,

the proceeds shall be carefully forwarded to Kentucky, for the objects referred to in this appeal.

Newcastle, 10 *Mo.*, 11*th*, 1859.

The last stanza of the following sweet song, is that which was sung by little Laura the day before she died:

I

Do they miss me at home?—do they miss me?
    'Twould be an assurance most dear,
To know at this moment some loved one
    Were saying, I wish he were here.
To feel that the group at the fireside
    Were thinking of me as I roam—
O yes, 'twould be joy without measure,
    To know that they missed me at home.

II

When twilight approaches, the season
    That ever is sacred to song,

Does some one repeat my name over,
  And sigh that I tarry so long?
And is there a chord in the music
  That's missed when my voice is away,
And a chord in each heart that awaketh
  Regret at my wearisome stay?

III

Do they set me a chair near the table
  When evening's home pleasures are nigh,
When the candles are lit in the parlour,
  And the stars in the calm azure sky?
And when the "good nights" are repeated,
  And all lay them down to their sleep,
Do they think of the absent, and waft me
  A whispered "good night" while they weep?

IV

Do they miss me at home?—do they miss me
  At morning, at noon, or at night?
And lingers one gloomy shade round them,
  That only my presence can light?
Are joys less inviting and welcome,
  And pleasures less hale than before,
Because one is missed from the circle,—
  Because I am with them no more?

JULIA COLMAN AND
MATILDA G. THOMPSON

~~❧❀❧~~

(BIOGRAPHIES AND DATES UNKNOWN)

Julia Colman and Matilda Thompson's work, *The Child's Anti-Slavery Book: Containing a Few Words about American Slave Children, and Stories of Slave-Life* (1859) represents a complex and interesting collection of re-covered juvenile abolitionist texts published on the eve of the Civil War. Its three short stories, "Little Lewis: The Story of a Slave Boy," "Mark and Hasty; or, Slave-Life in Missouri," and "Aunt Judy's Story: A Story from Real Life"[1] suggest that on the eve of the national strife, Colman and Thompson (about whom no biographical information has surfaced)[2] felt confident walking the tightrope as women authors of abolitionist texts that depict slavery as un-Christian and un-American.

Claiming to have their origins in true stories, these sentimental, juve-nile pseudoslave-narratives capture the psychological distress that slave children as well as their mothers and fathers experience. Echoing au-thentic slave narratives such as Frederick Douglass, *The Autobiography of Frederick Douglass* and Harriet Jacobs, *Incidents in the Life of a Slave Girl*, Colman and Thompson's stories describe the conditions of servitude, in particular its violation of family bonds; the events that lead to a child's awakening of his or her status as a slave; the emotional crisis and rami-fications of this awakening; and the process by which the child attains freedom.

Matilda Thompson's "Mark and Hasty" and Julia Colman's "Little Lewis" achieve an unparalleled level of complexity in the portrayal of the slave family unit, its rupture, and the stalwart efforts that slave parents make to protect their child's best interests. "Mark and Hasty" is the only abolitionist text recovered to date that begins with a complete slave fam-ily unit: Mark (father), Hasty (mother), and Fanny (daughter). However, both "Mark and Hasty" and "Little Lewis" document the slave mother's extreme psychological suffering on separation from her husband and children, respectively. These two works, then, spotlight the collaboration between slave mothers and white women, as Colman and Thompson depict how Fanny and Lewis's mothers affect their child's liberation. Hasty utters a deathbed wish to Mrs. Jennings, which results in her "adopting" Fanny and then moving to Chicago to work for the abolitionist cause. Nelly plants the seed of Lewis's liberation when she encourages him to use the necessary deception to attain an education, which he ultimately secures through Mrs. Ford, who not only teaches Lewis to read but also affects his escape.

Matilda Thompson's piece, "Aunt Judy's Story"[3] reflects the domestic abolitionists' tradition of casting mothers as storytellers and revisionist historians. This fascinating story contrasts Mr. and Mrs. Ford's strategies for educating their children about history. The father figure, Mr. Ford, narrates an abbreviated history about Native Americans, whom he casts as oppressors rather than victims, for whom his children originally express compassion. In contrast, the mother figure, Mrs. Ford, initially refuses to tell the children about Aunt Judy's history because "it is not in my power to do so, as I am not very well acquainted with her history" (352). After learning Aunt Judy's history, Mrs. Ford tells the heartbreaking story about "Aunt Judy's attempts to remain with her husband (who dies after being violently beaten and sold), the forceful separation from her children, and her re-enslavement (despite her free papers)" (De Rosa 92). Unlike other abolitionist mother-historians who overtly critique slavery, its laws, and those who perpetuate it, Mrs. Ford (i.e., Thompson) arouses antislavery sentiments (evident from the tears that she and her children shed) by documenting Aunt Judy and her family's suffering.

THE CHILD'S ANTI-SLAVERY BOOK: CONTAINING A FEW WORDS ABOUT AMERICAN SLAVE CHILDREN AND STORIES OF SLAVE-LIFE (1859)

"A FEW WORDS ABOUT AMERICAN SLAVE CHILDREN"

Children, you are free and happy. Kind parents watch over you with loving eyes; patient teachers instruct you from the beautiful pages of the printed book; benign laws protect you from violence, and prevent the strong arms of wicked people from hurting you; the blessed Bible is in your hands; when you become men and women you will have full liberty to earn your living, to go, to come, to seek pleasure or profit in any way that you may choose, so long as you do not meddle with the rights of other people; in one word, *you are free children!* Thank God! thank God! my children, for this precious gift. Count it dearer than life. Ask the great God who made you free to teach you to prefer death to the loss of liberty.

But are all the children in America free like you? No, no! I am sorry to tell you that hundreds of thousands of American children are *slaves*. Though born beneath the same sun and on the same soil, with the same natural right to freedom as yourselves, they are nevertheless SLAVES. Alas for them! Their parents cannot train them as they will, for they too have MASTERS. These masters say to them:

"Your children are OURS—OUR PROPERTY! They shall not be taught to read or write; they shall never go to school; they shall not be taught to read the Bible; they must submit to us and not to you; we shall whip them, sell them, and do what else we please with them. They shall never own themselves, never have the right to dispose of themselves, but shall obey us in all things as long as they live!"

"Why do their fathers let these masters have their children? My father wouldn't let anybody have me," I hear one of my little free-spirited readers ask.

Simply, my noble boy, because they can't help it. The masters have banded themselves together, and have made a set of wicked laws by which nearly four millions of men, women, and children are declared to be their personal chattels, or property. So that if one of these slave fathers should refuse to let his child be used as the property of his master, those wicked laws would help the master by inflicting cruel punishments on the parent. Hence the poor slave fathers and mothers are forced to silently witness the cruel wrongs which their helpless children are made to suffer. Violence has been framed into a law, and the poor slave is trodden beneath the feet of the powerful.

"But why did those slaves let their masters bring them into this state? Why didn't they fight as our forefathers did, when they threw off the yoke of England's laws?" inquires a bright-eyed lad who has just risen from the reading of a history of our Revolution.

The slaves were not reduced to their present servile condition in large bodies. When our ancestors settled this country they felt the need of more laborers than they could hire. Then wicked men sailed from England and other parts of Europe to the coast of Africa. Sending their boats ashore filled with armed men, they fell upon the villages of the poor Africans, set fire to their huts, and, while they were filled with fright, seized, handcuffed, and dragged them to their boats, and then carried them aboard ship.

This piracy was repeated until the ship was crowded with negro men, women, and children. The poor things were packed like spoons below the deck. Then the ship set sail for the coast of America. I cannot tell you how horribly the poor negroes suffered. Bad air, poor food, close confinement, and cruel treatment killed them off by scores. When they died their bodies were pitched into the sea, without pity or remorse.

After a wearisome voyage the survivors, on being carried into some port, were sold to the highest bidder. No regard was paid to their relationship. One man bought a husband, another a wife. The child was taken to one place, the mother to another. Thus they were scattered abroad over the colonies. Fresh loads arrived continually, and thus their numbers increased. Others were born on the soil, until now, after the lapse of some two centuries, there are nearly four millions of negro slaves in the country, besides large numbers of colored people who in various ways have been made free.

You can now see how easy it was for the masters to make the wicked laws by which the slaves are now held in bondage. They began when the slaves were few in number, when they spoke a foreign language, and when they were too few and feeble to offer any resistance to their oppressors, as their masters did to old England when she tried to oppress them.

I want you to remember one great truth regarding slavery, namely, that a slave is a human being, held and used as property by another human being, and that *it is always* A SIN AGAINST *God to thus hold and use a human being as property!*

You know it is not a sin to use an ox, a horse, a dog, a squirrel, a house, or an acre of land as property, if it be honestly obtained, because God made these and similar objects to be possessed as property by men. But God did not *make man to be the property of man*. He never gave any man the right to own his neighbor or his neighbor's child.

On the contrary, he made all men to be free and equal, as saith our Declaration of Independence. Hence, every negro child that is born is as free before God as the white child, having precisely the same right to life, liberty, and the pursuit of happiness, as the white child. The law which denies him that right does not destroy it. It may enable the man who claims him as a slave to deprive him of its exercise, but the right itself remains, for the wicked law under which he acts does not and cannot set aside the divine law, by which he is as free as any child that was ever born.

But if God made every man, woman, and child to be free, and not property, then he who uses a human being as property acts contrary to the will of God and SINS! Is it not so, my children?

Yet that is what every slaveholder does. *He uses his slaves as property.* He reckons them as worth so many dollars, just as your father sets a certain money value on his horse, farm, or merchandise. He sells him, gives him away, uses his labor without paying him wages, claims his children as so many more dollars added to his estate, and when he dies wills him to his heirs forever. And this is SIN, my children—a very great sin against God, a high crime against human nature.

Mark what I say! the sin of slavery does not lie merely in whipping, starving, or otherwise ill-treating a human being, but in using him as property; in saying of him as you do of your dog: "He is my property. He is worth so much money to me. I will do what I please with him. I will keep him, use him, sell him, give him away, and keep all he earns, just as I choose."

To say that of a man is sin. You might clothe the man in purple, feed him on manna from Heaven, and keep him in a palace of ivory, still, if you used him as your property, you would commit sin!

Children, I want you to shrink from this sin as the Jews did from the fiery serpents. Hate it. Loathe it as you would the leprosy. Make a solemn vow before the Saviour, who loves the slave and slave children as truly, as he does you, that you will never hold slaves, never apologize for those who do. As little Hannibal vowed eternal hatred to Rome at the altar of a false god, so do you vow eternal enmity to slavery at the altar of the true and living Jehovah. Let your purpose be, "I will rather beg my bread than live by the unpaid toil of a slave."

To assist you in carrying out that purpose, and to excite your sympathy for poor slave children, the following stories were written. The characters in them are all real, though their true names are not always given. The stories are therefore pictures of actual life, and are worthy of your belief.

D. W.[4]

"LITTLE LEWIS: THE STORY OF A SLAVE BOY"

By Julia Colman

"A, B, C," said little Lewis to himself, as he bent eagerly over a ragged primer. "Here's anoder A, an' there's anoder, an' there's anoder C, but I can't find anoder B. Missy Katy said I must find just so many as I can. Dear little Missy Katy! an' wont I be just so good as ever I can, an' learn to read, an' when I get to be a man I'll call myself white folks; for I'm a most as white as Massa Harry is now, when he runs out widout his hat; A, B, C." And so the little fellow ran on, thinking what a fine man he would be when he had learned to read.

Just then he heard a shrill laugh in the distance, and the cry, "Lew! Lew! where's Lew?"

It was Katy's voice, and tucking his book in his bosom, he ran around the house toward her with light feet; for though she was often cross and willful, as only daughters sometimes are, she was the only one of the family that showed him even an occasional kindness. She was, withal, a frolicsome, romping witch, and as he turned the corner, she came scampering along right toward him with three or four white children at her heels, and all the little woolly heads of the establishment, numbering something less than a score.

"Here, Lew!" she said, as she came in sight, "you take the tag and run."

With a quick movement he touched her outstretched hand, and he would have made the others some trouble to catch him, for he was the smartest runner among the children; but as he turned he tripped on a stone, and lay sprawling. "Tag," cried Hal, Katy's cousin, as he placed his feet on the little fellow's back and jumped over him. It was cruel, but what did Hal care for the "little nigger." If he had been at home he would have had some little fear of breaking the child's back, for his father was more careful of his *property* than Uncle Stamford was.

Before Lewis could rise, two or three of the negro boys, who were always too ready to imitate the vices of their masters, had made the boy a

"Little Lewis Sold"
Courtesy, American Antiquarian Society.

stepping stone, and then Dick, his master's eldest son, came down upon him with both knees, and began to cuff him roundly.

"So, you black scamp, you thought you'd run away with the tag, did you!" Just then he perceived the primer that was peeping out of Lewis's shirt bosom. "Ha! what's here?" said he; "a primer, as I live! And what are you doing with this, I'd like to know?"

"Missy Katy give it to me, and she is teaching me my letters out of it. Please, massa, let me have it again," said he, beseechingly, as Dick made a motion as if to throw it away. "I would like to learn how to read."

"You would, would you!" said Dick. "You'd like to read to Tom and Sam, down on a Louisiana plantation, in sugar time, when you'd nothing else to do, I suppose. Ha, ha, ha!" and the young tyrant, giving the boy a vigorous kick or two as he rose, stuffed the book into his own pocket, and walked off.

Poor Lewis! He very well knew the meaning of that taunt, and he did not open his mouth. No threat of a dark closet ever frightened a free child so much as the threat of being sold to a Southern plantation terrifies the slave-child of Kentucky.

Lewis walked slowly toward the kitchen, to see Aunt Sally. It was to her he used to go with all his troubles, and sometimes she scolded, and sometimes she listened. She was very busy dressing the vegetables for dinner, and she looked cross; so the little fellow crept into the chimney corner and said nothing; but he thought all the more, and as he thought, the sad tears rolled down his tawny cheeks.

"What is the matter now, little baby?" was Aunt Sally's tender inquiry.

Lewis commenced his pitiful tale; but as soon as Aunt Sally heard that it was about learning to read, she shut him up with "Good enough for you! What do you want of a book? Readin' isn't for the likes of you; and the less you know of it the better."

This was poor sympathy, and the little fellow, with a half-spiteful feeling, scrambled upon a bench near by, and tumbled out of the window. He alighted on an ashheap, not a very nice place to be sure, but it was a retired corner, and he often hid away there when he felt sad and wanted to be alone. Here he sat down, and leaning his head against the side of the house, he groaned out, "My mother, O my mother! If you ain't dead, why don't you come to me?"

By degrees he calmed down, and half asleep there in the sunshine, he dreamed of the home that he once had. His mother was a noble woman, so he thought. Nobody else ever looked so kindly into his face; he was sure nobody else ever loved him as she did, and he remembered when she was gay and cheerful, and would go all day singing about her work. And his father, he could just remember him as a very pleasant man that he used to run to meet, sometimes, when he saw him coming home away down the road; but that was long ago. He had not seen him now for years, and he had heard his mother say that his father's master had moved away out of the state and taken him with him, and maybe he would never return. Then Lewis's mother grew sad, and stopped her singing, though she worked as hard as ever, and kept her children all neat and clean.

And those dear brothers and sisters, what had become of them? There was Tom, the eldest, the very best fellow in the world, so Lewis thought. He would sit by the half hour making tops, and whistles, and all sorts of pretty playthings. And Sam, too! he was always so full of fun and singing songs. What a singer he was! and it was right cheerful when Sam would borrow some neighbor's banjo and play to them. But they were all gone; and his sad, sweet-faced, lady-like sister Nelly, too, they were all taken off in one day by one of the ugliest negro-drivers that ever scared a little slave-boy's dreams. And it was while his mother was away from home too. How she did cry and take on when she came back and found them all gone, and she hadn't even the chance to bid them good-by! She said she knew her master sent her off that morning because he was going to sell her children.

Lewis shuddered as he thought of that dreadful night. It was hardly two years ago, and the fearful things he heard then burned into his soul with terrible distinctness. It seemed as if their little cabin was deserted after that, for Tom, and Sam, and Nelly were almost grown up, and the rest were all little ones. The next winter his other sister, Fanny, died; but that wasn't half so sad. She was about twelve years old, and a blithesome, cheerful creature, just as her mother had been. He remembered how his master came to their cabin to comfort them, as he said; but his mother told him plainly that she did not want any such comfort. She wished Nelly was dead too. She wished she had never had any children to grow up and suffer what she had. It was in vain her master tried to soothe her. He talked like a minister, as he was; but she had grown almost raving, and she talked to him as she never dared to do before. She wanted to know why he didn't come to console her when she lost her other children; "three all at once" she said, "and they're ten times worse than dead. You never consoled me then at all. Religion? Pooh! I don't want none of *your* religion."

And now she, too, was gone. She had been gone more than a year. It was said that she was hired out to work in another family; but it wasn't so. They only told her that story to get her away from the children peaceably. She was sold quite a distance away to a very bad man, who used her cruelly.

Ned, who was some two years younger than Lewis, and the only brother he had left, was a wild, careless boy, who raced about among the other children, and did not seem to think much about anything. Lewis often wished he could have somebody to talk with, and he wondered if his mother would ever come back again.

Had he been a poet he might have put his wishes into verses like the following, in which Mrs. Follen has given beautiful expression to the wishes of such a slave boy as Lewis:

"THE SLAVE BOY'S WISH"

I WISH I was that little bird,
    Up in the bright blue sky,
That sings and flies just where he will,
    And no one asks him why.

I wish I was that little brook,
    That runs so swift along,
Through pretty flowers and shining stones,
    Singing a merry song.

I wish I was that butterfly,
    Without a thought or care,
Sporting my pretty, brilliant wings,
    Like a flower in the air.

I wish I was that wild, wild deer,
    I saw the other day,
Who swifter than an arrow flew,
    Through the forest far away.

I wish I was that little cloud,
    By the gentle south wind driven,
Floating along so free and bright,
    Far, far up into heaven.

I'd rather be a cunning fox,
    And hide me in a cave;
I'd rather be a savage wolf,
    Than what I am—a slave.

My mother calls me her good boy,
    My father calls me brave;
What wicked action have I done,
    That I should be a slave?

I saw my little sister sold,
    So will they do to me;
My heavenly Father, let me die,
    For then I shall be free.

So talking to himself he fell into a doze, and dreamed about his mother. He thought her large serious eyes were looking into his, and her long black hair falling over his face. His mother was part Indian and part white, with only just enough of the black to make her hair a little curly.

It don't make much difference what color people are in the slave states. If the mothers are slaves the children are slaves too, even if they are nine-tenths white.

From this pleasant dream Lewis was roused by a splash of cold water, and Aunt Sally, with her head out of the window, was calling, "Here you lazy nigger! come here and grind this coffee for me." And the little boy awoke to find himself a friendless orphan, in a cold world with a cruel master.

The next morning Lewis was playing about the yard with as good a will as any of the young negroes. Children's troubles don't last long, and to see him turning somersets, singing Jim Crow, and kicking up a row generally, you would suppose he had forgotten all about the lost primer and his mother too.

He was in the greatest possible glee in the afternoon, at being sent with another boy, Jim, to carry a package to Mr. Pond's. Then he was trusted, so he put himself on his dignity, and did not turn more than twenty somersets on the way. In coming back, as they had no package to carry, they took it into their heads to cut across lots, though it was no nearer than the road. Still it made them plenty of exercise in climbing fences and walking log bridges across the brooks. While doing this they came in sight of some white pond-lilies, and all at once it occurred to Lewis that it would be right nice to got some of them for Miss Katy, to buy up her good-will, for he was afraid she would be very angry when she found that he had lost the primer. So he waded and paddled about till he had collected quite a handful of them, in spite of Jim's hurrying up, and telling him that he would get his head broke, for missus had told them to be quick.

When he had gathered a large handful he started on the run for home, stopping only once or twice to admire the fragrant, lovely flowers; and he felt their beauty quite as much, I dare say, as Miss Katy would.

When they were passing the quarters, as the place is called where the huts of the slaves are built, Aunt Sally put her head out of the cabin door, and seeing him, she called out, "Here, Lew, here's your mother."

The boy forgot his lilies, dropped them, and running to the door, he saw within a strange woman sitting on a bench. Was *that* his mother? She turned her large dark eyes for a moment upon him, and then she sprang to meet him. His little heart was ready to overflow with tears of joy, and he expected to be overwhelmed with caresses, just as you would if you should meet your mother after being separated from her more than a year.

Imagine his terror, then, as she seized him rudely by the wrists and exclaimed, "It's you, is it? a little slave boy! I'll fix you so they'll never get you!"

Then she picked him up in her arms and started to run with him, as if she would throw him into the well. The little fellow screamed with fright. Aunt Sally ran after her, crying at the top of her voice, "Nancy, O Nancy! don't now!" And then a big negro darted out of the stables, crying "Stop her there! catch her!"

All this hubbub roused the people at the house, and Master Stamford forthwith appeared on the verandah, with a crowd of servants of all sizes. Amid the orders, and cries, and general confusion that followed, Nancy was caught, Lewis was taken away, and she was carried back to the cabin, while the big negro was preparing to tie her. As she entered the cabin, her eye caught sight of a knife that lay there, and snatching it up, she gave herself a bad wound with it. Poor woman, she was tired of her miserable life. I don't wonder that she wanted to die.

Was it right, you ask, for her to take her own life? Certainly not. But let us see what led to this attempt.

For a long time she had been separated from Lewis and Ned, the last of her children that remained to her. To be sure, the other three were probably living somewhere, and so was her husband. But she only knew that they had gone into hopeless servitude, where she knew not. Indeed, she did not know but that they were already dead, and she did not expect ever to hear, for slaves are seldom able to write, and often not permitted to when they can. If there had only been hope of hearing from them at some time or other she could have endured it. But between her and those loved ones there rested a thick cloud of utter darkness; beyond that they might be toiling, groaning, bleeding, starving, dying beneath the oppressor's lash in the deadly swamp, or in the teeth of the cruel hounds, and she could not have the privilege of ministering to the least of their wants, of soothing one of their sorrows, or even dropping a silent tear beside them. If she could have heard only *one* fact about them it would have been some relief. But she could not enjoy even this poor privilege. And then came the dead, heavy stillness of despair creeping over her spirits.

Do you wonder that she became perfectly wild, and beside herself at times? How would you feel if all you loved best were carried off by a cruel slave-driver, and you had *no hope* of hearing from them again in this world?

During these dreadful fits of insanity she would bewail the living as worse than dead, and pray God to take them away. Then she would curse herself for being the mother of slave children, declaring that it would be far better to see them die in their childhood, than to see them grow up to suffer as she had suffered.

She lived only a few miles from her old home; but her new master was an uncommonly hard man, and would not permit her to go and see her children. He said it would only make her worse, and his slaves should learn that they were not to put on airs and have whims. It was their business to live for him. Didn't he pay enough for them, and see that they were well fed and clothed, and what more did they want? This he called kind treatment. Very kind, indeed, not to allow a mother to go and see her own children! But when she was taken with those insane spells, and would go on so about her children that she was not fit to work, indeed could not be made to work, it was finally suggested to him that a visit to her children would do her good.

This was the occasion of her present visit, and it was because she was insane that she attempted to take her own life. The wound, however, was not very deep, and Nancy did not die at this time. After the doctor had been there and dressed her wound, and affairs had become quiet, Lewis stole to the door of the cabin. He was afraid to go in. He hardly knew, any of the time, whether that strange wild woman could be his mother, only they told him she was. There was blood spattered here and there on the bare earth that served as a floor to the cabin, and on a straw mattress at one side lay the strange woman. Her eyes were shut, and now that she was more composed, he saw in the lineaments of that pale face the features of his mother. But her once glossy black hair had turned almost white since she had been away, and altogether there was such a wild expression that he was afraid, and crept quietly away again.

He then went to find his brother, who, of course, did not remember so much about her. But it was touching to see the two little lone brothers stand peeping in wonderingly at their own mother, who was so changed that they hardly knew her. Then they went off behind the kitchen to talk about it, and cry over it.

The strange big negro was Jerry, who belonged to the same master with Nancy, and he had come to bring her down. He was afraid that his master would be very angry if he should go back without her; but the doctor said the woman must not be moved for a week, and he wrote a letter for Jerry to carry home to his master, while Nancy remained.

The next day, as they gained a little more courage, the brothers crept inside of the cabin. Their mother saw them, and beckoned them to her bed-side. She could scarcely speak a word distinctly, but taking first one and then the other by the hand, she said inquiringly: "Lewis?" "Ned?"

They sat there at the bed-side by the hour that day. Sometimes she would hold their hands lovingly in hers; then again she would lay her hand gently on the heads of one and the other, and her eyes would wander lovingly over their faces, and then fill with tears.

After a day or two little restless, fun-loving Ned grew tired of this, and ran out to play; but Lewis stayed by his mother, and she was soon able to talk with him.

She showed him her wrists where they had been worn by the irons, and her back scarred by the whip, and she told him of cruelties that we may not repeat here. She talked with him as if he were a man, and not a child; and as he listened his heart and mind seemed to reach forward, and he became almost a man in thought. He seemed to live whole years in those few days that he talked with his mother. It was here that the fearful fact dawned upon him as it never had before. *He was a slave!* He had no control over his own person or actions, but he belonged soul and body to another man, who had power to control him in everything. And this would not have been so irksome had it been a person that he loved, but Master Stamford he hated. He never met him but to be called by some foul epithet, or booted out of the way. He had no choice whom he would serve, and there would be no end to the thankless servitude but death.

"Mother," said the boy, "what have we done that we should be treated so much worse than other people?"

"Nothing, my child, nothing. They say there is a God who has ordered all this, but I don't know about that." She stopped; her mother's heart forbade her to teach her child infidel principles, and she went on in a better strain of reasoning. "Perhaps he allows all this, to try if we will be good whether or no; but I am sure he cannot be pleased with the white folk's cruelty toward us, and they'll all have to suffer for it some day."

Then there was a long pause, when both mother and son seemed to be thinking sad, sad thoughts. Finally the mother broke the silence by saying: "Well, here we are, and the great question is how to make the best of it, if there is any best about it."

"I know what I'll do, mother," said Lewis earnestly, "I'll run away when I'm old enough."

"I hope you may get out of this terrible bondage, my child," said the mother; "but you had better keep that matter to yourself at present. It will be a long time before you are old enough. There is one thing about it, if you're going to be a free man, you'll want to know how to read."

Lewis's heart was full again, and he told his mother the whole story of the primer.

"And did Missy Katy never ask about it afterward?" inquired the mother.

"No, she never has said a word about it."

"O well, she don't care. There are some young missies with tender hearts that do take a good deal of pains to teach poor slaves to read; but she isn't so, nor any of massa's family, if he is a minister. He don't care any more about us than he does about his horses. You musn't wait for any of them; but there's Sam Tyler down to Massa Pond's, he can read, and if you can get him to show you some, without letting massa know it, that'll help you, and then you must try by yourself as hard as you can."

Thus did the poor slave mother talk with her child, trying to implant in his heart an early love for knowledge.

But the time soon came when Nancy was well enough to go back to her cruel servitude. This visit had proved a great good to little Lewis. The entire spirit of his thoughts was changed. He was still very often silent and thoughtful, but he was seldom sad. He had a fixed purpose within, which was helping him to work out his destiny.

His first effort was to see Sam Tyler. This old man was a very intelligent mulatto belonging to Mr. Pond. For some great service formerly rendered to his master, he was allowed to have his cabin, and quite a large patch of ground, separated from the other negroes, and all his time to himself, except ten hours a day for his master. His master had also given him a pass, with which he could go and come on business, and the very feeling that he was trusted kept him from using it to run away with.

Mr. Pond was very kind to all his servants, as he called them, and a more cheerful group could not be found in the state. It would have been well if the Rev. Robert Stamford and many of his congregation had imitated Mr. Pond in this respect, for his servants worked more faithfully, and were more trustworthy than any others in the vicinity. There was one thing more that he should have done; he should have made out free papers for them, and let them go when they pleased.

When Lewis mentioned his wish to Sam Tyler, the old man was quite delighted with the honor done to his own literary talent. "But you see," said he, "I can tell ye what is a sight better; come over to Massa Pond's Sunday school. I'd 'vise ye to ask Massa Stamford, and then ye can come every Sunday."

Lewis had a notion that it would not be very easy to get his master's permission, so the next Sunday he went without permission.

It was a right nice place for little folks and big ones too. Nearly all Mr. Pond's servants were there punctually. It was held an hour, and Mr. Pond himself, or one of his sons, was always there. He read the Bible, taught them verses from it, sung hymns with them, and of late, at their urgent solicitation, he had purchased some large cards with the letters and easy readings, and was teaching them all to read.

The first day that Lewis went he crept off very early, before his master was up, telling Aunt Sally where he was going, so that if he should be inquired for she could send Ned after him. Aunt Sally remonstrated, but it was of no avail; he was off, and she really loved him too well to betray him.

That day young master Pond was in the Sunday school, and he spoke very kindly to Lewis, commending his zeal, and asking him to come again. But when he told his father that one of Mr. Stamford's boys was there, Mr. Pond's reply was that "this matter must be looked into."

Mr. Pond was there himself on the next Sunday, and though he spoke very kindly to the boy, yet he told him very decidedly that he must not come there without a written permission from his master. "Well, then, I can't come at all, sir," said Lewis sorrowfully.

"Ask him, at any rate," was the reply. "I'd like to have you come very well; but I'm afraid he will think I want to steal one of his boys, if I allow you to come here without his consent."

It was with much fear that Lewis made known his wish to his master, and he was received, as he expected to be, with abuse.

"You would like to be a smart nigger, I suppose; one of the kind that talks saucy to his master and runs away. I'll make you smart. I'm smart enough myself for all my niggers; and if they want any more of the stuff, I'll give them some of the right sort," said he with vulgar wit, as he laid his riding-whip about the shoulders of poor Lewis.

But when Mr. Stamford found that Lewis had already been to Mr. Pond's Sunday school, he made a more serious matter of it, and the poor boy received his first severe flogging, twenty-five lashes on his bare back.

"I hope now," said Aunt Sally, while dressing his welted and wounded back with wet linen, "that you'll give up that silly notion of your'n, that of learnin' to read. It's of no use, and these 'ere learned niggers are always gettin' into trouble. I know massa'd half kill one, if he had 'im. Now, if you belonged to Massa Pond 'twould be different." And so she went on; but the more she talked the more firmly Lewis made up his mind that he would learn to read if he could, and the words of his mother came to his mind with authority: "If you're going to be a free man you'll want to know how to read."

About two months after this he paid another visit to Sam Tyler. Sam's plot of ground and cabin was near the division line between the two farms, and Lewis took his time to go down there after dark. He asked Sam to teach him to read.

"I should think you'd got enough of that," said Sam. "I shouldn't think it would pay."

"What would you take for what you know about readin'?" asked Lewis.

"Well, I can't say as I'd like to sell it, but it would only be a plague to you so long as you belong to Massa Stamford."

By dint of coaxing, however, Lewis succeeded in getting him to teach him the letters, taking the opportunity to go to him rainy nights, or when Mr. Stamford was away from home. That was the end of Sam's help. He had an "idea in his head" that it was not good policy for him to do this without Massa Stamford's consent, after what Mr. Pond had said about Lewis's coming to Sunday school. Sam was a cautious negro, not so warm-hearted and impulsive as the most of his race. He prided himself on being more like white folks.

Lewis was soon in trouble of another sort. He had found an old spelling-book, and Sam had shown him that the letters he had learned were to be put together to make words. Then, too, he managed to get a little time to himself every morning, by rising very early. So far so good, and his diligence was deserving of success, but the progress he made was very discouraging. C-a-n spelled sane, n-o-t spelled note, and g-o spelled jo. "I sane note jo;" what nonsense! and there was no one that could explain the matter intelligently. He perseveres bravely for a while, finding now and then a word that he could understand; but at last his book was gone from its hiding place; he knew not where to get another; and in short he was pretty much discouraged. These difficulties had cooled his ardor much more than the whip had done, and by degrees he settled down into a state of despondency and indifference that Mr. Stamford would have considered a matter of the deepest regret, had it befallen one of his own children.

Years passed on—long, dreary, cheerless years. Lewis was now a boy of seventeen, rather intelligent in appearance, but melancholy, and not very hearty. In spite of repeated thinnings out by sales at different times to the traders, the number of Mr. Stamford's slaves had greatly increased, and now the time came when they must all be disposed of. He had accepted a call from a distant village, and must necessarily break up his farming establishment.

It was a sad sight to see these poor people, who had lived together so long, put up at auction and bid off to persons that had come from many different places. Here goes the father of a family in one direction, the mother in another, and the children all scattered hither and thither. And then it was heartrending to witness their brief partings. Bad as had been their lot with Mr. Stamford, they would far sooner stay with him than be separated from those of their fellow-slaves whom they loved.

A lot at a time were put up in a row, and one after another was called upon the block, and after a few bids was handed over to a new master, to be taken wherever he might choose.

Ned and Jim and Lewis stood side by side in one of those rows. Ned had grown up to be a fine sprightly lad, and the bidding for him was lively. He was struck down to a Southern trader. Lewis listened despondently while the bidding for Jim was going on, expecting every moment to hear his own name called, when suddenly a strong hand was laid upon his shoulder from behind, and he was drawn from the row. After a thorough examination by a strange gentleman, in company with his master, he was bid to step aside. From some words that he heard pass between them, he understood that he had been sold at private sale, bartered off for a pair of carriage-horses.

The animals, a pair of handsome bays, were standing near by, and he turned to look at them. "Suppose they were black," said he to himself, "would they be any meaner, less powerful, less valuable, less spirited? I do not see that color makes much difference with animals, why should it make so much difference among men? Who made the white men masters over us?" He thought long and deeply, but there came no answer.

"Then, too, they are larger than I am, and there are two of them! What makes the difference that I should be higher priced? Ah, I have a *mind*, and it's my mind that they have sold," he added, with a sudden gleam of thought. "And what have I of my own? Nothing! They buy, and sell, and control soul and mind and body."

Lewis had yet to learn that even the poor slave may with all his soul believe on Jesus, and no master on earth could hinder him. Mr. Stamford had never given his slaves any religious teachings, and perhaps it was just as well that *he* did not attempt anything of that kind, for he is said to have taught his white congregation that it was no more harm to separate a family of slaves than a litter of pigs. His new master, whose name was Johns, lived about thirty miles distant, and nearly as much as that nearer the boundary line between Ohio and Kentucky, an item which the boy noticed with much satisfaction. On their way home Mr. Johns took special pains to impress on the mind of his new property the fact, that the condition of his being well treated in his new home would be his good behavior. "It's of no use," he says, "for my boys to go to showing off airs, and setting themselves up. I can't stand that. But if they are quiet and industrious, I give them as good allowances and as good quarters as anybody."

What Mr. Johns called good behavior in servants, was their doing promptly and precisely just as he told them to, without venturing to think for themselves anything about it. If any of them did venture an opinion before him he shut them up with a cut of the whip or a sharp word, so that the utmost extent of their conversation in his presence was a strict answer to his questions, and "Yes, massa," in reply to his commands.

Lewis was destined to assist in the garden. Mr. Johns was very fond of horticulture, but to have had his head gardener a slave, would have involved the necessity of talking with him, and consulting him too much to consist with his views of propriety. The slaves of families in the far South are not usually treated in this manner, but Mr. Johns was by birth an Englishman. The gardener, then, was a free, white man name Spencer, and Lewis found him a very pleasant master. It was not difficult for him to find his way into his good graces, so that Lewis did not suffer so much by the change as he expected. His heart was already hardened by the loss of so many friends, that he took this with unexpected indifference. But he did miss his brother Ned. More than once, in his dreams, did he hear him crying for help; but after a while he heard, through a fellow-slave, that Ned was serving as waiter in a hotel at Louisville. This was the last he ever heard of him.

Besides this, Lewis loved his new work. It was so delightful to see the shrubs, and trees, and plants flourish, and the flowers putting forth their gorgeous displays; and Spencer's kindness made the heaviest work seem light. It is very easy to serve a man that governs by kindness, but Lewis thought it would be much harder to serve Spencer if he had felt that he was his *owner*.

One morning, going earlier than usual to the garden, he found Miss Ford there, the governess of the children. She was promenading one of the wide alleys, and pensively reading a favorite author. This occurred morning after morning, and Lewis thought he would be so glad if she would only spend a few minutes teaching him to read! He knew that she was from the free states, where they did not keep slaves, and he thought, perhaps, if she knew his desire to read she would help him. But morning after morning passed, and she seemed to take very little notice of him. Finally, he one day observed her looking at a beautiful magnolia blossom, the first that had come out. It was quite on the top of the tree. She evidently wanted it, and Lewis drew near, hoping that she would ask him to get it for her, and so she did. Lewis was delighted, she thanked him so kindly. After this he found occasion to say: "I think missus must be very happy, she can read."

The lady looked surprised, and then pitiful. "And would you like to read?"

"Indeed, there is nothing in this world would make me more happy," said Lewis.

"It is a pity so simple a wish cannot be gratified," said she to herself. "Perhaps I could find time; if I thought so I might rise a little earlier. Could you come here by sunrise every morning?"

"O yes, missus, indeed I could."

"Come, then, to-morrow morning."

That was a happy day for Lewis. His first lesson was quite a success. He had not forgotten all his letters. After this he went on prosperously, having a half hour lesson every fair morning.

Lewis studied very hard, and made excellent progress. The difficulties that formerly troubled him now disappeared, for he had a teacher whom he could consult upon every word. Miss Ford gave him a few pence to buy candles with, and all his evenings were spent in assiduous devotion to his new task.

The thoughts of his new acquisitions made him so happy that he worked more diligently, and appeared far more cheerful than formerly. Mr. Johns observed it, and remarked that the boy had turned out "a better bargain than he expected."

When it was known in the house that Miss Ford was teaching Lewis, there was some consultation about it, and Mr. Johns approached the lady with a long face, to talk the matter over. However, she had altogether the advantage of him, for she laughed most uncontrollably at his concern, assured him that this was her intellectual play, and that she enjoyed the matter very much as she would teaching tricks to a parrot or monkey. "Surely, now, you would not deprive me of such an innocent amusement," said she, with mock lamentation.

"No; but my dear Miss Ford," said the gentleman, trying to appear serious, "it is not best for these people to know too much."

"O, that is too good!" she replied, with a laugh. "Do you expect him to rival a Henry Clay or an Andrew Jackson?" and then she went on telling some such funny mistakes and ludicrous blunders of the boy, that Mr. Johns could resist no longer, and he joined in the laugh. There was evidently no such thing as pinning her fast to serious reasoning on the subject, and as she stood very high in Mr. John's [sic] good graces, he concluded he might about as well let her do as she liked.

She had been a long time in the family, and as they had seen no ultra-abolition traits, they thought her "sound at heart" on that subject. And so she was; for had she known the true situation of the slaves, all the better feelings of her noble soul would have risen up in rebellion against the groundwork of the abominable "institution." But as the slaves were kept very much apart from the family, and by their master's peculiar training had very little to say when they did make their appearance, she had very little opportunity to study the workings of the system, if she had been disposed to do so, and very little to excite her curiosity about it.

As Lewis by degrees gained the good opinion of his teacher, and flattered her by his rapid progress, so she gradually became interested in his early history, and especially in his early failures in learning to read. She was quite indignant at the opposition he had experienced, and her expressions of surprise at the treatment he received, led him to tell of greater cruelties that he had seen practised on others, and so on to the story of his mother. She took a deep interest in all his details, and he was never at a loss for something to tell.

Could it be that slavery was so bad, that she was surrounded by these suffering creatures, and was doing nothing for them? She made inquiries of others prudently, and found that it was even so, and more too; that even she herself was not at liberty to speak out her sentiments about it. But she could think, and she did think. The great law of human, God-given *right* came up before her, and she acknowledged it. These poor creatures had a right to their own personal freedom, and she thought it would be doing God and humanity a service if she could help them to obtain that freedom. She did not know that in doing thus she would be sinning against the laws of her country, (!) and perhaps she would not have cared much if she had, for she was one of those independent souls that dare to acknowledge the law of right.

For months were these convictions gaining strength, but no opportunity occurred to assist any of them. Meanwhile she grew pensive and silent, oppressed by the helpless misery which she saw around her on every side.

One evening when Lewis came for his lesson he brought her an anonymous note. The writer professed to take a deep interest in the intelligent young slave Lewis, and asked the question if she would be willing to do anything to advance his freedom.

She unhesitatingly replied that she would be very glad to do so. Lewis knew where to carry the note, and she soon had an interview with the writer, Mr. Dean, of whom she had heard as the worst abolitionist in the neighborhood. Arrangements were soon made for running off the boy.

Miss Ford was to get leave of Mr. Johns to send Lewis to a neighbor of Mr. Dean's on an errand for herself in the evening. As this would keep him quite late, and he was to report to her on his return, no one else would be likely to miss him until morning. He was to proceed at once to Mr. Dean's house, whence, with face and hands dyed, and his clothes changed, he was to go with Mr. Dean in the capacity of a servant to Cincinnati, and he should then run his own chance of escape. In its main features the plan worked well, and Lewis escaped.

The next morning, when Lewis was missed at the house of his master, suspicion immediately fell upon Miss Ford. The plot was so simple that the truth could not well be concealed; but nothing was said about it until they might find some tangible evidence, and this was soon afforded by the imprudence of Dean. Two mornings after this he came to the garden fence by the arbor where she usually spent the morning, and threw over a note containing the words, "All right, and no suspicion."

But he was mistaken about the "no suspicion." He himself would have been arrested at the moment of his return, for one of his neighbors had seen and recognized them in Cincinnati; but they waited and watched to see if by some chance Miss Ford might not also be implicated. And it was done. There were more observers than he dreamed of, and Miss Ford, who from her window saw the note fall, saw it picked up a moment after by Mr. Johns himself. Mr. Dean was arrested before he reached home again, and both he and Miss Ford were sent to jail. Complaints were preferred against them, but many months passed before they were brought to trial. When at last the trial came off, Mr. Dean was sentenced to imprisonment for ten years, and five thousand dollars fine. Miss Ford's sentence was five years' [sic] imprisonment, but the governor finally granted a reprieve of the last two years.

After many adventures Lewis reached Boston, where he still lives, for ought I know, with a nice little woman of his own color for a wife, and three smart little boys. He labored so diligently in the cultivation of his mind that he became qualified for a teacher, and has been for a long time engaged in that pleasant and profitable occupation. But best of all, he has become a sincere Christian, rejoicing in the privilege of worshiping God according to the dictates of his own conscience, with none to molest nor make him afraid. He has heard once more from his parents. His father's master had returned to the neighborhood where his mother was, and they were again living together. His mother's mind was restored to sanity. She was more "like herself" than she had been before since the early days of their married life. In her later years she was brought to taste of the "liberty wherewith Christ has made us free," and went to her home above to be comforted after all her sufferings, while her cruel masters who enjoyed their ease here shall be tormented.

"MARK AND HASTY; OR, SLAVE-LIFE IN MISSOURI"

By Mathilda Thompson

Preface

The facts narrated in the following pages occurred in St. Louis a few years ago. They were communicated to the author by a friend residing temporarily in that city.

MARK AND HASTY
CHAPTER I

On a bright and pleasant morning in the month of November, Mrs. Jennings and her children were sitting in one of the bedrooms of a handsome dwelling in St. Louis. It was evident that preparations were being made for a long journey. Two large trunks, strapped and corded, stood in the center of the room, while folded and unfolded articles of clothing lay in confusion on the floor and chairs.

"Katy," said Mrs. Jennings to a colored girl, who had just entered the room, "I wish you would bring in the other trunk," so that it will be ready for the children's clothes when Hasty comes."

"Yes, missus," said Kate [sic], and then, as she was leaving the room, she turned and said: "There's Hasty comin' in de gate, though she aint got de clothes wid her; 'pears to me she looks awful sorrowful."

"Why, Hasty, what is the matter?" inquired Mrs. Jennings, as a pretty, but sad-looking mulatto woman made her appearance at the door.

"O missus!" she said, "you must please 'scuse me, kase I hasn't de clothes done; but I'se been so nigh distracted dis week, dat I aint had heart nor strength to do anything. My husband has been sold down South, and I specs I'll never see him again if he once get down dar, kase dey never gets back."

"Why, how did that happen, Hasty?" asked Mrs. Jennings. "Mark has always been such a trusty servant, and has lived so long in the family, that I thought nothing would have induced Mr. Nelson to part with him."

"Yes, missus, I knows all dat. Mark has been the faithfulest sarvant dat his massa ever had. But ye see, on Saturday night when he cum down to see me, little Fanny was berry sick, and I had been out washin' all day, and Mark wanted me to go to bed, but I didn't; we both sat up all night wid de chile. Well, early de next morning he started for his massa's, and got dere about church time, kase he had a good piece to walk. Den he hauled out de carriage, and fed de horses, and while dey was eatin', de poor crittur fell asleep. And after bit, Massa Nelson got mighty uneasy, kase he had to wait for de carriage, so he sent one of de men out to see whar Mark was; and dey found him asleep and went in and told his massa. Den he sent for Mark to cum into de parlor, and when he went in Massa Nelson axed him what right had he to go sleep, when it was time for de carriage to be round. And Mark said dat his chile had been sick, and he had sat up all night wid it, and dat was what made him so sleepy. Den Massa Nelson said he had no right to sit up, if it was gwine to interfere wid his work. And Mark stood right up and looked Massa Nelson in de face, and said: 'Massa Nelson; I think I hab as much right to sit up wid my sick chile, as you had to sit up de other night wid little Massa Eddie.' O my sakes alive! but Massa Nelson was mad den; he said: 'You, you black nigger, dare to talk to me about rights;' and he struck Mark over de face wid de big carrige whip, and said 'he'd 'tend to him in de mornin'.'"

"And did Mark say nothing more than that?" inquired Mrs. Jennings; thinking that Hasty, like any other wife, would endeavor to hide her husband's faults.

"No, missus, dat was every ting he said, and just went away and got de carriage round for Massa Nelson to go to church. Well, de next mornin' Massa Nelson told him to put on his coat and follow him, and he toted him down to old M'Affee's pen, and sold him to go down some river way down South; and I have cum dis mornin'," she said, looking up inquiringly into Mrs. Jennings's face, "to see if you, Missus, or Massa Jennings, wouldn't do something for him."

"Well, Hasty, I'm sorry, very sorry for you," said Mrs. Jennings; "but don't be down-hearted; I will postpone going East this week, and see what can be done for you; and if my husband can't buy Mark, he probably knows some one who wants a trusty servant, such as I know Mark to be. However, Hasty, you may be assured that I will do all in my power to prevent your husband from going."

Hasty dried her tears, and with many thanks took her departure, feeling much comforted by the confident tone with which Mrs. Jennings spoke.

After Hasty had gone, Mrs. Jennings pondered, as she had never before done, on the evil effects of slavery. She thought of Hasty's grief, as poignant as would have been her own, had her husband been in Mark's place, and which had changed that usually bright countenance to one haggard with suffering. She thought of the father torn from his wife and child; of the child fatherless, though not an orphan; of that child's future; and as it presented itself to her, she clasped her own little girl closer to her heart, almost fearing that it was to share that future. Ah! she was putting her "soul in the slave soul's stead."

CHAPTER II

Mrs. Jennings, true to her promise, acquainted Mr. Jennings with the transaction, and entreated him to make an effort immediately to rescue Mark from his fearful doom.

"Well, my dear," he answered, "it appears that the boy has been impudent, and I don't know that it would be right for me to interfere, but Mark has always been such a good servant that if I had been his master I would have overlooked it, or at least would not have punished him so severely. However, I'll go down to M'Affee and see about him."

Accordingly, the next morning, he went down to the slave "pen" to see the trader. He found him at the door of his office, a sleek, smiling, well-dressed man, very courteous and affable, having the appearance of a gentleman.

"Good morning, Mr. Jennings," said the trader, "what can I do for you to-day?"

"Why, M'Affee, I called down to see about a boy named Mark, one of Nelson's people. I heard you had him for sale, and as he is a good sort of a fellow, I wouldn't mind buying him, if you are reasonable."

"Want to keep him in St. Louis?" inquired the trader.

"O! certainly, I want him for a coachman; ours gets drunk, and my wife will not allow him to drive her."

"Well, Mr. Jennings, I am very sorry, but the fact is, Mr. Nelson was very angry at Mark, and pledged me not to sell him in the State. You see he was impudent, and you know that can't be allowed at all. I am right sorry, but I dare say I can suit you in one quite as good. There's Hannibal, one of Captain Adam's boys, he is a—

"No matter, I don't want him," interrupted Mr. Jennings; "I am not particular about purchasing this morning. I only wanted him to please my wife; she will be very much disappointed, as she has his wife washing for her, and she will be in great distress at parting with her husband."

"Yes, yes, I see! It's a pity niggers will take on so. I am sorry I can't accommodate Mrs. Jennings. If you should want a coachman, I should be glad if you would call down, as I have a good stock on hand of strong, healthy boys."

"Yes, when I want one I will give you a call. But do you really think that Mr. Nelson would refuse to have him remain even in the State? I really would like to keep the poor fellow from going down South, if I paid a hundred or two more than he is worth."

"O! there is no chance for him. Mr. Nelson was positive in his instructions. I don't think you need take the trouble to ask him, as I am almost sure he will refuse."

"Then I suppose nothing can be done. Good morning," said Mr. Jennings.

"Good morning, sir; I am sorry we can't trade."

Mr. Jennings went home, and acquainted his wife with the result of his mission. She was a kind mistress to her slaves, and had seen but little of the horrors of slavery. To be sure, she had heard of instances of cruelty, but they had made but little impression on her, and had soon been forgotten. But here was a case which outraged every womanly feeling in her breast, a case of suffering and wrong, occurring to persons in whom she was personally interested, and she was aroused to the wickedness of the system which allowed such oppression.

In the evening Hasty came up to see if anything had been done for her relief. As she entered the room, the sorrowful expression of Mrs. Jennings's face brought tears into her eyes, for she felt there was no hope.

"O poor Hasty!" said Mrs. Jennings.

"Don't say no more, missus, I see what's comin'. Poor Mark will go down South. Seems to me I knowed it would be so from de fust. O dear!

it'll go nigh breaking me down. 'Pears like I can't stand it no how," said Hasty, sobbing aloud.

Mrs. Jennings waited till the first burst of bitter grief was over, and then tried to comfort her as well as she was able, but she felt how hard it was to assuage such grief as this. She spoke to her of the hope of seeing her husband again in this world, and of the certainty at least, if both tried to do the will of God, of meeting in heaven. But her efforts were unavailing, and her consoling words fell on a heart that would not be comforted.

CHAPTER III

When Mrs. Jennings awoke the next morning, her first thoughts were of Hasty, and she determined that the day should not pass over without her making another effort for Mark. Accordingly, after breakfast she ordered the carriage, intending to make a visit to Mr. Nelson's.

"Where are you going, Maggie?" inquired Mr. Jennings of his wife, as he heard her give the order.

"I am going to Mr. Nelson's about Mark," she answered.

"Why, my dear, I told you what M'Affee said, that Nelson was implacable. And besides, I am afraid he will think it impertinent in you to meddle with his affairs."

"I shall make an apology for my visit," she answered, "but I cannot rest satisfied until I hear a direct refusal from his own lips. His conduct toward Mark seems more like revenge than punishment. I do not think he can persist in it."

"Well, I give you credit for your perseverance," he said, laughingly, "but I am afraid you will come home disappointed."

"If I do," she replied, "I shall feel less conscience-stricken than if I had remained at home, knowing that I have done all in my power to prevent his going."

As Mrs. Jennings rode along she felt that she had a disagreeable duty to perform, but, like a true Christian woman, she shrunk not, but grew stronger as she approached the dwelling of the lordly oppressor, and she prayed to God for strength to be true to him and to the slave. When she arrived, she entered the house of Mr. Nelson with strong hopes, but, much to her disappointment, was informed that he had left the city, and would be absent for some weeks. Her next thought was to see his wife, if she was at home. The servant said that his mistress was at home, but doubted if she could be seen.

"Present my card to her," said Mrs. Jennings, "and say to her that I have called on business, and will detain her but a few moments if she will see me."

The servant retired with the card, and in a few moments returned, saying that Mrs. Nelson would be glad to see her in the sitting-room. When Mrs. Jennings entered the room she apologized for the intrusion to a handsome, though slightly careworn lady, who arose to receive her.

"Madame," said Mrs. Jennings, "I have called on you this morning in relation to your servant Mark. I hope you will not think it impertinent in me to interfere in this matter, but I am very much interested in him. His wife has been my laundress for several years, and is exceedingly distressed at the idea of being separated from him. She came to me yesterday, and told me that he had been impertinent, and that Mr. Nelson intended selling him down South. I promised to use what influence I had to keep him in the city. And I have called this morning to see if I could persuade Mr. Nelson to overlook this offense, pledging myself for his future good conduct, for I really think that this will be a lesson to him that he will never forget."

"I can appreciate and sympathize with your feelings," said Mrs. Nelson, "for I have myself endeavored to change my husband's determination. But he is a rigid disciplinarian, and makes it a rule never to overlook the first symptom of insubordination in any of the servants. He says if a servant is once permitted to retort, all discipline ceases, and he *must* be sold South. It is his rule and he never departs from it. O! I sometimes feel so sick when I see the punishments inflicted that seem necessary to keep them in subjection. But we wives can do nothing, however great our repugnance may be to it. The children have begged me to take them to see Mark before he goes. I heard from one of the servants that his owner intended starting tomorrow, so that this will be the only opportunity they will have to see him, and I think I will gratify them and let them go."

Mrs. Nelson rang the bell, and in a few moments Sally had the children ready.

"I intended to go down myself," said Mrs. Jennings, "and if you have no objections, I will take the children down in my carriage, as it is waiting at the door."

"O, I thank you, that will suit me very well," said Mrs. Nelson, "as my engagements this morning will hardly permit me to go, and I was almost afraid to trust them with any of the other servants, now that Mark has gone."

Mrs. Jennings and the children immediately entered the carriage and drove to the yard. As the carriage drew up before the door, Mr. M'Affee came out and assisted the party to alight, and on hearing the business, summoned Mark to them.

"O! Massa Eddie and Missy Bell," said he joyfully, "I'se so glad you cum to see poor Mark; I was afeard I would never see you again."

"O yes," said Eddie, "we came as soon as mamma told us about it. You see we didn't know it until yesterday, when we went out to ride, and that cross old Noah drove us, and we couldn't tell what it meant; so as soon as we came home Bell asked mother about it, and she said that you had been naughty, and papa sent you away. But I don't care; I think pa might forgive you just this once."

"Yes, so do I," broke in Bell; "pa ought to let you stay, because little Fanny won't have any father to come and see at our house, and I like her to play with me."

"I'se afeard Fanny won't play any more," said Mark sadly. "She is berry sick; de doctor said it was de scarlet fever, and the oder night, when I was up home, she was out of her head and didn't know me."

"Why, is she sick?" asked Bell; "I didn't know that; I'll ask mamma if I can't go and see her when I get home. But mamma says maybe you'll come back one of these days. Won't you, Mark?"

"No, honey, I don't ever 'spec to get back; and if I do, it will be a long, long time. It's so far down where I'se sold to, down the Arkansas river, I believe."

"Are you sold there, Mark?" inquired Mrs. Jennings.

"Yes, missus, and I don't know what'll come of poor Hasty when she knows it. She was here dis morning, and said that you had gone to Massa Nelson's, and was going to try to get me off; but I knowed how it would be; but I couldn't bar to cast her down when she was so hopeful like, so I didn't tell her I was sold. O Missus Jennings! do please comfort de poor soul, she's so sick and weak, she can hardly bar up. I used to give her all the arnings I got from people, but I can't give her any more. O Lord! it comes nigh breakin' me down when I think of it," said Mark, the big tears coursing down his face.

"Don't cry, Mark," said little Bell, "Eddie and I will save up our money, and by the time we are big, we'll have enough to buy you; then I'll send Eddie down to bring you home."

"Yes," said Eddie, "and mamma will give us many a picayune, when we tell her what it's for."

Mrs. Jennings had been an interested spectator of the scene, and would have remained longer with Mark, to comfort him; but as it was after the dinner hour, she feared Mrs. Nelson would be anxious about the children, so she told them it was time to go, and that they must part with Mark.

"Well, Mark, if we *must* go," said the children, throwing their arms around his neck, "Good by."

"Good by, dear children," he said, "and please be kind to my poor little Fanny, that will soon have no father."

"We will," they answered, as they sadly passed from the yard.

CHAPTER IV

The following morning that sun rose warm and bright. All was bustle and excitement on the levee. Its broad top was crowded with drays and cabs conveying the freight and passengers to and from the steamboats, that lay compactly wedged together at its edge.

About ten o'clock the bell of the "Aldon Adams" announced that its time for starting had come. The cabs threaded their way through the piles of goods and bales of cotton to the plank, and delivered their loads of travelers flitting to the sunny South. The last package of freight was being carried aboard, and everything was ready for the start. But all who are going have not arrived. A sad procession is marching down to the boat. It is M'Affee's gang! the men handcuffed, the women and children walking double file, though not fettered. A little apart from the rest we recognise Mark, and by his side walks Hasty. Little is said by either, but O! they feel the more. At last they reached the plank that was to separate them forever, yes, forever.

At that same spot farewells had been exchanged; farewells, sad and tearful. Yet amid these tears, and with this sadness, hope whispered of a glad meeting in the future—of a joyful reunion. But here there was no such hope. Each felt that for them all was despair. Hark! the shrill whistle and the impatient puffing of the steam tell them they must part. The rest have taken their places on the deck, and they two are standing on the levee alone.

"Come, come, quit your parleying. Don't you see they are hauling in the plank! Jump aboard Mark, and don't look so glum. I'll git you another gal down in Arkansas," said the trader.

Had he seen the look which Hasty cast upon him, he might have been admonished by those words of Oriental piety; "Beware of the groans of a wounded soul. Oppress not to the utmost a single heart, for a solitary sigh has the power to overturn a world."

She turned from the trader, and, with a sob, as though the heart springs

"Hasty's Grief"
Courtesy, American Antiquarian Society.

were snapped, she threw herself into her husband's arms. Again, and again he pressed her to his heart, then gently unclasping her hands, he tottered along the plank, and nearly had he ended his saddened life in the rolling stream below, but the ready hand of his owner caught him, and hurried him aboard.

The plank was hauled aboard, and in an instant the boat was moving out into the stream. The passengers congregated on the hurricane deck, cheered, and waved their handkerchiefs to friends on shore, and her crew answered the shouts of those on the other boats as she rapidly passed them. Few saw, and those who did, without noting, the sorrowing woman, who, leaning against a bale of goods, with one hand shading her eyes, and the other pressed hard upon her heart, watching the receding boat, until it turned a bend in the river, and was hidden from her sight. Yet no watcher borne away upon the boat, nor any sorrowing one left upon the shore, turned away, as the last traces of the loved ones faded, with a heavier heart, or a feeling of such utter loneliness as did poor Hasty. Despairingly, she turned toward home. No tears, no choking sobs; but only that calm, frozen look to which tears and sobs would have been a relief.

The light, elastic step of but a week before was gone. She stopped not now to gaze into the gay windows, or to watch the throng of promenaders; but, with an unsteady pace, wended her way slowly to her humble home in the lower part of the city.

"Stop, Aunt Hasty," said a colored woman belonging to Mrs. Nelson, "missus gave me leave to cum down here dis afternoon to go home with you, kase she said you would take it so hard parting with your ole man."

Hasty looked up as she heard the well known voice of the kind-hearted Sally.

"O! Sally," she said, "I'se got no home now; they has taken him away that made me a home, and I don't keer for nothing now."

"You mustn't be down-hearted, Hasty," she said, "but look right up to de Lord. He says, Call on me in de day of trouble, and I will hear ye; and cast your burden on me, and I will care for ye. And sure enough dis is your time ob trouble, poor crittur."

"Yes," she answered, "and it has been my time of trouble ever since Mark was sold, and I has prayed to de Lord, time after time, to raise up friends to save Mark from going; but ye see how it is, Sally."

"Yes, I sees, Hasty, but ye mustn't let it shake your faith a bit, kase de Lord will bring it all right in his time."

Thus talking, and endeavoring to console her, Sally accompanied Hasty to her now desolate home. As she entered the room, the low moan of her child fell upon her ear, and awoke her to the necessity of action. It was well that there existed an immediate call on her, or her heart would have sunk under the heavy burden of sorrow. She went hastily to the side of the little sufferer, and passing her cold hand over the burning forehead of her child, whispered soothing words of endearment.

"Is father come?" asked Fanny. "I'se been dreamin', and I thought for sure he was here. 'Aint this his night to come home, mother?"

"No, honey, dis is Friday night," answered Hasty. "But never mind about father now, but go to sleep, there's a good girl."

And sitting down by the side of her child, Hasty, with a mother's tenderness, soothed her to sleep. All that long night she sat, but no sleep shed a calm upon her heart; but when morning came exhausted nature could bear up no longer, and she sank into a short but troubled slumber.

By the sick bed of her child,
  In her cabin lone and drear,
Listening to its ravings wild,
  Dropping on it a many tear,
Sat the mother, broken-hearted;
  Every hope was in its shroud.
From her husband she'd been parted,
  And to earth with grief she's bow'd.
Now within her ear is ringing
  Drearily hope's funeral knell,
And the night wind wild is singing
  Mournfully, the word *farewell.*

Day broke, and still mother and child slept on. Hasty's over-charged heart and brain were for the first time, for some days, lulled to forgetfulness. If this relief had not come, without doubt one would have broken, and the other been lost in madness. Fanny was the first to awake. The crisis of the disease had passed; the fever no longer scorched her veins, and her mind no longer wandered. She was, however, as weak as an infant, and as incapable of attending to her wants. For the first time for many days she felt a desire for food, and raising herself partly up, called to her mother to get her breakfast.

The voice of her child roused Hasty from her dreams of peace, to the dread realities of her bereavement. For a few moments she could not recall her scattered senses, but soon the remembrance of yesterday crowded upon her mind, and the anguish depicted upon her face showed that they had lost nothing of their intensity during their short oblivion.

"Why Fanny, child, is you awake? And de fever all gone, too? How is yer dis mornin', dear?" asked Hasty.

"O! I feel a heap better, mother," answered Fanny; "and I think I will be pretty near well by the time pappy comes to-night."

Every word her child uttered fell as a leaden weight upon her heart. Her mind instinctively reverted to the last time her husband had been there. Then no thought of separation clouded their minds, but together they watched beside their sick child, beguiling the long hours of the night with hopeful and loving converse. Then she thought of the incidents of the week as they followed each other in quick succession, the news of his sale, the trader's pen, the parting; all, all seemed burned upon her brain in coals of living fire, and with a moan of agony she sank insensible upon the bed.

A few moments after Mrs. Jennings entered the room. Ever since visiting Mark, and witnessing his anguish, she had constantly thought of Hasty, and longed for an opportunity of consoling her, and rendering her any assistance in her power. Feeling this morning uneasy at not hearing from her, she determined to go and see her. After some difficulty she at last found her, and, as we have seen, arrived very opportunely. Instantly, upon seeing the state of affairs, Mrs. Jennings ordered her coachman to go for a physician, while she and her maid, whom she had brought with her, used every means to restore Hasty to consciousness, and in a short time they succeeded in their efforts.

The doctor arrived shortly after, and advised rest and quiet as the best restoratives to her shattered nerves. The wants of Fanny were also attended to, and the cravings of her appetite satisfied from a basket of food which the thoughtful care of Mrs. Jennings had provided. Mrs. Jennings's next thought was to procure a nurse for Hasty. Here she had no difficulty, for the neighbors of Hasty willingly offered their services. Selecting one who appeared thoughtful and tidy, Mrs. Jennings returned home with a heart lightened by a consciousness of duty well performed.

For some days Hasty lay in a kind of stupor, without taking any notice of transpiring events, or seeming to recur to those of the past. She was daily supplied with various little dainties and luxuries suitable to an invalid, and received many other attentions from the kind-hearted Mrs. Jennings. Fanny's health improved each day, and, as the buoyancy of youth threw off the remains of disease, she regained her strength, and at the end of the following week she was able to take almost the entire charge of her mother. Hasty's eyes followed every movement of her child with the intensest eagerness, as if fearing that she too would be taken from her.

When Fanny was fully recovered she learned the fate of her father. She did not weep, or sob, or complain, but for the first time she realized the shadow that slavery had cast over her; and the change was instantaneous, from the mirthful, happy child, to the anxious, watchful slave girl. Hereafter there was to be no trusting confidence, no careless gayety, but this consciousness of slavery must mingle with every thought, with every action.

One day, about a week after Hasty was taken sick, her mistress entered her room. This lady was the widow of a Frenchman, one of the early settlers of St. Louis, who had, by persevering industry, gained a competency. Before he had an opportunity of enjoying it he died, and left his property, consisting of a dwelling, five or six negroes, and a good sum in the stocks, to his widow. Mrs. Le Rue, on breaking up housekeeping, allowed Hasty to hire her time for two dollars a week, on condition that at the end of each month the required sum was to be forthcoming, and in the event of failure, the revocation of the permission was to be the inevitable consequence.

The monthly pay-day found Hasty prostrated on a bed of sickness, and of course it passed without the payment of the stipulated sum. This was the immediate cause of her visit.

The anxiety depicted in the countenance of Mrs. Le Rue did not arise from any sympathy for the emaciated and suffering woman before her, but only from that natural vexation with which a farmer would regard the sudden falling lame of a valuable horse. The idea of commiserating Hasty's condition as a human being, as a sister, never for a moment occurred to her; indeed, the sickness of the little poodle dog, which she led by a pink ribbon, would have elicited far more of the sympathies of her nature. In Hasty she saw only a piece of property visibly depreciated by sickness.

"What is the matter with you, girl? Why have you not come to pay me my money?" she asked harshly, as she took the seat that Fanny had carefully dusted off.

"O missus! I'se been too sick to work dis two weeks; but I'se got five dollars saved up for you, and if ever I get well I kin pay you the rest soon."

"Pay the rest soon! Yes, you look very much like that. You are just making a fool of yourself about your husband; that is the way you niggers do. You are just trying to cheat me out of the money. I'll never let one of my women get married again."

While the much-injured lady was delivering this speech, the poodle, who had been intently watching the face of his mistress, and thinking some one must be the offender, sprang at Fanny, viciously snapping at her feet. She, poor girl, had watched every expression in the face of her mistress, with the same anxiety as the courtiers of the sultan watch that autocrat, who holds their lives and fortunes in his hand; and surprised at this assault from an unlooked-for quarter, she jumped aside, and in doing so trod upon the paw of her tormentor, and sent him howling to the lap of his mistress.

This was the last drop that caused the cup of wrath to overflow. Without heeding the protestations of Fanny, she seized her by the arm, and boxed her ears soundly.

"What did you tread upon the dog for, you great clumsy nigger? I'll teach you what I'll do, if you do anything of the kind again; I'll give you a good whipping."

Then turning to Hasty, whose feeble nerves had been intensely excited by this scene, she said: "I want you to get to work again pretty soon, and not lie there too lazy to work. You need not think I am going to lose my money by your foolishness. I shall expect your month's payment as usual, and if I don't get it, I will hire you out like the rest. And there is another thing I have to say; you are not going to keep this lazy girl here to hinder you, and to spend money on. A lady I know wants just such a girl to go to the door, and to wait on her, who will give me two dollars a month for her, and it is quite time she was doing something. I will not take her away now, but next week do you tidy her up and send her to me."

CHAPTER V

Hasty was dying. She knew that it was to be so. For herself it was a release which she hailed gladly; but the thought of leaving her child rent her heart with anguish. She could see what the lot of that poor waif of childhood, cast upon the sea of Southern despotism, would be, and she longed to protect her from it. Yet what is a slave mother's protection to her child? What blow can she arrest? What temptation avert? None. Even a mother's claim is unrecognized, and the child's affection unregarded. Hasty's strength gradually declined until Sunday, when, feeling that death was near, she sent Fanny for Mrs. Jennings, for the purpose of bidding her farewell, and asking her protection for her daughter. Mrs. Jennings, on learning from Fanny the condition of Hasty, immediately complied with the request. On entering the room she was surprised and shocked at the ravages that mental and bodily suffering had made on the once handsome woman. Seating herself by the bedside, Mrs. Jennings inquired in what way she could ease the mind of the dying mother. With earnestness did Hasty plead that her child might be rescued from her present condition. She entreated Mrs. Jennings to buy Fanny from Mrs. Le Rue, and bring her up in the fear of God, and beyond the reach of a slave girl's perils.

All this Mrs. Jennings promised, and with many a word of comfort she smoothed the passing of the immortal spirit into the unknown country.

She pointed to the Saviour, and told of his wondrous love, of the equality of all in his sight, and of the saving power of his grace extended to all, whether bond or free.

Just as the sun threw his last rays upon the spires of the city, Hasty's spirit was released, and she was *free*. Fanny gave herself up to a child's grief, and refused to be comforted. To the slave, the affections are the bright spots in his wilderness of sorrow and care; and as an Arab loves the oasis the better that it is in the midst of the desert, so the slave centers the whole strength of his nature in his loved ones, the more so that he is shut out from the hopes of wealth, the longings of ambition, and the excitements of a freeman's life.

Mrs. Jennings verified her promise to Hasty, and soon after her death purchased Fanny. But her whole soul revolted at a system which could cause the suffering she had seen; and in the course of a few months she prevailed upon her husband to close his business in St. Louis, and remove to Chicago, where she is an active worker among the anti-slavery women in that liberty-loving city. She has instilled the principles of freedom for all men into the minds of her children, and recently wrote the following verses for them on the occasion of the celebration of the Fourth of July:[5]

"Little children, when you see
　　High your country's banner wave,
Let your thoughts a moment be
　　Turned in pity on the slave.

"When with pride you count the stars,
　　When your hearts grow strong and brave,
Think with pity of the scars
　　Borne in sorrow by the slave.

"Not for him is freedom's sound;
　　Not for him the banners wave;
For, in hopeless bondage bound,
　　Toils the sad and weary slave.

"All things round of freedom ring—
　　Winged birds and dashing wave;
What are joyous sounds to him
　　In his chains, a fettered slave?"

"AUNT JUDY'S STORY: A STORY FROM REAL LIFE"

By Matilda G. Thompson

CHAPTER I

"Look! look! mother, there comes old Aunt Judy!" said Alfred, as an old colored woman came slowly up the gravel walk that led to the handsome residence of Mr. Ford, of Indiana.

The tottering step, the stooping back, and glassy eye, betokened extreme age and infirmity. Her countenance bore the marks of hardship and exposure; while, the coarse material of her scanty garments, which scarcely served to defend her from the bleak December wind, showed that even now she wrestled with poverty for life. In one hand she carried a small pitcher, while with the other she leaned heavily on her oaken stick.

"She has come for her milk," said little Cornelia, who ran out and took the pitcher from the woman's hand.

"Let me help you, Auntie, you walk so slow," said she.

"Come in and warm yourself, Judy," said Mrs. Ford, "it is cold and damp, and you must be tired. How have you been these two or three days?"

"Purty well, thank ye, but I'se had a touch of the rheumatiz, and I find I isn't so strong as I was," said Judy, as she drew near the grate, in which blazed and crackled the soft coal of the West, in a manner both beautiful and comforting.

Mrs. Ford busied herself in preparing a basket of provisions, and had commenced wrapping the napkin over it, when she paused and leaned toward the closet, in to which she looked, but did not seem to find what she wanted, for, calling one of the boys, she whispered something to him. He ran out into the yard and down the path to the barn; presently he returned and said,

"There are none there, mother."

"I am very sorry, Judy, that I have not an egg for you, but our hens have not yet commenced laying, except Sissy's little bantam," said Mrs. Ford.

Now Cornelia had a little white banty, with a topknot on its head and feathers on its legs, which was a very great pet, of course; and Sissy had resolved to save all banty's eggs, so that she might hatch only her own chickens. "For," said she, "if she sets on other hen's eggs, when the chickens grow big they will be larger than their mother, and then she will have so much trouble to make them mind her."

"Aunt Judy's Husband Captured"
Courtesy, American Antiquarian Society.

Now, when she heard her mother wish for an egg, the desire to give one to Judy crossed her mind, but it was some moments before she could bring herself to part with her cherished treasure. Soon, however, her irresolution vanished, and she ran quickly to her little basket, and taking out a nice fresh egg, she laid it in Judy's hand, saying,

"There, Judy, it will make you strong."

Mrs. Ford marked with a mother's eye the struggle going on in the mind of her daughter, but determined not to interfere, but let her decide for herself, unbiased by her mother's wishes or opinions. And when she saw the better feeling triumph, a tear of exquisite pleasure dimmed her eye, for in that trifling circumstance she saw the many trials and temptations of after life prefigured, and hoped they would end as that did, in the victory of the noble and generous impulses of the heart.

When the basket was ready, and Aunt Judy regaled with a nice cup of tea, one of the boys volunteered to carry it home for her, a proposal which was readily assented to by Mrs. Ford, whose heart was gladdened by every act of kindness to the poor and needy performed by her children, and who had early taught them that in such deeds they obeyed the injunction of our Saviour: "Bear ye one another's burdens."

CHAPTER II

Several weeks had passed away since Judy's visit, when, one day, as Cornelia stood leaning her little curly head against her mother's knee, she said:

"Mother, who is Judy? Has she a husband or children?"

"I do not know of any, my daughter. She may have some living; but you know Judy was a slave, and they have probably been sold away from her, and are still in slavery."

"In slavery, mother! and *sold?* Why, do they sell little children away from their mothers?"

"Yes, Cornelia, there are persons guilty of such a wicked thing; mothers and children, and whole families, are often separated from each other, never, perhaps, to meet again!"

"So Judy was a slave, mother?"

"Yes, Cornelia, she was: and from all I have learned of her history, I am sure she has led a very unhappy and sorrowful life."

"O! now I understand what you meant when you said that she had a thorny path through life. Have you ever heard her history, mother? if you have, won't you tell it to us?"

"Yes, do, mother, do!" exclaimed the children together.

"I should like very much to gratify you, my dear children, but it is not in my power to do so, as I am not very well acquainted with her history. But I will tell you how we can arrange it. Judy will be here tonight, as I promised to give her some Indian cakes, of which she is very fond, and I have no doubt that she will tell you the story of her sad life."

The idea of hearing Judy's story occupied the mind of the children all the afternoon, and the evening was looked forward to with great impatience by them.

It was twilight, and Mrs. Ford and the children had gathered around the warm, comfortable grate to await the return of papa. The wind whistled without, and the snow-flakes fell silently and steadily to the frozen ground.

"Mother, can't I bring in the lights?" asked Cornelia, who was getting a little impatient; only a little, for Cornelia was remarkable for her sweet and placid disposition.

"Yes, dear, I think you may. Hark! yes, that is his footstep in the hall. Go, Alfred, and tell Bessie to bring up the tea. And you, Cornelia, bring your father's dressing-gown and slippers to the fire."

"Yes, wife, let us have some of Bessie's nice hot tea, for I am chilled through and through; and such a cutting wind! I thought my nose would have been blown off; and what would my little girl have said if she had seen her papa come home without a nose? Would you have run?" asked Mr. Ford.

"No, indeed, papa, if your nose were blown off, and your teeth all pulled out, and you were like 'Uncle Ned,' who had 'no eyes to see, and had no hair on the top of his head,' I would just get on your lap as I do now; so you see you could not frighten me away if you tried ever so hard," said Cornelia, laughingly.

Supper was hastily dispatched by the children, who were eager and impatient for the coming of Aunt Judy.

"O mother! *do* you think she will come?" asked Alfred, as his mother arose from the table to look at the weather.

"Well, indeed, Alfred, I am sorry to disappoint you, but I think there is little probability of seeing Judy to-night."

"Why, no, mother, I thought that as soon as I saw what a stormy night it was; and although it will disappoint us very much, I hope she will not come," said little Cornelia.

"Why, how you talk, sis! *Not come*, indeed! Humph! I hope she *will*, then. This little snow wouldn't hurt me, so it wouldn't hurt her," said the impetuous Alfred.

"You must remember, my son, that Judy is old and infirm, and subject, as she says, to a 'touch of the rheumatiz.' But I am sorry that she has not come to-night. She may be sick; I think I will call down and see her to-morrow," said Mrs. Ford, drawing out the table and arranging the shade on the lamp, so that the light fell on the table and the faces of those around it. They were cheerful, happy faces, and everything around them wore the same look; and from the aspect of things, it seemed as if they were going to spend a pleasant and profitable evening.

"Dear papa, tell us a story with a poor slave in it, won't you? and I will give you as many kisses as you please," said Cornelia, twining her arms around her father's neck.

"No, no, papa, not about the slave, but the poor Indian, who has been far worse treated than the slave was or ever will be. Only to think of the white people coming here, plundering their villages, and building on their hunting grounds, just as if it belonged to them, when all the while it was the Indians'. Now, if they had bought it and paid for it, honorably, as William Penn did, it would have been a different thing; but they got it meanly, and I'm ashamed of them for it," said Alfred, his eyes flashing and his cheeks glowing with indignation.

"All that you have said is true, my son, but the Indians were also guilty of great cruelty toward the white people," said Mr. Ford.

"But, papa, don't you think the Indians had good cause for their hatred to the whites?" asked Harry.

"Why, Harry, they had no reason sufficient to justify them in their cruel and vindictive course; but they did no more than was to be expected from an entirely barbarous nation, and I am sure they had no good example in the conduct of the white people, from whom much better behavior might have been expected."

"Well, papa, what were some of the wrongs that the Indians endured!"

"The Indians regarded the whites as intruders, and maddened by some acts of injustice and oppression committed by the early settlers, they conceived a deadly hatred, which the whites returned with equal intensity; and for each crime committed by either of them, the opposite party inflicted a retribution more terrible than the act which provoked it, and the Indian, being less powerful, but equally wicked, was the victim."

"Well, although I think the Indians were very wicked, I pity them, but I feel a great deal more for the poor slave," said little Cornelia.

"I think they were very cruel, sis, but I still think that they were very badly treated," said Alfred.

"There is no doubt of that," answered his father; "but, my son, when you began the argument you said that you thought the Indians were more deserving of compassion than the Africans. Now this is the difference. The Indians were always a warlike and treacherous race; their most solemn compacts were broken as soon as their own purposes had been served. And they were continually harassing the settlers; indeed they have not ceased yet, for at the present time they are attacking and murdering the traders who cross the plains, if they are not well armed, and in sufficiently large companies to keep them in check. Now the Americans had never his cause of complaint against the Africans, for, although like all heathen, they were debased, and were cruel and warlike among each other, they never annoyed us in America. And the Americans had not, therefore, even this insufficient excuse for enslaving them. The Indians were robbed of their lands, and driven from their homes; but the Africans not only lost their country, but were compelled to work in slavery, for men to whom they owed no allegiance, in a different climate and with the ever-galling thought that they were once free. It argues well for their peaceable disposition, that they have not long ago revolted, and by a terrible massacre shaken off their yoke as they did in St. Domingo. Now, which was the worst used in this case?"

"O! the slave, papa. I willingly surrender," said Alfred, laughing.

"Well, if you have finished, I move we go to bed, and thence to the land of dreams," said Mrs. Ford, rising and putting away her sewing.

It was unanimously agreed that this was the best plan, and after giving thanks to God for his many mercies, they retired.

CHAPTER III

"Good morning, father," said Alfred; "I have been thinking that I surrendered too soon last night; I did not bring out all my forces, because I forgot something I heard that old Baptist minister say when he was lecturing here a few days ago. He said that the Creek Indians would not send the poor fugitives back to their masters. It is true they made a treaty with our government to do so, but they had too much humanity to keep it; and for not doing so, the government withheld two hundred and fifty thousand dollars, which was due to the Indians for some lands, and used it to pay the masters. But that made little difference to them, for they still persisted in disobeying the 'Fugitive Slave Law.' Now don't you think *that* was a good trait in their character?"

"Yes, Alfred, I do; they manifested a very generous and humane disposition."

"Well, but I think it was very dishonorable for them to break any treaty," said Harry.

"You see, Harry there is where you and I differ. I think it a great deal better to break a bad promise than to keep it," answered Alfred.

"Come in to breakfast, papa," said Cornelia, peeping her little curly head in at the door, "Mamma wants you to come right away, because she has to go to Judy's."

"Very well, we will go now, and not keep mother waiting. Just look at the snow! How it sparkles! Jack Frost has been here, for the windows are all covered and the water in the pitcher is frozen."

"Yes, papa, and see what funny shapes the icicles are in, and the trees and bushes look as if they had their white dresses on," said little Cornelia.

"It will be a splendid morning for a sleigh ride. Would you like to take one, mother?" asked Harry, after their breakfast was over and family prayer ended.

"Yes, my son, I should; I have to go to Judy's this morning; so we can take the children to school first, and then pay my visit. I should like to have the sleigh at the door pretty early, as I have several places to go to after coming from Judy's."

"Very well, mother, you, shall have it immediately. Now bundle sis up warm, for there is a cutting wind, and I think it looks like snowing again. And O! mother, I had nearly forgotten it, there was a poor Irish family coming off the boat last night, who seemed destitute of both clothing and food. If we have time this morning, won't you go and see them?"

"Perhaps I will," said his mother; and Harry ran off, but soon returned, calling, "Come, mother, the sleigh is waiting, and the horse looks as if he was in a hurry to be off."

"Yes, Harry, I am coming; I only went back to get a little milk for Judy; she is so weak that I think she needs it."

"O mother!" said Alfred as they drove along, "What is more enlivening than the merry jingling of the sleigh bells on a clear frosty day?"

"It is, indeed, very pleasant, Alfred; but while we are enjoying our pleasant winter evenings, and our many sleigh rides, the thought comes to our minds that however much we may like the winter time, there are hundreds in our city who think of its approach with fear and, trembling, and who suffer much from cold and hunger, until the pleasant spring time comes again. But you were telling me, Henry, about those poor people, and I was too much occupied to attend to you. Do you know where they live?" asked Mrs. Ford.

"Yes, just along the bank, mother; it is a wretched-looking house, and very much exposed. Poor things! I pitied them very much; they appeared so destitute, and even the children had a care-worn look on their thin faces."

"What! in that old house, Harry?" exclaimed Alfred. "Why the windows have hardly any panes in them, and there are great holes in the walls."

"Yes, Ally, that is the place, and it is, as you say, a rickety old house; but I suppose it is the best they can get. But here we are at school, Ally; you get out first, and I will hand sissy out to you. Take hold of her hand, for the path is slippery."

The children alighted, and then Harry and his mother, after a pleasant ride round the city, drove up to Aunt Judy's cottage.

"O Miss Ford! am dat you? Now who'd a thought on't? I'se sure you's de best woman I ever see'd; now jist tell me what you cum'd out on sich a day as dis for!" asked old Judy as Mrs. Ford entered the cottage. As for

Harry, he drove the horse back to the stable until noon, when he was to call for his mother on his way from school with Ally and Cornelia.

"Why, Judy, we came to see you; I thought that if you were sick, I could perhaps comfort you."

"Wal, I *has* been sick wid de rheumatiz. O marcy! I'se had sich orful pains all through me, and dats de reason I didn't cum last night. But, bless us! honey, here I'se been standing telling you all my pains and aches, and letting you stand in your wet feet; now come to de fire, my child."

"My feet are not wet, Auntie, only a little cold. Harry brought me around in the sleigh, and we were well wrapped up. Now, Judy, here are a few things for you, some tea and sugar, a loaf of bread, and a bit of bacon."

"Thanks, Missy Ford, I'se so glad to see a little tea; it's so long since I tasted any. And a bit of bacon too! Wal, now I *will* have a dinner!"

"Do not wait till dinner time, Judy; I want you to make a cup of tea now, and rouse yourself up, and try to recollect all that has passed and happened to you since your childhood, for I promised the children that I would tell them your history."

"Yes, missy, I'll try," said Judy, taking her little cracked earthen teapot, and making her tea.

After it was made, and Judy was refreshed with a good breakfast, she began and told Mrs. Ford the history of her sorrows and troubles, which we will let Mrs. Ford tell to the children herself. It was quite a long narrative.

CHAPTER IV

Judy had just finished speaking when they were interrupted by the entrance of Harry, who had returned for his mother. Judy followed them to the sleigh, for she said she "must cum out and see de chil'en, spite of her rheumatiz."

"Auntie," said little Cornelia, "have my little banty's eggs hatched yet?" Cornelia had sent the little banty and her eggs to aunt Judy, that the chickens might be hatched under her care.

"Laws, yes, honey, I'll go in and get 'em for you to see; but I think you had better not take them home yet, till they get bigger," said Judy, going back into the house. In a little while she appeared with a little covered basket in her hand. She unwrapped the flannel from around the basket, and there lay six beautiful little white banties.

"O mamma! look at the little things! Are they not little beauties?" said Cornelia, picking up one of them, and laying its soft feathery head to her cheeks.

"Yes, my dear; but you must give them back, and not keep Auntie waiting in the cold."

Cornelia hesitated a little while, and then was giving it back reluctantly, when her mother gently said, "Cornelia!" and she instantly returned the basket to Judy.

After they were all seated in the sleigh, and Harry had touched the horse with the whip, they heard someone calling after them, and on looking behind there was poor old Judy carrying two hot bricks in her hand.

"Get out, Ally, and take them from her, and do not let her come so far in the snow."

But while he was getting free from the entanglement of the buffalo skin, Judy had come up, and, handing them to Mrs. Ford, said:

"Here, Missy, is these ar bricks. I heated 'em for you, and forgot 'em till you was gone; take 'em honey; you's got more than a mile to go, and I knows you will be cold."

Mrs. Ford thanked her, but gently reproved her for exposing herself. They watched her as she trudged back in the snow, and then waving their hands to her as she disappeared in the turn of the road, Harry touched the horse, and in a few minutes they seemed as if they were actually flying over the frozen surface.

When they arrived at home Bessie had a smoking dinner on the table for them, which they partook of with great relish. After they had finished their dinner, their mother said that as they had but one session at school, they would have ample time to perform their tasks before tea-time. Harry was to chop the wood, while Alfred was to pile it on the porch; and Cornelia would finish the garters that she was kniting [sic] as a Christmas present for papa. And after that they were to study their lessons for the next day, so that they would be at leisure in the evening. All cheerfully obeyed, and before tea-time their tasks were all performed and lessons learned.

After the tea-things had been removed, "Now," said Mr. Ford,

'Stir the fire, and close the shutters fast,
Let fall the curtain, and wheel the sofa round,' "

"And be ready for Aunt Judy's story," added Alfred. "Come, mother, come; we are all waiting."

"Have a little patience, my son, I will be there in a few minutes."

She soon reappeared, and was greeted with "three cheers" from the children, and seating herself in the large comfortable rocking-chair, she began:

"On the eastern side of the beautiful Roanoke was the residence of Mr. Madison, and here the first few years of Judy's life was passed. She had a kind master, and, while in his service, had a very happy time. She had, like most of her race, a strong native talent for music, and was frequently called upon to exercise it by singing songs, and dancing, for the amusement of General Washington and the other officers of the Revolution who visited at her master's house. Judy was then quite young, and greatly enjoyed a sight of the soldier's gay uniform.

"Her master died when she was a child. Her mistress was then in very ill health, and little Judy spent most of the time in her room, in attendance upon her. One day her mistress was seized with a violent fit of coughing. Judy ran to her assistance, and finding that the cough did not yield to the usual remedies, called for help, but before aid was obtained, Mrs. Madison was dead! She died with her arms around the neck of her faithful attendant.

"Mrs. Madison had made provisions for the emancipation of Judy, and after her death she received her free papers, which she carefully guarded.

"After her mother's death, the daughter of Mrs. Madison determined to remove to Kentucky, and Judy, being much attached to her and the family, accompanied them.

"Soon after her arrival there, Judy married a slave on the plantation of Mr. Jackson, which was several miles distant from that of Judy's mistress. John's master was very cruel to him; he would not allow him to leave the estate, nor was Judy permitted to come to see him; and thus they lived apart for several months; but the brutal treatment of his master at last rendered John desperate, and he determined to run away. It was a fearful risk, but if he succeeded, the prize, he thought, would be sufficient compensation.

"One morning he had a pass from his master to go to a neighboring town on business, and he thought this a good opportunity to execute the project he had so long entertained. He started, and traveled all night, and lay concealed in the woods all day, and on the third day after he had left home he ventured on to the estate of Judy's mistress. He went into one of the hen-houses, and it was not long before he saw Judy come out to feed the poultry. She was very much frightened when she saw him, and thought of the consequences that might arise from his master's rage if he found him. However, she hid him in the barn, supplying him with food at night. He stayed there more than a week, intending to leave Kentucky after his master's pursuit should have ceased. But one morning his master came to the house, and told Judy's mistress that one of his slaves was concealed on the place, and asked permission to hunt him, which was granted. He soon found him by the aid of one of the slaves who had noticed Judy carrying food to the barn, and watched her till he had discovered her husband, and then informed against him."

"O how mean to betray him!" exclaimed Alfred.

"Yes, Ally, it was; but I suppose it was the hope of reward that induced him to be guilty of such a base act."

"And *was* he rewarded?" asked Cornelia, "for I am sure if he was he did not deserve it."

"I do not know that he was, my daughter," answered Mrs. Ford. "John was taken to jail and locked up until his master should return home. Judy obtained a permit to enter the jail, and stayed with him in the cold, damp cell, cheering him with her presence. She could not bear the thought of being again separated, and determined to accompany him, let the consequences be what they might. Her husband was taken to a blacksmith's shop on the next day after his recapture, and a heavy pair of handcuffs placed upon him, and a chain (having at the end a large iron ball) was then fastened to his leg to prevent him from running, and in this condition they started for home. They walked for six days, she with her infant in her arms, and he, heavily loaded with irons. And she told me that often her dress was one cake of ice up to her knees, the snow and rain being frozen on her skirts. Her husband's shoes soon gave way, and his feet bled profusely at every step. Judy tore off her skirt, piece by piece, to wrap them in, for she loved him tenderly. But the anguish of their bodies was nothing in comparison with that of their minds. Fear for the consequences of the attempt, and regret that it had not been successful, filled their hearts with grief, and they journeyed on with no earthly hope to cheer them.

"Just think, my children, what they must have suffered through those long dreary days, John going back to slavery and misery, and Judy not knowing what her own fate might be. But she had comforted herself with the thought that when John's master saw what a condition he was in, he would relent toward him. But she was sadly mistaken, for he took him, weary, sick, and suffering, as he was, and whipped him cruelly, and then left him in an old shed."

"O mamma!" said little Cornelia, burying her face in her mother's lap, and sobbing aloud, "Do they do such wicked things?"

"I wish I had hold of him," said Alfred, "wouldn't I give it to him?"

"I should feel very much grieved if I saw you harm him in any way, Ally. Do you forget what our blessed Saviour said about returning good for evil?" asked his mother.

"Well, but mother, I am sure it would have been no more than fair just to give him a good cowhiding, so as it did not kill him."

"No more than he deserved, perhaps, but my son, you should remember that Jesus taught us that we should forgive the greatest injuries.

"After this cruel treatment of John, Judy, with the aid of one of the other slaves who sympathized with her and John, carried him to a little hut that was not so much exposed as the one in which he had previously lain. He had a razor with which he had attempted to kill himself, but Judy came in at that moment, and as he was very weak, she easily took it from him; but he said:

"'O let me die! I would rather be in my grave, than endure this over again.'

"He was sick and helpless a long time, but he would have suffered much more if Judy had not been free, and had it in her power to nurse him. There is many a poor slave that has fallen a victim to this kind of barbarity, with no eye to witness his distress but his heavenly Father's.

"To add to John's misery was the brutal treatment of a little brother; a smart active child of eight years of age, who was owned by the same man. Mr. Jackson was a great drunkard, and when under the influence of liquor no crime was too great for him. One day, for some slight offense, he took the child, marked his throat from ear to ear, and then cut the rims of his ears partly off and left them hanging down. A little while after this, a gentleman, who had been in the habit of visiting at the house, rode up, and noticing the child's throat, asked him how it happened. He said, "Massa did it." The gentleman was so enraged, that he immediately mounted his horse, rode away, and had him arrested.

"When John was able to leave his bed, his mistress, a kind and humane woman, whose slave he had been before her marriage, took him and hid him in a cave that was on the plantation, and supplied him with food, intending to send him away as soon as she could do so safely.

"He was there several weeks, and his master supposed he had again escaped, and was hid somewhere in the woods, but he had become so much dissipated that he took no interest in his business affairs, and never explored the hiding-places on his own plantation. One day a gentleman by the name of Mr. Lawrence of Vincennes, came to Mr. Jackson's to purchase a servant to take with him to Indiana."

"Why, mother, I thought that they would not allow anyone to hold slaves here," said Ally.

"No, they do not, my son, but this gentleman was to take him as a bound servant for a term of years, and he probably supposed that poor John's legal rights would not be very carefully examined. John was sold in the woods for a small sum. After the bargain was concluded, Mr. Lawrence asked if the slave had a wife on the plantation, and was told that he had. Judy was pointed out to him. He asked her if she knew where her husband was, and she told him that she did; for she thought it was better for him to leave his cave, as it was damp and comfortless. So that night, with new hope in her heart, Judy went to his lone and dreary hiding-place, and told him of the bargain. Any change was a relief to him, and he came willingly out, and made preparations for going with Mr. Lawrence. He waited until his master was in bed, and too deeply stupefied with liquor to heed what was passing, and then came to the place appointed. Mrs. Jackson gave him some clothes, and made what provision she could for his comfort on the way. John had a horse given him to ride upon, but Judy was taken no notice of; yet she determined to walk the three days' journey, rather than be separated from John.

"Mr. Lawrence, when he perceived Judy was following them, tried to persuade her to return, for she had a young child with her, and he was afraid she would be troublesome. He told her that after her husband was settled in Vincennes, he would send for her, but she had learned to place no confidence in promises made to a slave; so she resolved she would go, believing if she lost sight of her husband she would never see him again.

"They had to cross the Ohio in a ferry boat, and Judy strained every nerve to reach it before them. She did so; and hurrying up the stairs with her baby, she clasped the railings, resolved to stay there, unless compelled by violence to leave the boat. But no one noticed her, and she arrived safely on the other side. After walking some miles, poor Judy became tired and weary, and her strength failed her, and she was afraid that after all she had gone through, for the sake of her husband, she would be left at last. But she thought she would make another effort, so she told Mr. Lawrence that if he would buy her a horse to ride upon, she would bind herself to him for six months after they arrived in Indiana. He agreed to do so, and bought her a horse. After they reached Vincennes, and Judy had worked out her six months, she again bound herself to him to serve out her husband's time, for he was very weak and feeble, and was suffering with a severe cough, and Judy longed to see him own his own body. But God freed him before the year was out. He had suffered so much from severe whipping and abuse of every kind that he wasted away and died of consumption.

"After his death Judy remained with his master for some time, but she finally became dissatisfied, and longed to go back to Mrs. Madison's daughter, and see her home once more. She mentioned this to Mr. Lawrence, but he took no notice of it until, one day, he came to her and said:

"'Judy, I want you to come down to the auction rooms, I have bought a few things to-day, and I want you to carry them home; and you might as well bring little Charley along with you, he can help you.'

"The little Charley here spoken of was a smart child of five or six years of age. Judy and Charley accompanied Mr. Lawrence to the rooms. When they arrived there Judy observed a number of strange-looking men who appeared to be earnestly conversing on some subject which interested Mr. Lawrence deeply. But Judy suspected nothing, and had begun arranging the things so that she could carry them more conveniently, when her master turned round to her and said:

"'Judy, you have become dissatisfied with me, and I have got you a new master.'

"Judy was frightened, and attempted to run, but one of them caught her, and dragging her to a trap door, let her down. Little Charley, not knowing what had become of his mother, began to cry, but one of the men held him and told him to stop making such a noise.

"Judy remained in the cellar until a vessel came along, and she was then taken out, and a handkerchief tied tightly over her mouth to prevent her from screaming or making any noise. She was then hurried on board of the boat, with a cargo of slaves bound for the far South. It seemed now as if her 'cup of bitterness was full.' As she was on the deck, in grief and terror, she heard some one calling 'Mother! mother!' and on looking up, there was her darling boy. She asked him how he came there; he answered:

"'A naughty man that put you down in the cellar carried me to his house, and locked me up, and then brought me here.'

"Poor Judy! she knew in a moment that both were to be sold, and no language can describe her anguish; her free papers were left behind, and another one of her children, her little daughter Fanny. She did not know what would become of her, or where she was going. After sailing for several weeks, they arrived at a place which she thinks was called Vicksburg; here they were taken off the boat, and carried to the auction rooms, where a sale was then going on. In a little while after they came in, a gentleman walked up to them, and after looking at little Charley, placed him on the block. Poor Judy's heart was almost bursting; but when she saw a man buy and carry away the pride and joy of her heart, she became frantic, and screamed after him, but he was picked up and carried from her sight. It was too much for her; all was a mist in a moment, and she sank senseless to the floor. When she revived she found herself lying on an old pile of cotton in one corner of the auction rooms. The auctioneer, seeing that she had arisen, bade her stand in the pen, along with the other negroes. Judy mechanically obeyed, and took her place with the others, and was sitting like one in a dream, when she was aroused by a man slapping her on the back.

" 'Come, look spry, old woman, said he.'

" 'Could you look spry, massa, if your child, your son you loved as well as your life, was torn away from you? O God!' said she, burying her face in her hands, 'have mercy on me, and help me to be resigned.'

" 'Yes, I'll make you resigned,' said he, sneeringly, slapping her across the back. 'Now you follow me, and don't let me hear a word out of your head.'

"Judy obeyed, and after arriving at the wharf, they went on board a vessel that was bound for New Orleans. In about a week after they had started, they arrived at Mr. Martin's plantation, where Judy saw about one hundred and fifty slaves at work in the field. Without being allowed a moment to rest herself, after her long walk from the boat, she was given a basket and ordered to the field. Poor Judy's head was aching severely, and when she was exposed to the scorching rays of the sun of the south, her temples throbbed wildly, and O! how she longed for some quiet shady place, where she could bathe her fevered brow and rest her weary limbs. But she must not think of stopping a moment to rest, for the eyes of the brutal overseer were upon her, and the thought of the stinging lash, the smart and pain, came across her mind, and urged her on, and made her work with greater swiftness than before. At last the weary, weary day drew to a close, and it was getting quite dark, and the dew was beginning to fall, and Judy was expecting every moment to hear the order for them to return home. But still they worked on, and hour after hour passed, until it was almost midnight, and not till then did the joyful summons come for them to stop."

"Why, mamma, do they make them work so late as that?" asked Cornelia.

"Yes, my daughter, in the busy season the poor slaves are often kept out very late. After they had received the order to return home, Judy, with aching limbs, joined the other slaves who were wearily wending their way to the little out-house where the overseer was weighing their cotton. As they presented their baskets to be weighed, they watched eagerly to see if their baskets were approved of. Judy gladly heard that hers was the full weight, and after ascertaining where she was to sleep, and receiving her allowance of corn, she went to the shed pointed out to her. She made her cakes for her supper and for the next morning, and then laid down upon her bed, or rather on a pile of straw with an old piece of sheet spread over it. Judy was much exhausted, and soon fell asleep, notwithstanding the roughness of her bed. But it seemed as though she had scarcely closed her eyes before the plantation bell rang, and called them to another weary day's work.

"Thus many, many months passed, of toiling from day to day, and from morning till night. One morning they saw one of the house servants running toward them; he told them that their master was dead! He had died suddenly from a fit of appoplexy [sic]. The tidings were received by Judy with joy. You must pardon her, my children, for this man had been a cruel master to her, and she thought that, as he had neither wife nor children, his slaves would be sold, and perhaps she would get farther north, and in the neighborhood of her old home, and might meet with some of her old friends who would prove that she was free.

"A few days after Mr. Martin's funeral there was a meeting of his heirs, and they determined to sell the slaves. Accordingly the next morning they were marched down to the wharf, where they found a boat at anchor, and all went on board. We will pass over the wearisome trip of several days, and imagine them to be at the end of their journey at Memphis. Here they were taken off the boat, and placed in jail until auction day. In a few days they were again taken out and tied in couples, and taken to the auction. Judy was sitting very disconsolate, thinking of her past misfortunes and coming sorrows. The hope of seeing any of her old friends, or of being reunited with her children, she had almost given up. The auctioneer called to her, and she stepped on the block. Her strong and well-proportioned figure, and comely, though dejected and sad appearance, instantly raised a dozen bids. First here, now there, might be heard the voice of the competitors; the noise of the hammer ceased, and Judy was the property of Mr. Carter. After his purchase Mr. Carter was taking Judy to the boat when she felt some one catching hold of her arm; she turned around and immediately recognized the person as a gentleman whom she had known while living with Mrs. Madison's daughter. He said to her:

" 'Why, Judy, where are you going?'

"She answered in a kind of wicked despair:

" 'To hell, I believe.'

"This gentleman inquired about her condition, and finally rescued her, and sent her to Vincennes, where she labored for many years and found some good friends, but she never felt safe after she had been stolen away from there. She made inquiries about her children, but never learned anything of them. Not having anything to attach her to Vincennes, she left and came to Terra Haute, where she resided a little while, and then came further into the interior of the state.

"Her children are scattered, and gone she knows not where; and after a long life of toil and suffering she is here, old, infirm, and a beggar. Every wrinkle on her brow could tell a tale of suffering; her youth is gone; her energies are all spent, and her long life of toil has been for naught."

Mrs. Ford ceased, her tears were falling fast, and the children were sobbing around her. The fire, from neglect, had gone out, and there were only a few smoking embers left in the fire-place, reminding them of the time that had been spent in hearing "Aunt Judy's Story."

"ME NEBER GIB IT UP!"[6]

"Please, massa, teach me to read!" said an aged negro one day to a missionary in the West Indies.

The missionary said he would do so, and the negro became his scholar. But the poor old man, trained in ignorance through threescore years, found it difficult to learn. He tried hard, but made little progress. One day the missionary said:

"Had you not better give it up?"

"No, massa," said the negro, with the energy of a noble nature, "me neber gib it up till me die!'

He then pointed to these beautiful words in his Testament: "God so loved the world that he gave his only begotten [sic] Son, that whosoever believeth on him should not perish, but have everlasting life." "There," he added, with deep feeling, "it is worth all de labor to be able to read *dat one single verse!*"

Noble, godly old man! Though once a slave he had a freeman's soul, and richly merited that freedom which England so righteously gave to her West Indian slaves some years ago. Let us hope the time is not far distant in which the colored people of our own happy land will also all be free, all able to read the Bible, all possess that soul freedom with which

Christ makes his disciples free. God has many dear children among the slaves, many of whom feel that slavery is worse than death. May he in his wisdom provide for their early deliverance from the terrible yoke which is about their necks!

NOTES

1. For analyses of these texts, see chapters 2 and 3 of De Rosa.

2. According to Carol Mattingly, Julia Colman led the Department of Temperance Literature for the Women's Christian Temperance Union from 1875 to 1890, gave public lectures across the country, and wrote more than 500 books and pamphlets (68). However, I have been unable to verify if she is the same Julia Colman who authored stories in *The Child's Anti-Slavery Book*.

3. See MacCann's brief reference to "Aunt Judy's Story: A Story from Real Life" ("White Supremacy" 60).

4. D. W. has not been identified to date.

5. This poem also appears in *Aunt Lizzie's Stories* (1863). Asa Bullard, brother-in-law to Reverend Henry Ward Beecher (Bullard 152), secretary for the Massachusetts Sabbath School Society, and compiler of many children's books (frequently published by Boston's Lee and Shepard), edited *Aunt Lizzie's Stories*, volume 10 of the Sunnybank Stories series. Each text in *Aunt Lizzie's Stories* (such as "Oranges," "He Thinks It Is Saturday," "Way to Obey," and "The Drunkard's Boy") portrays an adult narrator who utters deliberate moral lessons on biblical principles and Christian behavior. Like Elizabeth Margaret Chandler, "Looking at the Soldiers" and Jane Elizabeth Jones, *The Young Abolitionist; or Conversations on Slavery*, this mother-historian challenges the highly patriotic concept of Independence Day with a blunt reminder of the racially violated "freedom and justice for all" proclamation. In a brief but meaningful way, she rewrites history for nineteenth-century American children.

6. The text does not indicate whether Colman or Thompson wrote this short work.

LIST OF SELECTED LIBRARIES THAT OWN ORIGINAL EDITIONS OF WORKS IN THE ANTHOLOGY

American Antiquarian Society

Aunt Mary: *The Edinburgh Doll and Other Tales for Children* (1854)

Kate Barclay: *Minnie May: With Other Rhymes and Stories* (1856)

Julia Colman and Matilda Thompson: *The Child's Anti-Slavery Book: Containing a Few Words about American Slave Children and Stories of Slave-Life* (1859)

Eliza Lee Cabot Follen: *Hymns, Songs, and Fables, for Young People* (1846); *The Liberty Cap* (1846); *Sequel to "The Well-Spent Hour", or, The Birthday* (1832)

Sarah Josepha Buell Hale: *Poems for Our Children: Designed for Families, Sabbath Schools, and Infant Schools: Written to Inculcate Moral Truths and Virtuous Sentiments* (1830)

Amelia Opie: *The Negro Boy's Tale* (1825?)

Ann Preston [Cousin Ann]: *Cousin Ann's Stories for Children* (1849)

Anna H. Richardson: *Little Laura, the Kentucky Abolitionist: An Address to the Young Friends of the Slave* (1859)

S.C.C.: *Louisa in Her New Home* (1854)

Harriet Beecher Stowe: *Pictures and Stories from Uncle Tom's Cabin* (1853); *Little Eva, The Flower of the South* (185?)

Hannah and Mary Townsend: *The Anti-Slavery Alphabet* (1846 and 1847)

Boston Athenaeum

Aunt Mary: *The Edinburgh Doll and Other Tales for Children* (1854)

Columbia University

Eliza Lee Cabot Follen: *Hymns, Songs, and Fables, for Young People* (1846)

Cornell University

Harriet Newell Greene Butts: *Ralph: or, I Wish He Wasn't Black* (1855)
Anna H. Richardson: *Little Laura, the Kentucky Abolitionist: An Address to the Young Friends of the Slave* (1859)
S.C.C.: *Louisa in Her New Home* (1854)

Duke University

Kate Barclay: *Minnie May: With Other Rhymes and Stories* (1856)
Grandmother: *Grandmother's Stories for Little Children* (1854)
Jane Elizabeth (Hitchcock) Jones: *The Young Abolitionists; or Conversations on Slavery* (1848)

Free Library of Philadelphia

Ann Preston [Cousin Ann]: *Cousin Ann's Stories for Children* (1849)

Harvard University

Eliza Lee Cabot Follen: *The Liberty Cap* (1846); *May Morning and New Year's Eve* (ca. 1857)

Library Company of Philadelphia

Hannah and Mary Townsend: *The Anti-Slavery Alphabet* (1846 and 1847)

The Newberry Library (Chicago)

Amelia Alderson Opie: *The Negro Boy's Tale* (1825?)

University of Chicago

Eliza Lee Cabot Follen: *Sequel to "The Well-Spent Hour", or, The Birthday* (1832)

University of Tennessee

[Madame]: *Jemmy and His Mother, A Tale for Children* (1858)

University of Wisconsin, Madison

Sarah Josepha Buell Hale: *Poems for Our Children: Designed for Families, Sabbath Schools, and Infant Schools: Written to Inculcate Moral Truths and Virtuous Sentiments* (1830)

BIBLIOGRAPHY

Abbot, Anne Wales, ed. "A Massachusetts Slave." *The Child's Friend.* 8.5 (Aug. 1847): 233–38.

Aunt Mary. *Aunt Mary's Multiplication.* Providence, RI: Weeden and Peck, 1850–1859?

———. *The Edinburgh Doll and Other Tales for Children.* Boston: J. P. Jewett, 1854.

Bacon, Margaret Hope. "Anne Preston: Pioneer Woman Doctor." *Friends Journal.* 45 (October 1999): 20–23.

[Bailey, Gamaliel?]. [Last Installment of *Uncle Tom's Cabin*]. *The National Era* [Washington, DC] 1 Apr. 1852: 54.

Balfour, Clara L. *Women Worth Emulating.* New York: American Tract Society [1877?], 74–89.

Barclay, Kate. "The Lost Child." *The Ladies' Wreath and Parlor Annual.* New York: Burdick and Scovill, [1856].

———. *Minnie May: With Other Rhymes and Stories.* Boston: John P. Jewett, 1856.

———. *The Odd Fellow's Token: Devoted to Friendship, Love and Truth.* Auburn, NY: James M. Alden, 1850, ca. 1846.

———. *The Odd Fellow's Token: Devoted to Friendship, Love and Truth.* Geneva, NY: G. H. Derby, 1846.

———. *The Temperance Token, or, Crystal Drops from the Old Oaken Bucket.* Auburn, NY: J. C. Derby, 1848, ca. 1846.

Bardes, Barbara A., and Suzanne Gossett. *Declarations of Independence: Women and Political Power in Nineteenth-Century American Fiction.* New Brunswick: Rutgers UP, 1990.

Bardes, Barbara A., and Suzanne Gossett. "Sarah J. Hale, Selective Promoter of Her Sex." *A Living of Words: American Women in Print Culture.* Ed. Susan Albertine. Knoxville: U of Tennessee P., 1995. 18–35.

Baym, Nina. *Woman's Fiction: A Guide to Novels by and about Women in America, 1820–1870*. Ithaca: Cornell UP, 1978.

[Bennett, James Gordon?]. "Anti-Slavery and Abolitionism in the Theatres." *The New York Herald* 28 Aug. 1852: [np].

Born, Donna. "Sara Jane Clarke Lippincott: (Grace Greenwood)." *American Newspaper Journalists, 1690–1874*. Ed. Perry J. Ashley. [*Dictionary of Literary Biography*] Vol. 43. Detroit, MI: Gale, 1985.

Bowerman, Sarah G. "Elizabeth Margaret Chandler." *Dictionary of American Biography*. Ed. Allen Johnson and Dumas Malone. Vol. 2. New York: Scribner's, 1930. 613.

Boyer, Paul S. "Hale, Sarah Josepha Buell." *Notable American Women 1607–1950*. Ed. Edward T. James. 3 vols. Cambridge: Harvard UP, 1971.

Bradburn, Eliza Weaver. *Pity Poor Africa: A Dialogue for Children in Three Parts*. 2nd. ed. London: John Mason, 1831.

Brown, Lois, ed. *Memoir of James Jackson, the Attentive and Dutiful Scholar, Who Died in Boston, October 31, 1833, Aged Six Years and Eleven Months*, by his teacher Susan Paul. Cambridge, MA: Harvard UP, 2000.

Buck, Claire, ed. *The Bloomsbury Guide to Women's Literature*. New York: Prentice, 1992. 879.

Butts, Harriet Newell Greene. *Chancun Son Nid: Jue du Père Castor*. [Paris]: Flammerion, 1936.

———. *Little Harry's Wish, or, "Playing Soldier."* 2nd ed., enl. and improved. [Hopedale], MA: Hopedale Age Office, 1868.

———. *Plouf, Canard Sauvage*. Paris: Flammarion, 1935.

———. *Ralph: or, I Wish He Wasn't Black*. Hopedale, MA: E. Gay, 1855.

———. *Thwing Family Thanksgiving: At the House of Almon Thwing, Hopedale, 1854*. [Hopedale, MA: Community P], 1854.

C.W.K. [Uncle Tom in Painting and Statuary]. *The Liberator* 23 Dec. 1852: 203.

Chandler, Elizabeth Margaret. "An Appeal to the Ladies of the United States." Lundy 17–21.

———. "The Child's Evening Hymn." Lundy 72.

———. "Christmas." Lundy 124–25.

———. "A Lesson from the Flowers." *The Liberator* 14 May 1831.

———. "Looking at the Soldiers." Lundy 109–10.

———. "Oh Press Me Not to Taste Again." Lundy 108–109.

———. "The Slave Ship." *The Casket* (1825?).

———. "The Sugar-Plums." Lundy 108.

———. "What Is a Slave, Mother?" *Genius of Universal Emancipation*. May 1831: 13.

———. "What Is a Slave, Mother?" *The Liberator*. 4 June 1831: 90.

Child, Lydia Maria. *An Appeal in Favor of That Class of Americans Called Africans*. New York: Allen and Ticknor, 1833.

Colman, Julia, and Matilda G. Thompson. *The Child's Anti-Slavery Book: Containing a Few words about American Slave Children, and Stories of Slave Life.* New York: Carlton & Porter, 1860.

Constitution of the American Reform Tract and Book Society, with Reasons for its Organization. Cincinnati: Board of Directors, 1853.

Cousin Ann [Ann Preston]. *Cousin Ann's Stories for Children.* Philadelphia: J. M. McKim, 1849.

———. "Henry Box Brown." *Cousin Ann,* 22–26.

———. "Howard and His Squirrel." *Cousin Ann,* 13–14.

———. "Tom and Lucy: A Tale for Little Lizzie." *Cousin Ann,* 14–17.

De Rosa, Deborah. *Domestic Abolitionism and Juvenile Literature, 1830–1865.* New York: State U of New York P, 2003.

Dillon, Merton L. *Benjamin Lundy and the Struggle for Negro Freedom.* Urbana: U of Illinois P, 1966.

———. "Elizabeth Chandler and the Spread of Antislavery Sentiment to Michigan." *Michigan History* 39 (1955): 481–94.

———. "Elizabeth Margaret Chandler." *Notable American Women, 1607–1950: A Biographical Dictionary.* Ed. Edward T. James. Vol. 1. Cambridge: Belknap P of Harvard, 1975. 319–20.

Douglas, Ann. *The Feminization of America.* New York: Doubleday, 1977.

Douglass, Frederick. *Narrative of the Life of Frederick Douglass; An American Slave: Written By Himself.* New York: Signet, 1968.

[Dwight, J.S.?]. [Notice: Collier's *Eva's Parting*]. *Dwight's Journal of Music* [Boston] 31 Jul. 1852.

Eberle, Roxanne. "Amelia Opie's *Adeline Mowbray*: Diverting the Libertine Gaze; or, the Vindication of a Fallen Woman." *Studies in the Novel* 26.2 (Summer 1994): 121–52.

———. "'Tales of Truth?': Amelia Opie's Antislavery Poetics." *Romanticism and Women Poets: Opening the Doors of Reception.* Eds. Harriet Kramer Linkin and Stephen C. Behrendt. Lexington: UP of Kentucky, 1999. 71–91.

Emilio, Manual. *Little Eva Song. Uncle Tom's Guardian Angel.* Words by John G. Whittier. Boston: John P. Jewett, 1852.

Filler, Louis. Crusades *Against Slavery: Friends, Foes, and Reform, 1820–1860.* Algonac, MI: Reference Publication, 1986.

Finley, Ruth E. *The Lady of Godey's: Sarah Josepha Hale.* Philadelphia: Lippincott, 1931.

Fisher, Philip. "Making a Thing into a Man: The Sentimental Novel and Slavery." *Hard Facts: Setting and Form in the American Novel.* New York: Oxford UP, 1987. 87–127.

Florence. "The Infant Abolitionist." *The Oasis.* Ed. Lydia Maria Child. Boston, MA: Allen & Ticknor, 1834. 201.

Follen, Eliza Lee Cabot. "And the Days of Thy Mourning Shall Be Ended." New

York: American Anti-Slavery Society, 1855. Anti-Slavery Tracts Series 1: Nos. 1–20, 1855–1856. Tract no. 12. Westport, CT: Negro UP, 1970. 5–6.

———. *Anti-Slavery Hymns and Songs*. New York: American Anti-Slavery Society, 1855. Anti-Slavery Tracts Series 1: Nos. 1–20, 1855–1856. Westport, CT: Negro UP, 1970.

———. "Auld Lang Syne." New York: American Anti-Slavery Society, 1855. Anti-Slavery Tracts Series 1: Nos. 1–20, 1855–1856. Tract no. 12. Westport, CT: Negro UP, 1970. 4.

———. "Billy Rabbit to Mary." *Hymns, Songs, and Fables, for Young People* 91–92.

———. "Children in Slavery." *Hymns, Songs, and Fables, for Young People* 54–55.

———. "Dialogue." *The Liberty Cap* 23–30.

———. "How Shall Children Do Good?" *The Child's Friend* 2.4 (July 1844): 109–13.

———. *Hymns, Songs, and Fables, for Children*. Boston: Carter, Hendee, & Babcock, 1831.

———. *Hymns, Songs, and Fables, for Young People*. Rev. and enl. from the last ed. Boston: William Crosby and H. P. Nichols, 1848. 91–92.

———. "The Land of the Free and the Home of the Brave." New York: American Anti-Slavery Society, 1855. Anti-Slavery Tracts Series 1: Nos. 1–20, 1855–1856. Tract no. 12. Westport, CT: Negro UP, 1970. 1–2.

———. *The Liberty Cap*. Boston: Leonard C. Bowles, 1846.

———. "Lines on Hearing of the Terror of the Children of the Slaves at the Thought of Being Sold." *The Liberty Cap* 22.

———. "The Little Slave's Wish." *Hymns, Songs, and Fables, for Young People* 69–71.

———. *Little Songs, for Little Boys and Girls*. Boston: Leonard C. Bowles, 1833.

———. "Lord Deliver." *Anti-Slavery Hymns and Songs*. New York: American Anti-Slavery Society, 1855. Anti-Slavery Tracts Series 1: Nos. 1–20, 1855–1856. Westport, CT: Negro UP, 1970. 7.

———. *May Morning and New Year's Eve*. Boston: Whittmore, Nichols, and Hall, 1857.

———. "The Melancholy Boy." *The Child's Friend* 2. 2 (1844): 37–41.

———. *Nursery Songs*. New York: S. Colman, 1839.

———. "On Hearing of the Sadness of the Slave-Children from the Fear of Being Sold." *Anti-Slavery Hymns and Songs*. New York: American Anti-Slavery Society, 1855. Anti-Slavery Tracts Series 1: Nos. 1–20, 1855–1856. Westport, CT: Negro UP, 1970. 8.

———. "Picnic at Dedham." *The Liberty Cap* 10–21.

———. "Remember the Slave." *Hymns, Songs, and Fables, for Young People* 50–52.

———. *Sequel to "The Well-Spent Hour", or, The Birthday.* Boston: Carter and Hendee, 1832.

———. *Sequel to "The Well-Spent Hour", or, The Birthday.* Boston: J. Munroe, 1848.

———. "Soliloquy of Ellen's Squirrel, on Receiving His Liberty;—Overheard by a Lover of Nature and a Friend of Ellen." *Hymns, Songs, and Fables, for Young People* 76–77.

———. "Three Little Kittens." *Little Songs, for Little Boys and Girls.* Boston: Leonard C. Bowles, 1833.

———. "To Mothers in the Free States." New York: American Anti-Slavery Society, 1855. Anti-Slavery Tracts Series 1: Nos. 1–20, 1855–1856. Tract no. 8. Westport, CT: Negro UP, 1970. 1–4.

———. *True Stories About Dogs and Cats.* Boston: Whittmore, Niles, & Hall, 1856.

———. *Twilight Stories.* Boston: Whittmore, Niles, and Hall, n.d.

———. *The Well-Spent Hour.* New ed. Boston: J. Munroe, 1838.

———. "Where Is Thy Brother." New York: American Anti-Slavery Society, 1855. Anti-Slavery Tracts Series 1: Nos. 1–20, 1855–1856. Tract no. 12. Westport, CT: Negro UP, 1970. 1.

Ford, Paul Leicester, ed. *The New England Primer: A Reprint of the Earliest Known Edition, with Many Facsimiles and Reproductions, and an Historical Introduction.* New York: Dodd, Mead, 1899.

Frost, Maria Goodell. *Gospel Fruits; or, Bible Christianity Illustrated: A Premium Essay.* Cincinnati: American Reform Tract and Book Society, 1856.

Fullard, Joyce. "Ann Preston: Pioneer of Medical Education and Women's Rights." *Pennsylvania Heritage* 8.1 (Winter 1982): 9–14.

Garrison, William Lloyd. *Juvenile Poems, for the Use of Free American Children of Every Complexion.* Boston: Garrison and Knapp, 1835.

[Garrison, William Lloyd?]. [Notice about *Uncle Tom's Cabin*]. *The Liberator* [Boston] 2 Jul. 1852: 106.

[Gay, Sidney Howard?]. [*Uncle Tom's Cabin*]. *The National Anti-Slavery Standard* [New York] 15 Jul 1852: 31.

Grandmother. *Grandmother's Stories for Little Children.* Boston: John P. Jewett, 1854.

Gray, Janet. "Grace Greenwood." *The Oxford Companion to Women's Writing in the United States.* Ed. Cathy N. Davidson and Linda Wagner-Martin. New York: Oxford UP, 1995.

"Great Excitement—The Negro Brigade and *Uncle Tom's Cabin.* Washington, Special Dispatches to 'The Press.'" *The Philadelphia Press* 19 May 1863: 2.

Hale, Sarah Josepha (Buell). *The Genius of Oblivion, and Other Original Poems.* Concord, NH: Jacob A. Moore, 1823.

———. "Independence." *The School Song Book. Adapted to the Scenes of the School Room. Written for American Children and Youth.* Boston: Allen and Ticknor, 1834.

————. *Liberia; or, Mr. Peyton's Experiments.* New York: Harper, 1853.

————. "My Country." *Poems for Our Children* 14–15.

————. *Northwood: A Tale of New England.* Boston: Bowles & Dearborn, 1827.

————. *Northwood; or, Life North and South: Showing the True Character of Both.* New York: H. Long, 1852.

————. *Poems for Our Children: Designed for Families, Sabbath Schools, and Infant Schools: Written to Inculcate Moral Truths and Virtuous Sentiments.* Boston: Marsh, Capen and Lyon, 1830.

"Harriet Beecher Stowe." *Bibliography of American Literature.* Comp. Jacob Blanck. Ed. and compiled Michael Winship. Vol. 8. New Haven: Yale UP, 1990.

Hersh, Blanche Glassman. *The Slavery of Sex: Feminist-Abolitionist in America.* Urbana: U of Illinois P, 1978.

Hoganson, Kristin. "Garrisonian Abolitionists and the Rhetoric of Gender, 1850–1860." *American Quarterly* 45.4 (Dec. 1993): 558–95.

Howard, Carol. "'The Story of the Pineapple': Sentimental Abolitionism and Moral Motherhood in Amelia Opie's *Adeline Mowbray.*" *Studies in the Novel* 30.3 (Fall 1998): 355–77.

Howard, Susan K. "Amelia Opie." *British Romantic Novelists, 1789–1832.* Vol. 116. Detroit, MI: Gale, 1992. 228–33.

Hughs, Mrs. [Aunt Mary]. *Aunt Mary's Stories for Children.* Boston: Phillips, Sampson, 1850.

————. *Aunt Mary's Stories for Children Chiefly Confined to Words of Two Syllables.* London: William Darton, 1823.

————. *Aunt Mary's Tales for the Entertainment and Improvement of Little Girls, Addressed to Her Nieces.* New York: D. Bliss, 1817.

Jacobs, Harriet A. *Incidents in the Life of a Slave Girl, Written by Herself.* Ed. Jean Fagan Yellin. Cambridge, MA: Harvard UP, 1987.

James, F. *Eva's Parting Words.* Words by Mary A. Collier. [N.p.]: Geo. P. Reed, 1852.

Jensen, Joan M. "Not Only Ours but Others: The Quaker Teaching Daughters of the Mid-Atlantic, 1790–1850. *History of Education Quarterly* 24.1 (Spring 1984): 3–19.

Jones, Jane Elizabeth. *Address to the Women's Rights Committee of the Ohio Legislature.* Columbus, OH: Harris and Hurd, 1861.

————. *The Wrongs of Women: An Address Delivered before the Ohio Women's Convention, at Salem, April 19th, 1850. Ohio Women's Convention Proceedings.* Cleveland, OH: Smead and Cowles, 1850. 30–48.

————. *The Young Abolitionists; or Conversations on Slavery.* Boston: Published at the Anti–Slavery Office, 1848.

Jones, Mary Patricia. "Elizabeth Margaret Chandler: Poet, Essayist, Abolitionist." Diss. U of Toledo, 1981.

Jordan, John W., ed. "Longstreth-Townsend Family." *Colonial Families of Philadelphia*. Vol. 2. New York: Lewis, 1911. 1532–40.

Kelly, Gary. "Discharging Debts: The Moral Economy of Amelia Opie's Fiction." *The Wordsworth Circle* 11.4 (Autumn 1980): 198–203.

Kerber, Linda. *Women of the Republic: Intellect and Ideology in Revolutionary America*. Chapel Hill: Published for the Institute of Early American History and Culture, U of North Carolina P, 1980.

Lenz, Millicent. "Harriet Beecher Stowe." *American Writers for Children before 1900*. Ed. Glenn E. Estes. [*Dictionary of Literary Biography*] Vol. 42. Detroit, MI: Gale, 1985.

Low, Mary, and Harriet Beecher Stowe. *A Peep into Uncle Tom's Cabin*. Boston: John P. Jewett, 1853.

———. *A Peep into Uncle Tom's Cabin*. London: Sampson, Low and Sons, 1853.

Lundy, Benjamin, ed. *The Poetical Works of Elizabeth Margaret Chandler; with a Memoir of Her Life and Character by Benjamin Lundy, and Essays, Philanthropic and Moral, by Elizabeth Margaret Chandler, Principally Relating to the Abolition of Slavery in America*. Philadelphia: Lemuel Howell, 1836.

Lutz, Alma. *Crusade for Freedom: Women of the Antislavery Movement*. Boston: Beacon P, 1968.

M.A.F. *Gertrude Lee; or, The Northern Cousin*. "By a Lady." Cincinnati: American Reform Tract and Book Society, 1856.

MacCann, Donnarae C. "The White Supremacy Myth in Juvenile Books about Blacks, 1830–1900." Diss. U of Iowa, 1988.

[Madame.] *Jemmy and His Mother, A Tale for Children and Lucy; or, the Slave Girl of Kentucky*. Cincinnati: American Reform Tract and Book Society, 1858.

Mattingly, Carol. *Well-Tempered Women: Nineteenth-Century Temperance Rhetoric*. Carbondale: Southern Illinois UP, 1998.

Melder, Keith E. "Jones, Jane Elizabeth Hitchcock." *Notable American Women, 1607–1950: A Biographical Dictionary*. Ed. Edward T. James. Vol. 1. Cambridge, MA: Belknap P of Harvard, 1975. 285–86.

Milton, John. "Song on May Morning." *English Minor Poems: Paradise Lost. Samson Agonistes, Areopagitica*. Chicago: Encyclopedia Brittanica, 1955, ca. 1948.

Moe, Phyllis. "Eliza Cabot Lee Follen." *American Women Writers: A Critical Reference Guide from Colonizing Times to the Present*. Ed. Lina Mainiero. Vol. 2. New York: Ungar, 1980. 58–60.

Moser, I. Kathleen. "J. Elizabeth Jones: The Forgotten Activist." Undergrad thesis, Kent State University Honors Program, August 1996.

[Notice about *Uncle Tom's Cabin*]. *The Daily Tribune* [New York] 15 Jul. 1852: [np].

O'Connell, Catherine E. "The Magic of the Real Presence of Distress: Sentimentality and Competing Rhetorics of Authority." *The Stowe Debate: Rhetorical Strategies in Uncle Tom's Cabin*. Ed. Mason I. Lowance, Jr., Ellen

E. Westbrook, and R. C. De Prospo. Amherst: U of Massachusetts P, 1994. 13–36.

O'Keefe, Doris. "Re: Hannah and Mary Townsend." E-mail to the author. 28 Feb. 2003.

Okker, Patricia. *Our Sister Editors: Sarah J. Hale and the Tradition of Nineteenth-Century American Women Editors.* Athens: U of Georgia P, 1995.

Opie, Amelia Alderson. *Adeline Mowbray; or, The Mother and Daughter, a Tale.* London: Longman, Hurst, Rees and Orme; A. Constable, 1804.

———. *The Black Man's Lament; or, How to Make Sugar.* London: Harvey and Darton, 1826.

———. *The Father and Daughter, a Tale in Prose.* Boston: S. G. Goodrich, 1827.

———. *The Father and Daughter, a Tale in Prose: With an Epistle from the Maid of Corinth to Her Lover, and Other Poetical Pieces.* London: Davis, Wilks and Taylor, 1801.

———. "The Negro Boy's Lament." New York: AMS Press, 1974, 1843.

———. *The Negro Boy's Tale: A Poem Addressed to Children.* London: Harvey and Darton, 1824.

———. *The Negro Boy's Tale: A Poem Addressed to Children.* New York: S. Wood and Sons, [1825?].

———. *Valentine Eve.* London: Longman, Hurst, Rees, Orme and Brown, 1816.

———. "A Wife's Duty." *Tales of the Heart.* London: Longman, Hurst, Rees, Orme, and Brown, 1820.

Papashvily, Helen Waite. *All the Happy Endings: A Study of the Domestic Novel in America, the Women Who Wrote It, the Women Who Read It in the Nineteenth-Century.* New York: Harper, 1956.

Paul, Susan. *Memoir of James Jackson, The Attentive and Dutiful Scholar, Who Died In Boston, October 31, 1833, Aged Six Years and Eleven Months.* Boston: James Loring, 1835.

Preston, Ann. "Woman's Rights and Wrongs." *National Anti-Slavery Standard* 17 June 1852.

Reiman, Donald H. Introduction. *Elegy to the Memory of the Late Duke of Bedford [by Amelia Opie]; [and] Psyche, with Other Poems [by Mary Tighe].* By Amelia Opie and Mary Tighe. Detroit, MI: Garland, 1978. v–xv.

"Review of Poems by Amelia Opie." *Edinburgh Review* 1 (Oct. 1802): 113–21.

Richardson, Anna H. *Little Laura, the Kentucky Abolitionist: An Address to the Young Friends of the Slave.* Newcastle: Printed by Thomas Pigg & Co., 1859.

Roberts, Bette B. "Lydia Maria Francis Child." *American Women Writers: A Critical Reference Guide from Colonial Times to the Present.* Ed. Lina Mainiero. Vol. 1. New York: Ungar, 1979.

S.C.C. *Louisa in Her New Home. By the Author of The Wonderful Mirror.* Philadelphia: Pennsylvania Anti-Slavery Society, 1854.

————. *A Visit to the Country: A Tale, by the Author of Letters to a Mother, Ellen, Happy Valley, etc.* Boston: William Crosby, 1839.

————. "The Wishing-Cap." *The Child's Friend* 9 (1847): 66–69.

————. *The Wonderful Mirror. By the Author of a Visit to the Country.* Boston: n.p., 1855.

Schlesinger, Elizabeth Bancroft. "Two Early Harvard Wives: Eliza Farrar and Eliza Follen." *New England Quarterly* 38 (June 1965): 147–67.

Schlipp, Madeline Golden, and Sharon M. Murphy. "Sarah Josepha Hale: First Woman's Magazine Editor [1788–1879]." *Great Women of the Press.* Carbondale: Southern Illinois UP, 1983. 37–48.

Shackelford, Lynne P., and Everett C. Wilkie, Jr. "John P. Jewett and Company." *American Literary Publishing Houses, 1638–1899.* Ed. Peter Dzwonkosk. [*Dictionary of Literary Biography*] Vol. 49. Detroit, MI: Gale, 1978. 226.

Simmons, James R., Jr. "Amelia Opie." *British Short Fiction Writers, 1800–1880.* Ed. John R. Greenfield. Vol. 159. Detroit, MI: Gale, 1996. 261–64.

Smedman, M. Sarah. "Sarah Josepha Hale." *American Writers for Children before 1900.* Ed. Glenn E. Estes. Vol. 42. Detroit, MI: Gale, 1985. 207–17.

Staves, Susan. "British Seduced Maidens." *Eighteenth Century Studies* 14.2 (Winter 1980–81): 109–34.

Stille, Darlene R. *Extraordinary Women of Medicine.* New York: Children's P, 1997. 20–24.

Stone, Witmore. "John Kirk Townsend." *Dictionary of American Biography.* Ed. Dumas Malone. Vol. 9 (part 2). New York: Scribner's, 1935–36. 617–18.

[Stowe, Harriet Beecher?]. *Little Eva: The Flower of the South.* New York: Vincent L. Dill, [between 1853 and 1855?].

————. *Little Eva's First Book for Good Children.* Exeter [England]: Drayton and Sons, High Street, ca. 1855.

————. *Little Eva's First Book for Good Children.* New York: Stereotyped by Vincent L. Dill, 1853 and 1855.

————. *Pictures and Stories from Uncle Tom's Cabin.* Boston: John P. Jewett, [1853?].

————. *True Stories from Uncle Tom's Cabin.* London: Darton and Co., 1860.

————. *Uncle Tom's Cabin: Authoritative Text, Backgrounds and Contexts, Criticism.* Ed. Elizabeth Ammons. New York: Norton, 1994.

Tompkins, Jane. *Sensational Designs: The Cultural Work of American Fiction, 1790–1860.* New York: Oxford UP, 1985.

Townsend, Hannah, and Mary Townsend. *The Anti-Slavery Alphabet.* Philadelphia: Printed for the Anti-Slavery Fair, Merrihew and Thompson, 1847.

[Uncle Tom's Companions]. *The Independent* [New York] 23 Dec. 1852: 207.

Wells, Susan. *Out of the Dead House: Nineteenth-Century Women Physicians and the Writing of Medicine.* Madison: U of Wisconsin P, 2001. 57–79.

————. "Women Write Science: The Case of Hannah Longshore." *College English* 58.2 (Feb. 1996): 176–91.

INDEX

About the Author

DEBORAH C. DE ROSA is Assistant Professor of English at Northern Illinois University. She is the author of *Domestic Abolitionism and Juvenile Literature: 1830–1865* (2003) in addition to book chapters and journal articles.